UNIFIED NOTATION

Class Diagram

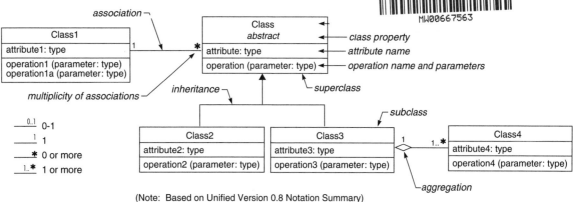

(Note: Based on Unified Version 0.8 Notation Summary)

OMT NOTATION

Object Model

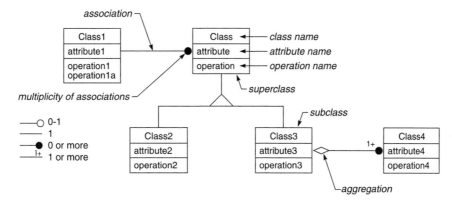

UNIFIED NOTATION, OMT NOTATION

Message Trace

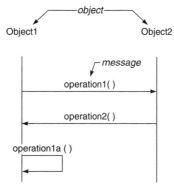

(Note: OMT calls this an "Event Trace Diagram.")

Object Models

Object Models

Strategies, Patterns, and Applications
Second Edition

Peter Coad

with David North and Mark Mayfield

YOURDON PRESS
Prentice Hall Building
Upper Saddle River, New Jersey 07458

Editorial/production supervision: *Harriet Tellem, Craig Little*
Cover design: *DEFRANCO Design*
Manufacturing manager: *Alexis Heydt*
Acquisitions editor: *Paul W. Becker*
Editorial assistant: *Maureen Diana*
Cover photography: *Don Rogers, Don Rogers Photography, Austin, TX, USA.*

Published by Prentice Hall P T R
Prentice-Hall, Inc.
A Simon & Schuster Company
Upper Saddle River, New Jersey 07458

The publisher offers discounts on this book in bulk quantities.
For more information contact:

Corporate Sales Department
Prentice Hall P T R
1 Lake Street
Upper Saddle River, New Jersey 07458

Phone: 800-382-3419
FAX: 201-236-7141, e-mail: corpsales@prenhall.com

The poem "Sermons We See" is reprinted from *Collected Verse of Edgar A. Guest*, by Edgar A. Guest, ©1934. Used with the kind permission of Contemporary Books, Inc., Chicago, IL, USA.

All object models in Coad notation were prepared using Together®/C++, a product of Object International Software Ltd.

Playground® and the Coad Letter® are registered trademarks of Object International, Inc. Together® is a registered trademark of Object International Software Ltd.

Printed in the United States of America

10 9 8 7 6 5 4

ISBN 0-13-840117-9

Prentice-Hall International (UK) Limited, *London*
Prentice-Hall of Australia Pty. Limited, *Sydney*
Prentice-Hall Canada Inc., *Toronto*
Prentice-Hall Hispanoamericana, S.A., *Mexico*
Prentice-Hall of India Private Limited, *New Delhi*
Prentice-Hall of Japan, Inc., *Tokyo*
Simon & Schuster Asia Pte. Ltd., *Singapore*
Editora Prentice-Hall do Brasil, Ltda., *Rio de Janeiro*

Dedication

To Amy Ellen Coad,
My artistic, beautiful, and perceptive one.
Love, Daddy

—Peter Coad

To Beverly North,
The object of my desire. Thanks for all your extra effort.
Love, David

—David North

To Michael Geoffrey Mayfield,
I've been so busy. Let's play!
Love, Dad

—Mark Mayfield

Sermons We See
by Edgar A. Guest

I'd rather see a sermon than hear one any day;
I'd rather one should walk with me than merely tell the way.

The eye's a better pupil and more willing than the ear,
Fine counsel is confusing, but example's always clear;

And the best of all the preachers are the ones who live their creeds,
For to see good out in action is what everybody needs.

I soon can learn how to do it if you'll let me see it done;
I can watch your hands in action, but your tongue too fast may run.

And the lecture you deliver may be very wise and true,
But I'd rather get my lessons by observing what you do.

For I might misunderstand you and the high advice you give,
But there's no misunderstanding how you act and how you live.

Contents

Acknowledgments

Acknowledgments are very special—a place to thank those who helped us during the development of this book.

We thank and acknowledge the kind help from these colleagues:

Andy Carmichael (Object UK Ltd.), for his help with keeping notation expressive, yet to the point.

Ward Cunningham (Cunningham & Cunningham), for his example of building object models.

Peter Durcansky (Object Intl.) for his attention to detail and help in symbol design.

Michael Kao (OCLC), for suggesting a way to incorporate scenarios into the object model itself.

Thomas Klenner (DFS), for his help in developing control structures for scenario views.

Linda Martz (Hughes Aircraft), for her insights on scenarios and dynamics.

Jill Nicola (JEN Consulting), for her insights on reuse through view management.

Roland Racko (DP Research), for his encouragement to continue with simplicity, brevity, and clarity, and for suggesting that we add strategies for discovering new strategies and patterns.

Ken Ritchie (KCR Consulting), for his help with patterns, including the fundamental pattern.

Hans Rohnert and Frank Buschman (Siemens), for exchanging research results with us and for the lively discussions that followed during the early stages of this work.

Thomas Wikehult (ABB Network Control AB), for his insights on patterns and adornments.

Rebecca Wirfs-Brock (Digitalk), for her work on stereotyping.

We thank our workshop participants and customers, for their encouragement, for their insights, and for allowing us to serve. The German proverb is true: "You learn the most when you teach." We offer special thanks to:

Klaus Golinski, Frank Hogelucht, Perdita Löhr, Thomas Klenner, Andreas Langer, and Hartmut Uhr (DFS)

Doug Heins (HP)

Ben Stivers and Scott Pruitt (Harris Data)

Mats Weidmar (Enea Data)

Charlie Whiting (OCLC).

We thank AIG's Tuesday morning object model workshop participants.

We thank the developers of Together/C++, the tool that we used throughout the development of this book:

> Dietrich Charisius, Rolf Gebhardt, Dietmar Deimling, Alexander Aptus, Günther Wannenmacher, Maxas Volodin, and Michael Gerasimov (Object Intl. Software Ltd.).

We also thank the developer of Playground, the new shareware object model tool included with this book: Peter Durcansky (Object Intl.). We thank the rest of Object International's team members, especially Henry Machicek, Andrea Peoples, Pam Perez, and Kay Smith.

We thank Cherrie Chiu (Computer Literacy Bookstores), for her encouragement during the final months of this project.

We also thank each member of our immediate families, for their loving support—especially during the development of this book:

> Judy, Ben, Amy, and David Coad
> Beverly, Michelle, David, and Daniel North
> Karen, Michael, Casey Lee, and Stephen Alexander Mayfield.

We thank our editor and the book production team:

> Paul Becker (Prentice Hall), for his encouragement, help, and wise advice along the way.
> The production team, especially Harriet Tellem (Prentice Hall) and John Morgan (Morgan Cain) for all their hard work in getting this book out so quickly.

David thanks:

> Robert Barcum, Bob Baker, and Russ Reinhardt (AIG), for your support and encouragement.

Finally, Peter thanks:

> Hanspeter Siegrist and Dietrich Charisius (Object Int'l Software Ltd.), for your vision, commitment, and friendship.
> Steve and Paula Clarner (Perceptive Scientific), for a great time in Cozumel. (Ernesto's is a state of mind.)

Preface

Strategies, Patterns, and Applications

APPLICATIONS

How do people really learn? A proverb in Latin says it best: "The example educates."

Truly, the example educates. It's a wonder if anything else ever does. Educating by example is what true education is all about.

An elementary education innovator startled us with these words:

"Educate right at the moment someone can apply it with success."

This book is a book of education by example.

You won't find the obligatory 125 pages about object philosophy. You won't find page after page of icons and adornments. Why? Because the purpose of this book is to communicate *how to build effective object models*. And the only way to do that is to give you good examples, presenting key "lessons" right at the moment you can apply them with success.

The best shortcut to building effective object models is to study real-life examples of building effective object models. That's why this book presents applications—along with strategies and patterns, applied along the way.

The core of this book is its six application chapters. Each example is a real-life example of building an object model. Each application has enough detail in it, so that you might read it and say, "Yes, I get it. I can build real systems this way." Moreover, each application is one that, by analogy, is applicable to most businesses and industries. For example, "point of sale" and "warehouse" are applications that nearly every business needs.

Chapters 1 to 6 present the applications, delivering new strategies and patterns at the moment you can apply them with success. Chapter 1, "Connie's Convenience Store," presents a point-of-sale application (nearly every business has one, in one form or another). Chapter 2, "Wally's Warehouse," presents a warehousing application (again, nearly every business has one). Chapter 3, "Ollie's Order Center," presents an order processing application (nearly every business has one). Chapter 4, "Dani's Diverters," presents a soft real-time application: a sensor-and-diverter system (nearly every manufacturing or shipping business has one). Chapter 5, "Andi's Autopilot," presents a hard real-time application: an autopilot system (many hard real-time systems have similar needs). Chapter 6, "All Five Applications, At High Speed," presents instructions for building initial object models entirely with patterns, resulting in object models that are ready for subsequent refinement with strategies.

STRATEGIES AND PATTERNS

As you read through the applications, you'll also discover specific strategies and patterns, practical and repeatable "how to" advice that will help you develop an intuitive feel for building object models. Strategies and patterns are nuggets of wisdom about building object models. In this book, you'll learn 148 strategies and 31 patterns, which appear in sequence in Chapter 7.

A *strategy* is a plan of action intended to accomplish a specific objective.

A *pattern* is a template, one worthy of emulation. "'Pattern'" can apply to the plans for a product rather than to the creations made from its specifications. The word often suggests blueprints or templates to be followed in constructing the product. More generally, the word indicates the design or configuration that something takes in actuality. But the word can also refer to the perfect representative of a type, or to any example thought worthy of emulation" (*Use the Right Word*). Observe that:

   – A pattern is a plan, rather than a specific implementation.
   – A pattern is a *template*, to be followed during construction.
   – A pattern is something observed from something in actuality.
   – A pattern is *an example worthy of emulation.*[1]

An *object-model pattern* is a template of objects with stereotypical responsibilities and interactions; the template may be applied again and again, by analogy.

Object patterns are repetitive forms, just like those in music. They occur again and again and again. You'll learn how to use them to your advantage, in building effective object models.

Strategies and patterns express examples of good practice, ones that can be used to help object modelers develop more effective results. Both help developers gain an intuitive understanding, a "gut feel," for good object models.

Strategies and patterns make it possible to communicate object-modeling expertise effectively. Without such patterns, that much-needed expertise is only acquired by trial-and-error. Where did these strategies and patterns come from? From continual introspection, while building hundreds of object models over a five-year period.

Through time, strategies and patterns join the language of analysts and designers, even when discussing the architectural aspects of an object model. For example, as soon

---

[1]Some researchers have suggested that a pattern is "a solution to a problem in a context," citing Chris Alexander's work in architecture (see the bibliography). Here are some thoughts on this.

(1) A pattern is a template, not a specific solution.

(2) Alexander's "pattern" theory remains unaccepted by his peers.

(3) No dictionary supports his definition of the word "pattern." (Although it is true that one may assign any meaning to any word, when a word's meaning has been established over several millennia of human experience, it is probably unwise to do so.)

(4) Although "a solution to a problem in a context" is a compelling writing style—after all, nearly every sales letter follows it—that does not make an instance of that writing style a "pattern."

as someone on the team describes a pair of objects as "participant-transaction," others on the team immediately know what kinds of objects and stereotypical responsibilities are involved.

Strategies and patterns move object-model building to something more than just "one object a time."

Chapter 7 is a strategy and pattern handbook. The appendices address supporting issues: notation, patterns in other fields, data management, the executive decision to adopt object technology, and a histogram of initial object modeling. A glossary defines key terms.

WHY READ THIS BOOK?

What makes this book unique? In other words, why read this book?

It teaches *a software method by example—entirely by example.*

– This is the world's first software method book to do so. It's about time!

It presents *applications that occur in nearly every industry.*

– You'll find it easy to relate to the applications.
– You'll find it easier to transfer what you learn to your own software development projects.

It uses real-world applications, with *a depth that readers can say, "Yes, it can be done."*

– The book selectively explores specific aspects of each application, to expose you to specific strategies and patterns.
– No trivial examples!
– No rambling case studies, either (the applications expose strategies and patterns, not mind-numbing minutia).

It delivers *148 strategies and 31 patterns*—practical, ready-to-use insights for building effective object models.

– This is the world's first (and only) methods book to do so.
– It's a no-BS guide that really helps.
– It delivers tangible chunks of "how to" advice, designed to help you more quickly develop an intuitive sense in building effective object models.
– It offers practical insights into how to build better object models, no matter what notation you use.

It presents *four activities and four object model components*—not steps and phased models.

– You're free to follow the development path that best suits your customer, your company, your project—and your time-to-market needs.
– You apply four activities—purposes and features, objects, responsibilities, and scenarios—following whatever path best fits your project needs.
– You work with objects in four model components—problem domain, human interaction, data management, and system interaction—as you see fit, on your project.

– You get the "separation of concerns" benefit of "analysis and design" approaches—without forcing people to work with those considerations in separate phases or steps.

It presents the Coad notation, *fully integrating class diagrams, object interaction diagrams, and object timing diagram*—one model, from concept to code.

– Such a unified notation is an essential ingredient, an absolute must:
  – for delivering frequent, tangible, working results—and corresponding risk reduction.
  – for acquiring and using tools that support continuously up-to-date object models and object-oriented programming.
– Chapter 1 describes the notation, right when you need it. In addition, Appendix A summarizes it.

All six application chapters present *object model results in all three leading notations: Coad, OMT, and Unified.* Here's why:

– To communicate better with those readers already familiar with any of these notations.
– To facilitate multinotation literacy, for all readers.
– To demonstrate that the heart and soul of effective object models is its strategies and patterns (not the shape of an icon or the number of adornments).

AUTOMATED TOOL, INCLUDED ON DISKETTE

This book comes with automated tool support, called Playground™.

Playground is a low-cost, easy-to-use tool for building objects models. It's shareware. And you can use it free, while working through the examples in this book.

Playground is especially suited for teams of domain experts and object modelers, working together during the early stages of a new project. It's a great way to get started with building effective object models.

– Features: Drag-and-drop classes, attributes, services, connections; multiple views, always in-sync; view management, with view categories, selective hiding/showing, and view update options; full control over connections, including routing points, right-angled or diagonal connections, and more; and extensive customization with preferences.
– Requirements. Windows with Win32s, 486-33 or better, 8 MB RAM, 4 MB disk space. Maximum recommended model size: 50 classes.
– Tech support for Playground is provided by e-mail (playground@oi.com) or regular mail only.
– Try it out for free. Use Playground for free, while working out examples in this book or using it in a classroom. The "Classroom and Personal Study ONLY" version is included with this book on diskette (the newest version is at ftp://ftp.oi.com/pub/oi/playground).
–Registered version benefits package. Diskette of most recent release, priority tech support, automatic notification of upgrades—and freedom

from the "Classroom and Personal Study ONLY" watermark (a tiny label that appears at the bottom of windows and printed outputs).

– Registered version pricing. For individual use: $40. For individual use within a company or organization: $95. The registration fee applies only to the version you receive at that time. Site licenses are available.

– Guarantee. Full 30-day money-back guarantee.

– How to register. Send your name, address, e-mail address, and payment to Object Intl., Inc. Payment by check (US funds) or Visa/MC/Amex (for credit card orders, be sure to include both your card number and its expiration date).

For object models and C++, we use Object International's Together™/C++, the tool for continuously up-to-date object modeling and C++ programming.

Contact Object International, Inc., 1720 Leigh Drive, Raleigh NC 27603 USA (om-book@oi.com or visit http://www.oi.com).

ADDITIONAL STRATEGIES AND PATTERNS

What about updates, including additional strategies and patterns?

As a reader of this book, you qualify for a free one-year subscription to The Coad Letter®, a continuing series of special reports on object technology.

Enjoy reading about new advances in object technology. Recent issues include "Amplified Learning" (16 pages on accelerating mastery of "object think") and an advance copy of the hypertext version of the "Strategies and Patterns Handbook."

Delivered by e-mail. To subscribe: just send a message to us at majordomo@oi.com. The body of the message should read: subscribe coad-letter.

(If you don't have e-mail and would like to receive an issue whenever we print one, please feel free to send in your contact information.)

OBJECT MODEL WORKSHOPS

What about object workshops, for the latest advances in strategies and patterns?

Announcing: lively and engaging workshops that deliver practical insights into building better object models.

In each hands-on session, you'll learn and apply specific strategies and patterns for building objects models (applicable with whatever notation you prefer: Coad, Booch, or Rumbaugh).

Peter Coad and Mark Mayfield will personally work with your team. Your team will "learn-by-doing," building actual project results, mastering more and more strategies and patterns, including new breakthroughs, not yet in print.

Delivered at your site or ours. Money-back guarantee. Our goal is customer delight. "I've been working with OOA/OOD and C++ for 3 years, yet I learned more in this workshop than in all that time!" (sr. developer in a "big 3" C++ software company).

Contact Object International, Inc., 1720 Leigh Drive, Raleigh NC 27603 USA (om-book@oi.com or visit http://www.oi.com).

CREATIVITY AND INNOVATION

Creativity and innovation are essential. The global marketplace demands them from all of us.

Methods, at their best, help people move to greater heights of creativity and innovation. We hope that this method—the Coad method—might serve you in this way.

Peter Coad
Object International, Inc., Raleigh NC USA
coad@oi.com   http://www.oi.com
PGP fingerprint:
```
3D BA 3B DD 57 B6 04 EB
B7 30 9D 06 A1 E1 05 50
```

David North
Applied Intelligence Group, Oklahoma City OK USA
dnorth@aig.com

Mark Mayfield
Austin TX USA
mlm@oi.com
PGP fingerprint:
```
B1 CB BE 43 1E 74 22 57
08 AF 7E CE 5B DA A5 3B
```

Connie's Convenience Store (A Point-of-Sale Application)

GETTING STARTED

Here's what you need to know before you plunge into the first application:
    What's an object? What's a class?

        An object is a person, place, or thing.
        A class is a description that applies to each of some number of objects.[1]

    What are strategies and patterns, and why are they important?

        A strategy is some specific advice that you can use to achieve a specific objective.
        A pattern is a template of interacting objects, one that may be used again and again by analogy.
        The purpose of strategies and patterns is to reduce the amount of time it takes to become proficient at building object models.

IN THIS CHAPTER

In this chapter, you'll learn and apply strategies and patterns that fit within these four major activities of building object models:

    – Identifying system purpose and features.
    – Selecting objects.
    – Establishing responsibilities.
    – Working out dynamics with scenarios.

---

[1]Classes and objects form an outline, a skeleton, an organizational framework that is easy to understand and likely to be much more stable over time when compared to software organized around data, functions, or external interfaces. According to classification theory, "In apprehending the real world, [people] constantly employ three methods of organization, which pervade all of people's thinking: (1) the differentiation of experience into particular objects and their attributes, e.g., when they distinguish between a tree and its size and spatial relations to other objects, (2) the distinction between whole objects and their component parts, e.g., when they contrast a tree with its component branches, and (3) the formation of and the distinction between different classes of objects, e.g., when they form the class of all trees and the class of all stones and distinguish between them" ("Classification Theory," *Encyclopaedia Britannica*, 1986).

Welcome— to Connie's Convenience Store!

Figure 1–1: Connie's Covenience Store.

IDENTIFYING SYSTEM PURPOSE AND FEATURES

Connie's Convenience Store needs a point-of-sale system. And you're going to build an object model for her.

You could call Connie a domain expert (well, perhaps not to her face; you might not want her to get a big head about all of this). Why? She knows the business. And she has working experience in that business, including experience using automated systems which (at times purportedly) support and help people run such a business. You see, Connie knows how things work in a convenience store. And she has some actual experience using an automated point-of-sale system.

Where do you begin?

Work together with Connie, to identify the purpose and features for the system under consideration.

Identify the purpose of the system

#2. "System Purpose" Strategy	identifying purpose and features
• Develop an overall purpose statement in 25 words or less. Why this system? Why now?	
• Keep the overall goal, the critical success factor, always before you.	
• "To support, to help, to facilitate, . . ."	

That large, numbered box with a single border is a strategy box. You'll see these boxes from time to time, just when you need them, within the application chapters. The number in the upper left corner is the strategy number; it's there for easy reference. This strategy is #2. In the application chapters, you'll learn and apply the strategies and patterns as you read them not (necessarily) in sequential order. Chapter 7 lists all strategies, #1 to #148, sequentially.

And now, back to Connie. Ask some purpose-setting questions:

(Peter) What would you like an automated system to do for you?

(Connie) Do all the work! Be my own personal cash machine!

(Peter) Dream on! Really, Connie. What capabilities would help you do a better job?

(Connie) How about if I sketch a "wish list" on the white board? Here it goes:

- scan items and automatically price them
- know whether an item is on sale
- automatically total the sale and calculate tax
- handle purchases and returns
- handle payment with cash, check, or charge
- authorize checks and cards
- calculate change, when working with cash or checks
- record all of the information about a customer transaction
- balance the cash in the drawer with the amount recorded by the point-of-sale system.

(Peter) Why do you want to do this? I'm asking why so I can better understand what you really want.

(Connie) I want these features for a variety of reasons. Mainly, though, I want to:

- speed up checkout time
- reduce the number of pricing errors
- reduce the labor required to ticket the items with a price, originally and when prices change.

(Peter) Okay. Let's see if we can work together to come up with a statement of the purpose of the system, in 25 words or less. How about:

> "To help each cashier work more effectively during checkout."

(Connie) Actually, it's more than that. Let's describe it this way:

> "To help each cashier work more effectively during checkout, and to keep good records of each sale."

(Peter) Actually, it's more than that. We'll want to assess the business results, too. How about:

> "To help each cashier work more effectively during checkout, to keep good records of each sale, and to support more efficient store operations."

(Connie) Very good.

Identify system features

#6. "Four Kinds of Features" Strategy	identifying purpose and features
• Be certain to include features that cover the following: 1. Log important information. 3. Analyze business results. 2. Conduct business. 4. Interact with other systems.	

Identify features for logging important information

Ask domain experts about information that the system needs to log for them.

(Peter) Now let's work out some features, ones that identify a sense of scope for the project under consideration. Let's begin with this question: what are some of the things that you'd like to keep track of?

(Connie) I need a lot of basic business information.

(Peter) Let's work together to identify some specific needs, stated as features of the system under consideration. For example: "to maintain what items we sell in a store."

(Connie) Easy enough. I'd include these "needed information" features:

– "needed information" features
  – to maintain prices, based upon UPC (universal product code)
  – to maintain tax categories (categories, rates, and effective dates)
  – to maintain the authorized cashiers
  – to maintain what items we sell in a store
  – to log the results of each sale in a store.

Identify features for conducting business

(Peter) So what happens when you put all of that needed information to work? How do you use it to conduct your business? What profitable use do you make of it?

(Connie) Hold on. You asked three questions. Let me give you one answer: I use it to keep track of what I sell.

(Peter) Could the system do some number crunching for you, putting all that information to more profitable use?

(Connie) Yes!

(Peter) What kinds of things could the system do to help you conduct your business?

(Connie) Oh, the day-to-day basics of running a convenience store:

– "conducting business" features
  – to price each item, based upon its universal product code (UPC)
  – to subtotal, calculate sales tax, and total
  – to accept payment by cash, check, or charge.

Identify features for analyzing business results

(Peter) What happens after the fact? What kind of analysis of business results would help you run your business more efficiently?

(Connie) Let's face it. Analyzing business results is the key to improving our operations. It's the only way I can measure how my business is doing and determine what actions I should take. This area really affects our bottom line. Can you help me here?

(Peter) Sure. Let's work on it together. How about something like this:

– "analyzing business results" features
  – to count how many of each item sold
  – to count how much we received in cash, check, or credit card sales
  – to assess how each cashier is performing
  – to assess how each store is performing.

Identify features for working with interacting systems

(Peter) Connie, what other systems do you work with?

(Connie) Other systems? Oh, the check and credit-authorization systems we use. Yes, our new point-of-sale system should automatically interact with whatever check and credit-authorization systems we might want to use.

(Peter) Let's put this into another objective. How about this?

- "interacting system" objective
    - to obtain authorization from one or more credit (or check) authorization systems.

(Connie) That sound fine.

An observation about system purpose and features

(Connie) Now that we have identified the purpose and features for my system, does that firmly identify the scope?

(Peter) It does identify scope—for now, not forever. Stuff happens: needs change, competitors change, governments change. And our understanding about what's really needed in this system will evolve over time, too.

(Peter) It's reasonable to assume that neither of us is omniscient. Right? So we'll use the system purpose and features to guide us in understanding what's within the responsibilities for the system under consideration.

(Peter) We'll learn more about what's really needed as we learn more about what this system is all about.

(Connie) Okay. Proceed!

SELECTING OBJECTS

It's time to start putting together an object model.

What objects do you need in your object model?

Where do you begin? Apply some strategies, then some patterns.

Use object model components to guide and organize your work

What kind of partitioning works well within an object model?

Use these model components:

- problem domain (PD)
    (classes relating to the business at hand)
- human interaction (HI)
    (windows and reports)
- data management (DM)
    (databases)
- system interaction (SI)
    (other systems)
- "not this time" (NT)
    (outside of scope for this system).

#25. "Object-Model Components as a Guide" Strategy	selecting objects (model components)
• Use object-model components as a working outline for organizing your search for objects. • PD: problem domain HI: human interaction DM: data management SI: system interaction (and NT: not this time).	

Each class fits into just one of these model components.

Why use model components? Use them to partition the classes into meaningful, loosely coupled subsets. Here's an overview (Figure 1–2) of how it works:

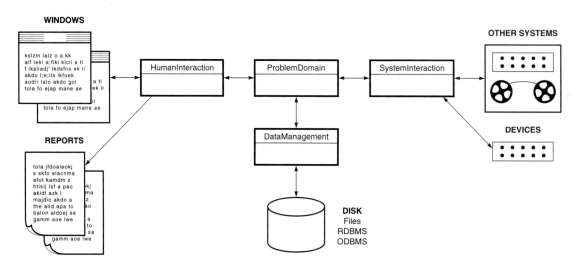

Figure 1–2: Object model components and their interactions.

The problem-domain (PD) component contains the objects that directly correspond to the problem being modeled. Objects in this component are technology-neutral. They have little (or no) knowledge about objects in the other components (human interaction, data management, and system interaction).

The human-interaction (HI) component contains objects that provide an interface between problem-domain objects and people. In an object model, such objects most often correspond to specific windows and reports.

The data-management (DM) component contains objects that provide an interface between problem-domain objects and a database or file-management system. In an object model, such objects most often correspond to specific problem-domain objects that need support for persistence and searching.

The system-interaction (SI) component contains objects that provide an interface between problem-domain objects and other systems or devices. A system-interaction object encapsulates communication protocol, keeping its companion problem-domain object free of such low-level, implementation-specific detail.

That's four object-model components. There is a fifth one. It's the "not this time" component. It's a bucket that holds objects that are interesting, ones that you consider, yet that for one reason or another (be it technical, sociological, or economic), you've decided not to include at this time. By using this component along with the others, you can show what's included—and what's not.

By organizing classes this way, you facilitate simpler modeling this time (within each model component).

You also increase the likelihood of reuse next time. Why? Here's an example. Next time, you might want to reuse certain problem domain classes, even though you may choose to work with different human interaction classes.

What's the alternative? Smash the model components together. But then the overall model is harder to understand; and in the future, unless you choose the same problem-domain, human-interaction, data-management, and system-interaction approach, reuse is very unlikely. Ouch!

So, use model components. Use them as an overall outline, a guide for selecting objects. And use them to keep your classes well-organized, for understanding, and for reuse (Figure 1–3):

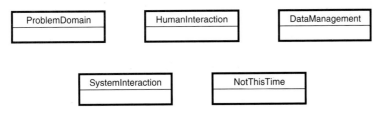

Figure 1–3: Model components.

You can use these model components to organize your approach to building the model.

In this chapter, you'll go from PD to HI to DM to SI. In each case, you'll use strategies and patterns to help you:

- select objects
- establish responsibilities
- work out dynamics with scenarios.

SELECTING PROBLEM-DOMAIN OBJECTS

Take a walk on the wild side inside Connie's Convenience Store. Look for objects, one that the system might need to know or do something about.

Coming up, you'll apply strategies for selecting objects:

- actors and participants
- places
- things.

For now, consider PD objects. (Later in this chapter, you'll consider HI, DM, and SI objects, too.)

Select actors and participants

An actor is a person, an organization, or some other thing that participates in one or more ways over time. A participant participates in a specific way, plays a role, fulfills a specific mission.

What are the actors and participants in this system?

#13. "Select Actors" Strategy	selecting objects (pattern players)
• Look for actors: people and organizations that act as participants within the system under consideration. • Examples: person, organization (agency, company, corporation, foundation).	

Here, the actor is:

– person.

Organization could be interesting, too. Maybe later.

#14. "Select Participants" Strategy	selecting objects (pattern players)
• Analyze how each actor participates, in ways that might be of interest to the system under consideration. • Why. Each actor participates in one or more ways through time. It's the same actor, just different ways of participating. People talk about wearing "different hats" during the day. That's exactly what such participation is all about. • Examples: agent, applicant, buyer, cashier, clerk, client, civilian, customer, dealer, delegate, distributor, donor, employee, investor, manufacturer, member, officer, official, order clerk, owner, participant, policy holder, professional, prospect, recipient, retailer, sales clerk, sales rep, shipper, student, subscriber, supervisor, supplier, suspect, teacher, wholesaler, worker.	

In what interesting ways does a person participate when using a point-of-sale system? Why, there's:

– cashier
– head cashier
– customer.

What objects do you need? The system purpose and features give you a standard, a checkpoint, for making that decision. Here's how. If an object fits within the context of the system's responsibilities, then include it. If not, then (1) add to the system features or (2) put that object in the "not this time" model component.

Consider cashier, head cashier, and customer.

Cashier, head cashier

Cashier objects are a must; the system will assess each cashier's performance.

What about head cashier? What should you do here?

One choice: you could model it as another kind of participant. In fact, you could model a head cashier as a special kind of, a specialization of, a cashier. When would you do this?

Check out potential attributes.

#68. "Partially Applicable Attribute" Strategy	establishing responsibilities / what I know (consider and challenge)
• Attribute that applies only to certain objects in a class? • Do you have an attribute which applies only to certain kinds of objects? • Do you have an attribute that may have the value "not applicable"? • If so, factor out the specialized attribute into a specialization class.	

Check out potential services.

#121. "Partially Applicable Service" Strategy	establishing responsibilities / what I do (consider and challenge)
• Do you have a service that applies only to certain objects in a class? • Do you have a service that applies only to certain kinds of objects? • Do you have a service which tests for what kind it is, and then acts accordingly? • If so, factor out the specialized service into a specialization class.	

Add another participant class? Only if a head cashier object knows or does something different from what a cashier object knows or does. (Hmmm. No difference here.)

Another choice: you could model it along with some other participant. Express simple variation with attribute values. In this case, you could treat a head cashier as a cashier with a greater level of authorization. The only difference is the value of its authorization level. This second choice makes sense here: at this point, just a difference in value seems to be enough.

Customer

What about the customer? Adding "customer" makes sense only if you have some way to find out who Connie's customers are, or at least who some of her customers are.

#47. "Way to Know" Strategy	selecting objects (consider and challenge)

- You need a way to know each object—and its attribute values.
- If you have no way to know an object, either find a way to know about it or put the object in the "not this time" model component.
- Example: customer. You must have a way to know about customer objects; otherwise, put customer in the "not this time" model component.

If each and every customer comes into a store, participates anonymously, and leaves again, then there is no reason to have a customer object in an object model. Why? Because the system would not be responsible to know or do anything about that customer.

But what if Connie's new system could know the identity of at least some of her customers, especially some of her better customers? What then?

How could Connie's cashiers find out about who their customers are? What could Connie do to make this happen? She could offer a check guarantee card. Or she could launch a special "frequent shopper" program. Either way, Connie could issue cards with machine-readable codes. The cashier (or even the shopper) could run the card through a scanner.

Connie could use that information to better serve her customers.

This looks like a change in scope. Better check it out with Connie.

(Peter) How about a frequent buyer program?

(Connie) Nice idea. But not this time! I'm dealing with enough changes right now.

(Peter) Understood. Have a nice day.

(Peter, to himself) And don't be so cranky. Good grief. I'm just doing my job.

Okay, then. To the problem-domain component, add person and cashier. To the "not this time" component, add organization, customer, and head cashier (Figure 1–4):

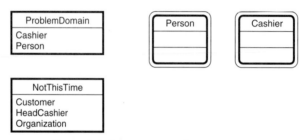

Figure 1–4: Select actors and participants.

About class names:

#38. "Use the Domain Vocabulary" Strategy	selecting objects (names)
• Use the domain vocabulary. • Encourage domain experts to eliminate names of things that aren't their own. • Don't put words in your domain expert's mouth. • Don't change the vocabulary unless the domain expert feels the need to do so. • Don't change the domain vocabulary—unless your domain experts choose to change their own vocabulary.	

About the class-with-objects symbol: the bold inner-rounded rectangle represents a class; the outer-rounded rectangle represents one or more objects in a class. The class name goes in the top section; attributes go in the middle; services go in the bottom.

Select places

#15. "Select Places" Strategy	selecting objects (pattern players)
• Look for places where things come to rest, places that contain other objects. • Examples: airport, assembly-line, bank, clinic, depot, garage, geographic entity, hangar, hospital, manufacturing site, plant, region, sales outlet, service center, shelf, station, store, warehouse, zone.	

What places are important?

Here's what to look for. Look for places where things come to rest. And look for places that hold or contain other objects.

At Connie's, that sounds a lot like:

– store
– shelf.

Both of these classes are in the problem domain. So far, so good.

#42. "System Responsibility" Strategy	selecting objects (consider and challenge)
• Is the object something that your system is responsible to know or do anything about? • If not, put it in the "not this time" model component.	

Is the system responsible to know or do anything about a store or shelf, to meet one of its features?

A store is a container of things.

#22. "Select Container Objects" Strategy	selecting objects (pattern players)
• Use a domain-based container, one that holds other objects. • Examples: airport, aircraft, aisle, bank, bin, building, cabinet, folder, garage, hangar, hospital, locker, room, safe, store, warehouse.	

A store is a container of many things, including cashiers, registers, and items for sale. Consequently, a store object is a good place to put calculations that apply across all of the objects contained in a store—just the part of the calculations that apply across the overall collection. Based upon the calculation needs expressed by the system features, it looks like you need this in your model. Add store to the problem-domain component.

A shelf could be important too, especially if the system is responsible for assessing the performance of each shelf. A shelf could know its contents and the layout of its contents. Yet such responsibilities are outside of the purpose and features of the system under consideration. Rather than get carried away with the joy of object modeling, constrain yourself and put shelf in the "not this time" model component (Figure 1–5):

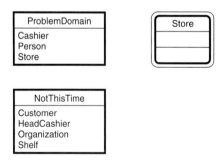

Figure 1– 5: Select places.

Note: many figures in this chapter (and other application chapters) illustrate a selected view, just a portion of the overall model. Such figures highlight a specific aspect of the object model. From time to time, you'll find a "progress at this point" figure, showing the entire object model, too.

What's next? Consider kinds of stores.

#34. "Select Kinds of Objects" Strategy	selecting objects (kinds of objects)

- Use generalization-specialization (gen-spec) to find additional classes.
   - Look at each class as a generalization. Name its specializations, ones that fit with system objectives.
   - Look at each specialization. Name its generalizations, ones that fit within system objectives.
- Use gen-spec for domain-based reuse within an application; use configuration management for reuse across multiple applications, even multiple problem domains.
- Use gen-spec to show domain-based "what's the same, what's different," within an application.
- Examples: equipment, kinds of equipment; participants, kinds of participants; transactions, kinds of transactions.

A store is a kind of sales outlet. Perhaps over time, Connie will expand to other kinds of sales outlets (for example, catering centers or catalog sales). Connie might choose to do this in the future.

Stores might be specialized into kinds of stores (for example, superstore, grocery store, convenience store). Connie might choose to do this in the future, too.

Note how generalization-specialization is a useful tool for exploring what could happen, with success over time.

For now, leave store as is.

Select things
Tangible things

#16. "Select Tangible Things" Strategy	selecting objects (pattern players)

- Look for tangible objects, ones used in the problem domain.
- Take a walk through the business. Select objects from the tangible ones around you.
- Examples: account, cash box, cash drawer, item, plan, procedure, product, schedule, scheduled event.

What are the tangible things in the store?
   – item
   – register
   – cash drawer.

(Note: a register consists of a number of data entry devices: a mag stripe reader, an item scanner, a keypad, and a receipt printer. You don't need these in your object model; all of these are just data entry device "nuts and bolts.")

Kinds of things, too

You might be interested in categories of items, such as:

– perishability: perishable, nonperishable
– taxability: taxable, nontaxable
– type: dairy, produce, canned goods, frozen foods.

Should you add some additional classes, representing these different kinds of items?

Here's how. For each category, consider the following:

– If you don't care about the distinction, forget about it.
– If all you care about is the category value, add an attribute.
– If a category implies added attributes, then add a specialized class; put the added attributes in it.
– If a category implies different services, then add a specialized class; put the added services in it.

In this case, based upon the system features, you don't really care about the distinctions. Just add item, for now.

Descriptive things

#19. "Select Items and Specific Items" Strategy	selecting objects (pattern players)
• Look for items, descriptive objects with values that apply to some number of specific items and actions that apply across those specific items.	
• Examples: aircraft–specific aircraft, loan description–specific loan, job description–specific job, video description–videotape, price category item–specific item, tax category item–specific item.	

What kinds of catalog descriptions or descriptive tables of values do you need to do business?

In this system, it's tax tables. Yuck!

Anyway, you really do have to keep track of tax categories, and the taxable rate that applies for each one. Add a tax category object, so you can keep track of each category, its rate, and its effective date. Add your "tangible things" and "descriptive things" to your object model (Figure 1–6):

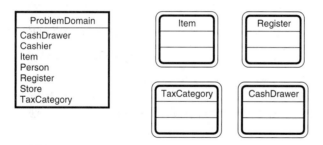

Figure 1–6: Select tangible things and descriptive things.

About transactions as things

What's a transaction, in the context of building an object model?

A "transaction" is a recording or logging of any event of significance; hence, you could call it "a significant event remembered." A "transaction object" knows about a significant event, knows who the players are in that event, and calculates things pertaining to that event.

#17. "Select Transactions" Strategy	selecting objects (pattern players)

- Look for transactions, "events remembered," events that the system must remember through time. A transaction is a moment in time (for example, a sale) or an interval of time (for example, a rental).

- Look for an entry in a historical record or log, an entry that must be maintained. Why? To answer questions or to perform assessments.

- Examples: agreement, assignment, authorization, contract, delivery, deposit, incident, inquiry, order, payment, problem report, purchase, refund, registration, rental, reservation, sale, shift, shipment, subscription, time charge, title, withdrawal.

- Note: Nearly all transactions consist of a number of transaction line items.

- Note: Where do these transactions come from? The possibilities are:
    A window (the event logged is based upon human interaction at some point in time)
    Another object, monitoring for a significant event, then logging that such an event
        occurred
    Another system, one that your system can interact with regarding events it logs.

So the question is: what are the transactions, the notable events that must be recorded by your system?

Consider Connie's Convenience Store. What significant transactions, events remembered, occur every day? How about:

- sale
- payment (a companion to any sale at Connie's)
- session (from logon to logoff).

Sale

One of the transactions is sale. Check it out.

> (Peter) Connie, what are the main things you do with a customer?
> (Connie) We sell items.
> (Peter) Do you have a special name for that?
> (Connie) A special name? "Sale." (Now isn't that special.)
> (Peter) Does it include only items you sell to a customer?
> (Connie) Now that you mention it, a sale may include both sales and returns.

Hold it! The domain vocabulary is "sale." Someone on our team might argue that you should use a more accurate term, "sales transaction." Advice? Don't do it. Key point: don't ever change domain vocabulary unless your customer sees the need for and wants to make the change (otherwise you'll be forever mapping her words to your words; that's both counterproductive and a real nuisance).

Most transactions have parts, called transaction line items. A sale is no exception. A sale is a collection of some number of sale line items. Add the classes: sale and sale line item (Fig. 1-8).

Kinds of sales

#34. "Select Kinds of Objects" Strategy	selecting objects (kinds of objects)

• Use generalization-specialization (gen-spec) to find additional classes.
    Look at each class as a generalization. Name its specializations, ones that fit with system objectives.
    Look at each specialization. Name its generalizations, ones that fit within system objectives.
• Use gen-spec for domain-based reuse within an application; use configuration management for reuse across multiple applications, even multiple problem domains.
• Use gen-spec to show domain-based "what's the same, what's different," within an application.
• Examples: equipment, kinds of equipment; participants, kinds of participants; transactions, kinds of transactions.	

Consider the kinds of sales:

> – sales, returns.

Do you need to distinguish between a sale and a return?

> (Peter) What's the difference between a sale and a return?
> (Connie) The only difference is whether the amount is positive or negative.

You don't need to add classes for both "sale" and "return." At this point, the system's responsibilities for them appear to be identical. The only difference is whether the amount is positive or negative.

Payment

Payments are important, too. No kidding!

> (Peter) What kinds of payments do you accept?
> (Connie) Cash, check, charge, or a combination of those.
> (Peter) Really, a combination?
> (Connie) Yes, especially in the wee hours of the morning. You'd be surprised.
> (Peter) I'll take your word for it.

Cash, check, and charge are kinds of payments.

Do you need to know and do different things, based upon the kind (or kinds) of payment? Probably so. So add these specialized classes to your object model. As you go along, you might end up sliding them over into the "not this time" bucket. And that's okay. You're learning more and more about what's really needed for this system under consideration.

Here's how to model gen-spec (Figure 1–7):

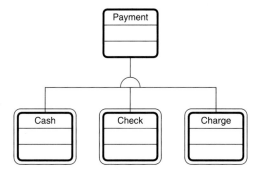

Figure 1–7: Gen-spec.

The gen-spec icon is a semicircle. Generalizations connect to the rounded edge; specializations connect to the straight edge.

By convention, a generalization class may or may not have objects; lowest-level specialization classes must have directly corresponding objects. Here, the generalization class does not have directly corresponding objects.

Session

Sessions? Are they important?

Yes. Based upon the system features, you need to assess cashier performance. To make that calculation, you will probably want to know all of the corresponding sessions for that cashier.

Adding transactions to your object model

Add the following classes to your object model:

> – sale, sale line item
> – payment, check, cash, charge
> – session.

See Figure 1–8:

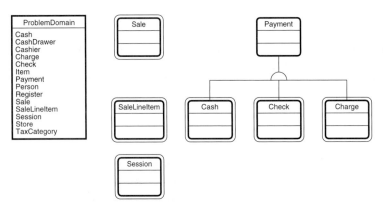

Figure 1–8: Select transactions.

APPLYING PATTERNS: SELECT AND ORGANIZE PROBLEM-DOMAIN OBJECTS

You've selected a number of objects (and formed classes of them).

Now, take an initial look at some patterns. An object-model pattern is a template of objects with stereotypical responsibilities and interactions; the template may be applied again and again by analogy.

Use some patterns, initially, at this point, just to connect some of the pieces together in a meaningful way. You might discover some additional objects along the way, too.

Participant-transaction

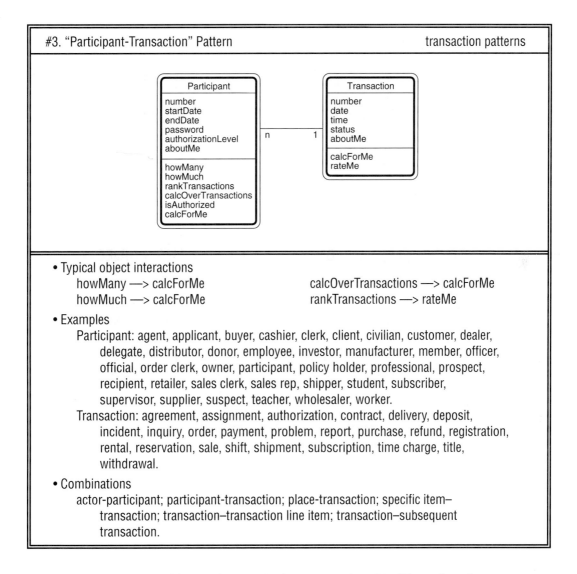

That large, numbered box with a double border is a pattern box. You'll see these boxes from time-to-time, right when you need them, within the application chapters. The number in the upper left corner is a pattern number; it's there for easy reference. See Chapter 7, "Strategies and Patterns Handbook," for more.

Session and its participants

A session is a transaction object. What are its participants?

The participants are a cashier and a register. A cashier starts a session on a specific register at a specific date and time.

Apply the participant-transaction pattern (Figure 1–9):

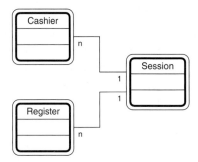

Figure 1–9: Cashier, register-session.

Note: the connecting lines are object connections. An object connection is a graphical attribute, showing that one object knows about some number of other objects.

Note: the markings at the end of each object connection are called object connection constraints; each constraint is placed next to each object, expressing what it knows about other objects. Here, a session knows one cashier and one register; a cashier object knows some number of session objects; a register object knows some number of session objects, too (Figures 1–10 and 11):

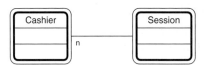

Figure 1–10: An object connection with a constraint.

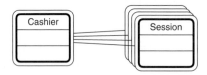

Figure 1–11: What an object connection and its constraint represents.

Another note: this is just the opposite of the entity-relationship convention for what that approach calls "multiplicities." Why? There is a good reason for this. (Actually, the credit for this goes to our clients and seminar participants. They asked us again and again: if you're constraining a session, why are you marking it on the other end of the line? That got us thinking. And it helped us to change.) You see, entity-relationship markings reflect "table think": one row here keys to some number of rows there. Some object methods continue that tradition; that's not enough. Here, you are working with objects. For each object, you consider "what I know; who I know; what I do." The first is represented by attributes; the second is represented by object connections; the third is represented by services. Constraints on "who I know" belong next to the object being constrained. That's the convention used here. It better supports "object think."

By placing the constraint next to the object being constrained, each object's responsibilities for "who I know" comes through much more clearly.

#73. "Show Who I Know" Strategy	establishing responsibilities / who I know (fundamentals)

- Show "who I know" graphically, with an object connection.

    Include constraints, placed next to each object being constrained: 1   0-1   n   1-n
        <blank>   ordered n   [XOR A] 1   [OR B] 2   [C] ordered n   all

    "n" is the same thing as "0-n" (it's just easier to write it as "n").
    A <blank> constraint indicates that an object has no need to know the other objects
        (this may occur, notably for a part in an aggregate).
    ordered n   an ordered collection of some number of connections
    [XOR A] 1 indicates an exclusive or, pertaining to all object connections labeled
        with the same tag (in this example the tag is "A"). Place whatever constraint
        applies to the right of the brackets, e.g., [XOR A] 1.
    [OR B] 2   two connections, selected from the connections labeled "B".
    [C] ordered n   an ordered collection of some number of connections (any connection
        from that object that is labeled "C").

- Or show "who I know" textually, with an attribute.

    Use this format whenever an object connection spans across model components — or
        any other time that an object connection would be cumbersome, visually.
    For a textual representation, use this format:
        "<class name, beginning with a lowercase letter>"
    Make it singular or plural, reflecting the number of objects that the object may
        know.

Another example: a cashier object knows about its corresponding session object (the current one), as well as some number of session objects (one for each and every time the cashier logs onto the system). This is a common situation in life: "I know many, yet one is most important to me right now." What can you do about it? Use both a "current session" attribute and a cashier-session object connection.

Place-transaction

A store is a place where a sale happens. It's an instance of place-transaction.

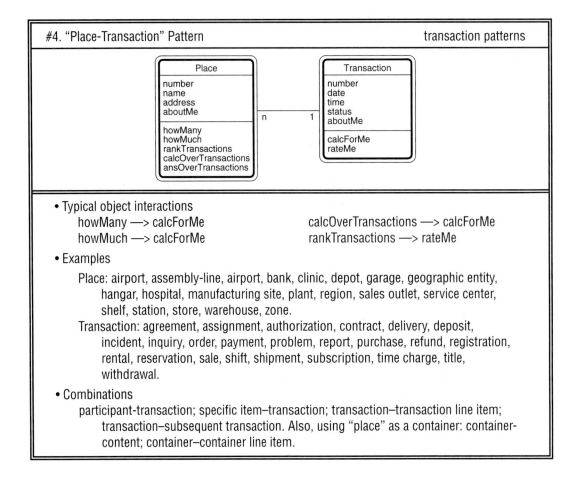

Connect the players (Figure 1–12):

Figure 1–12: Store-sale.

Transaction–subsequent transaction

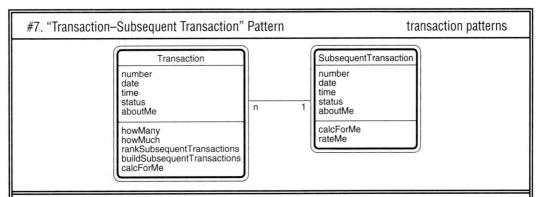

#7. "Transaction–Subsequent Transaction" Pattern   transaction patterns

- Typical object interactions

  howMany —> calcForMe   calcOverSubsequentTransactions —> calcForMe

  howMuch —> calcForMe   rankSubsequentTransactions —> rateMe

- Examples

  Transaction: agreement, assignment, authorization, contract, delivery, deposit, incident, inquiry, order, payment, problem, report, purchase, refund, registration, rental, reservation, sale, shift, shipment, subscription, time charge, title, withdrawal.

  Transaction–subsequent transaction: application-issue; intermediate result–final result; order-shipment; purchase-payment; reservation-sale; traffic citation–payment.

- Combinations

  participant-transaction; place-transaction; specific item–transaction; transaction–transaction line item; subsequent transaction–subsequent transaction line item.

- Notes

  Work out transactions in time sequence (the order they usually occur in).

  If subsequent transaction and its line item objects correspond 1-to-1 with transaction and its line item objects, combine them.

Session and the subsequent transactions

Consider a session object.

A session is a transaction. What are its subsequent transactions? In other words, what "event remembered," what significant moment in time occurs after a session?

What follows a session transaction? Hopefully, one or more sales.

What follows a sale transaction? Hopefully, one or more payments.

Connect the objects, using two instances of the transaction–subsequent transaction pattern (Figure 1–13):

Figure 1–13: Session-sale and sale-payment.

Container-content

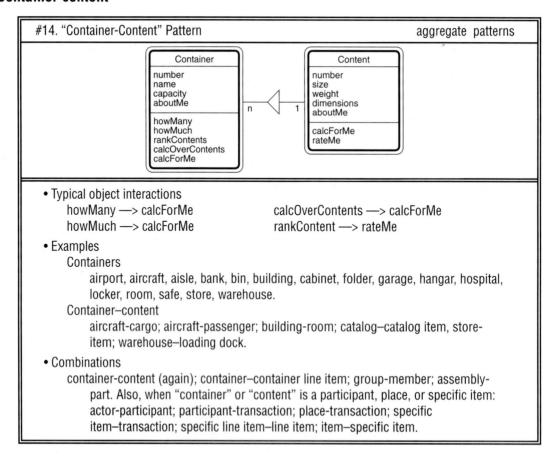

A store, as content

Consider a store as content, then as a container.

A store is a part of a chain. "Chain" would be interesting, especially if you wanted to do a calculation across a collection of stores. Not this time, however.

A store, as a container

A store is a domain-based container.

Think of the store as a large container. What does it contain? Look inside. A store contains registers, items, cashiers (Figure 1–14).

Store is a domain-based container. Domain-based containers are a convenient place for expressing responsibilities across a collection of other domain objects, ones that are not already taken care of by some other collection. Eventually, you may want add to the kinds of objects that a store object knows.

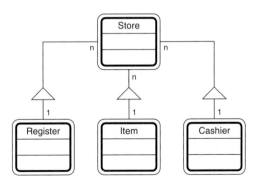

Figure 1–14: Store–register, item, cashier.

Note that a store object knows its registers, items, and cashiers. That makes sense. On notation: in each case, the triangle points from a part to a whole.

Transaction–transaction line item

A sale is a transaction.

Nearly all transaction objects have corresponding transaction line items.

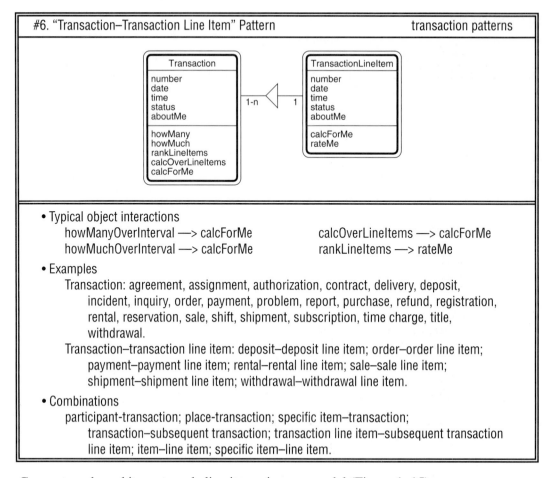

#6. "Transaction–Transaction Line Item" Pattern   transaction patterns

- Typical object interactions
      howManyOverInterval —> calcForMe   calcOverLineItems —> calcForMe
      howMuchOverInterval —> calcForMe   rankLineItems —> rateMe

- Examples
      Transaction: agreement, assignment, authorization, contract, delivery, deposit,
            incident, inquiry, order, payment, problem, report, purchase, refund, registration,
            rental, reservation, sale, shift, shipment, subscription, time charge, title,
            withdrawal.
      Transaction–transaction line item: deposit–deposit line item; order–order line item;
            payment–payment line item; rental–rental line item; sale–sale line item;
            shipment–shipment line item; withdrawal–withdrawal line item.

- Combinations
      participant-transaction; place-transaction; specific item–transaction;
            transaction–subsequent transaction; transaction line item–subsequent transaction
            line item; item–line item; specific item–line item.

Connect a sale and its parts, sale line items, in your model (Figure 1–15):

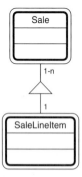

Figure 1–15: Sale-sale line item.

Note that a sale object knows one or more sale line item objects.

Actor-participant

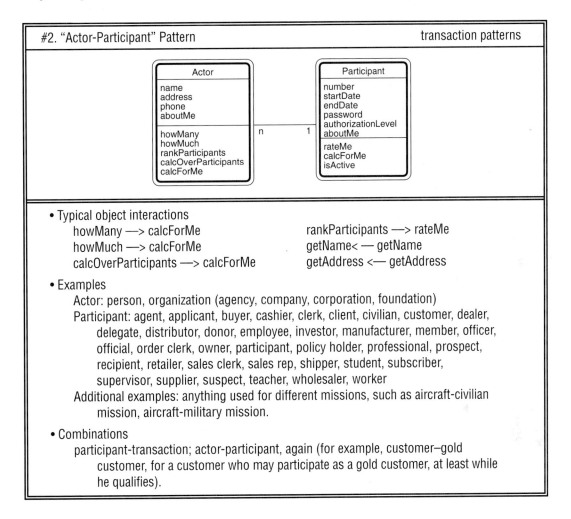

Here, the actor is person; the participant is cashier.

Use the pattern to lay out these objects in a standard configuration (Figure 1–16):

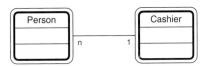

Figure 1–16: Person-cashier.

Note that a person could know more than one cashier object. When? Suppose that you keep track of start and end of employment, for each cashier object. Then one person object might know a number of cashier objects over time.

However, if you don't keep track of start and end dates, then an object connection constraint of "1" for person objects makes sense (Figure 1–17):

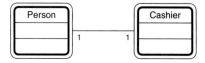

Figure 1–17: person object knows one cashier object (and vice versa).

Progress at this point

You've selected objects, using strategies and patterns. Take a look at where you are (Figure 1–18):

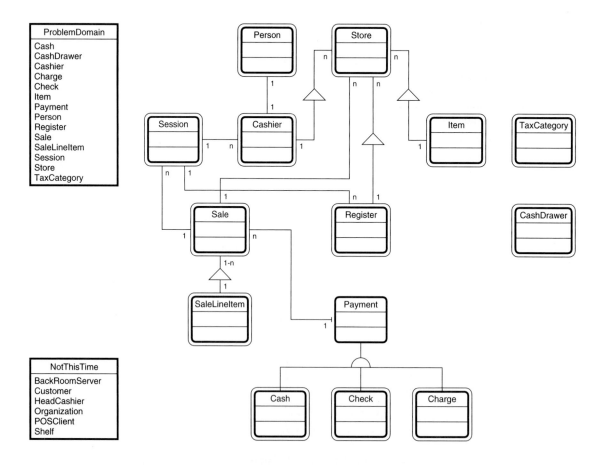

Figure 1–18: Progress at this point.

ESTABLISHING RESPONSIBILITIES FOR PROBLEM-DOMAIN OBJECTS

Every object in an object model has specific responsibilities.

An object knows things about itself.
An object knows other objects.
An object does things, too: by itself or in collaboration with others.

Your job: establish responsibilities, reflecting your system's responsibilities to know and do. To get this done, use strategies for establishing responsibilities for:

– what I know
– who I know
– what I do.

Responsibilities for actors and participants

Actor: person

Establish responsibilities: "what I know."

#52. "Establish Actor and Participant Attributes" Strategy	establishing responsibilities / what I know (pattern players)
• For actor, consider: name, address, phone. • For participants, include: number, date and time (perhaps an ending date and time), password, authorization level.	

What do you need to know about each person?

Whether a cashier or a customer, you're likely to need some of the same information each time (Figure 1–19):

– name
– address
– phone.

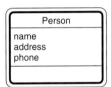

Figure 1–19: Person: "what I know."

Establish responsibilities: "who I know."

Who does a person object know?

#72. "Establish Objects I Know" Strategy	establishing responsibilities / who I know (fundamentals)

• This is an aspect of a software object coming to life: "I know other objects, ones that are related to the actual object that I'm an abstraction of."
 	
 • Select connecting objects to satisfy these two purposes:
   To directly know "to whom to send a message" (within one or more scenarios).
   To answer a query about objects that are directly related to it.	

Here's some specific help.

#74. "Establish Actor and Participant Object Connections" Strategy	establishing responsibilities / who I know (pattern players)
• For an actor, include an object connection to: its participants. • For a participant, include an object connection to: its actor, its transactions.	

A person object knows its participant objects. And each participant object knows its corresponding person object (Figure 1–20):

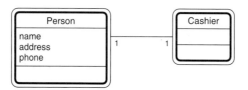

Figure 1–20: Person: "who I know."

Establish responsibilities: "what I do."

#89. "Basic Services" Strategy	establishing responsibilities / what I do (fundamentals)
• The basic service, done by all, are not shown in an object model, except within specific scenario views that might use them. • The basics: get, set; add (a connecting object), remove (a connecting object); create (something a class does) and initialize, delete. • Note: attributes are private, by convention. In scenarios, use "get <attribute name>" and "set <attribute name>" services to access attribute values. • The basic DM services—for data management objects—are: search, load, and save.	

What does a person object do?

The same basics that every object does:

- get . . . an attribute value
- set . . . an attribute value
- add . . . a connection to another object
- remove . . . a connection to another object
- delete . . . that object.

What does the person class itself do? The same basics that every class does:

- create (and initialize) . . . a new object.

You don't need these basic services in your object model. You will find occasional use for them within a scenario view.

What if you did put them everywhere? You'd have to add a half dozen labels to every class with objects. Ugh! That's a lot of added model complexity, with little gain in model effectiveness. You see, notation is not free; every piece must pay its way, improving understanding enough to warrant the added complexity. As one person so eloquently put it:

> "The ability to simplify means to eliminate the unnecessary so that the necessary may speak."
>
> *—Hans Hoffman*

What about for person and participant?

#94. "Establish Actor and Participant Services" Strategy	establishing responsibilities / what I do (pattern players)
• For an actor or participant, include: calculate for me, rate me, is <value>. • For an actor as a collection, include: how many, how much, rank participants, calculate over participants (plus services to enforce business rules across that collection). • For a participant as a collection, include: how many, how much, rank transactions, calculate over transactions (plus services to enforce business rules across that collection).	

Usually, the more interesting "what I do" behavior is done by the participant objects.

Participant: cashier
Establish responsibilities: *"what I know."*

#50. "Select Attributes from Actual Ones" Strategy	establishing responsibilities / what I know (fundamentals)
• This is an aspect of a software object coming to life: "I know selective things that describe the actual object that I'm an abstraction of." • Select the attributes for your software objects, taken from the abundance of the attributes that could be used to describe a corresponding actual (real-world) object. • Consider attributes from a broad-sweeping perspective; then work your way into the specific ones you need. Look at attributes in general, in this domain, and ultimately just within this system's responsibilities.	

Okay. What do you need to know about each cashier?

– number
– password
– authorization level

and, as discussed earlier in the chapter, an attribute to distinguish that one session has special meaning, namely:

– current session.

Model it (Figure 1–21):

Figure 1–21: Cashier: "what I know."

Establish responsibilities: *"who I know."*

Who does a cashier object know?

It knows its sessions, the ones it participates in. (And each session knows its cashier.)

It knows its corresponding person object, too (Figure 1–22):

Figure 1–22: Cashier: "who I know."

Establish responsibilities: "what I do."

What does a cashier object do?

Yes, it does the basics: get, set, add, remove, and delete.

And yes, the class does its basic action: create.

Anything else?

#86. "Do It Myself" Strategy	establishing responsibilities / what I do (fundamentals)
• This is an aspect of a software object coming to life: "I do those things that are normally done to the actual object that I'm an abstraction of." • Here's why. "Doing it myself" encapsulates attributes with the services that work on those attributes. That results in lower coupling and stronger cohesion. • If you are building a simulation system, then a software object will mimic what an actual object does. In most systems, this is not so. Software objects do those things that the system is responsible to do with regard to that object.	

What about the actions done to an actual cashier? How about:

– is authorized? (to perform a specific action)

– assess performance over interval.

Using personification and a first-person perspective, for the cashier object, the one that is an abstraction of an actual cashier, you can think of this as:

"I'm a cashier."

"I know my employee number, my name, my password, my authorization level, and my sales over time."

"I determine whether or not I'm authorized to do something."

"I assess my performance."

Hold on a minute. Someone out there is whining, "But cashiers don't authorize themselves. And we certainly wouldn't let a cashier assess his own performance."

No kidding! Please reconsider the difference between actual objects and abstraction objects. What they know is often the same; what they do is often remarkably different.

Take a closer look at what's going on here. An actual cashier is one who actually works at Connie's Convenience Store, a living, breathing human being. In an object model (and later, in code), a cashier object is an abstraction; it's not the real thing; it's a figment of your imagination.

A cashier object "knows" and "does" things that the system needs to do, pertaining to the actual cashier. The cashier object and an actual cashier match up perfectly. The cashier object's attributes and the actual cashier's attributes match up, too.

#50. "Select Attributes from Actual Ones" Strategy	establishing responsibilities / what I know (fundamentals)
• This is an aspect of a software object coming to life: "I know selective things that describe the actual object that I'm an abstraction of." • Select the attributes for your software objects, taken from the abundance of the attributes that could be used to describe a corresponding actual (real-world) object. • Consider attributes from a broad-sweeping perspective; then work your way into the specific ones you need. Look at attributes in general, in this domain, and ultimately just within this system's responsibilities.	

The cashier object's services and the actual cashier's services match up, too—but only if you are developing a simulation system. Otherwise, and that means for most applications, the services are remarkably different.

Why? Because the services for an object in an object model are those services that it must fulfill to do its part in achieving the system's responsibilities. And the services that an object in an object model is best suited for are the ones which take advantage of and fully utilize what that object knows and who that object knows. Then an object comes to life with what it does.

You want to ask the question "Is authorized?" Which automated object should you turn to? Or you want to send the command "assess performance for a time interval." Who does this work for you?

The worker is a cashier object, of course. It's the one with sufficient knowledge to coordinate getting these services accomplished. (Otherwise, without this approach, you end up with a model of data-holding "objects" and function-blob "objects." Yuck!)

By letting a cashier object take on these services itself, you get lower coupling, stronger cohesion, and domain-based partitioning of services (not just domain-based partitioning of attributes). What a deal!

A side note: personification is a vital aspect of "object think." It's one of the most important principles on where to place a service. It helps object modelers strive for distributed attributes and services, based upon the domain-based partitioning of classes. It helps people let go of "DFD think" and "ERD think."[2] Moreover, personification itself is extremely engaging. Try it out, especially when working out dynamics with scenarios.

What kind of services do you need for cashier?

---

[2]DFD stands for data flow diagram and ERD stands for entity-relationship diagram. These are both part of design methods that separate data and functions. Yuck!

#90. "Service as a Question" Strategy	establishing responsibilities / what I do (fundamentals)

- Ask: what questions can an object answer?
- Some good starting words to choose from: has, how many, how much, includes, is.
- Why: stronger encapsulation, better partitioning of services; fewer objects that are mere data holders.

One useful cashier service answers the question "Is authorized?" Write it down like this:

    – is authorized.

What's another?

#91. "Service as a Verb" Strategy	establishing responsibilities / what I do (fundamentals)

- Some good service name verbs to choose from:
  activate (initialize, initiate, open, start)
  answer (reply, respond)
  assess (appraise, assay, evaluate, value)
  calculate (compute, count, estimate, rate, tally)
  deactivate (close, end, shut down, terminate)
  determine (decide, figure out, observe, resolve)
  find (get, look for, pinpoint)
  measure (bound, gauge, limit)
  monitor (conduct, direct, manage, observe, operate, supervise, watch)
  qualify (characterize, differentiate, discriminate, distinguish, mark)
  select (choose, cull, elect, opt for, pick).
- Append "over interval" for services that apply to different time intervals.

Another useful cashier service is:

    – assess performance.

If a service is something that could be applied over many intervals of time, add "over interval" to the service name (Figure 1–23).

Revised, a cashier's services are:

    – is authorized
    – assess performance over interval.

Model it.

Figure 1–23: Cashier: "what I do."

Participant: customer

Connie has already decided to hold off on finding a way to know about specific customers.

Yet, what if you had a customer object? It could do some interesting things for you, though.

#88. "Why, Why, Why" Strategy	establishing responsibilities / what I do (fundamentals)

• Add value by asking "why, why, why?"
   Why, why, does the system need this object anyway?
   What useful questions can it answer? What useful actions can it perform?
   What is done to an actual object, something that this object could do itself?	

It's the active side of objects that's the exciting aspect; the active side tells you more about the "why, why, why" of having that object in the object model. A customer object could:

- tally purchases over interval
- tally purchase rate over interval
- tally number of returns over interval
- tally number of bad checks over interval.

Such services all fall under one important heading, "assess customer" or "qualify customer."

Note: "assess" is a stereotypical behavior for a participant; look for "assess" services whenever you consider the active side of a participant object.

Responsibilities for places
Store

Why do you need a store object?

Yes, you could keep track of the name, address, and other attribute values for a store.

More importantly, a store object gives you a place to put those calculations that apply across a collection of what a store contains: registers, items, and cashiers.

#102. "Service across a Collection" Strategy	establishing responsibilities / what I do (where to put)
• Service across a collection of objects? Add a service to a collection object, an object that knows and does things across that collection. Let each worker within a collection do its fair share—as much as it can, based upon what it knows. • Be sure the collection does just those things that apply across a collection; makes its workers do as much work as they know enough to accomplish. • Across its workers: enforce business rules that may apply to its participation.	

Establish responsibilities: "what I know."

#53. "Establish Place Attributes" Strategy	establishing responsibilities / what I know (pattern players)
• For location, include: number, name, address (perhaps latitude, longitude, altitude).	

Just include the name of the store; that's enough for now.
   – name.

Establish responsibilities: "who I know."

#75. "Establish Place Object Connections" Strategy	establishing responsibilities / who I know (pattern players)
• For a location, include object connections to objects which come to rest at a location . . . or are contained by a location. • For a location, include object connections to transaction objects, to show that location's participation in that transaction.	

Who does a store object know? A store object, as a container, knows its contents:
   – registers (zero or more)
   – items (zero or more)
   – cashiers (zero or more).

It also needs to know its transactions—so it can answer questions and perform calculations across its collection of transactions:

    – sales made in the store (zero or more).

It also needs to know some descriptive objects:

    – tax categories that apply to the store (zero or more).

(From the other direction, each register, item, cashier, and sale knows a corresponding store. A sale knows its corresponding store. A tax category knows its corresponding stores.)

Establish responsibilities: "what I do."

#95. "Establish Place Services" Strategy	establishing responsibilities / what I do (pattern players)
• For a place, include: calculate for me, rate me, is <value>. • For a place as a collection, include: how many, how much, rank transactions, rank contents, rank container line items, calculate over transactions, calculate over contents, calculate over container line items (plus services to enforce business rules across that collection).	

What useful things can a store object do, to support a point-of-sale system?

A couple of things come to mind. How about:

    – get item for UPC
    – get cashier for number.

What useful things can a store object do, with calculations across its collection of objects? It can do plenty. As you investigate the content for each window and report, you can add services that span "across the collection of things in a store" to store itself.

Add store responsibilities to the model (Figure 1–24):

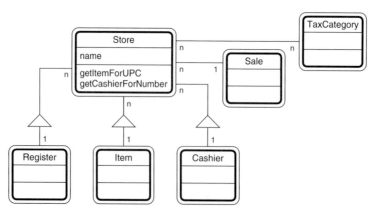

Figure 1–24: Store: what I know, who I know, what I do.

Responsibilities for tangible things

Establish responsibilities for tangible things in the store:

>   – item
>   – register
>   – cash drawer

and

>   – tax category.

You'll work on sale and other transactions, immediately after that.

Item

Establish responsibilities: "what I know."

An actual item is described by its item number, description, universal product code (UPC), expiration date, price, and whether it's taxable or not.

An item object "knows" its values for those same attributes (Figure 1–25):

>   – number
>   – description
>   – UPCs
>   – prices
>   – taxable (either it's taxable or it's not).

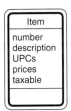

Figure 1–25: Item: "what I know."

Wait a minute!

Some of these attributes seem to have repeating values. That's a good place to look for additional objects.

Consider UPC

An item object potentially knows a collection of UPC values.

Using an attribute which has a number of repeating values is not a problem.

#64. "Attribute with Repeating Values" Strategy	establishing responsibilities / what I know (consider and challenge)

• An attribute that may have a number of values?
 	
 • Add a new class to your model. Add an object connection. Look for additional attributes that may apply.
       Add a new class, even if it has only one attribute for now.
       Why: make the most of problem-domain partitioning; pave the way for
         accommodating future change gracefully.
 	
 • Example: Item with the attribute UPCs. Add a UPC class. Add an object connection between an item and its UPCs.	

If you potentially could have attributes for each repeating value, then go ahead and split what's being described as another class in your model. It's domain-based partitioning. Even if the new class has only one attribute, go ahead and add it anyway. As you find a need for additional attributes and services, you'll already have this domain-based partitioning in your model. And that's a good deal.

Here, UPC is the repeating value. An item in Connie's Convenience Store may correspond to many manufacturer-issued UPCs. Could you have potentially many attributes for each UPC? Absolutely. A UPC could be described by its code, its bit-map image, its originator, and its date of first usage.

Right now, within this system's responsibilities, suppose that all you care about is the UPC itself. No matter. Go ahead and add a UPC class, with the attribute "upc."

How about an object connection, too? Yes, you need one. An item knows its UPC objects. And a UPC object knows its items. Connect item and UPC with an object connection (Figure 1-26).

Consider price

An item object knows many prices. Hey, you don't believe it? Check it out with Connie!

(Peter) Tell me about the prices of an item.

(Connie) An item has a regular price, beginning on an effective date; we keep track of past, present, and future regular prices. In addition, an item often has a promotional price, good from an effective date through an expiration date; we keep track of past, present, and future promotional prices. We pride ourselves in giving our customers the best price that applies at the time of purchase.

(Peter) Do you plan prices in advance? When would you add them to the system?

(Connie) We plan ahead. And we definitely need to enter the new prices in advance of their effective dates.

So what does all of this mean to your object model?

An item knows its price objects.
An item knows its regular prices (with price and effective date).
An item knows its promotional prices (with price, effective date, and expiration date).

So what should you add to your model?

Add a price class, with the attributes:

– price
– effective date.

Add a specialization class, promo price, with the attributes:

– price
– effective date
– expiration date.

But wait! A specialization class inherits the attributes, connections, services, and messages that apply to its generalization class. You see, a gen-spec structure communicates "what's the same; what's different."

What's the same:

– price
– effective date.

What's different:

– expiration date.

Add it to your model.

What about object connections? An item knows its price objects. And a price object knows its item. So connect item and price with an object connection (Figure 1–26):

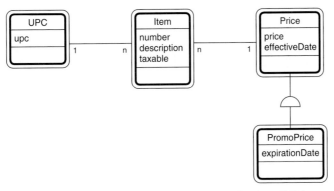

Figure 1–26: Discovering additional objects and responsibilities.

On describing each attribute

At some point along the way, you might add some descriptive information about each attribute.

First things first, however. Pick good attribute names, ones that communicate exceedingly well. A well-chosen name is far more helpful than an abundance of descriptive words. (Hey! And that means if you need a long-winded attribute description, you should find a better attribute name.)

Nevertheless, you may want to add attribute descriptions, more fully communicating what each attribute is all about.

#58. "Describe Attributes with a Template" Strategy	establishing responsibilities / what I know (descriptions)

- Describe each attribute, using a template as your guide.
  description
  legal values (range; limit; enumeration of values)
  unit of measure
  data type
  tolerance
  required (yes or no)
  get/set constraints
  how to get a default value from another source, in the event a custom value is
      not known
  applicable states (for state-dependent attributes)
  traceability codes (to a requesting document, if any).

You might choose to write this in natural language; you might choose to write this in a formal specification language (like Object-Z, if you're a "zed-head"). Or you might just want to sketch it out with programming language syntax.

You may as well get in the habit of writing down some short descriptions. And you may even find some additional attributes and services along the way. (Ah! Some immediate gratification from doing this grunt work. That would be nice. Read on.)

Work out some attribute descriptions for item's attributes.

Begin with number and description:

- number: an identifying number, uniquely assigned by Connie's
    required: yes
- description: a name for the item (it may be a brand name)
    required: yes
    length = 20 characters
- taxable: an indication whether or not this item is taxable
    enumeration of values: yes or no
    default: yes.[3]

Hmmm. Something seems suspicious here.

#61. "Yes/No Attribute" Strategy	establishing responsibilities / what I know (consider and challenge)

- Attribute has values "yes or no?"
  The attribute name itself may be a value for some other attribute name
  Example: taxable (yes or no); change to tax status (taxable, tax-exempt, resale).
  Why bother: added detail now, added ease of change in the future.

---

[3]You'll see very few attribute or service descriptions like this in this book. Writing descriptions is pretty straightforward. Reading them is unbelievably boring (and that's not something for *this* book). Nevertheless, for some systems and organizations, detailed attribute (and service) descriptions are required writing. So be it.

"Taxable" is a "yes/no" attribute, that is, it has the value "yes" or "no."

Check it out. "Taxable" is the name of a value: an item is "taxable" or "nontaxable." Using a value as an attribute name is boring; it's a "yes/no" kind of thing. Moreover, using a value as an attribute is unwise; as soon as you've got additional values, you're in trouble; at that point, your object model will become more complex than it needs to be.

Think about what happens at a store you visited recently. Are all items taxed at the same rate? Or do special taxes apply to certain categories of items?

That's it! Some categories of items may be taxable, while others are not. Instead of taxable, what an item object really needs to know is its tax category. Model that "need to know" with an object connection to tax category.

Carefully examining each attribute does pay off. And writing attribute descriptions certainly gets one to consider that kind of detail. Based upon the added insight, here's what item looks like now (Figure 1–27):

Figure 1–27: Item: "what I know."

Establish responsibilities: "who I know."

Who does an item object know?

It knows:

    – UPC (zero or more).
    – price (zero or more).
    – tax category (zero or more).
    – sale line item (zero or more).

Yes, each UPC, price, and tax category object knows its items. A sale line item knows its item, too (Figure 1-28).

Establish responsibilities: "what I do."

Why do you need this abstraction, an item object?

Certainly one reason is to remember the values of the attributes of an item.

Yet there is a far more important reason why you might add an item object. And that reason is to capture some system dynamics. What does the system really need to do regarding its items?

Hopefully, an item is something more than just a data holder. Look for something more than that.

What can this abstraction do for you?

Apply the "do it myself" strategy. Here it is again (it's important):

#86. "Do It Myself" Strategy	establishing responsibilities / what I do (fundamentals)

- This is an aspect of a software object coming to life: "I do those things that are normally done to the actual object that I'm an abstraction of."

- Here's why. "Doing it myself" encapsulates attributes with the services that work on those attributes. That results in lower coupling and stronger cohesion.

- If you are building a simulation system, then a software object will mimic what an actual object does. In most systems, this is not so. Software objects do those things that the system is responsible to do with regard to that object.

Consider the actions done to a real item. Then turn them around, letting your abstraction, the one that comes to life in software, actually do those actions to (or for) itself.

List some of the things done to an actual object (in this case, an item):

    – figure out the price for a given date- calculate a total for a given number
         of items.

So let the item abstraction do something useful for you:

    – get price for date
    – how much for quantity.

You could just ask for the price. Yet "how much for quantity" is a good way to encapsulate quantity-sensitive pricing for an item.

Add item responsibilities to your object model (Figure 1-28):

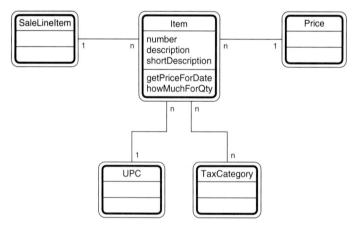

Figure 1–28: Item: "what I know; who I know; what I do."

Register
Establish responsibilities: "what I know."

What does a register object know? It knows its:

> – number (e.g., register number 2).

Establish responsibilities: "who I know."

Who does a register object know? It knows its:

> – store (one)
> – session (zero or more)
> – cash drawer (one, in this system).

(From the other direction, each session, and cash drawer knows its register. A store knows its registers, too.)

Establish responsibilities: "what I do."

What does a register object do?

It provides basic services (get, set, add, remove, delete).

What else could it do?

A register object knows its session objects. So it could do something across that collection of objects, something like this:

> – how much (money collected) over interval
> – how many (sales) over interval.

Add register responsibilities to the model (Figure 1–29):

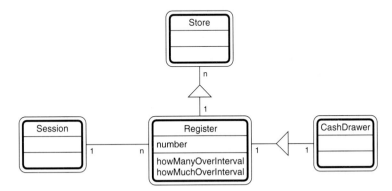

Figure 1–29: Register: "what I know; who I know; what I do."

Cash drawer
Establish responsibilities: "what I know."

What does a cash drawer object know? It knows its:

> – balance
> – position (open, closed)
> – operational state (okay, jammed, missing).

An important note about operational state

Whenever an object represents an interacting system or device, it needs to know its "operational state." You'll need to add service descriptions that portray state-dependent behavior (keywords: precondition, trigger, terminate, postcondition).

Establish responsibilities: "who I know."

A cash drawer object knows its:

> – register.

Establish responsibilities: "what I do."

What does a cash drawer do?

> – open.

When you tell a cash drawer object, an abstraction, to open itself, what happens? The cash drawer object sends an electrical signal to the actual cash drawer device, activating it, so it will open.

(Peter) Hey, Connie, how about a cash drawer that closes automatically?

(Connie) Nice idea, especially if someone leaves their drawers open in public. (Sorry about that.) Anyway, automatically closing cash drawers are not available.

Go ahead and add cash-drawer responsibilities to your model (Figure 1–30):

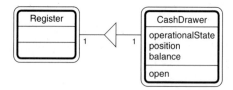

Figure 1–30: Cash drawer: "what I know; who I know; what I do."

Tax category
Establish responsibilities: "what I know."

A tax category object knows its category, its rate, and its effective date.

Note: a combination of category and rate values might occur again and again, on various dates. This makes it a good candidate for an item-specific item pattern (although this is not pursued further in this chapter).

Establish responsibilities: "who I know."

A tax category object knows its:

> –items.

(And yes, an item knows its tax categories.)

Establish responsibilities: "what I do."

What does a tax category do? Just the basic services: get, set, add (a connection), remove (a connection), and delete.

Add tax category responsibilities to your model (Figure 1–31):

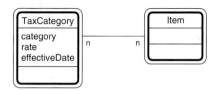

Figure 1–31: Tax category: "what I know; who I know; what I do."

Responsibilities for problem-domain transactions

Transactions are moments in time in which objects interact, moments in time that a system is responsible to remember for some future need.

Investigate your transactions:

> – sale (and its part, sale line item)
> – payment
> – session.

Sale

Establish responsibilities: "what I know."

#54. "Establish Transaction Attributes" Strategy	establishing responsibilities / what I know (pattern players)
• For transactions, include: number, date, time, status. • For line items, include: quantity (if it knows an item, rather than a specific item), status.	

What do you need here, for a sale? In this case, add these two attributes:

> – date and time.

What about total? Here's the strategy:

#66. "Calculable Result" Strategy	establishing responsibilities / what I know (consider and challenge)

• An attribute for holding a calculable result? At first, don't show it in the object model.
 	
• At some point, you may want to add the attribute. Here's how:
 Add an explicit "get <attribute>" service for it.
  Specify that service so it:
   checks for an attribute value—and returns it, if it has one
   otherwise, invokes a calculate service, saves the result, and returns the result
    to the sender.
  Add an explicit "calculate <attribute>" service, too—so you can tell the object to do the
   calculation you want it to do.	

You could add "total" as an attribute and "get total" as a service. Here, though, keep it simple and just plan on adding a "calculate total" service to your model.

Establish responsibilities: "who I know."

In general, who does a transaction object know?

#76. "Establish Transaction Object Connections" Strategy	establishing responsibilities / who I know (pattern players)
• For a transaction, include object connections to: participants, transaction line items, a companion transaction, one that occurs at the same moment in time. • For a transaction line item, include object connections to: the transaction, a companion "item description" object, a subsequent transaction line item.	

How about this time, for a sale? Well, previously, using patterns, you discovered who a sale knows:

    – session
    – payment
    – sale line items.

That's that.

Establish responsibilities: "what I do."

#96. "Establish Transaction Services" Strategy	establishing responsibilities / what I do (pattern players)
• For a transaction, include: calculate for me, rate me, is <value>. • For a transaction as a collection, include: how many, how much, rank transaction line items, rank subsequent transactions, calculate over transaction line items, calculate over subsequent transactions (plus services to enforce business rules across that collection). • For line items, include: calculate for me, rate me.	

So what about for this point-of-sale system? What useful things could a sale do? How about:

- – calculate subtotal for the sale (without tax)
- – calculate the discount for the sale
- – calculate tax for the sale
- – calculate total for the sale (total amount due with tax)
- – commit.

Add sale responsibilities to your object model (Figure 1–32):

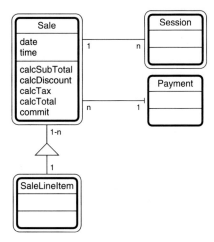

Figure 1–32: Sale: "what I know; who I know; what I do."

Sale line item

Establish responsibilities: "what I know."

In general, what does a transaction line item know? Usually, it knows:

- – a date and time, if needed for each line item
- – quantity
- – tax status (regular, resale, tax-exempt, and the like).

How about in this case? What does a sale line item know?

- quantity
- tax status.

Establish responsibilities: "who I know."

In general, who does a transaction line item know?

It knows:

- an item (or some other tangible thing), the one for which the transaction line item knows a quantity value
- a subsequent line item.

How about in this case? Who does a sale line item know?

- an item.

A sale line item could know a return line item. Hold onto that thought. You'll get a chance to pursue it in a few pages.

Meanwhile . . .

A sale line item knows:

- an item
- a sale.

(And each sale and item knows some number of sale line items.)

Establish responsibilities: "what I do."

Now turn to the active side of a sale line item. What useful things could a sale line item do? How about:

- calculate subtotal (for this sale line item).

Add sale line-item responsibilities to your model (Figure 1–33):

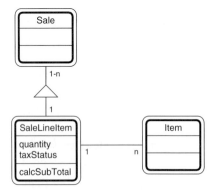

Figure 1–33: Sale line item: "what I know; who I know; what I do."

On describing each service

A good service name goes a long way toward describing what a service is all about.

At some point along the way, you can add some service descriptions, too. After all, you and others need to know what you really intend for each service.

#116. "Describe Services with a Template" Strategy	establishing responsibilities / what I do (descriptions)

• Describe each service, using a template as your guide.
    input, output parameters
    description (including pseudo-code or actual code, detailing the algorithm to be applied)
    traceability codes to preceding documentation, if any
    visibility: public, protected, private.	

Here, consider what it takes to describe the "calculate total" services for sale and for sale line item.

Using structured language, you can develop a description that looks something like this:

```
sale.calcTotal ( ; total)
    calcSubtotal ( ; subtotal)
    calcDiscount (subtotal ; discount)
    total = subtotal - discount
    calcTax (total ; tax)
    total = total + tax
sale.calcSubtotal ( ; subtotal)
    subtotal = 0
    for each saleLineItem that I know:
        saleLineItem.calcSubtotal ( ; lineItemTotal)
        subtotal = subtotal + lineItemTotal.
```

Sale line item, revisited

A sale line item may be for a sale or for a return.

Do you need any specializations of a sale line item? Check it out. A generalization class shows "what's the same." A specialization class shows "what's different."

Consider what's the same, what's different. In particular, with any kind of transaction, consider how much control, or lack of control, you have in the situation being recorded.

You've got pretty good control over a purchase: you have the item, a customer wants to buy it; you're in control.

Returns are the real challenge: you're getting an item you've had no control over; you don't have as much control; a lot of unusual things can happen. For example:

– A customer may return an item to a different location than where he purchased it.
– A customer may return an item which had a different price when he purchased it.
– A customer may return an item that Connie's no longer carries.
– A customer may return an item that was individually marked down, perhaps because it was slightly damaged.
– A customer may return an item and be charged a return fee.

A return line item knows what a sale line item knows, plus:
- return price
- reason code
- sale date
- sale price.

Sounds like a great use of gen-spec. It's domain-based. Some responsibilities are the same; some are different.

#67. "Common Attributes" Strategy	establishing responsibilities / what I know (consider and challenge)
• Classes with common attributes? • If the attributes have the same name and meaning, and if you can find a generalization-specialization that makes good sense, then add a generalization class and factor out the commonality.	

#120. "Common Services" Strategy	establishing responsibilities / what I do (consider and challenge)
• Classes with common services? If the services have the same name and meaning, and if you can find a generalization-specialization that makes good sense, then add a generalization class and factor out whatever commonality you discovered.	

If the service name is the same, yet the details of the service are different, then show the service name in both the generalization and the specialization.

Add a return line item, a specialization of a sale line item (Figure 1–34):

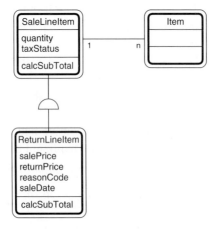

Figure 1–34: Sale line items and return line items: what's the same, what's different.

Payment and kinds of payments

What about payments and the three kinds of payments: cash, check, and charge?

Consider what's the same, what's different.

Establish responsibilities: "what I know."

What's the same? Each payment knows its:

> – amount paid.

What's different?

Each cash object knows its:

> – cash tendered.

Each check object knows its:

> – bank routing number
> – account number
> – amount tendered
> – authorization code.

Each credit object knows its:

> – card type
> – card number
> – expiration date
> – authorization code.

Note that two specializations, check and credit, have a common attribute: authorization code. If these attributes are the same in name and in meaning, and if you can add a domain-based generalization, add a new generalization to the gen-spec structure.

Here it is:

> payment
> > cash
> > authorized payment
> > > check
> > > credit.

By doing this, you explicitly express commonality (Figure 1–35). Good show!

Establish responsibilities: "who I know."

What's the same? Each payment knows its corresponding:

> – sale.

(And yes, a sale knows about its corresponding payments. Remember, at Connie's, a customer may make several payments, with some combination of cash, check, and charge.)

Okay, what's different for the kinds of payments? Nothing comes to mind here. Onward!

Establish responsibilities: "what I do."

What's the same? Just the basic services.

What's different?

At some point, an authorized payment needs to be authorized. So you can think of an authorized payment object as one that can authorize itself. Add a service called:

> – authorize.

Add payment (and kinds of payment) responsibilities to the object model. Be sure to include authorized payment, too (Figure 1–35):

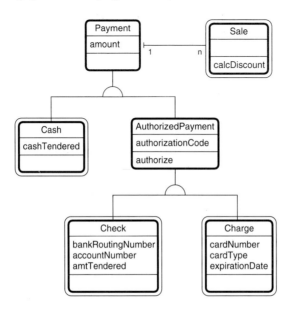

Figure 1–35: Payments and kinds of payments: "what I know; who I know; what I do."

Session

After all of that, a session will seem like a cakewalk.

It is.

Establish responsibilities: "what I know."

What does a session object know?

> The attributes are:

>> – start date
>> – start time
>> – end date
>> – end time.

Establish responsibilities: "who I know."

Who does a session know?
    A session knows its:

- register
- cashier.

(And yes, each register and cashier knows about its sessions.)

Establish responsibilities: "what I do."

What does a session do?
    A session is a collection of its sales (the sales made during the session). So it can provide these services:

- how much (money collected) over interval
- how many (sales) over interval.

    Add session responsibilities to your object model (Figure 1–36):

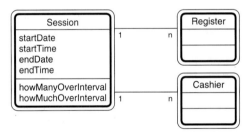

Figure 1–36: Session: "what I know; who I know; what I do."

APPLYING PATTERNS: ESTABLISH PROBLEM-DOMAIN RESPONSIBILITIES

At this point, you've established a number of responsibilities for each PD object, spanning "what I know, who I know, and what I do."
    Now consider patterns. A pattern includes stereotypical responsibilities for each object in the pattern. Check it out, with collection-worker.

Collection-worker

Consider the fundamental pattern of object modeling: collection-worker.

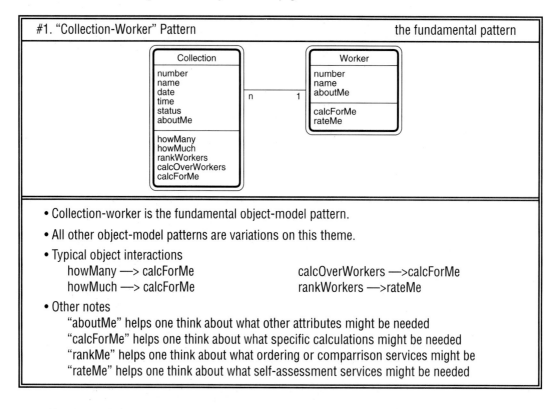

#1. "Collection-Worker" Pattern   the fundamental pattern

- Collection-worker is the fundamental object-model pattern.

- All other object-model patterns are variations on this theme.

- Typical object interactions
  - howMany —> calcForMe   calcOverWorkers —>calcForMe
  - howMuch —> calcForMe   rankWorkers —>rateMe

- Other notes
  - "aboutMe" helps one think about what other attributes might be needed
  - "calcForMe" helps one think about what specific calculations might be needed
  - "rankMe" helps one think about what ordering or comparrison services might be
  - "rateMe" helps one think about what self-assessment services might be needed

A collection object knows about some number of workers.

A collection object only does those things which apply across its collection of workers, e.g., it calculates, rates, and selects.

A worker does all that it can do with what it knows, or with what others may tell it in combination with what it knows.

How do you find places to apply a pattern? Just look for potential pattern players!

In this case, look for objects that know some number of objects. Such a "knowing" is indicated with an object connection (or a special kind of object connection, a whole-part connection) that has an upper-bound constraint of "many."

Many patterns are collection-worker patterns. Apply some here.

Participant-transaction

Okay, you worked with this one a bit earlier. Consider cashier and session. A cashier object knows all of the sessions it has participated in. So a cashier object is the logical place to put any service that needs to do something across such a collection of sessions. For example, you could ask a cashier object to calculate the quantity sold over a specified interval. You could also let a cashier object calculate its total amount of sales made over a specified interval. Hence:

– cashier (collection) . . . of its sessions
    how much (money collected) over time
    how many (sales) over time.

What's next?

Transaction–transaction line item

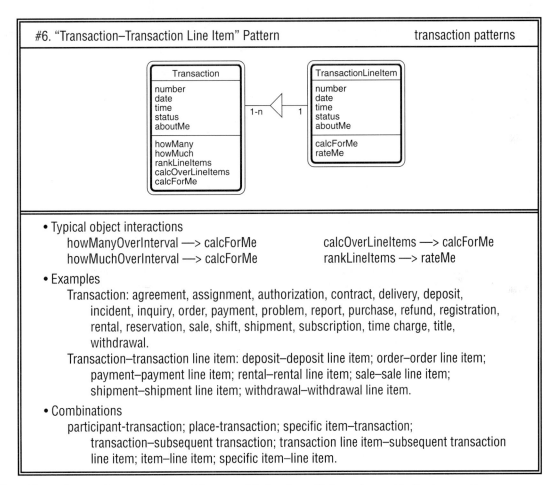

Consider what each transaction object could do, in collaboration with its transaction line items.

    Continuing, take a look at sale–sale line item:

– sale (collection) . . . of its line items
    calculate subtotal
– sale line item (worker)
    calculate subtotal.

Item–line item

Okay. What's next? How about this:

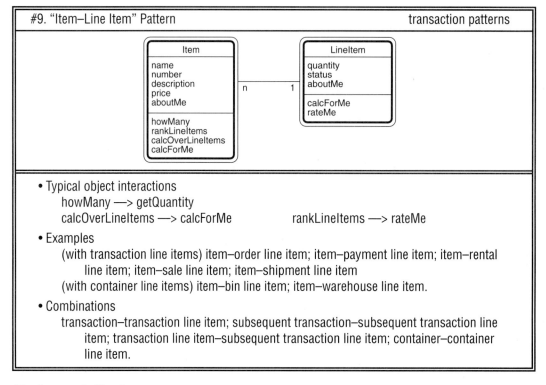

For item–sale line item:
- item (collection … of its sale line items)
   how much over interval
- sale line item (worker)
   how much over interval.

Add services to item and sale line item, and by analogy to cashier, session, and sale (Figure 1–37):

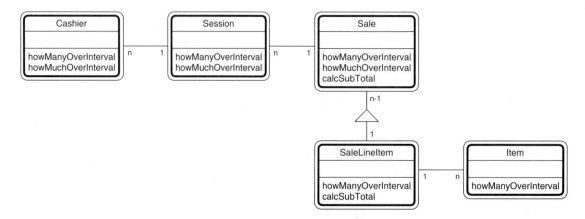

Figure 1–37: Some pattern instances.

Progress at this point

You've now selected objects and established responsibilities for the problem domain objects.

Here's your progress at this point (Figure 1–38):

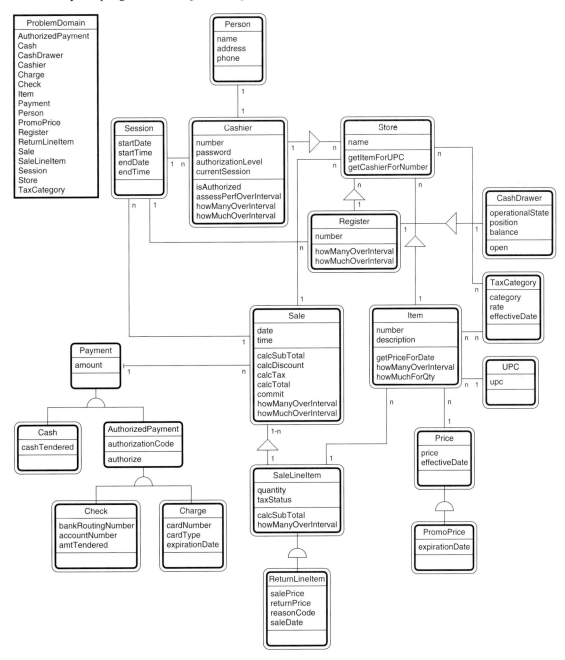

Figure 1–38: Progress at this point.

WORKING OUT PROBLEM-DOMAIN DYNAMICS WITH SCENARIOS

A scenario is a time-ordered sequence of object interactions to fulfill a specific need. It describes a needed capability, one which is accomplished by some number of objects working together.

Why use scenarios? Here's why:

- To find additional objects.
- To better distribute and refine responsibilities.
- To gain better understanding of system dynamics.
- To assess model completeness.
- To test an object model (ultimately, to test the system itself).

Develop and describe each scenario with a scenario view. A scenario view is simply a view on an object model, called out to portray a scenario.

It's not possible or practical to consider every scenario within a system of any significant size. So focus on the key scenarios, ones that give you:

- Insight into critical object interaction sequences

    You may want to consider several scenarios, perhaps as many as a couple dozen.

- Insight into object-model completeness

    After some initial scenarios, you should experience a decreasing number of discoveries of additional objects and responsibilities.

Select key scenarios

#127. "Select Key Scenarios" Strategy	working out dynamics with scenarios

- Work out and demonstrate the satisfaction of a system feature.
    Include scenarios that get you to work through the object interactions that are required to deliver a feature of the system under consideration.
    Consider using subscenarios, to make a scenario easier to work with and easier to understand.
- Stretch the model, examining it for completeness.
    Include scenarios that really stretch your object model; use them to check out the overall completeness of your model.
- Examine key object interactions within your model.
    Include scenarios that let you investigate dynamics for important services in your model.

Admittedly, the most interesting scenarios are those which start with a human interface or a system interface, and wind their way through the objects in your system.

Yet at this point, all you've developed are PD objects. Yet even within the PD objects, you can work out some meaningful scenarios. Just look for a service that needs some help from other objects to get its job done. For example, for a sale, you could choose to take a closer look at its calculate total service. Then you can consider scenarios that begin with human interaction, as we will later in this chapter.

Scenario: sale calculates its total

Okay. So check it out.

(Pete) How do you calculate the total for a sale?

(Connie) Well, it is not too hard. You have to calculate the subtotal of all of the line items and add to it the total taxes due on that amount.

A scenario view shows:

> – the objects participating in the scenario (across the top of the view)

followed by a time sequence (going down the page) with the following:

> – sending service, a message arrow, a receiving service, and arguments
> – sending service, a message arrow, a receiving service, and arguments
> – sending service, a message arrow, a receiving service, and arguments.

You get the idea.

Please note that there is a leveling of detail here. Scenario views fully expose the object interactions. Service descriptions present the details of a specific service. So, it's time to build a scenario view.

Here's a good way to do it. Begin with the services within the "recognizer." Then expand the scenario, to include interacting objects, too. Consider sale and its messaging (hey, it's not very exciting, but it's a start). Develop a scenario view (Figure 1–39):

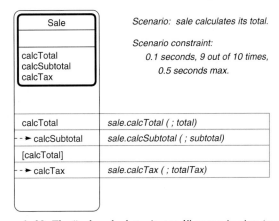

Figure 1–39: The "sale calculates its total" scenario view (round I).

Here's how to read it:

> A specific sale object is told to calculate its total.
>
> The "calcTotal" service invokes the "calcSubtotal" service.
> The "calcSubtotal" service returns "subtotal."
>
> The "calcTotal" service invokes the "calcTax" service.
> The "calcTax" service returns "totalTax."
>
> The "calcTotal" service returns "total."

Here are some scenario view conventions and notes:

- The "recognizer" object is in the left-most column.
- The first service in the scenario is listed immediately below the "class with objects" symbol, in that first column.
- A sending service is the service name that precedes the tail of a message arrow. Within an object symbol, when you need to explicitly identify which service is the sending service, use square brackets, identifying the sending service.
- The argument list consists of inputs, followed by a semicolon, then outputs.

Now expand this scenario. What does it take for a sale to calculate its subtotal?

Remember the pattern at work here. Sale–sale line item is an instance of the transaction–transaction line item pattern.

A sale tells each of its items to calculate its total.

Does a sale line item know enough to calculate its total? No. What else does it need? It needs the item's price. Who knows the price? An item does (indirectly; it needs to work with its price objects).

What do you really want an item to do for you? Instead of giving you a value, what answer or what result do you need? It's this: how much for quantity and date.

Now we're getting somewhere. That's one of the system features. Yes!

Work out the scenario view, this time for sale, sale line item, and item (Figure 1–40):

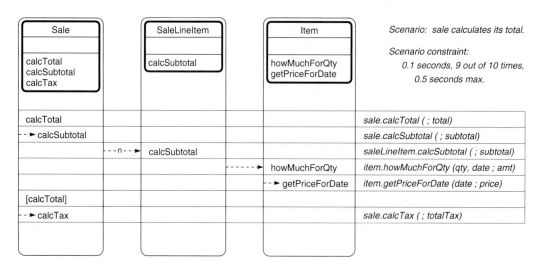

Figure 1–40: The "sale calculates its total" scenario view (round II).

Here's how to read it:

A sale object is told to calculate its total.

The "calcTotal" service invokes the "calcSubtotal" service.

The "calcSubtotal" sends a "calcSubtotal" message to a sale line item
object (it repeats this for all of its sale line items).

A sale line item is told to calculate its subtotal.

The "calcSubtotal" service sends a "howMuchForQty" message to an
item object, giving it a quantity and a date.[4]

An item object is told to calculate its amount for quantity.

The "howMuchForQty" service invokes the "getPriceForDate"
service, giving it a date.

The "getPriceForDate" service returns a price.

The "howMuchForQty" returns an amount.

The "calcSubtotal" service returns a subtotal.

The "calcSubtotal" service returns "subtotal."

The "calcTotal" service invokes the "calcTax" service.

The "calcTax" service returns "totalTax."

The "calcTotal" service returns "total."

Here's another scenario view convention:

– The "n" on a message arrow indicates that a message may be sent to
some number of objects (Figure 1–40).

So when you see (Figure 1–41):

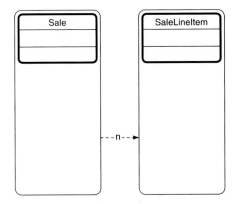

Figure 1–41: Sending a message to some number of objects.

---

[4]Note that "how much for qty" requires that the quantity be passed to it, as an argument. One
might cry out, "just ask for the value and reduce the argument coupling." But wait; argument
coupling is not the full story here. Consider the following. Would it be generally useful for an
item to be able to calculate "how much for qty?" Yes. And as the business rules become more
complicated, what object will eventually know enough so it can calculate quantity discounts for
a particular item? An item object (line items never need to know about detail like that).

Very cool.

What's being expressed is this (Figure 1–42):

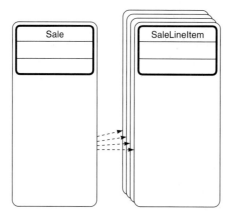

Figure 1–42: Picturing messages to some number of objects in a class.

So far, so good.

What's next? What other sale service needs your attention? It's time to calculate tax.

(Peter) How do you calculate the tax for a sale?

(Connie) Actually, tax collection varies from country to country. Here's what we do in the States. We calculate the subtotal for each tax category. Then we apply the tax rate to each tax category. Finally, we add up the results, to get the tax for a specific sale.

(Peter) Yuck!

Tax matters always complicate things. Welcome to the real world.

Sketch it out:

> A sale asks a store for its tax categories.
> A sale tells a sale line item to calculate its tax for a specified tax category.
>> A sale line item tells its item to calculate its amount in a tax category.
>> An item gets its price for that date.
> A sale asks a tax category for its rate.

You've got some new players: tax category and store (store acts as a collection of tax categories).

Expand the scenario view accordingly (Figure 1–43):

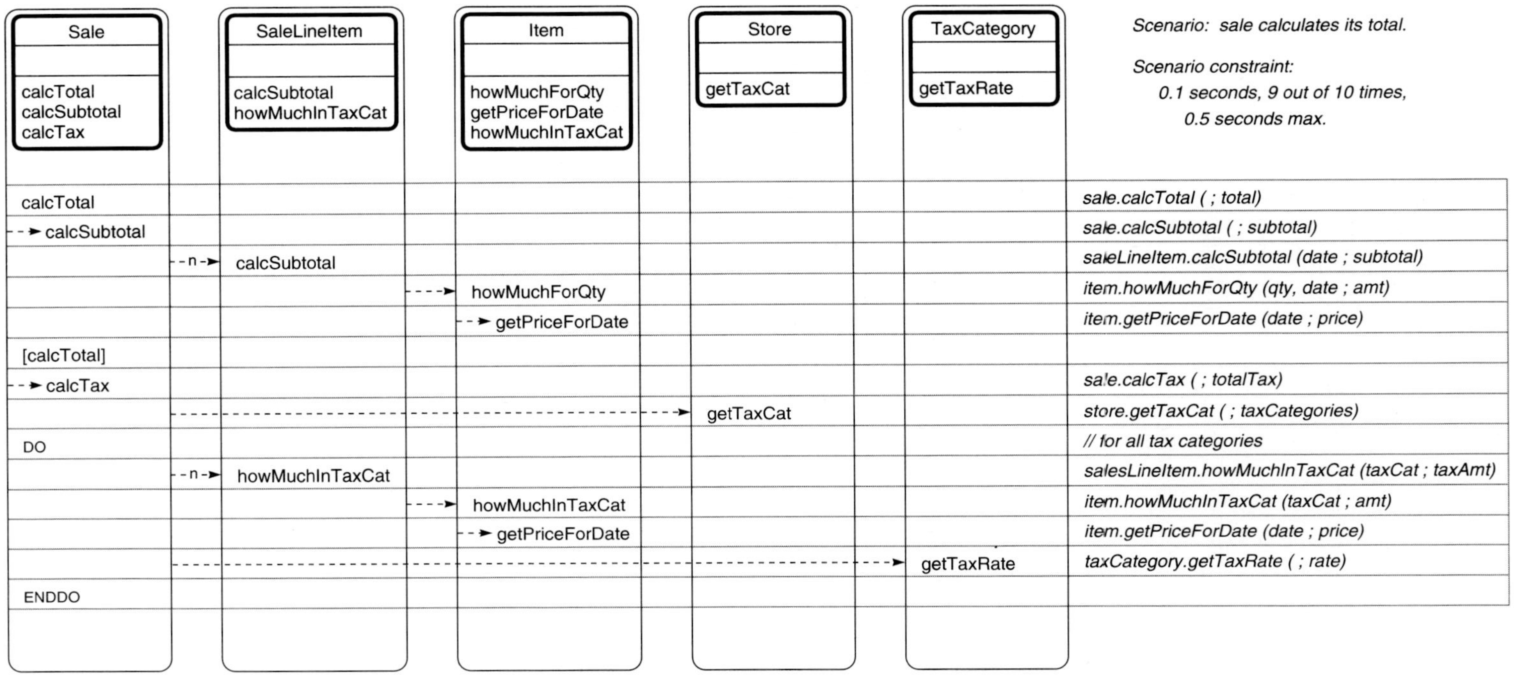

Scenario: *sale calculates its total.*

Scenario constraint:
0.1 seconds, 9 out of 10 times,
0.5 seconds max.

Figure 1–43: The "sale calculates its total" scenario view (final round).

Wow!

By now, you know how to read a scenario view.

This scenario view expands upon these two lines from the previous rounds:

> The "calcTotal" service invokes the "calcTax" service.
> The "calcTax" service returns "totalTax."

Here's what happens now:

> Within a sale object, the "calcTotal" service invokes the "calcTax" service.

> The "calcTax" service sends a "getTaxCat" message to a store object.

>> A store is told to get its tax categories.
>> The "getTaxCat" service returns a collection of tax categories.

> The "calcTax" service sends a "howMuchTaxInCat" message to a sale line item object (and it may do this a number of times), giving it a tax category.

>> A sale line item is told to calculate its tax for a given category.
>> The "howMuchInTaxCat" service sends a "howMuchInTaxCat" message to an item object, giving it a tax category.

>>> An item object is told to calculate its amount within a tax category.
>>> The "howMuchInTaxCat" service invokes the "getPriceForDate" service, giving it a date.

>>> The "getPriceForDate" service returns a price.
>>> The "howMuchInTaxCat" service returns an amount.

>> The "howMuchInTaxCat" service returns a tax amount.
>> The "getTaxRate" service returns a tax rate for that category.
> The "calcTax" service returns "totalTax."

Yes!

Scenarios are vitally important for building effective object models. You work out system dynamics. And you find additional objects and responsibilities along the way. What a deal!

SELECTING HUMAN-INTERACTION OBJECTS

Finally, you are ready to check out some human-interaction objects.

Actually, you might choose to find human-interaction objects; then you could work on problem-domain objects next. Or you might work back and forth, finding objects and dropping them into the HI or PD "buckets." Anyway, at this point it's time to check out some human-interaction objects. In today's systems, human-interaction objects are most often windows or reports.

Select windows

What windows should you consider?

Consider these strategies for selecting windows.

#27. "Select Windows: A First Cut" Strategy	selecting objects (model components)

- Add windows for each problem-domain object that you are working with.

- If an object has line items, model both with a single window.

#28. "Select Logon Window" Strategy	selecting objects (model components)

- Add a logon window—if the system needs to know who is using the system, for access control and accountability.

- Examples: cashier logon window, customer logon window, order clerk logon window—or simply a logon window.

#29. "Select Setup Windows" Strategy	selecting objects (model components)

- Add system setup windows.
    Create and initialize the objects you need, to get the system ready to go.
    Add system administration services for adding users and privileges.

- Add activate and deactivate actions.
    Do this for whatever human interaction might be needed for activating or deactivating
        an interacting system or device.
    Put the actions with a window that knows objects that can carry those actions out.

- Note: Don't include data entry "nuts and bolts," such as screen, monitor keyboard, mouse, mag-stripe reader, and the like.

#30. "Select Core Windows" Strategy	selecting objects (model components)

- Consider who (audience) needs what (content), and why (purpose).

- Add "conducting business" windows.
    Include transaction windows. Examples: sale window, session window, payment
        window.

- Add "analyzing business results" windows.

- Consider combination windows, when content is closely related in time.
    Examples: a transaction and its line items; a sale and payment window.

Window objects for this system

What's needed at Connie's Convenience Store?

> – a logon window
> – a transaction window
> – a sale (and payment) window
> – some transaction participant windows
>> a store window
>> a cashier window
>> a register window
>> a cash drawer window
>> a tax category window
>> a UPC window
>> an item (and price) window
> – a results window
>> a store assessment window.

Select reports

What kind of reports might you need?

> – legally required reports
> – business-required reports.

You don't need to attempt to model all of the reports you may eventually get with ad hoc queries to a database. That would be silly. You don't need batch-checking reports of an existing system. You don't need hardcopy "nut and bolts" like printers.

Report objects for this system

What's needed this time?

#31. "Select Reports" Strategy	selecting objects (model components)
• Put together key summaries and specialized outputs, meeting specific legal or business needs.	
• Look carefully at who (audience) needs what (content), and why (purpose).	
• Don't include every ad hoc query that someone might eventually ask; don't include outdated batch reports.	

A cashier works with one important report:

> – a receipt.

What other reports do you need? Check out the system features. These reports support those objectives:

> – a store report
> – an item report
> – a cashier report

where each report spans a requested time interval, whatever that interval might be.

Add windows and reports to the human interaction component (Figure 1–44):

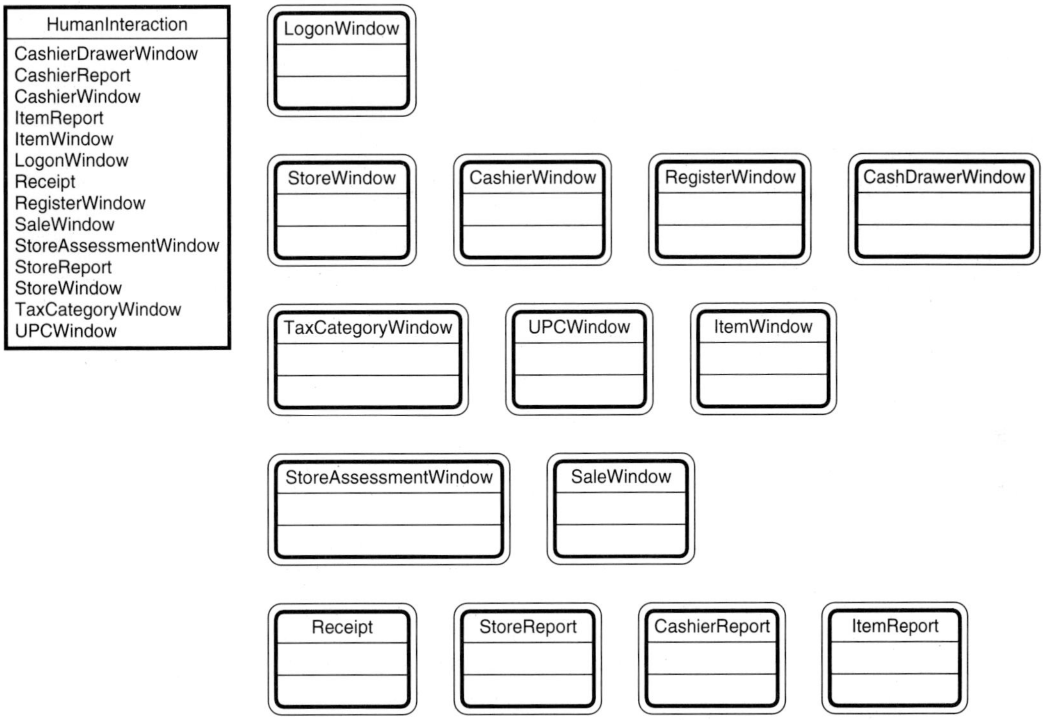

Figure 1–44: Select human interaction windows and reports.

ESTABLISHING HUMAN INTERACTION RESPONSIBILITIES

Responsibilities for windows

How to model a window effectively

In an object model, a window knows what it holds: its components and its screen layout.

Consider a window's components. A window may contain many objects, including views, panes, edit fields, list boxes, menus, buttons, and the like. These objects all work together to create the effect of one large object, a window.

You could build a rather large and complex model for each window. But why? Face it: the tool of choice for building windows in most applications is a GUI builder, one that generates C++ or Smalltalk code. (The only time you would write something yourself, with the help of some graphic class libraries, is when you are building an application that requires some specialized graphics manipulation.)

A far better approach? Here it is:

– In your object model, establish what each window knows and does.
– While working with your GUI builder, select mechanisms (views, panes, edit fields, list boxes, menus, buttons, and the like) so that a window fulfills its responsibilities.

Logon window

Establish responsibilities: "what I know."

#57. "Establish Window or Report Attributes" Strategy	establishing responsibilities / what I know (model components)
• For windows or reports, include: search fields, data entry fields, or both.	

For the logon window, you need these fields:

 – cashier number
 – cashier password
 – register number.

Establish responsibilities: "who I know."

#79. "Establish Window or Report Object Connections" Strategy	establishing responsibilities / who I know (model components)
• For a window or report, include an object connection (expressed as an attribute) to: the contents of the window, the objects it knows directly, to get the content it needs to do its job (note that a window can use those objects to get to other objects, indirectly).	

Here the objects a logon window needs to know include:

 – store (a collection of cashiers, with the ability to search for a cashier, given a cashier number)
 – cashier.

One could model this "who I know" aspect with object connections. Yet object connections that span across object-model components are usually shown textually (so that they are easier to read and understand).

Establish responsibilities: "what I do."

Here's how.

For a window, the "what I do" are those the window-specific menu actions for that window.

In addition, every window object knows how to display itself. And every window class knows how to create (and initialize) a new object in that class.

Here, all you need to add is:

 – logon.

Add the logon window and its responsibilities to the object model (Figure 1–45):

Figure 1–45: Logon window: "what I know; who I know; what I do."

Sale window

Establish responsibilities: "what I know."

Consider a sale window.

What does it know?
> It knows values, ones that it eventually sends as message arguments:

> > – upc
> > – session.

Establish responsibilities: "who I know."

Who does a sale window know?
> Here's the scoop: objects, ones that it eventually sends messages to.
> A sale window needs to send messages to:

> > – sale
> > – sale line item
> > – item
> > – payments.

Establish responsibilities: "what I do."

What does a sale window do?
> Here are the services:

> > – commit
> > – cancel.

> Add sale window responsibilities to the model (Figure 1–46):

Figure 1–46: Sale window: "what I know; who I know; what I do."

For additional windows, follow the same basic strategies, again and again.

Responsibilities for reports

Receipt

Establish responsibilities: "what I know."

Here's how.

For a report, the "what I know" consists of:

– values, ones that it eventually sends as message arguments.

The "who I know" consists of:

– objects that I can send messages to.

Hence, for a receipt, you need this attribute:

– sale.

Establish responsibilities: "what I do."

Here's how.

For a window, the "what I do" are those the report-specific output actions for a window.

Here, it's:

– generate

which internally invokes:

– add heading lines
– add line item line
– add subtotal line
– add tax line
– add total line
– add payment line.

Add receipt and its responsibilities to the object model (Figure 1–47):

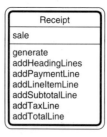

Figure 1–47: Receipt: "what I know; who I know; what I do."

WORKING OUT HUMAN-INTERACTION DYNAMICS WITH SCENARIOS

Find meaningful human interaction scenarios

To begin with: where can you find ideas for meaningful scenarios?

Here's how. Human-interaction scenarios begin with some human interaction.

#128. "Where to Begin a Scenario" Strategy	working out dynamics with scenarios
• Begin with a PD object's service, an HI object's service, or an SI object's service.	

So what human interaction do you need, to get something useful done, like make a sale?

– log on
– make a sale
– log off.

Scenario: log on

Here you go.

Start on the scenario view.

First, get the corresponding cashier object and ask it to verify the password that was entered (Figure 1–48):

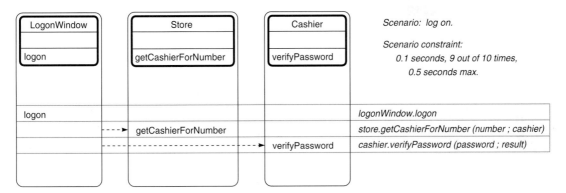

Figure 1–48: The "log on" view (round I).

Next, create a session; then tell the register object to remember it.

To create and initialize a new object in a class, just send the class the message:

    Class.create (initial values ; object).

Here it goes (Figure 1–49):

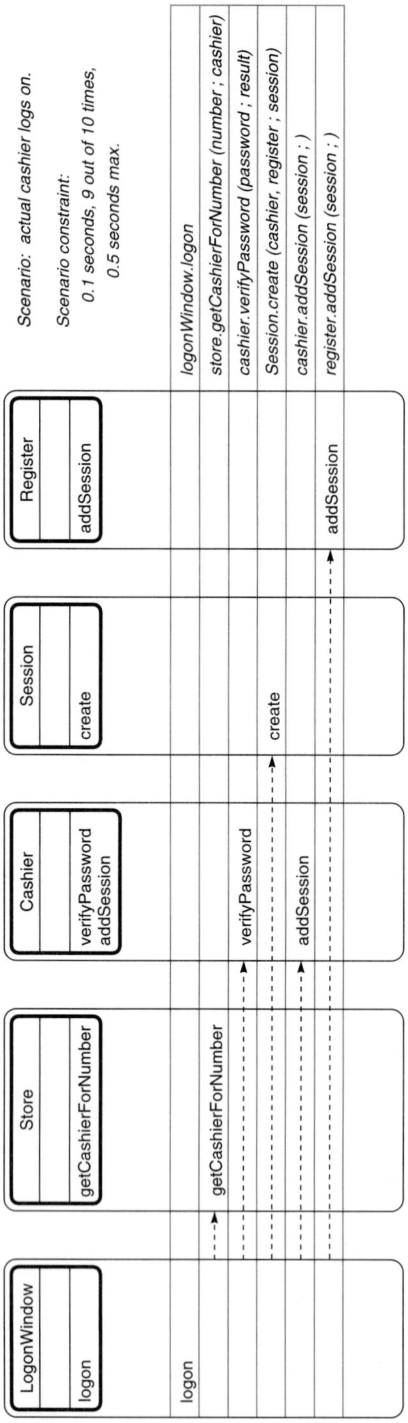

Figure 1–49: The "log on" view (round II).

Now add in the other housekeeping activities, putting together the full scenario (Figure 1–50):

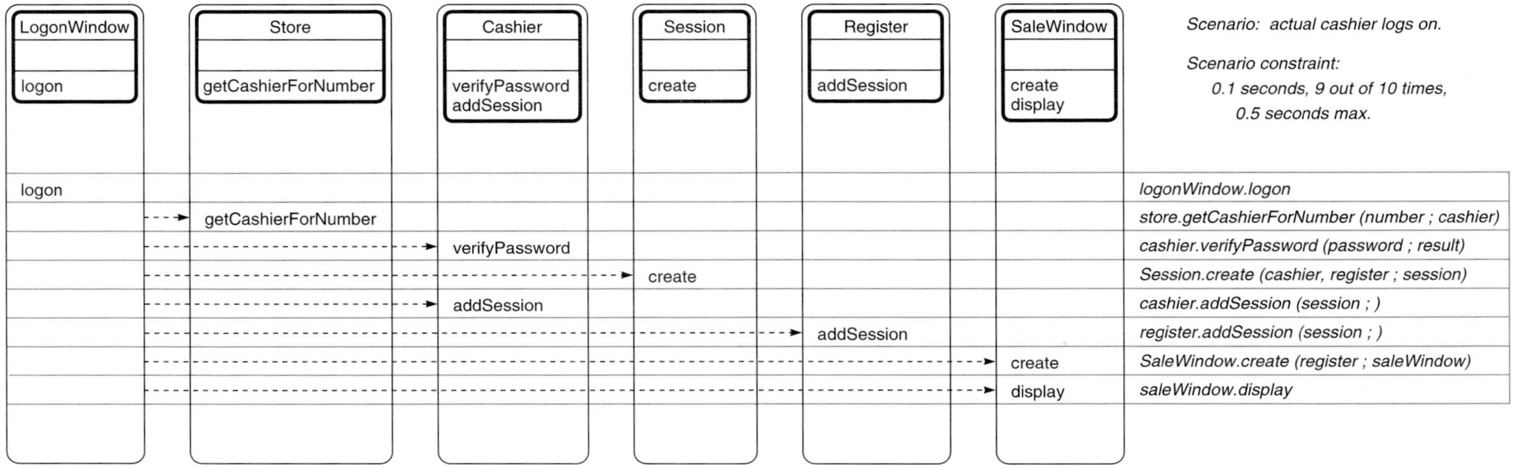
LogonWindow
logon
Store
getCashierForNumber
Cashier
verifyPassword
addSession
Session
create
Register
addSession
SaleWindow
create
display
Scenario: actual cashier logs on.
Scenario constraint:
0.1 seconds, 9 out of 10 times,
0.5 seconds max.
logon
getCashierForNumber
verifyPassword
create
addSession
addSession
create
display
logonWindow.logon
store.getCashierForNumber (number ; cashier)
cashier.verifyPassword (password ; result)
Session.create (cashier, register ; session)
cashier.addSession (session ;)
register.addSession (session ;)
SaleWindow.create (register ; saleWindow)
saleWindow.display

Figure 1–50: The "log on" view (final round).

Scenario: make a sale

This scenario consists of a number of shorter scenarios:

      – start sale
      – sell item
      – total the sale
      – gets payment by check
      – complete the sale.

"Start sale" scenario

Here is the scenario view (Figure 1–51):

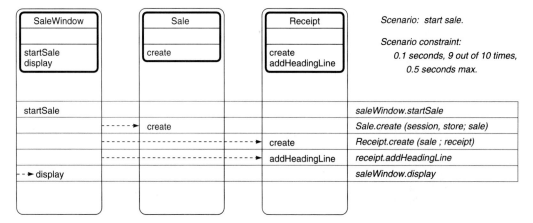

Figure 1–51: The "start sale" scenario view.

    Note that a sale window knows its corresponding receipt. That's something new, something you need to add to the object model.

    Note also that basic services (for an object: get, set, add a connection, remove a connection; for a class: create) appear in scenarios as needed. That's just fine.

"Sell item" scenario

Here is the scenario view (Figure 1–52):

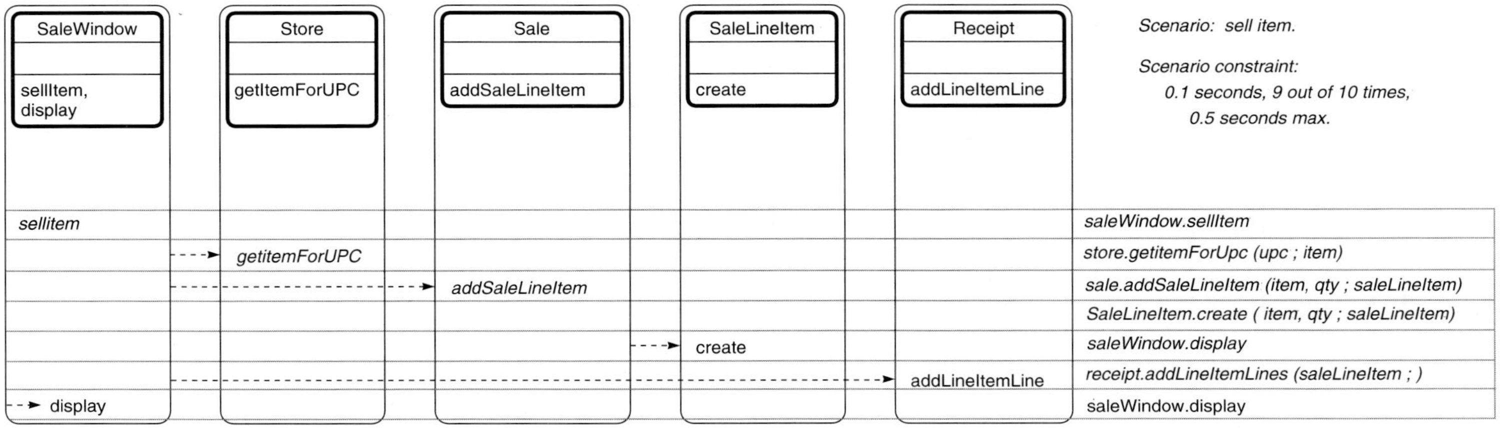

Figure 1–52: The "sell item" scenario view.

Scenario: sell item.

Scenario constraint:
0.1 seconds, 9 out of 10 times,
0.5 seconds max.

saleWindow.sellItem	
store.getItemForUpc (upc : item)	
sale.addSaleLineItem (item, qty ; saleLineItem)	
SaleLineItem.create (item, qty ; saleLineItem)	
saleWindow.display	
receipt.addLineItemLines (saleLineItem ;)	
saleWindow.display	

SaleWindow
sellItem,
display

Store
getItemForUPC

Sale
addSaleLineItem

SaleLineItem
create

Receipt
addLineItemLine

sellItem

getItemForUPC

addSaleLineItem

create

addLineItemLine

display

"Total the sale" scenario

Here is the scenario view (1–53):

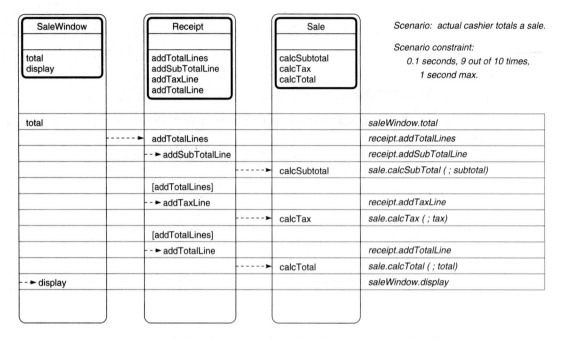

Figure 1–53: The "total the sale" scenario view.

"Get payment by check" scenario

It's just about time for another scenario view.

But first, note that you need to get the authorization done. Add an authorization system object to take care of it (more on this in the pages ahead).

Meanwhile, here is the scenario view (Figure 1–54):

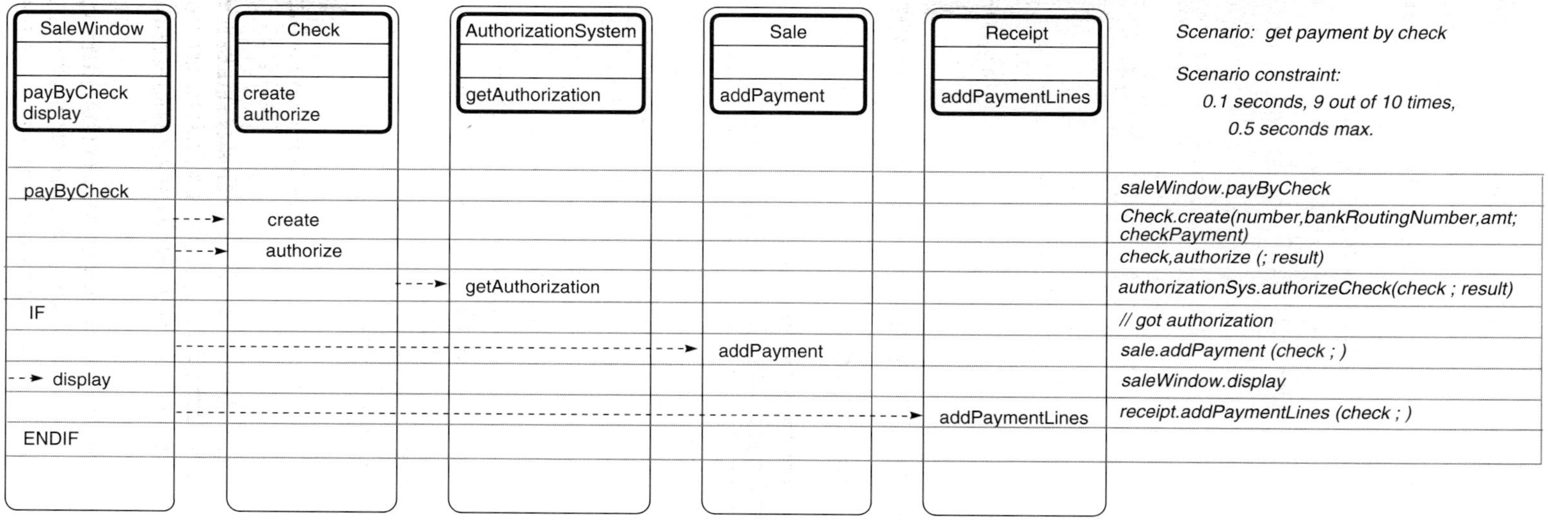

Scenario: get payment by check

Scenario constraint:
0.1 seconds, 9 out of 10 times,
0.5 seconds max.

saleWindow.payByCheck

Check.create(number,bankRoutingNumber,amt; checkPayment)

check.authorize (; result)

authorizationSys.authorizeCheck(check ; result)

// got authorization

sale.addPayment (check ;)

saleWindow.display

receipt.addPaymentLines (check ;)

SaleWindow	AuthorizationSystem	Sale	Receipt
payByCheck	getAuthorization	addPayment	addPaymentLines
display			

Check
create
authorize

payByCheck

create

authorize

getAuthorization

IF

display

ENDIF

addPayment

addPaymentLines

Figure 1–54: The "get payment by check" scenario view.

Hold it! A sale window needs to know its values for a payment. Add a payment attribute.

"Complete the sale" scenario

Here is the scenario view (Figure 1–55):

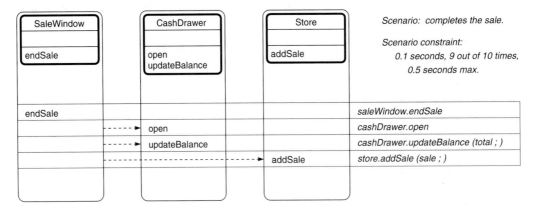

Figure 1–55: The "complete the sale" scenario view.

Scenario: log off

One more time.

Here is the scenario view (Figure 1–56):

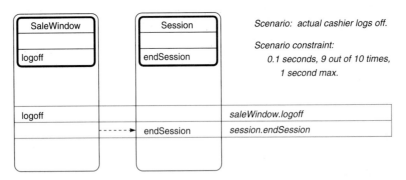

Figure 1–56: The "log off" scenario view.

Another service! Add "end session" to session.

Way to go! This object model is really beginning to take shape.

Scenarios drive you to significant detail—and better object models. Cool!

SELECTING SYSTEM-INTERACTION OBJECTS

Interaction with other systems.

#33. "Select Interacting Systems or Devices" Strategy	selecting objects (model components)

• Select it.
    Look for other systems and pieces of equipment that your system must interact with.
    Look for interacting systems; look for devices needing data acquisition and control.
        (Skip display or printing "nuts and bolts.")
• Examples: aileron, avionics system, controller, diverter, elevator, radar, rudder, sensor, scanner.
• Model it.
    With a problem-domain object, and
    With a corresponding system-interaction (SI) object, encapsulating low-level communication detail.	

You need to interact with an authorization system.

  Add a problem-domain object: authorization system.

  Now add a system-interaction object, to encapsulate low-level communication needs: authorization system SI (Figure 1–57):

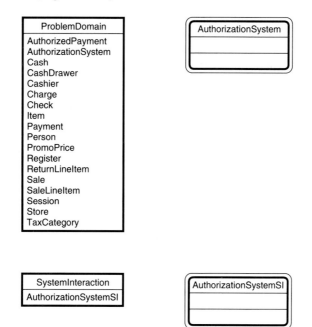

Figure 1–57: Selecting system interaction objects.

Interaction within this system

A point-of-sale application is a very likely candidate for a client-server architecture. However, do not build separate object models for the client and the server. Why? The models will be exactly the same—almost. And that's a waste of time and energy. Instead, you are far better off building one object model.

You might encounter a variety of client-server environments, including:

- object environments on client and server, with object communications support (ORB, SOM/DSOM, ODBMS)
- object environments on client and server, with nonobject communications support
- object environment on the client but not the server.

If you find that you must deal with a transition to nonobject technology (which is often the case), here's the basic approach to follow:

- allocate objects to the client or server
- decide which services will be allowed to run on which platform
- add both client and server objects, for translating in and out of your object technology.

If you have object-oriented environments on both client and server and your implementation environment supports an ORB, or you are using an object-oriented database that supports a client-server model, great news: you will not have to make any changes to your model, except minor changes to match any specific requirements of the environment you are using.

If you have object-oriented environments on both the client and the server, but there is no object communications support between them, then you need to add a "server" object for the client side, and a "client" object for the server side. These objects provide the transitions across the non-object communications boundaries. You need to decide which objects reside on each side of the boundary. You also need to define the client and server objects, to provide a communications link, one that routes messages between objects on different platforms.

If you have an object-oriented environment on the client and a relational database on the server, then use DM objects to provide the mapping and boundary to the non-object oriented server.

Use an object-modeling tool with view management, working out what's needed on each processor.

For this point-of-sale application, you get to take it easy (after all, this chapter needs to end at some point). Here's what you have to work with:

- an object-oriented environment on both the client and server
- access to an object-oriented communications mechanism.

Piece of cake!

No client object is needed here. No server object is needed here.

Move ahead and establish responsibilities for authorization system.

ESTABLISHING SYSTEM-INTERACTION RESPONSIBILITIES

Authorization system and authorization system SI

The point-of-sale system interacts with some number of authorization systems.

Establish responsibility: "what I know."

#56. "Establish Interacting System and Device Attributes" Strategy	establishing responsibilities / what I know (pattern players)
• For another system or device, include: number, name, operational state. • For its companion object, in the system interaction component, include: address, password.	

An authorization system knows its:

>   – type (check or credit card)
>   – cost per transaction
>   – vendor number
>   – operational state.

An authorization-system SI object knows its:

>   – address.

Establish responsibility: "who I know."

An authorization system object knows its authorization system SI object. Show this with an attribute (textually), rather than with an object connection (graphically).

Establish responsibility: "what I do."

#98. "Establish Interacting System or Device Services" Strategy	establishing responsibilities / what I do (pattern players)
• For an interacting system or device, include: activate, monitor (maintain), report, deactivate (plus calculate for me, rate me, is <value>). • For an interacting system or device as a collection, include: how many, how much, rank parts, calculate over parts. • Add a corresponding object in the system interaction (SI) component, to isolate specific interaction needs (examples: connect, logon, query, logoff, disconnect).	

An authorization system knows how to:

>   – get authorization (payment type, amount; authorization code).

An authorization system SI object knows how to connect, log on, query, log off, and disconnect.

Add both objects to your model (Figure 1–58):

Figure 1–58: Objects for an interacting system.

A collection of authorization systems

What if you want to work with many authorization systems, using the least expensive one first, then others on an as-needed basis? That's responsibility across a collection of authorization systems.

#23. "Select a Collection" Strategy	selecting objects (pattern players)

• What if you need a collection of objects, yet such a collection has no special name?
    Add a collection, using a plural form of the worker name. Example: authorization
        systems.
    Add a collection, using the worker name, followed by the word "collection" or "server."
        Example: authorization server.	

You need a collection of authorization systems. You could call it:

   – authorization system collection
   – authorization systems
   – authorization server.

Go ahead and use "authorization server." It sounds cool.

Establish responsibility: "what I know."

Nothing is needed here.

Establish responsibility: "who I know."

An authorization server knows its authorization system.

But what about an authorization system? Does it need to know who its server is? Not likely.

An object needs to know another object only when:

- "I know that object so others can ask me and I'll tell them about it." (The need to support basic queries is why most object connections are constrained in both directions.)
- "I know that object so I can send it messages to do some work on my be half."

In this case, ask this question: is the system responsible to answer the question: "For a specific authorization system, what's its server?" Not really. There's just one authorization server in this model. So don't include a constraint for authorization system to server; it just doesn't need to know.

Establish responsibility: "what I do."

An authorization system knows how to:

- get authorization (payment type, amount ; authorization code).

Add authorization server and its responsibilities to your object model, specifically to the system interaction component.

Add all of this to your model (Figure 1–59):

Figure 1–59: Authorization server: "what I know; who I know; what I do."

WORKING OUT SYSTEM-INTERACTION DYNAMICS WITH SCENARIOS

Both check and credit objects need help when told to "authorize." This is where the SI objects come into play.

Scenario: authorize payment

Here is the scenario view (Figure 1–60):

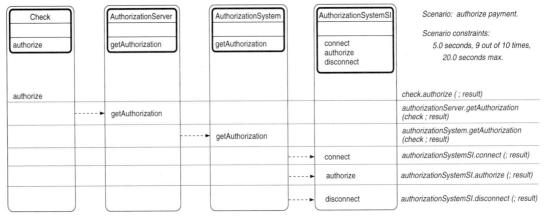

Figure 1–60: The "authorize payment" scenario view.

SELECTING DATA-MANAGEMENT OBJECTS AND RESPONSIBILITIES

Data-management (DM) objects are an important part of an object model.

#32. "Select Data Management Objects" Strategy	selecting objects (model components)
• Add a DM object for each problem-domain class of objects that you want to be persistent—stored between program invocations. • Why: use data management (DM) objects to encapsulate search and storage mechanisms across all of the objects within a problem-domain class. • Examples: cashier DM, sale DM, sale line item DM, item DM.	

Each DM class has just one object in that class. That object knows its corresponding PD objects, and is responsible for taking care of the data management needs across that collection of objects.

Here's what DM objects know and do:

    – Each DM object knows all of the objects in a corresponding problem-domain class.

        For example, a cashier DM object knows about all of the cashier objects.

    – Each DM object knows how to search.

        You can ask it to search for objects that you need.

    – Each DM object knows how to load and save.

        It loads and saves the problem domain objects it knows about.

        It usually does this if the underlying storage mechanism is not object-oriented.

So why are DM objects so doggone important?

– A DM object knows how to store and retrieve objects from whatever storage mechanism is to be used, whether flat file, indexed, relational, or object-oriented.
– A DM object isolates data management complexities from the rest of the application.
It interacts with local data management facilities and storage devices. When necessary, it interacts with an object that represents another system, to find objects located on an interacting system.
– A DM object isolates the transition from an object oriented environment to a nonobject-oriented environment
– And in systems that need such capability, a DM object could cache results when an interacting system is down.

For searching

If an object needs to search across all the objects in a class, and if no domain-based collection can be found to hold those objects, then let the object send a message to a DM object, asking it to do the search.

For persistence

This point-of-sale system also needs for some of its objects to be persistent, remembered over time, from one execution of the system to the next.

Here's the approach. If the underlying storage management is not object-oriented, then add a DM object for each class with objects that need to be persistent.

In this system, just add these DM objects:

– person DM
– cashier DM
– item DM
– register DM
– cash drawer DM
– sale DM
– sale line item DM
– session DM
– store DM
– tax category DM
– upc DM
– price DM
– payment DM.

Each DM object knows its corresponding PD objects.

#80. "Establish Data Management Object Connections" Strategy	establishing responsibilities / who I know (model components)
• For a data management object, include an object connection (expressed as an attribute) to the problem-domain objects (all of the objects in some problem-domain class) that it is responsible for.	

Each DM object does the DM basics: search, save, and load.

#100. "Establish Data Management Services" Strategy	establishing responsibilities / what I do (model component)
• For data management objects, include these services: search, save, load.	

Add DM objects and responsibilities to your model (Figure 1–61):

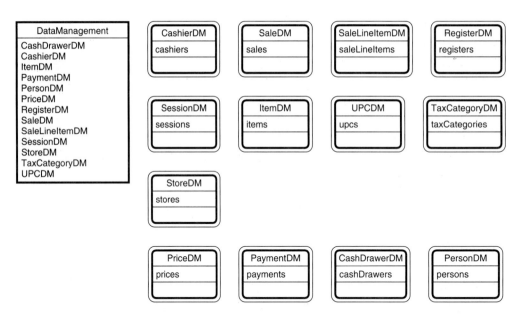

Figure 1–61: Data management objects and responsibilities.

For details on using the DM architecture with a wide variety of data-management systems (spanning files, relational databases, object databases, and SOM/DSOM), see the Data Management Appendix.

WORKING OUT DATA-MANAGEMENT DYNAMICS WITH SCENARIOS

Here's how.

To work out dynamics with DM objects:

Begin with a service in an HI component (for "save" and "load"), or

Begin with a search need from the PD component.

Here, consider a search need from a PD object:

> store.getCashierForID
> store.getItemForUPC.

Work out the dynamics for interacting with DM objects.

Scenario: get cashier for number

Here you go again. For this scenario, you need a "cashier DM" object. That object knows how to use the local file system to efficiently find the cashier object for the number. Here is the scenario view (Figure 1–62):

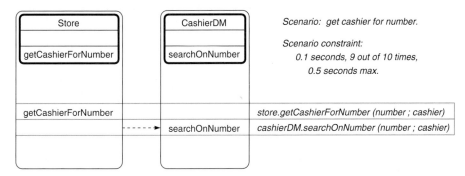

Figure 1–62: The "get cashier for number" scenario view.

Note that the basic search service, one that all DM objects provide, is made specific in the scenario view, using "search on <attribute name>."

Scenario: get item for UPC

This time, you'll need an "item DM" object.

The item DM knows how to use the local file system to efficiently find the item object for the UPC.

Here is the scenario view (Figure 1–63):

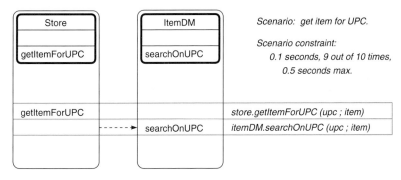

Figure 1–63: The "get cashier for id" scenario view.

PROGRESS AT THIS POINT

Here's the object model (Figures 1–64 to 69). Along with the scenarios in this chapter, this wraps up your work for Connie's Convenience Store.

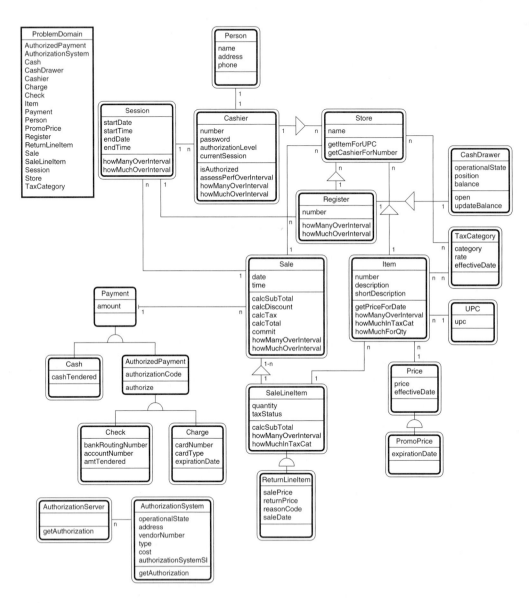

Figure 1–64: Progress at this point (Coad notation).

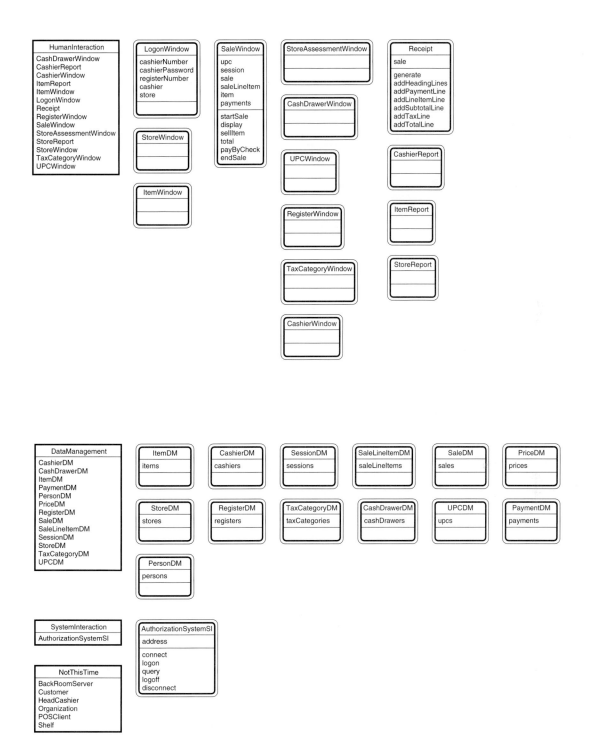

Figure 1–65: Progress at this point (Coad notation, continued).

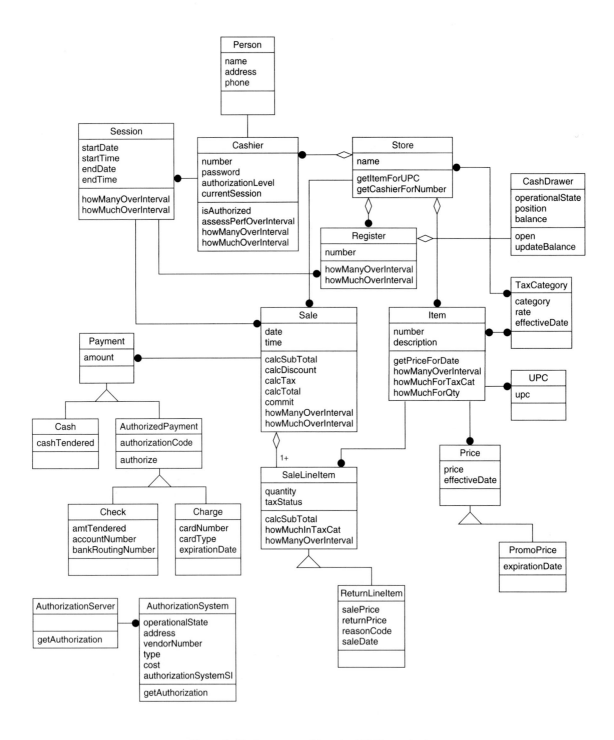

Figure 1–66: Progress at this point (OMT notation).

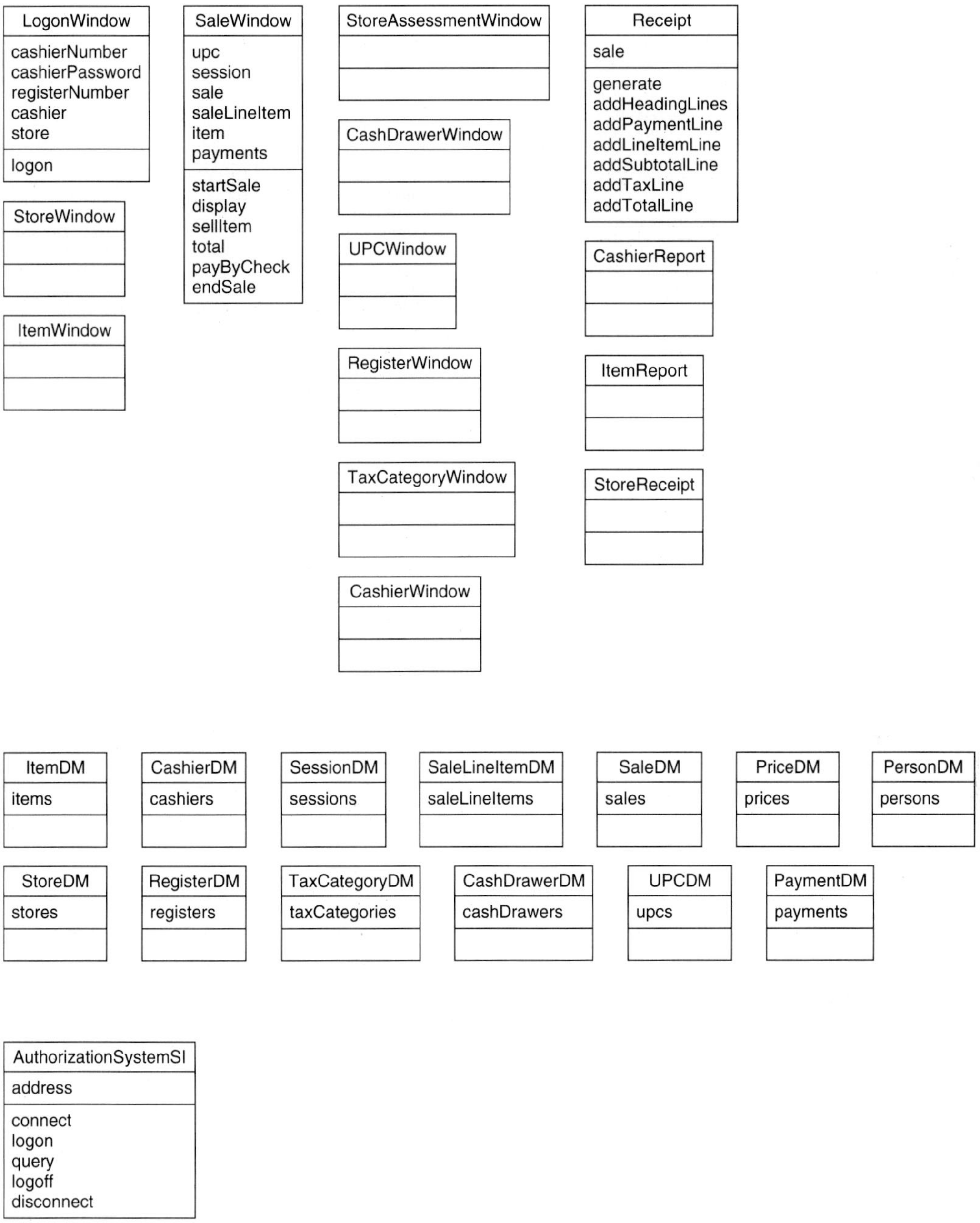

LogonWindow

cashierNumber
cashierPassword
registerNumber
cashier
store

logon

StoreWindow

ItemWindow

SaleWindow

upc
session
sale
saleLineItem
item
payments

startSale
display
sellItem
total
payByCheck
endSale

StoreAssessmentWindow

CashDrawerWindow

UPCWindow

RegisterWindow

TaxCategoryWindow

CashierWindow

Receipt

sale

generate
addHeadingLines
addPaymentLine
addLineItemLine
addSubtotalLine
addTaxLine
addTotalLine

CashierReport

ItemReport

StoreReceipt

ItemDM

items

CashierDM

cashiers

SessionDM

sessions

SaleLineItemDM

saleLineItems

SaleDM

sales

PriceDM

prices

PersonDM

persons

StoreDM

stores

RegisterDM

registers

TaxCategoryDM

taxCategories

CashDrawerDM

cashDrawers

UPCDM

upcs

PaymentDM

payments

AuthorizationSystemSI

address

connect
logon
query
logoff
disconnect

Figure 1–67: Progress at this point (OMT notation, continued).

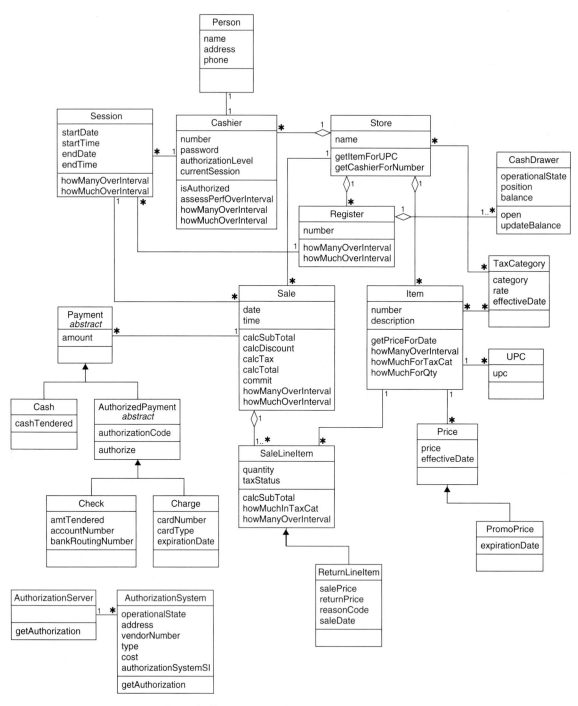

Figure 1–68: Progress at this point (Unified notation).

WRAP-UP

You did it! You built an object model for a point-of-sale application.

It's important! Nearly every business uses a point-of-sale application in one form or another. You can directly relate to (and, for some readers, you can directly apply) this object-modeling experience.

Along the way, you learned and applied four major activities (purpose and features, objects, responsibilities, scenarios) and four model components (problem domain, human interaction, data management, system interaction). You also learned and applied some strategies and patterns for developing more effective object models.

Excellent!

2

Wally's Warehouse
(A Warehouse Application)

In this chapter, you'll learn and apply strategies and patterns, ones that fit within these four major activities of building object models:

- Identifying system purpose and features
- Selecting objects
- Establishing responsibilities
- Working out dynamics with scenarios.

You'll also learn new strategies and patterns.

This chapter uses certain strategies from Chapter 1. It does not repeat them here. (Remember that Chapter 7, "Strategies and Patterns Handbook," has them all.) This chapter uses patterns from Chapter 1, too. Those patterns are repeated here right at the moment they are used (so you can see the spatial relationship of the pattern, just when you need to apply it).

By the way, you may have already discovered that the applications in this book apply in many businesses. All product- or service-based businesses need a point-of-sale system (in one form or another); that's Chapter 1. And all product- or service-based services need a warehouse system, too; that's Chapter 2.

Welcome—to Wally's Warehouse!

Figure 2–1: Wally's Warehouse.

Wally just purchased his business. He's ready to add a new system to help him run his business more efficiently and profitably.

IDENTIFYING SYSTEM PURPOSE AND FEATURES

Take a walk around Wally's warehouse

Take a walk on the wild side. (Well, maybe not; have you ever listened carefully to the lyrics of that song?)

Anyway, go for a walk around Wally's warehouse, listening carefully as he describes his business to you.

#3. "Field Trips, Pictures, and Examples" Strategy	identifying purpose and features
• Work with domain experts, ones well-versed in the business. • Ask for a guided tour; ask for a picture; ask for lots of examples.	

[At Wally's office]

(Peter) Wally, let's go for a walk around the warehouse. As we walk, just talk with me about how the operation works (or doesn't work). Let your surroundings prompt you for what's really important to your business.

(Wally) Let's go upstairs, then. I want to show you a bird's-eye view of the entire operation.

(Peter) That sounds promising.

[Upstairs]

(Wally) Check it out. My warehouse is organized into aisles. Each aisle is organized with bins. From up here, it looks like a grid of aisles and bins.

(Peter) How do you identify a particular aisle-and-bin combination?

(Wally) With a pair of numbers. For example, 12–10, meaning aisle 12, bin 10.

(Peter) That reminds me of a city map. Each location has an address. In this case, it's just a pair of numbers. And you use that number to identify a specific aisle-and-bin location. Good. Now the things that are stored at an aisle-and-bin location: where do they come from?

(Wally) Look over to your left. That area is the receiving dock.

(Peter) Is that the beginning point for items in your warehouse?

(Wally) Yes.

(Peter) Let's go downstairs and walk through the path that an item takes as it journeys through the warehouse.

[At the receiving dock]

(Peter) Okay, so items arrive here. What does your team do when items arrive at the receiving dock?

(Wally) Far too often, take a break. I think profit-sharing might help that problem, though. Anyway, a shipment of items arrives, we make sure we have a corresponding purchase order, mark it off, and then put the items away.

(Peter) You put away each item?

(Wally) We take a pallet, walk it through the warehouse, and unload each kind of item. It's really a time-consuming task.

(Peter) Do you just have one kind of item on a pallet? Or many kinds of items on a pallet?

(Wally) Many kinds of items on a pallet.

(Peter) What do you do when you put away a pallet of items?

(Wally) For each kind of item on a pallet, we look for an existing bin of those items, or an empty bin, and "put away" the items into a bin.

(Peter) So, there is usually only one kind of item in a bin?

(Wally) Yes, that's kind of how we know where things are.

(Peter) How do you choose a bin?

(Wally) You know, that's where we could use some help. My team puts them in locations that are close to the loading dock. Yet for pallets with lots of individual items, we'd save ourselves a lot of work by putting those pallets near the pickers, the ones who grab items for a shipment from the warehouse. Most of the time, my team knows where we usually keep a certain kind of item, and do their best to keep them close together—in the same bin or in nearby bins.

(Peter) Let me summarize:

> Your team receives pallets of items.
>
> Your team finds the corresponding purchase order and marks off the items.
>
> Your team "puts away" a pallet of items. For each kind of item, your team looks for:
>
> > – a "not yet full" bin of those items
> > – an empty bin
>
> and then they "put away" the items of that kind into the bin.

(Wally) Hey, you're catching on.

(Peter) Thanks. Let's continue our walk alongside the items, as they make their way through the warehouse.

(Wally) That means it's time to take you to an aisle-and-bin location.

[Aisle-and-bin location]

(Peter) So the items come to rest here, at an aisle-and-bin location.

(Wally) Yes, you're right, they do come to rest here. But not for very long! I've got to keep my investment in inventory down, as low as I can and yet fill my orders nearly all of the time (called my "fill rate"). It's a very delicate balance; done right, my profits improve; done poorly, and I go out of business.

(Peter) Fill rate? Sounds very important. What things do you do to improve your fill rate?

(Wally) In principle, it's simple: keep track of how many item I have and order just what I need. In practice, it is a real pain: walk down an aisle; count the items in each bin; tally results; place orders; and hope for the best.

(Peter) Please tell me more about counting: who does it, how often it's done, and the problems you face.

(Wally) A couple of my team members manually count the inventory, aisle-by-aisle, usually one aisle per day. It's a tough job. It's hard to find all the bins that hold a particular kind of item. Yet we must manually count, so we know how much we really have (the industry euphemism for missing items is called "shrinkage.") Accurate counts are another important part of achieving a better fill rate.

(Peter) Please tell me more about ordering.

(Wally) We order based upon a lot of factors: reorder levels, sales rate, replenishment time, and the like. That's something we could pursue in the future—not this time.

(Peter) Let's continue following items through your business. What's next?

(Wally) We get an order. Then someone on my team picks the order.

(Peter) What does a team member do, when picking an order? Better yet, walk me through an example.

[Order desk]

(Wally) First, I get an order from the order desk. My job is to pick the order.

[Aisle-and-bin locations]

(Wally) Next, I walk around the warehouse, looking for the items on my list.

(Peter) Oh, just like walking through an unfamiliar grocery store, looking for items on a shopping list. Now I understand some of the frustrations of this job.

(Wally) Good. Remember that feeling.

(Peter) So how do you find a kind of item? Wandering aimlessly?

(Wally) That's pretty much the case for new "pickers." After a while, it's more like walking through a grocery store that you are already familiar with. I know the basic areas to look in. Yet more often than I like, I waste time looking for an item I'm not familiar with. And get this: if none of us can find an item, it's lost—and orders for that item may go unfilled (and that affects our bottom line).

(Peter) So what happens when you find a bin with items that you need?

(Wally) I put the items into my tote.

(Peter) Yes, the grocery cart.

[Back at the order desk]

(Wally) And then I bring the tote back to the order desk (kind of like a checkout counter, I think).

(Peter) Right.

(Wally) Someone else packages the items and puts them on a truck.

(Peter) Really? So someone "bags the groceries" and takes them out to a "car."

(Wally) I think you've got it.

Identify the purpose of the system

What's the purpose of the system?

(Peter) Let's work on a statement of purpose.

> To improve warehouse profitability by helping team members put away and pick items more efficiently.

(Wally) It's more than that. How about this:

> To improve warehouse profitability by helping team members put away and pick items more efficiently . . . by keeping more accurate inventory counts, and by increasing fill rate.

IDENTIFY SYSTEM FEATURES

#8. "Best and Worst Features" Strategy	identifying purpose and features

• Ask users:
    What are the best features of the current system? Of competitive systems?
    What are the worst problems of the current system? Of competitive systems?
    What are the unneeded features of the current system? Of competitive systems?	

Identify the worst features of the current system.

For Wally's Warehouse, several "worst features" are time wasters:

The time it takes to put away items.

The time it takes to pick items.

The time it takes to count items.

For Wally's Warehouse, another "worst feature" is a missed opportunity:

Unfilled orders, ones that should be filled, but aren't, because an item couldn't be found.

Use these "worst features" to develop a key features list.

– to give put-away instructions

– to give picking instructions

– to maintain quantity for each kind of item, for each bin holding that kind of item

– to calculate fill rate, to assess efficiency.

SELECTING PROBLEM-DOMAIN OBJECTS
Select actors and participants

An actor, inside of Wally's Warehouse, is a person.

Think back to your walking tour of Wally's Warehouse. How did people participate? Consider the roles played by Wally's team:

– "put away-er"

– picker

– counter.

Are these participants within the system's responsibilities? The answer is yes, if (1) the system keeps track of who does what, or (2) if the system assesses performance for any of these roles played.

(Peter) Do you need to keep track of who does what? Or would you like to assess the performance of individual team members?

(Wally) No, at least not this time.

(Peter) In the future, we'll add them to the model, so we can keep track of them and assess their performance. (Meanwhile, we'll still study what these people do to other objects. Many times, actions upon an object are good clues for actions a software object will do to itself.)

What about actors outside of Wally's Warehouse? An actor could be:

   – a person
   – an organization.

(Peter) Do you work with outside organizations, individuals, or both?

(Wally) We work exclusively with organizations—companies, trusts, foundations, and the like.

   The actor is:

   – organization.

The participant is:

   – customer.

Do you need to know about customers? Yes! You need to know who the customer is, his purchase orders, and at some point, a loading dock for his orders.

Add organization and customer (anticipating the use of an actor-participant pattern) (Figure 2–2):

Figure 2–2: Select actors and participants.

Select places

What are the places where items come to rest in Wally's Warehouse?

   – receiving dock
   – pallet
   – bin
   – tote
   – loading dock.

#45. "Useful Questions" Strategy	selecting objects (consider and challenge)
• What useful questions could you ask this object, if you include it in your object model?	
• Examples: How many over interval? How much over interval? How good are you?	

What's needed in the problem domain component? Here's one way to check this out. Consider what useful questions each could answer for you:

   Receiving dock
      How many items need to be put away?
      How many pallets need to be put away?

Pallet
>What items and how many are you holding?

Bin
>What item and how many are you holding?

Tote
>What items and how many of each are you holding?

Loading dock
>What items and how many of each are you holding?
>What orders are you taking care of?

All of these could be of interest to Wally. Yet even Wally can't have it all.

(Peter) Given that preceding list of questions that the system could answer for you, which ones are most likely to affect your bottom line?

(Wally) The most important ones are: pallet, bin, and loading dock. Receiving dock and tote are interesting, I suppose, yet I'm not sure why I'd use them on a day-to-day basis.

(Peter) Okay.

For now, add pallet, bin, and loading dock to your model (Figure 2–3):

Figure 2–3: Select objects: places.

Select things
Tangible things

What tangible things are in the problem domain?
>Item (See Figure 2–4.)!

Figure 2–4: Select tangible things.

Containers

What are the containers of objects in this system?

– a warehouse contains loading docks
– a warehouse contains aisles, aisles contain bins, bins contain items.

You already have bin and loading dock.
Add warehouse and aisle (Figure 2–5):

Figure 2–5: Select objects: containers.

Here's an important point. At times, more than one strategy or pattern will point to the same object. Take note! This is gives added basis for including that object; it also suggests that the object may be of special significance within your object model.

Here, these notable objects are bin, item, and loading dock.

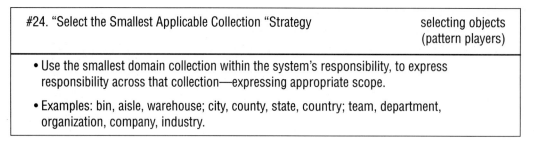

#24. "Select the Smallest Applicable Collection "Strategy	selecting objects (pattern players)
• Use the smallest domain collection within the system's responsibility, to express responsibility across that collection—expressing appropriate scope. • Examples: bin, aisle, warehouse; city, county, state, country; team, department, organization, company, industry.	

An item is the smallest element, one that's held in other containers. In such a situation, an item usually has one or more associated "line item" objects, ones that know of a specific quantity of that item.

Here, an item knows a bin line item object; a bin line item object is part of a bin.

Moreover, an item knows a pallet line item object; a pallet line item object is part of a pallet.

Add bin line item and pallet line item to your model (Figure 2–6):

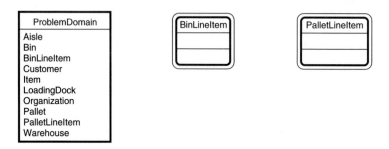

Figure 2–6: Select objects: item and its line items.

Transaction objects

What transactions, significant moments in time, need to be logged by the system?

Here's another way to look at it: what events are logged, information that is used to spur on additional business activity?

An order is something logged, information that is used to spur on additional business activity.

Okay. Now take transaction objects a step further, using them to find even more objects for your system under consideration.

Where do these transactions come from? The possibilities are:

- a window (the event logged is based upon human interaction at some point in time)
- another object, monitoring for a significant event, then logging that such an event occurred
- another system, one that your system can interact with regarding events it logs.

(Peter) Wally, where do orders come from? Do you get an order from some other system? Or do you enter it in yourself?

(Wally) Right now, we get the order from an order entry system.

(Peter) So that's where we should get the orders from?

(Wally) Right.

Later, you'll need a class called something like "order entry system," with responsibilities that include getting orders from it.

Order (and order line item)

Transaction objects usually consist of some number of transaction line item objects.

Consider order. An order has corresponding order line items (Figure 2–7):

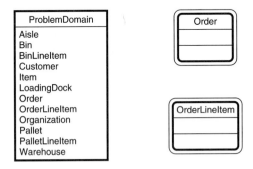

Figure 2–7: Select transaction objects.

APPLYING PATTERNS: SELECT AND ORGANIZE PROBLEM-DOMAIN OBJECTS

You've selected a number of objects (and formed classes of them).

Use some patterns to connect some of the pieces together in a meaningful way.

Actor-participant

You've already done some of this work, having anticipated using this pattern:

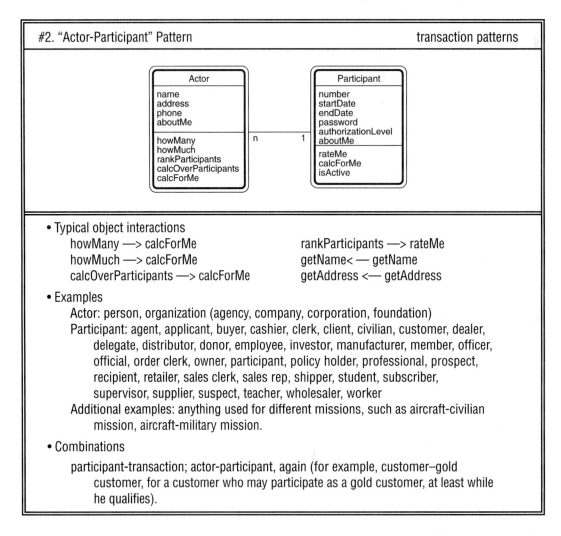

Here's an instance of this pattern (Figure 2–8):

    Actor: organization
    Participant: customer

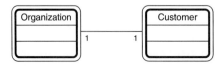

Figure 2–8: An instance of actor-participant.

Participant-transaction

First, take a look at the pattern:

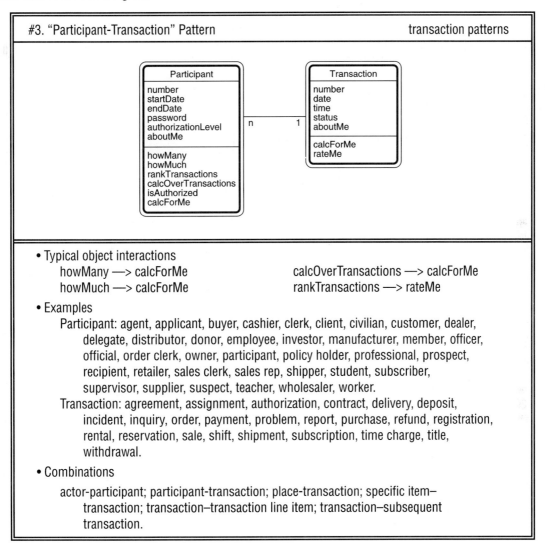

Here is an instance of this pattern (Figure 2–9):

Participant: customer
Transaction: order.

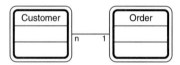

Figure 2–9: An instance of participant-transaction.

Place–transaction

Take a look at the pattern:

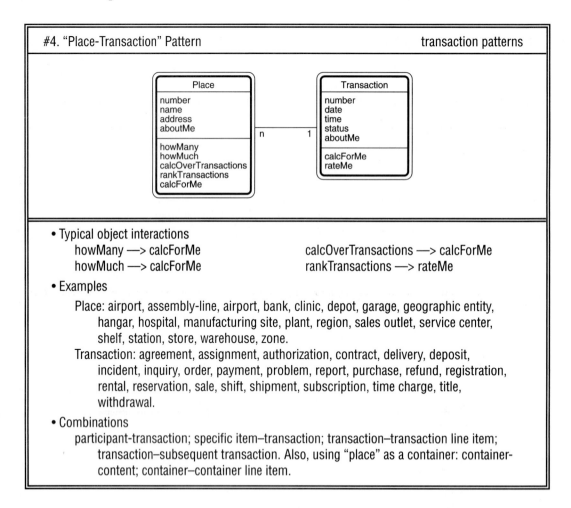

* Typical object interactions
    howMany —> calcForMe   calcOverTransactions —> calcForMe
    howMuch —> calcForMe   rankTransactions —> rateMe
* Examples
    Place: airport, assembly-line, airport, bank, clinic, depot, garage, geographic entity, hangar, hospital, manufacturing site, plant, region, sales outlet, service center, shelf, station, store, warehouse, zone.
    Transaction: agreement, assignment, authorization, contract, delivery, deposit, incident, inquiry, order, payment, problem, report, purchase, refund, registration, rental, reservation, sale, shift, shipment, subscription, time charge, title, withdrawal.
* Combinations
    participant-transaction; specific item–transaction; transaction–transaction line item; transaction–subsequent transaction. Also, using "place" as a container: container-content; container–container line item.

Here is an instance of this pattern (Figure 2–10):

Place: loading dock
Transaction: order.

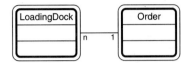

Figure 2–10: An instance of place-transaction.

Transaction–transaction line item

Apply the transaction–transaction line item pattern.

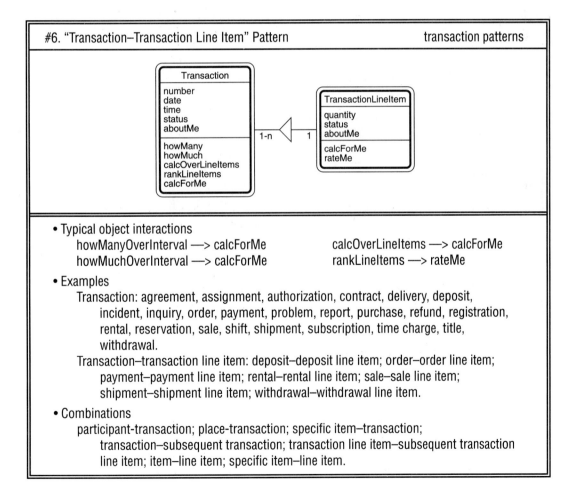

You've already identified the key players:

– order–order line item.

Add a pattern instance (Figure 2–11):

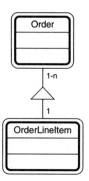

Figure 2–11: An instance of transaction–transaction line item.

Container–container line item

Apply the container–container line item pattern.

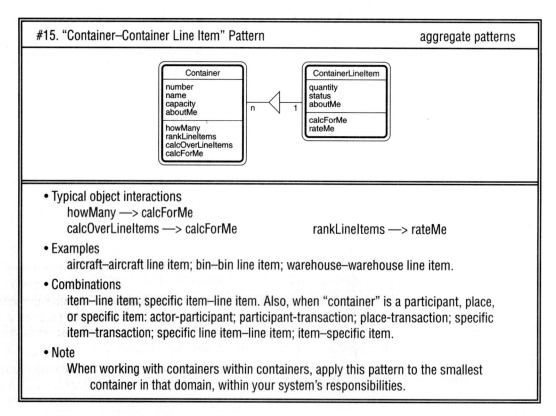

You've already identified the key players:

– bin–bin line item
– pallet–pallet line item.

Add two pattern instances (Figure 2–12):

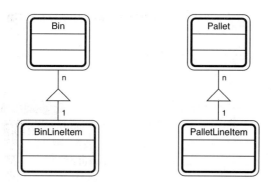

Figure 2–12: Two instances of container–container line item.

Container-contents

Apply the container-content pattern.

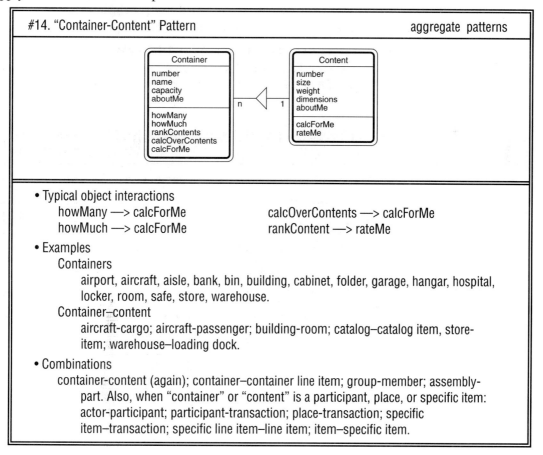

You've already identified the players:

- warehouse–loading dock
- warehouse-pallet

– warehouse-aisle

– aisle-bin.

Add these pattern instances to your model (Figure 2–13):

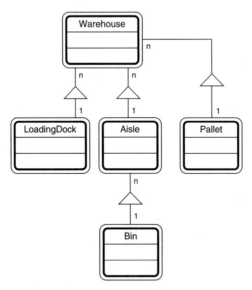

Figure 2–13: Four instances of container-contents.

Item–line item

Apply the item–line item pattern.

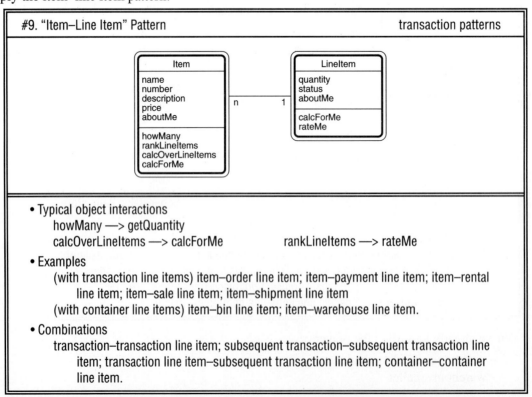

You've already identified the players:

– item–bin line item
– item–pallet line item
– item–order line item.

Add three pattern instances to your model (Figure 2–14):

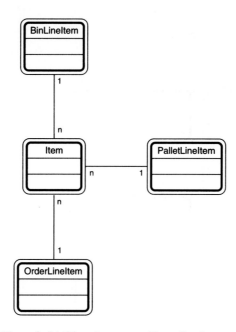

Figure 2–14: Three instances of item–line item.

Progress so far

Here is what your model looks like at this point (Figure 2–15):

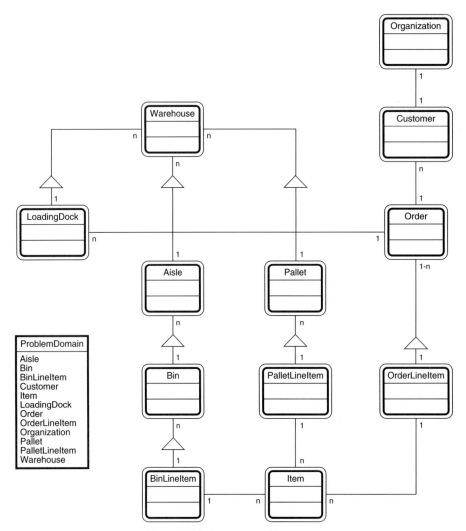

Figure 2–15: Progress at this point.

ESTABLISHING RESPONSIBILITIES FOR THE PROBLEM-DOMAIN OBJECTS
Responsibilities for actors and participants

It's time to play "what I know; who I know; what I do."

Do it for actors (person and organization). Do it for participants (customer).

Actor: organization

Just do it.

What I know: name.
Who I know: customer.
What I do: just the basics.

Add these responsibilities (Figure 2–16):

Figure 2–16: Establishing responsibilities for an organization.

Participant: customer

Again.

> What I know: number, address.
> Who I know: organization, orders.
> What I do: the basics, once again.

Add these responsibilities (Figure 2–17):

Figure 2–17: Establishing responsibilities for a customer.

Responsibilities for places

Now consider responsibilities for places, specifically those places where things come to rest: pallet, bin, and loading dock.

Pallet

Play the trio, once again.

> What I know: number.
> Who I know: pallet line item, warehouse.
> What I do: consider this one.

In a manual system, someone unloads items from a pallet to some bins. Flip it. In an automated system, your pallet object comes to life: it unloads items into a bin.

So what I do is this: unload items into a bin (Figure 2–18):

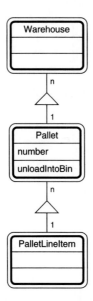

Figure 2–18: Establishing responsibilities for a pallet.

Bin

Check out the responsibilities for a bin.

What I know: number.
Who I know: aisle, bin line item.
What I do: work on this a bit.

What kind of useful questions could this object answer for you? How about: is empty?

What actions are done to an actual bin, that as your abstraction could do to itself? In the real world, items are added to a bin. Flip it. A bin object can add items to itself.

What I do: is empty, add items.

Add these responsibilities (Figure 2–19):

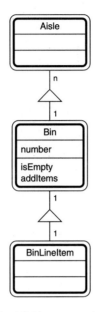

Figure 2–19: Establishing responsibilities for a bin.

Loading dock

Put the trio to work again.

> What I know: number.
> Who I know: warehouse, orders (the ones that ship from this loading dock)
> What I do: just the basics.

Add these responsibilities (Figure 2–20):

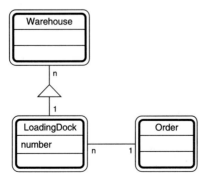

Figure 2–20: Establishing responsibilities for a loading dock.

Responsibilities for tangible things

Item

Time once again for the trio.

> What I know: number, description, universal product code (UPC).
> Who I know: bin line item, pallet line item, order line item.
> What I do: how many available; find bins for quantity.

> What else does an item do? Consider the actions done to a real item: unload from a pallet, load from a bin to a tote.

> Flip the actions. Now your abstraction, an item object, knows how to unload itself from pallet to bin and how to load itself from bin to tote.

> Hence, here's a "what I do" update: how many available; find bins for quantity; unload from a pallet to bin (but, no totes to work with in this system) (Figure 2–21):

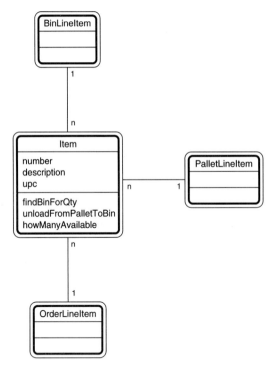

Figure 2–21: Establishing responsibilities for item.

Responsibilities for containers

Check out the responsibilities for the containers you are working with:

> – warehouse
> – aisle
> – bin (and bin line item)
> – pallet (and pallet line item).

Some containers have inventoried contents. They need line items, just to keep track of specific quantities of items within them. Bin and pallet are like that.

Warehouse

Consider the usual trio.

What I know: name.

Who I know: aisles, loading docks, pallets.

What I do: find bin for pallet (find an available bin that one can unload a pallet into), find next aisle to count (find the next aisle that someone should count, to get accurate inventory numbers).

Add these responsibilities (Figure 2–22):

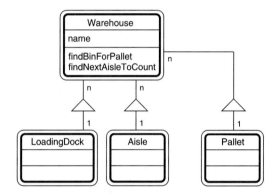

Figure 2–22: Establishing responsibilities for a warehouse.

Aisle

Consider the usual trio.

What I know: number.

Who I know: bins, warehouse.

What I do: find bin for pallet, rate myself as next aisle to count.

Add these responsibilities (Figure 2–23):

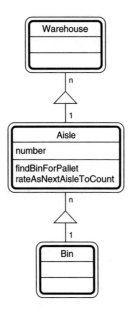

Figure 2–23: Establishing responsibilities for an aisle.

Bin (and bin line item)

You've already established the responsibilities for a bin. Now consider the specific responsibilities for a bin line item.

What I know: quantity (plus date and time, if within the system's responsibilities).
Who I know: item, bin.
What I do: the basics.

Add these responsibilities (Figure 2–24):

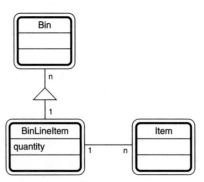

Figure 2–24: Establishing responsibilities for "bin line item."

Pallet (and pallet line item)

You've already established the responsibilities for a pallet. Now consider the specific responsibilities for a pallet line item.

What I know: quantity (plus date and time, if within the system's responsibilities).
Who I know: item, pallet.
What I do: unload into a bin.

Add these responsibilities (Figure 2–25):

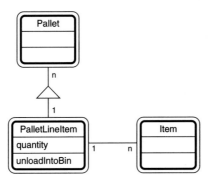

Figure 2–25: Establishing responsibilities for "pallet line item."

Repeating pattern instances

Hold on there!

Bin and pallet seem more and more alike in this model—especially when you consider similar pattern instances:

  – bin–bin line item–item
  – pallet–pallet line item–item.

And note that these pattern instances overlap, too: item is the common player.

#44. "Reengineer with Objects" Strategy	selecting objects (consider and challenge)
• Look for objects (and repeating instances of a pattern) that are likely to have the same responsibilities—and actually reflect an organizational boundary or previous system boundary. • Model the objects once—for a simpler object model. Make recommendations for reengineering the organization, too.	

Does the business really need both bin and pallet? Or is there a better way?

What's the same about these pattern instances? Item.

What's different about these pattern instances? The containers, that's all.

Does the system really need to keep track of both kinds of containers? Or could Wally improve his business by storing a pallet of items in a bin (rather than storing just one kind of item in a bin)?

Provided that the warehouse can physically accommodate this change, this would be a real business process improvement, saving Wally time, money, and headaches.

The impact to your model? Check it out. You still need both pallet and bin. You'll first find out about a pallet, then its pallet line items, and then its bins. Yet you don't need bin line items any longer; it's now exactly the same thing as a pallet line item. Zap it.

But can you simplify things this far?

(Peter) What if I suggested that you change your operation, always storing an entire pallet in a bin? That would make the put-away a lot simpler, right?

(Wally) You software weenies sure come up with the strangest ideas. Let me take you for a walk down the aisle (of the warehouse!).

(Peter) Okay.

(Wally) Take a look at the bins we use. Big ones, little ones—different sizes. The "pallet in a bin" approach won't work here. And even if it could, I'm certain that we'd have a warehouse of near-empty bins, and spend most of our days consolidating those bins to make room for more.

(Peter) Agreed.

Okay, so you can't go so far as to make pallets and bins the same.

Consider the next best thing: dump an entire pallet of items into a bin. You could take pallet line items (on a shipping form, verified at the receiving dock) and dump them into bin line items.

(Peter) Wally, what if I suggested that you change your operation, always adding an entire pallet of items to a bin—provided that all of them would fit? That would make put-away a lot simpler, wouldn't it?

(Wally) Sure, that makes put-away a lot simpler—if we had the option to put an entire pallet away into one bin. When we exercised that option, we'd already know the quantities and items that we're adding (from the shipping form). But how will we keep track of what quantities and items are in what bins?

(Peter) We'll let the system do that. Then, when it's time to pick an order, we'll let the system generate a pick list, a list of bins, with the quantities and items to pick up at each bin.

(Wally) If you order it, kind of the way a super-shopper organizes his grocery-store shopping list, then my team can pick more efficiently.

(Peter) That's the idea.

(Wally) Let's do it.

Pick list

Is a pick list simply a human interaction object, just a view of order and item information, and nothing more?

Or is a pick list more important, something about which the system needs to know and do something about, over time?

#46. "More Than a Report" Strategy   selecting objects (consider and challenge)

- Is that report simply a human interaction object, just a view of problem-domain values and calculation results? Or does it embody something about which the system needs to know and do something through time?

- Add to your object model, when your system is responsible for both producing and remembering the content expressed in that report.

The system needs to know about pick lists. Here's why.

- It needs to know what pick lists have already been issued:
  - to avoid overpicking the bin
  - to keep track of what bin to pick from.
- It needs to know what pick-list line items were filled and which ones were not filled—so a warehouse (knowing all of its pick lists) can calculate its own fill rate.

What I know: date.
Who I know: pick-list line items, warehouse.
What I do: remove items from bins,

Pick-list line item

Do the trio, again.

What I know: quantity needed, quantity picked.
Who I know: item, bin line item, pick list.
What I do: remove item from bin.

Add these responsibilities (Figure 2–26):

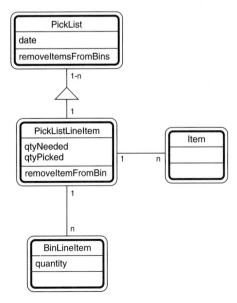

Figure 2–26: Establish responsibilities for pick list and pick-list line item.

Responsibilities for transactions

Turn your attention to transactions and transaction line items.

Consider order and order line item, then pick list and pick-list line item.

Order

Strike up the trio.

What I know: number, shipping date, shipping address (if different from a customer's normal shipping address).

Who I know: order line items, customer.

What I do: check this out.

In a manual system, someone would take an order and write up a pick list. In an automated system, your order object comes to life: it builds its own pick list.

So "what I do" is this: build a pick list, the specific sequence of:

– which bin to go to
– the quantity of items to get there.

Add these responsibilities (Figure 2–27):

Figure 2–27: Establishing responsibilities for an order.

Order line item

Apply the trio again.

What I know: quantity ordered.

Who I know: order, item, pick-list line items.

What I do: check this out.

In a manual system, someone would take an order line item and write up a pick-list line item. In an automated system, your order object comes to life: it builds its own pick-list line item.

So "what I do" is this: build pick-list line item.

Add these responsibilities (Figure 2–28):

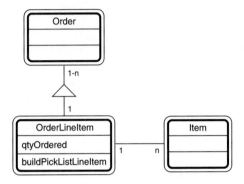

Figure 2–28: Establishing responsibilities for an order line item.

Transaction–subsequent transaction

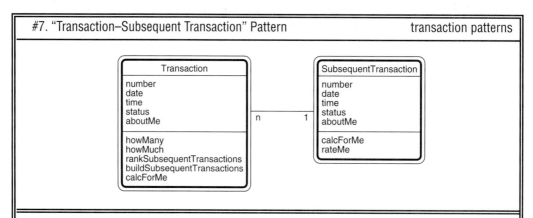

#7. "Transaction–Subsequent Transaction" Pattern — transaction patterns

Transaction
number
date
time
status
aboutMe

howMany
howMuch
rankSubsequentTransactions
buildSubsequentTransactions
calcForMe

n — 1

SubsequentTransaction
number
date
time
status
aboutMe

calcForMe
rateMe

- Typical object interactions
    howMany —> calcForMe
    howMuch —> calcForMe

    calcOverSubsequentTransactions —>calcForMe
    rankSubsequentTransactions —>rateMe

- Examples

    Transaction: agreement, assignment, authorization, contract, delivery, deposit, incident, inquiry, order, payment, problem, report, purchase, refund, registration, rental, reservation, sale, shift, shipment, subscription, time charge, title, withdrawal.

    Transaction–subsequent transaction: application–issue; intermediate result–final result; order–shipment; purchase–payment; reservation–sale; traffic citation–payment.

- Combinations

    participant-transaction; place-transaction; specific item-transaction; transaction–transaction line item; subsequent transaction–subsequent transaction line item.

- Notes

    Work out transactions in time sequence (the order they usually occur in).

    If subsequent transaction and its line item objects correspond 1-to-1 with transaction and its line item objects, combine them (transaction and its line items, with start and stop dates and times).

This pattern captures a pair of transactions, ones that occur together, or one after another.

These transaction occur:

- at the same time (example: sale and payment, when payment is required at the time a sale is made), or
- in a customary sequence (example: order, then pick list).

You've already selected order and pick list. You've got the players. Now put together an instance of this pattern:

Transaction: order

Subsequent transaction: pick list.

These transactions occur in a chronological sequence. An order is first. The pick list is later. An order may have a corresponding pick list. A pick list always has a corresponding order.

Show the chronological sequence and existence dependency with object connection constraints (Figure 2–29):

An order object knows about zero or one pick lists—0-1.

A pick list object knows exactly one order—1.

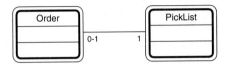

Figure 2–29: An instance of transaction–subsequent transaction.

As noted a bit earlier, at times you'll find that more than one strategy or pattern will point to the same object. Take note! This gives an added basis for including that object; it also suggests that the object may be of special significance within your object model.

Progress at this point

You've now selected objects and established responsibilities for the problem domain object.

Here's your progress at this point (Figure 2–30):

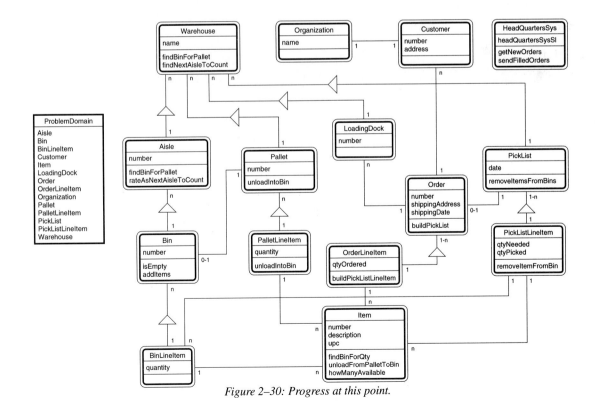

Figure 2–30: Progress at this point.

WORKING OUT PROBLEM-DOMAIN DYNAMICS WITH SCENARIOS

Consider the features of this system.

- to give put-away instructions
- to give picking instructions
- to maintain quantity for each kind of item, for each bin holding that kind of item
- to calculate fill rate, to assess efficiency.

The features are the starting point for many scenarios.

Yet that might be too much to start with at first. So, use the features to help you identify services to be provided by a problem domain object. Work out the dynamics for these more interesting services.

Specifically, for this chapter, take a look at:

- find bin for pallet
- build pick-list line items.

Using scenarios, work out the dynamics required for these services to get their jobs done.

Scenario: find bin for pallet

Okay. So a warehouse object is going to get an available bin for you.

A warehouse is a container. It holds all of the bins.

So what? Why not have a galaxy object: it's a container of most everything you might work with, and you could put all behavior across a collection in that object.

Why not? Simply this: you end up with a gigantic function blob; you lose problem domain partitioning of services; and your resulting systems will be increasingly brittle.

A better approach?

#103. "Service in the Smallest Applicable Container" Strategy	establishing responsibilities / what I do (where to put)

• Begin with a problem-domain object.
 	
 • Identify the smallest problem-domain collection that it's a part of.
 	
 • Add the "service across a collection" to that object.
 	
 • Does the collection include all of the objects you need to work with?
    If yes, you're done.
    If not, do it again, letting the collection be the problem-domain object for the next pass.	

Establish a "service across a collection" with the smallest problem-domain containers that hold those objects. Then consider those container objects, and apply this strategy again: find the next largest problem-domain container that holds those smaller container objects, and so on.

Okay. So how about in this situation?

Round 1.

> The domain object is a bin.
>
> The smallest problem domain container of bins is an aisle.
>
> Add the "find bin for pallet" service to an aisle object.
>
> Does an aisle object include all of the bins you might need to consider?
>> No. Carry on.

Round 2.

> The domain object is an aisle.
>
> The smallest problem domain container of aisles is a warehouse.
>
> Add the "find bin for pallet" service to a warehouse object.
>
> Does a warehouse object include all of the bins you need to work with?
>> Yes—mission accomplished.

All of this leads to new understanding about warehouse, aisle, and bin.

A warehouse object has the service "find bin for pallet." It collaborates with its aisle objects.

An aisle object has the service "find bin for pallet." It collaborates with its bin objects.

A bin object needs a service, too: "is available for pallet."

Hey wait a minute! If you distribute responsibility, doesn't effective reuse means working with small, collaborative collections of objects? Right you are. Reuse of just one object is just too narrow; nearly every object needs some help from its friends. Moreover, the fundamental tenant of reuse is understandability. Hence, you use problem-domain partitioning—classes—to partition attributes and services in an understandable and meaningful way.

Add these responsibilities to your object model (Figure 2–31):

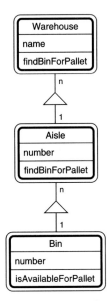

Figure 2–31: Adding responsibilities discovered while working out a scenario.

Now, work out the scenario. Here's what happens:

– Someone asks a warehouse to find a bin for a pallet.

  – A warehouse asks an aisle to find a bin for a pallet.

    – A bin checks to see if it is available for a pallet.[1] It's available if:

       the bin does not have an associated pallet (at this time)

       the bin has enough room

          simplest algorithm: the bin is empty (no line items).

    – If all is well, a bin assigns a pallet to itself, by remembering the pallet.

  – (At some later time, once the actual pallet is unloaded into an actual bin, someone asks a bin to release its associated pallet.)

Here's the scenario view (Figure 2–32):

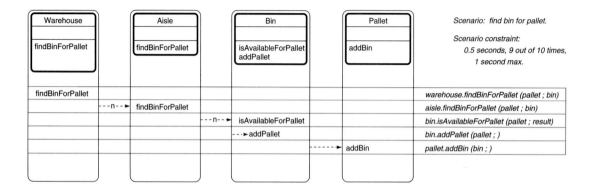

Figure 2–32: The "find bin for pallet" scenario view.

---

[1]Note that there may be multiple concurrent requests to a warehouse to find a bin for a pallet. That's fine. A bin needs to apply concurrency control over its decision whether or not it is available.

"Find bin for pallet" is a service that could be quite simple. For example, it could look for and return the first empty bin that it finds. Over time, though, you could make it much more sophisticated, taking into consideration the volume of items on a pallet, the available volume in a bin, kinds of items already stored within a bin, and the like. Note that the object model and scenario view would still be much the same—some parameters would change, and some service descriptions would change, too. Note the resilience to change (a very wonderful thing).

Scenario: build pick-list line items

Sketch out what happens:

– An order asks an order line item to build a pick-list line item
  – An order line item asks an item to build pick-list line item.
    – An item finds a bin (bin line item) with enough items[2]
      – An item asks a bin line item if it has the quantity available
        A bin line item gets the quantity currently being picked from
          the previously-assigned pick list line items
        A bin calculates the quantity available and returns it
      – An item asks a pick list to add a pick-list line item.
        A pick list asks the pick-list line item class
          to create and initialize a pick-list line item.

Here is the scenario view (Figure 2–33):

[2]Note that there may be multiplie concurrent requests for an item to build pick-list line items. That's fine. An item needs to apply concurrency control over its assignment of bins for picking.

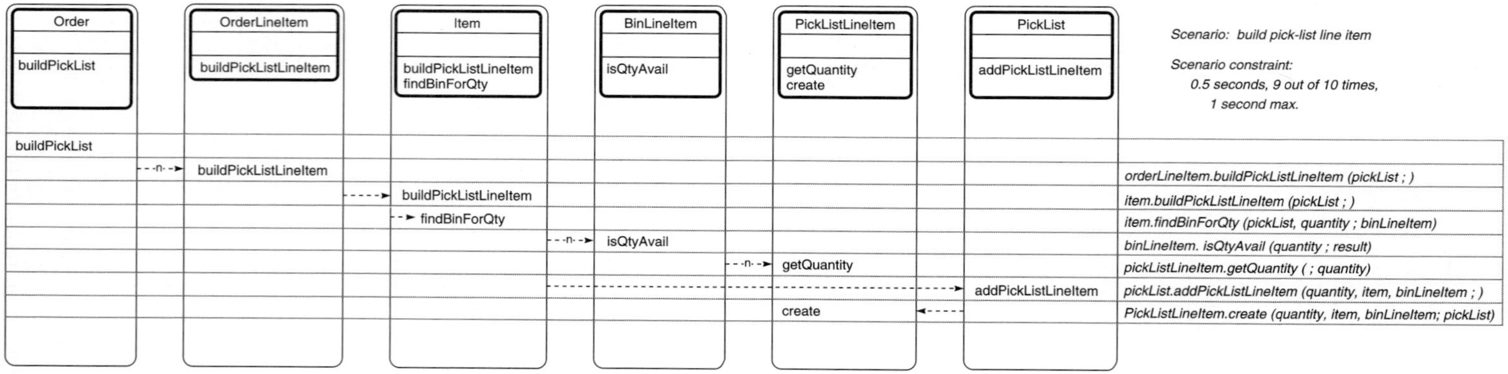

Figure 2–33: The "build pick-list line items" scenario view.

SELECTING HUMAN-INTERACTION OBJECTS AND RESPONSIBILITIES

You've read that purposes and features, objects, responsibilities, and scenarios are activities, not steps.

That means you can work on them in whatever order you choose. And you can apply whatever activity helps you get the job done.

You're ready to work with human-interaction objects, responsibilities, and scenarios. Do it differently.

You learn a lot about objects and responsibilities whenever you work with scenarios. So why not begin with scenarios this time, using them to help you find objects and establish responsibilities along the way?

Do it!

A note on data-entry windows and scenarios

What about data-entry windows?

For Wally's Warehouse, add these objects to your object model:

- a warehouse window
- an aisle window
- a pallet window
- a bin window
- an item window
- an order window.

Add these windows (Figure 2–34):

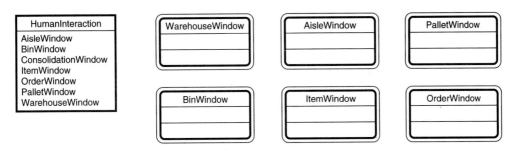

Figure 2–34: Add data-entry windows.

What about data-entry scenarios? One could spend weeks writing up scenario views. Very impressive volume of work. Very little content. Ugh!

So many scenarios, so little time. You could investigate an incredible number of scenarios, many of which would be downright boring (and fairly unproductive).

What should you do about it? Look for scenarios that do more than create objects and initialize values. Look instead for scenarios that exercise interesting system dynamics—so you learn more about what your system is really about.

WORKING OUT HUMAN-INTERACTION DYNAMICS WITH SCENARIOS

Consider the features of this system.

> – to give put-away instructions
> – to give picking instructions
> – to maintain quantity for each kind of item, for each bin holding that kind
>   of item
> – to calculate fill rate, to assess efficiency.

The features are the starting point for many scenarios that begin with some human interaction, for example:

> – Putting away scenarios
> – Picking scenarios
> – Bin consolidation scenarios (offering suggestions on what bins to com-
>   bine, for more efficient operations).

"Putting away" scenarios

A pallet has arrived at the warehouse. What's next? It's time to find a bin to put the contents of the pallet into. This is called "putting away."

For the putting away scenarios, you'll need a pallet window. Here's why:

> – to capture data entry about a pallet and its pallet line items
> – to display the put-away instruction
> – to accept input about where the pallet was put.

Now consider what's needed for the scenario itself:

> From a pallet window: create a new pallet, add pallet line items (easy and
>   somewhat boring).
> From a pallet window: ask a warehouse to find bin for pallet (work this one
>   out).
> From a pallet window: ask a pallet to unload itself (work this one out).

Scenario: find bin for pallet

What happens this time?

This scenario view is much like the one you worked out earlier. Find an available bin in the warehouse. Assign the pallet to that bin. This time, add a pallet window to tell the full story (Figure 2–35):

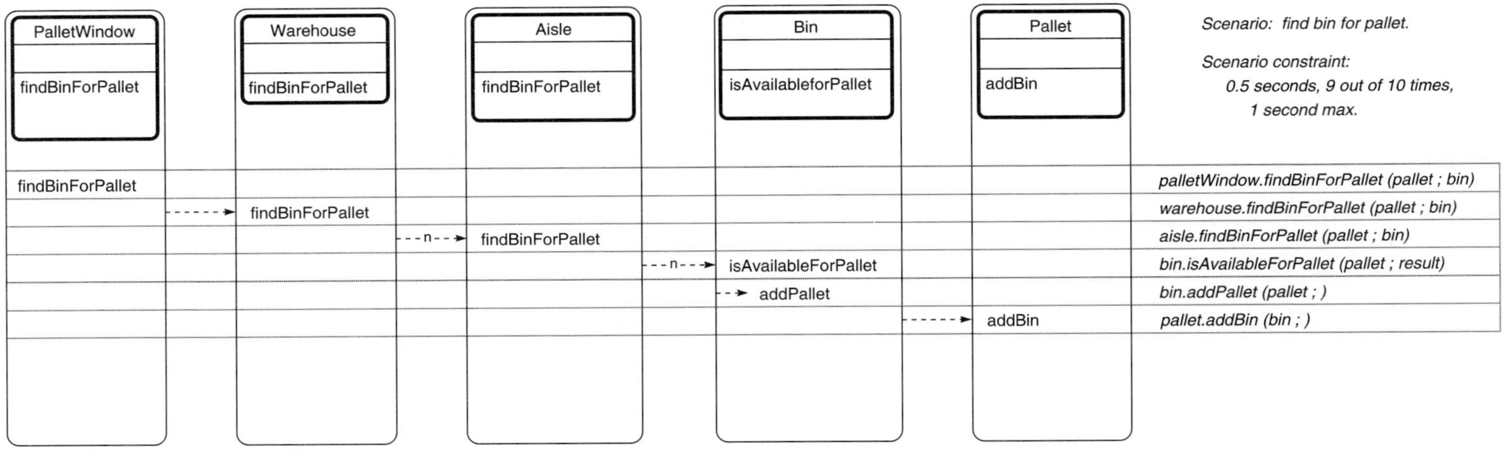

Figure 2-35: The "find bin for pallet" scenario view (with human interaction).

135

Scenario: unload pallet

Time passes. You arrive at the bin in the warehouse, the one you're really going to put the contents of the pallet into. You unload the pallet into a specific bin. Then you enter the bin number, telling the pallet window that you've done your duty.

What happens next?

- The pallet window checks to see if the bin it knows is the same as the one that the pallet was previously assigned to.
  - If not, it releases that bin.
- The pallet window tells a pallet to unload itself.
  - A pallet tells each pallet line item to unload itself.
    A pallet line item sends that quantity and item to bin, so it can add a new line item (bin could first look for an existing line item for that item and just increment the quantity).
- The pallet window tells the warehouse to delete the pallet (no longer needed).
  - The warehouse tells the pallet to delete itself.
    The pallet tells the pallet line items to delete themselves.

Here is the scenarios view (Figure 2–36):

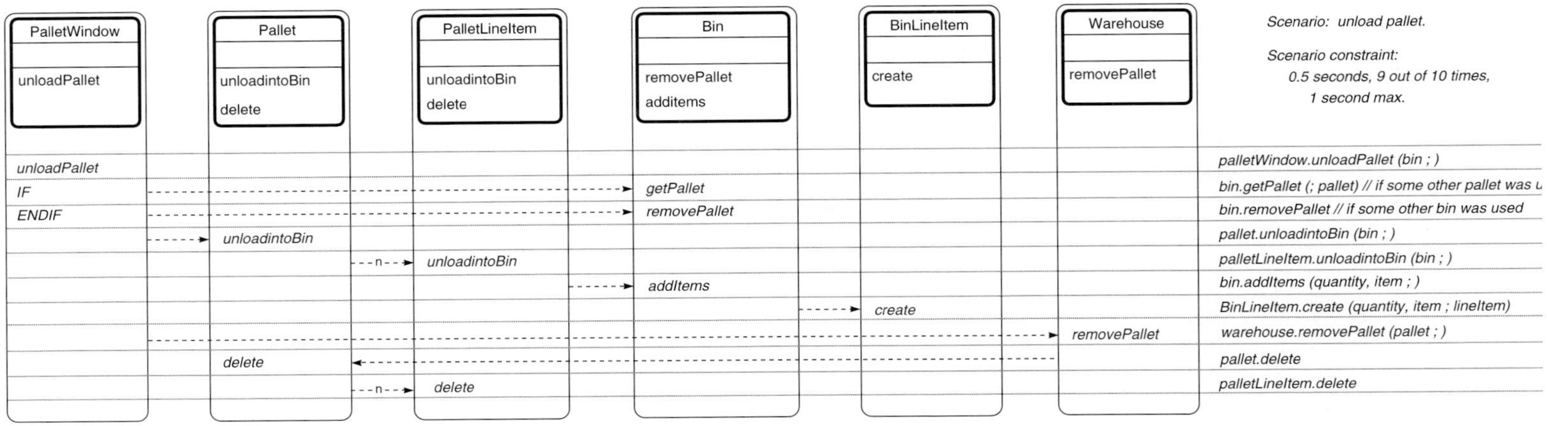

Figure 2–36: The "unload pallet" scenario view.

Picking scenarios

For the picking scenarios, you'll need an order window. Here's why:

> – to capture data entry about an order and its order line items
> – to display a pick list
> – to capture data that confirms the quantity picked.

Now consider what's needed for this scenario.

> From an order window: ask an order to generate a pick list (work this one out).
>
> From an order window: to confirm quantity picked (work this one out).

Scenario: generate pick list

So what happens here?

> – An order window asks an order to build its pick list itself.
> > – An order asks the pick list class to create and initialize a new object in that class.
> > > – An order asks an order line item to build pick-list line items.
> > > > You've already worked out this part of the scenario!
> > > > (Same old story, same old song and dance, my friend.)

Here's the scenario view (Figure 2–37):

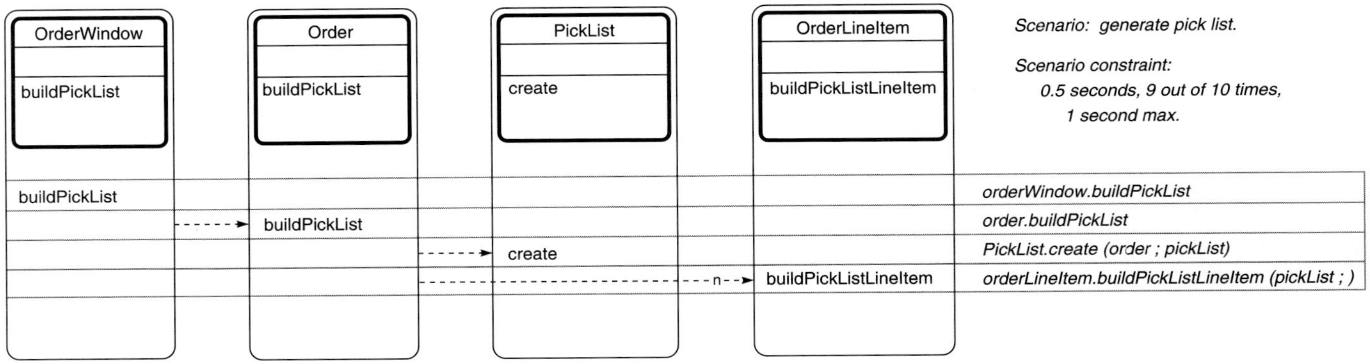

Figure 2–37: The "generate pick list" scenario view.

139

Scenario: confirm quantity picked

Here's what happens:

- In an overview window, a worker enters the actual quantity picked, for each pick-list line item.
  - An order window asks a pick-list line item to post the picked quantity.
    A pick-list line item updates its "quantity picked."
    A pick-list line item asks its bin line item to decrement its quantity by the quantity picked.

Here's the scenario view (Figure 2–38):

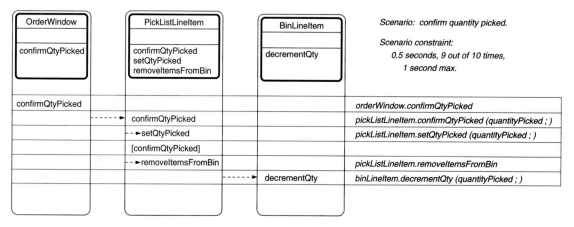

Figure 2–38: The "confirm quantity picked" scenario view.

Bin consolidation scenarios
Windows needed

For this scenario, you'll need a bin consolidation window:

- to capture data entry about "from" and "to" bins.

Keep asking questions

Find out a bit more about bin consolidation.

(Peter) I know we need to consolidate bins so that there will be empty ones to put pallets into. But how do you know what bins to consolidate?

(Wally) We look for bins that are close together that are almost empty.

(Peter) Okay. So you can look around and see what bins might be consolidated.

(Wally) That's right.

(Peter) Could we automate this in some way, say by volume of items and available volume in bins?

(Wally) Well . . .

(Peter) That sounds like something we could do, but shouldn't.

(Wally) I agree. Just let my team walk around. They will consolidate bins after hours—then notify the system of the changes that they make.

Observation: at first, letting the system determine what bins to consolidate sounded kind of fun. Yet, after considering the cost of adding that capacity and the cost of feeding it (with the dimensions of each item), it just didn't seem wise to do so. You need not automate everything in sight!

Sketch it out

So what happens here?

- A consolidation window captures a bin consolidation, from one bin to another.
- A consolidation window asks a bin to move its contents to another bin.
     - A bin asks its line items to move to another bin.
          A bin line item asks the move to bin to add a line item.
          A bin line item asks the move from bin to remove a line item.

Scenario view

Here is the scenario view (Figure 2–39):

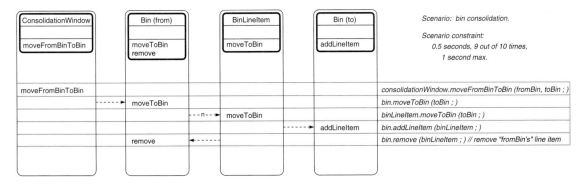

Figure 2–39: The "bin consolidation" scenario view.

This scenario view includes both "bin from" and "bin to"—one class, with different objects in that class playing different roles in the scenario.

When more than one object of a class participates in a scenario, it's often helpful to represent both objects in a scenario view (along with the role each one plays, in parentheses). Why? Doing this makes it easier to work out, express, and communicate the object interactions.

SELECTING DATA-MANAGEMENT OBJECTS AND RESPONSIBILITIES

Look for problem domain classes with objects that must be stored between program invocations.

Applying this strategy, add:

– aisle DM
– bin DM
– bin line item DM
– customer DM
– item DM
– loading dock DM
– order DM
– order line item DM
– organization DM
– pallet DM
– pallet line item DM
– pick list DM
– pick-list line item DM
– warehouse DM.

Each DM object knows its corresponding PD objects.

Each DM object does the DM basics: add, remove, and search.

Add DM objects and responsibilities to your model (Figure 2–40):

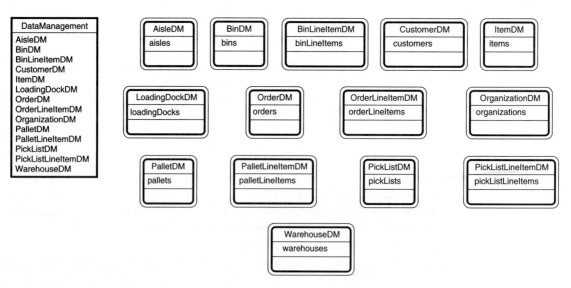

Figure 2–40: Data-management objects and responsibilities.

SELECTING SYSTEM-INTERACTION OBJECTS AND RESPONSIBILITIES

What about system-interaction objects and their responsibilities?

Earlier, you found a headquarters system, one your system can query, to get orders to be fulfilled.

Add a headquarters system object to the problem domain component.

Add a "headquarters system SI" object, a companion to take care of low-level system interaction (Figure 2–41):

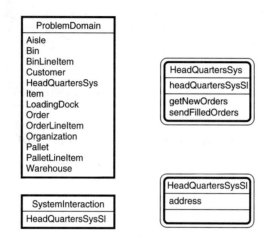

Figure 2–41: Interacting-system objects and responsibilities.

PROGRESS AT THIS POINT

Here's the object model. Along with the scenarios in this chapter, this wraps up your work for Wally's Warehouse (Figures 2–42 to 46).

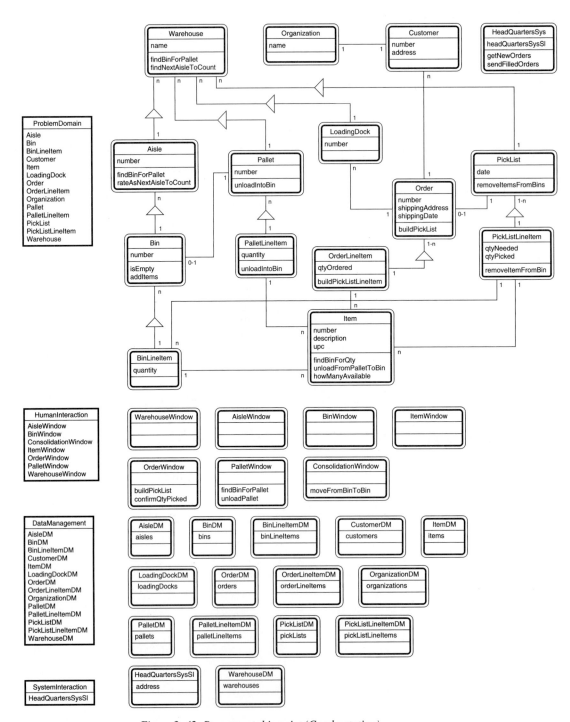

Figure 2–42: Progress at this point (Coad notation).

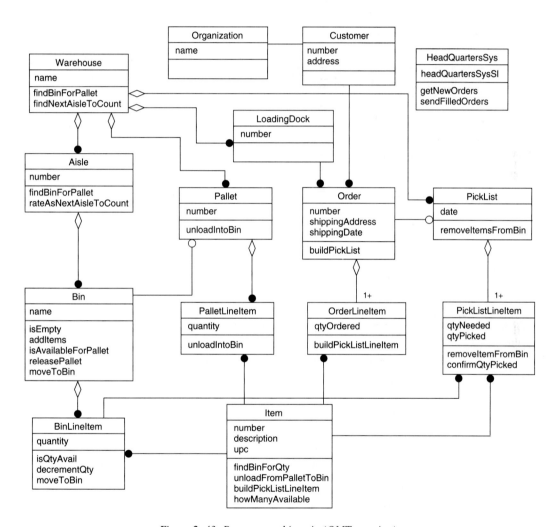

Figure 2–43: Progress at this point(OMT notation).

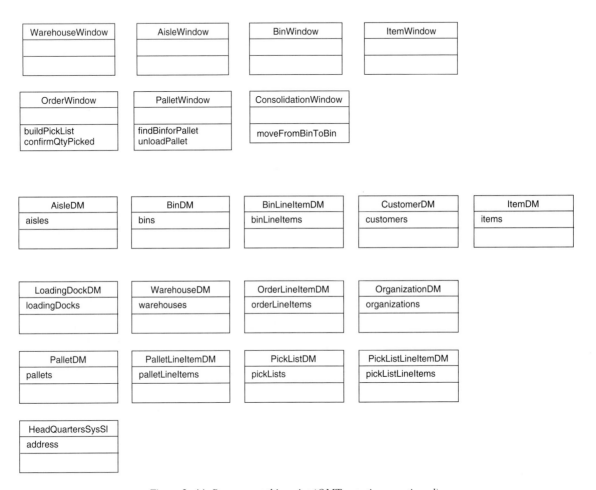

Figure 2–44: Progress at this point (OMT notation, continued).

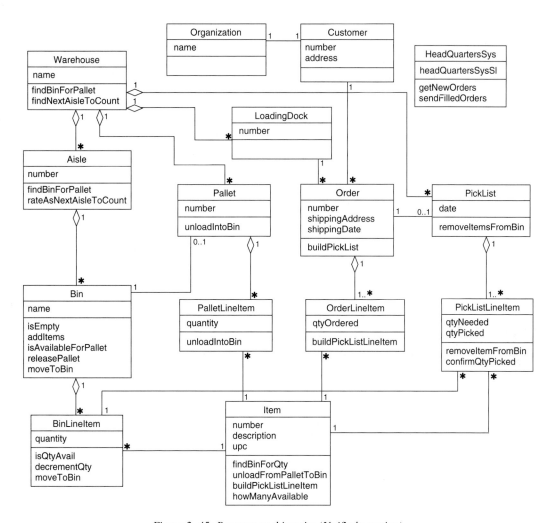

Figure 2–45: Progress at this point (Unified notation).

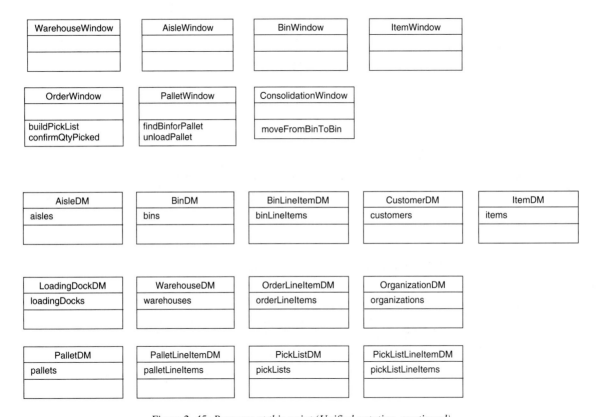

Figure 2–45: Progress at this point (Unified notation, continued).

Progress At This Point

Wally's Warehouse **149**

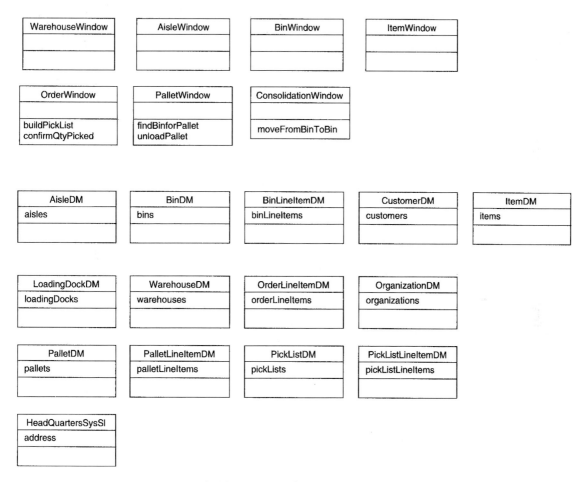

Figure 2–46: Progress at this point (Unified notation).

WRAP-UP

You did it! You built an object mode for a warehouse application.

It's important! Nearly every business uses a warehouse application, in one form or another. You can directly relate to (and for some readers, you can directly apply) this object modeling experience.

In this chapter, you learned and applied more strategies and patterns.

In addition, you saw that you can apply the same method again, this time in a different problem domain. You saw that strategies and patterns really do embody practical insights and experience into readily transferable guidelines that you can apply again and again with success.

Excellent!

3

Ollie's Order Center
(An Order-Entry Application)

GETTING STARTED

In this chapter, you'll build an object model for Ollie's Order Center.

The theme throughout the chapter is reuse, reuse, reuse. Specifically, you'll look for opportunities to:

– reuse a group of interacting objects—directly
    in other words: reuse of an instance of a pattern
– reuse a group of interacting objects—by analogy
    in other words, apply a pattern
    or, from the analogy, discover a new pattern
– reuse a class with inheritance, extending it with specialization
    specialization by kind
    specialization by usage.

Welcome to Ollie's Order Center!

Figure 3–1: Ollie's Order Center.

IDENTIFYING SYSTEM PURPOSE AND FEATURES

Welcome to Ollie's Order Center.

Ollie works at a local company. His job? He runs an order center, taking orders and processing them.

Identify purpose

(Peter) Hi, Ollie. I'd like to talk with you for a while, to see if an automated system might be of help to you.

(Ollie) Sounds good. A computer system might be real helpful. Just don't let it play the Laurel and Hardy theme song; that'd drive me crazy.

(Peter) Understood. So Ollie, what do you do?

(Ollie) I do about a hundred different things. Where do you want me to begin?

#9. "Top 10" Strategy	identifying purpose and features
• Build a list of features. • When you face an abundance of features (or classes, attributes, services), go after the top 10. • Why: avoid being overwhelmed by a sea of low-level details.	

(Peter) Sketch out a list of the "top ten" (or so) things that you do.

(Ollie) Okay. Let me work it out on the white board. Here's my list:

- Take an order over the phone and write it down on an order form.
- Total the order and tell the customer how much the order will cost.
- Get a purchase order (PO) number from the customer and write it down on the order form
- Decide what warehouse to send the order to.
- Fax the order to the warehouse for shipping.
- Get the number of items shipped, for each item shipped from the warehouse, via fax.
- Send the order form with the amount shipped to the accounts receivable department; they key it into an accounts receivable system.

(Peter) Just to make sure, please explain the term "accounts receivable."

(Ollie) Accounts receivable, also known as receivables, represent the amounts that we are to receive from others.

(Peter) Thanks. Let me ask you a few "why" questions. *Why* does a customer call you?

(Ollie) A customer calls me to place an order. Or he may call me to check my filing cabinet, to find out the status of a previous order.

(Peter) *Why* do you take orders over the phone?

(Ollie) Ninety percent of our orders come in over the telephone. The rest of the orders come in by fax, E-mail, and regular mail.

(Peter) *Why* do you total the order and give someone a price?

(Ollie) Great service! Actually, my customers demand it. It's a must. Besides, my prices vary over time, so it's good that I let him know up front exactly how much he's committing to spend with us.

(Peter) *Why* do you get a purchase order number from the caller?

(Ollie) I want to make sure that there's some corporate commitment behind the order. Otherwise, I might end up accepting an order that my company cannot collect on. That's bad for business—and for my profit sharing. I also add a purchase order number because many corporate customers use it to match an incoming shipment to a corresponding purchase order. I also add a purchase order number, doing whatever I can to encourage their prompt payment for the goods we deliver to them.

(Peter) *Why* do you select a warehouse?

(Ollie) I select the warehouse that's most cost-efficient to ship from. Generally speaking, that's the warehouse that is closest to the customer's shipping address.

(Peter) When do you make that decision?

(Ollie) I make that assignment for each new customer, right when I take his first order.

(Peter) I suppose that if we had shipping costs for different carriers on-line, we could ship a specific order from whatever warehouse would be least expensive to ship from.

(Ollie) Sure, although that's a little more extensive (and expensive) than what I'd expect from you, this first time out.

(Peter) *Why* do you fax an order to the warehouse?

(Ollie) I fax an order to the warehouse so the team there can do their best to fill it.

(Peter) *Why* does someone at the warehouse fax you back?

(Ollie) He faxes me with the actual number shipped, line item by line item.

(Peter) *Why* do you send the resulting information to the accounts receivable department?

(Ollie) Somebody needs to collect the amount due. And that somebody is the accounts receivable department.

#4. "Identify Major Sources of Stress" Strategy	identifying purpose and features
• Ask people about the most pressing problems that they face each day. "What stresses you out the most? What frightens you the most? What's the worst thing that could happen to you while your boss is watching?" • Look for ways to eliminate or reduce the impact of those problems.	

(Peter) What kinds of problems do you face?

(Ollie) I could give you a list a mile long.

(Peter) Let me ask it another way. What are the "top ten" or so problems that you face every day? I'm especially interested in those moments that cause a lot of stress or worry.

(Ollie) Really? Thanks for asking. I'm a bit surprised to hear that from a techno-geek. Let me sketch out a list on the white board. Here's what stresses me out the most:

- The warehouse ships the wrong merchandise—and blames it on my handwriting.
- The warehouse ships the wrong item—and blames it on me, because I didn't look up the right item number.
- The warehouse ships orders as they are received, first-in, first-out—not caring if they run out of stock before they get around to a priority order.
- Customers get cranky when they have to wait to place the order. I take a lot of heat for that.
- Customers want to know the exact status of their order. But I rarely know what's really going on. It's stressful for them and for me.

(Peter) Sounds like an automated system could help. Let's work on a statement of purpose. How about something like this:

> "To improve the efficiency and accuracy of taking orders and shipping orders."

(Ollie) Just make sure we ask for payment, too.

(Peter) You're absolutely right. How about this:

> "To improve the efficiency and accuracy of taking orders, shipping orders, and billing for orders."

(Ollie) That's what I'm looking for. Tell me more.

Identify system features

#6. "Four Kinds of Features" Strategy	identifying purpose and features
• Be certain to include features that cover the following: 1. Log important information. 3. Analyze business results. 2. Conduct business. 4. Interact with other systems.	

Identify features for logging important information

(Peter) What information do you need for your work, information that the system should log for you?

(Ollie) Here's my wish list, what I wish I had at my fingertips:

- "log important information" features
    to log items and prices
    to log tax categories (categories, rates, and effective dates)
    to log order clerk information

    – "log important information" features (continued)
        to log warehouse information
        to log customer information
        to log inventory, what's in each warehouse
        to log an order—and what we do with it.

Identify features for conducting business

#7. "Calculation Results and Decision Points" Strategy	identifying purpose and features
• Add features that deliver calculation results. Add features that support decision points.	

(Peter) What kinds of calculations do you do, calculations that the system could do for you?

    (Ollie) It could certainly do the calculations I do now.

    (Peter) Let's work it out.

        – "conducting business" features
           to price each order
           to subtotal, calculate sales tax, and total.

    (Peter) What decisions would you like help with?

    (Ollie) I'd really like to make sure that orders get filled on a priority basis, not simply first-in, first-out.

    (Peter) One more time, let's work it out.

        – "conducting business" features (continued)
           to select the next order to fill, based upon the priority of a customer
           and the order date.

Identify features for analyzing business results

(Peter) Now, as your team is busy working, or perhaps after hours each day, what kind of team member and business assessments do you do?

    (Ollie) I assess the performance of each clerk. I assess how each warehouse is doing. And I assess just how well my distributors are performing.

    (Peter) Good. Those are all things the system could help you with. You see, I'm looking for added value, something algorithmically interesting, something more than yet another data-holding system.

    (Ollie) I'll add those assessments to the features list.

        – "analyzing business results" features
           to assess clerk performance
           to assess warehouse performance
           to assess distributor performance.

Identify features for: working with interacting systems

(Peter) You've also got some other computer systems to deal with.

(Ollie) Yes, you're right. Anything you could do to simplify our work with the warehouse system and the accounts receivables system would be wonderful.

(Peter) Let's go ahead and add the corresponding features.

> – "interacting system" features
>> to interact with a warehouse system
>>> out: orders
>>> back: shipments.
>> to send updates to the accounts receivables system
>>> out: orders and shipments to customers.

Enough! You've got a system purpose and some system features. Time to start building up an object model.

Once again, your major activities are selecting objects, establishing responsibilities, and working out scenarios.

Go for it! And have some fun along the way.

SELECTING OBJECTS

Guess what you should do to get started? Yes, check out those object-model components. Use them as a guide, a working outline, for building your object model.

#1. "Four Major Activities, Four Major Components"   major activities and components

---

- Organize your work around four major activities, within four major components:

- Four major activities:

    Standard: Identify purpose and features, select objects, establish responsibilities, work out dynamics with scenarios.

    Variation 1: You may find it helpful to focus on working out dynamics with scenarios, establishing responsibilities along the way. This is especially suitable for real-time applications.

    Variation 2: You may find it helpful to select transaction, aggregate, and plan objects, then use the corresponding patterns to guide you through selecting additional objects, establishing responsibilities, and working out dynamics with scenarios.

- Four major components:

    Standard: Problem domain, human interaction, data management, system interaction.

    Variation 1: You may find it helpful to begin with human interaction, followed by problem domain, data management, and system interaction. This is especially suitable when your domain experts want to talk in terms of human interaction from the very start.

    Variation 2: You may find it helpful to begin with problem domain and system interaction, followed by human interaction and data management. This is especially suitable for real-time applications, when your domain experts are keenly interested in the data acquisition and control aspects of the system under consideration.

Model components: where to begin

Model components are indeed components, major groupings of classes that appear again and again in successful application development.

With four major model components, you might wonder where to begin. A recommendation: let the domain expert(s) be your guide.

When he talks about the problem domain (PD), add PD classes.

When he talks about human interaction (HI), add HI classes.

When he talks about interacting with other systems (SI), add SI classes.

It's comforting to have some sort of overall game plan. When it comes to object-model components, here's the one most often used:

     – problem-domain objects
     – human-interaction objects
     – system-interaction objects
     – data-management objects.

Here's an alternative. Use this overall game plan when the human-interaction needs are at the forefront of what the system is really all about:

     – human-interaction objects
     – problem-domain objects

– system-interaction objects
– data-management objects.

Here's another alternative. Use this overall game plan when interacting with other systems and devices is the focal point for the system under consideration:

– system-interaction objects
– problem-domain objects
– human-interaction objects
– data-management objects.

Strategies: where to begin

Purposes and features, objects, responsibilities, and scenarios are activities, not steps.

With four major strategy areas, you might wonder where to begin. Again, a recommendation: let the domain expert(s) be your guide.

When he talks about purposes and features, add them together.

When he talks about objects, add them together.

When he talks about responsibilities, add responsibilities—what I know, who I know, what I do—together.

Follow up on features, working out the required dynamics with scenarios.

Yet what's the overall game plan? Here's the most common overall approach:

– identify system purpose and features
– select objects
– establish responsibilities
– work out dynamics with scenarios.

Another path, one that focuses more attention on including just those responsibilities needed to deliver system features, is a reasonable alternate:

– identify system purpose and features
– selecting objects
– working out dynamics with scenario
– establishing responsibilities.

For this application

For this application, follow the most common overall approach, jumping between activities as needed along the way:

– model components: problem domain, human interaction, system interaction, data management
– strategies, applied component-by-component: purpose and features, objects, responsibilities, scenarios.

SELECTING PROBLEM-DOMAIN OBJECTS

Select actors and participants

Who are the actors? The actors are person and organization.

How do the actors participate? What roles do they play? A person might participate as a customer contact (a person with an organization) or an order clerk. An organization might participate as a customer or distributor.

Add classes (Figure 3–2):

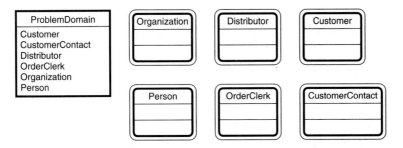

Figure 3–2: Actors and participants.

Select places where things come to rest

What are the places where things come to rest in this system? The warehouse (Figure 3–3):

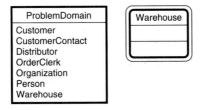

Figure 3–3: Select places where things come to rest.

Select things
Tangible things

What are the "tangible things" in this system? It's your good friend:

　　　– item.

Add it (Figure 3–4):

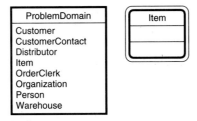

Figure 3–4: Select tangible things.

Transactions, transaction line items

Business systems revolve around business transactions.

What are the transactions, significant moments in time, needed here?

– order

– shipment.

Nearly all transactions have corresponding transaction line items.

Here, an order consists of one or more line items. A shipment contains one or more line items, too.

Add order, shipment, order line item, and shipment line item to the model (Figure 3–5):

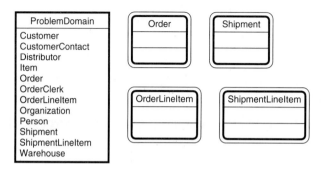

Figure 3–5: Select transactions.

REUSE, REUSE, REUSE

Just mention the word reuse—and the song "He's a Magic Man" comes to mind.

Somehow, people have gotten the impression that when one uses objects, then reuse magically happens along the way. Nothing could be further from the truth.

To gain leverage from reuse, pay attention to understandability, reuse granularity, and reuse mechanisms.

Understandability

Reuse can happen if and only if developers can find and understand something that is worth using again.

So reuse begins with simple things:

– choosing domain-based class names

– choosing less restrictive class names (generalizing the name, whenever the same responsibilities still apply)

– choosing domain-based generalization-specialization.

The foundation for good reuse practice: the realization that effective communication is a must. Understandability is the key.

Reuse granularity

What reuse building-block are you looking for? You can reuse:

- an attribute
- a service
- a class
- a pattern (a template for a group of collaborating objects)
- a pattern instance (a filled-in template, a group of collaborating objects)
- a scenario (or more likely, some portion of a scenario).

Attribute and service reuse is pretty meager.

Class reuse is okay—until you realize that no object (or class) is an island. For effective reuse, you need more than just a class at a time.

Pattern and pattern instance reuse is cool. You get reusable building blocks—Legos®—for software development.

Reuse mechanisms

You've got a choice of reuse mechanisms:

- inheritance
- components
- views.

Consider each mechanism, one-by-one.

Reuse mechanism #1: inheritance

Inheritance expresses "what's the same, what's different." That's a good thing.

You saw this kind of reuse back at Connie's Convenience Store:

- price, specialized into promo price
- sale line item, specialized into return line item
- payment, specialized into cash and authorized payment
- authorized payment, specialized into check and charge.

Each generalization class portrays the common attributes, services, and object connections. Each specialization class shows additional attributes, services, and object connections.

A generalization class explicitly captures commonality. And that's cool.

While inheritance is a helpful reuse mechanism, it's not the only one.

Very often, inheritance is not the best reuse mechanism.

What? Blasphemy? Not really. Read on.

The "coincidental generalization" problem

Sometimes a developer falls into the trap of using inheritance to factor out every bit of commonality in sight.

What happens? He sees common attributes, or common services, and factors them out—regardless of whether or not a domain-based generalization class is available.

Here are some examples:

- – a customer has a name, a boat has a name, so he adds a "named thing" class
- – a customer has an address, a boat has a location, so he adds "things with a location" class
- – a customer has status, a boat has a status, so he adds "things with a status" class.

He might save a couple of lines of descriptions and a couple of lines of code. But at what cost?

If the resulting classes do not portray domain-based generalization-specialization, problems follow. It's harder to understand. Lacking domain basis, it's not likely to hold up for subsequent applications, severely limiting future reuse.

Inheritance that expresses generalization-specialization is cool—easy to understand, more likely to remain stable over time.

Otherwise, leave it alone.

Inheritance is a great mechanism for expressing domain-based generalization-specialization—not for coincidental generalization.

The "coincidental specialization" problem

Sometimes developers use inheritance to express an application-specific version of a class.

That can help them claim that they are getting multiapplication ("enterprise wide") reuse.

This is certainly another way to explicitly represent commonality. But at what expense?

When you add a new application, you will probably need to change the existing class hierarchy in some way: add a class, move an attribute, move a service. Each time this happens, you've got two choices. One, you can make the change directly—and affect other applications (an expensive way to go). Two, you can make the change by adding more specializations—hacking in whatever your application needs.

Inheritance is a great mechanism for expressing domain-based generalization-specialization—not for coincidental specialization.

There must be a better way to work with commonality across multiple applications.

The "sometimes this kind, sometimes that kind" problem

Sometimes developers expect an object to transmute itself, converting itself from one specialization to another, over time.

That requires a messy set of create, copy, and release services—and fails to record what's happened over time.

A better approach is to add an object that has a collection of roles that it plays (the actor-participant pattern is a template for this approach).

The "ripple effect" problem

Sometimes developers forget that generalization classes can deeply affect what they are working on, somewhere lower in the class hierarchy.

It happens.

Just as soon as someone changes a generalization class, you've got to take care of the impact on the specialization classes.

The change ripples down the class hierarchy. The change ripples through your test harnesses, too.

That's why shallow (up to four levels), domain-based gen-spec structures make good sense.

And that's why the "coincidental specialization" approach falls apart so quickly (with ten or twenty levels of application-specific specializations, the "ripple effect" becomes more like a "tidal wave effect").

Is inheritance a total disaster?

After reading about its problems, you might think so.

Inheritance does pay off—when it's used in a reasonable context

So where does inheritance make sense?

Use inheritance within a single application, to capture domain-based generalization-specialization. Don't use it for view management (showing what you want to work with on a specific application).

When does inheritance fall apart?

- When it's blindly used to factor out commonality, without regard for domain-based generalization-specialization.
- When it's used to portray application-specific views.

Reuse mechanism #2: components

Another reuse mechanism is components.

In this case, an object consists of a number of components.

Here's a prime example. In everyday conversation, you might hear someone talking figuratively about all of the hats he wears. That's an object (a person) who participates in many ways (wears many hats). It's an object whose responsibilities are represented by a collection of ways of participation.

The "actor-participant" pattern is a template for component-based reuse.

Reuse with components is helpful, especially as you begin to reuse across multiple applications. For each application, you grab just the components that you need to work with.

Reuse mechanism #3: views

What about reuse across multiple applications?

It's a view-management issue. You can use specialization by usage. Or (even better) you can use a view-based configuration management tool.

Views, using "specialization by usage"

Consider item. Connie needs it. Wally needs it. And now Ollie needs it.

It sure seems like there must be some commonality in there somewhere. There is. The issue is how to best represent that commonality. One approach is "specialization by usage." Just add a specialization class for each usage, each application (Figure 3–6).

Item specializes into point-of-sale item, warehouse item, and order entry item.

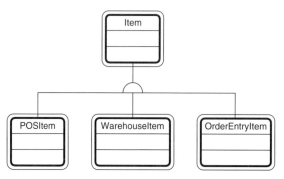

Figure 3–6: Specialization by usage.

Note that these are not domain-based specializations. Instead, they are application-based specializations, subject to the whim of a specific application. Reuse of specializations is most unlikely; each application will require its own specialization.

The problem with all of this is that there is a lot of commonality, a lot of potential for reuse, which remains untapped.

Yet if the only reuse tool you have is inheritance, it is a reasonable way to go.

However, there is a better way.

Views, using a view-based configuration management tool

What is the core issue here? Is it inheritance? Or is it views on an underlying model?

It sure isn't inheritance. Each application would be yet another "coincidental specialization." The change impact would be a real pain. No one wants continual changes, ones that impact more than one application at a time. The point: inheritance is ill suited for working with what is inherently a view-management problem.

Reuse across multiple applications is indeed a view-management issue. The underlying model includes all classes and responsibilities. Each application is a view.

With a view-based configuration management tool, for each class, you can select the subset of responsibilities that you need for a specific application.

This approach to reuse is at a higher plane than programming language syntax. One way to think about it is that every model element has an "application tag" associated with it. When you work within a specific application, you work with its tagged elements.

A configuration-management system can then assemble the classes for you, based upon your desired view or domain. Additional benefits include: no wasted space in the application; and no extraneous content from other applications, waiting for an opportunity to foul things up.

Reuse, for this application chapter

So what about reuse in this application chapter?

This chapter will assume best practice.

Use inheritance within this single application to capture domain-based generalization-specialization. Use a view-based configuration-management system, one that keeps track of all attributes and services for a class, across multiple applications—and lets you select the ones you want to work with this time.

ESTABLISHING RESPONSIBILITIES FOR PROBLEM-DOMAIN OBJECTS

Establish responsibilities, reusing some of the results you worked out in Chapters 1 and 2.

A number of the classes look very familiar:

> Connie's Convenience Store (Chapter 1)
>> person, cashier, sale, sale line item, item
> Wally's Warehouse (Chapter 2)
>> customer, order, item, warehouse.

Or you can reuse on a higher plane: reuse pattern instances, instead.

#37. "Select and Reuse a Group of Interacting Objects" Strategy	selecting objects (reuse)
• Reuse another instance of a pattern as is. • Reuse an instance of a pattern, specializing in one or more of its classes. • Reuse a pattern, by analogy.	

A number of pattern instances look very familiar. Remember Connie's Convenience Store (Chapter 1):

> – actor-participant
>> person-cashier
> – participant–transaction–transaction line item–item / associate–other associate
>> cashier–sale–sale line item–item–price.

Remember Wally's Warehouse (Chapter 2):

> – actor–participant–transaction–transaction line item–item
>> organization–customer–order–order line item–item
> – transaction–subsequent transaction–subsequent transaction line item–item
>> order–pick list–pick list line item–item
> – transaction line item–subsequent transaction line item
>> order line item–pick list line item
> – container-content
>> warehouse-order
> – container–container–container–container line item–item
>> warehouse–aisle–bin–bin line item–item.

Now look for similar pattern instances for Ollie's Order Center:

- actor–participant–transaction–transaction line item–item
  - organization–customer–order–order line item–item
  - person–order clerk–order–order line item–item
  - person–customer contact–order–order line item–item

- actor–participant–transaction–subsequent transaction–transaction line item–item
  - organization–customer–order–shipment–shipment line item–item
- transaction line item–subsequent transaction line item
  - order line item–shipment line item
- group-member
  - customer–customer contact
- actor-participant / group-member / container–container line item–item
  - organization–distributor–warehouse–warehouse line item–item
- container-content
  - warehouse-order.

So now what? Establish responsibilities, using patterns as a guide.

Actor–participant–transaction–transaction line item–item

Consider the responsibilities, class-by-class. Use the responsibilities in pattern instances in the applications in Chapters 1 and 2 as guides.

Organization–customer–order–order line item–item
Organization

Previously, you worked with this (Figure 3–7):

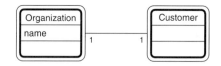

Figure 3–7: Organization—for Wally's Warehouse.

Now consider what you need for this application.
What I know.

- Reuse: name.

Who I know.

- Reuse: customer (actor-participant).
- Add: distributor (actor-participant).

What I do: just the basics.

Here's the result (Figure 3–8):

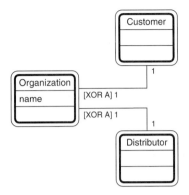

Figure 3–8: Organization—for Ollie's Order Center.

Check out those object connection constraints. "XOR" stands for exclusive or: one or the other, not both. The XOR applies to all object connections labeled with the same constraint tag, the letter that follows XOR.

Here's what it means in this example. An organization object knows a customer object or a distributor object—but not both. Either way, a customer object knows exactly one object, either a customer object or a distributor object.

Customer

Previously you worked with this (Figure 3–9):

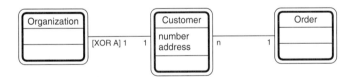

Figure 3–9: Customer—for Wally's Warehouse.

Ask about customer number.

#63. "Embedded Meaning in a Number" Strategy	establishing responsibilities / what I know (consider and challenge)
• Attribute is a number, with encoded meanings? • Add an attribute for each meaning. • Most often, include a number attribute, too (a sequence number, no longer a source of encoded meaning).	

(Peter) How do you identify customers?

(Ollie) We have this great customer numbering system. It works like this:

- first two letters are the customers initials
- then the warehouse number that we have assigned to them
- the next six are the file cabinet number that we use to file that customers orders.

(Peter) Hmmm—very interesting. Let's extract the meaning from that number: name, file cabinet number, and warehouse. We'll need:

- customer name
- a connection between order and warehouse.

(Peter) In addition, you'll need:

- a filing system based upon date (and sequence number, if order volume and retrieval frequency warrant it)—so you can access original pur chase order documents, when needed from time-to-time.

Next, investigate the active side of a customer object. It's a participant object. Take a look at what it might do to assess or qualify itself.

Ask Ollie about what he does to qualify a customer. Then see if the customer object could do it itself.

(Peter) What do you do to qualify a customer?

(Ollie) Using customer priority and credit rating, I assess whether he's good for the amount of the order.

(Peter) Okay. Then the system could help with some of that work. For a customer, it could figure out:

- Is this customer good for this amount?

What else could we do to qualify a customer in some way? How about:

- How many orders have you placed this year?
- How much money have you spent here, this year?

(Ollie) Good.

Finally, establish the responsibilities for each customer object.

What I know.

- Reuse: number.
- Add: priority, credit rating.

Who I know.

- Reuse: orders (participant-transaction)
- Add: customer contact (associate–other associate).

What I do. What are the questions you might ask an actual customer—if he could answer accurately, knowledgeably, and honestly (!) each time? How about:

- Which of your orders are still awaiting fulfillment?
- Are you good for the amount of this order?
- How many orders have you placed this year?
- How much money have you spent here this year?

Hence, the "what I do" for a customer object includes:

– get outstanding orders
– is good for amount
– how much (money) over interval
– how many (orders) over interval.

Add these responsibilities to your model (Figure 3–10):

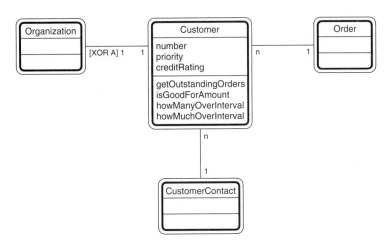

Figure 3–10: Customer—for Ollie's Order Center.

Order

Consider the pattern instances you've already worked with.

#36. "Select and Reuse an Analogous Class" Strategy	selecting objects (reuse)

- Look for a class that might apply.
- Consider synonyms.
- Consider a more general name, using "is a kind of."
- Consider metaphors (corresponding objects) within analogous systems (a system that has an analogous purpose).
- Caution: Watch out for metaphors based on what people are doing. Focus on what people act on instead, letting those objects do those things to themselves. (Reason why: do otherwise, and you'll end up with controller objects and data objects, resulting in weaker cohesion and higher coupling.)

For Connie's Convenience Store, you had "sale" (Figure 3–11). For Wally's Warehouse, you had "order" (Figure 3–12):

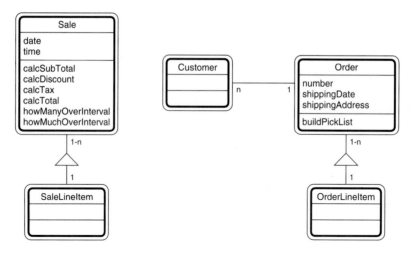

Figure 3–11: Sale—for Connie's Convenience Store.   Figure 3–12: Order—for Wally's Warehouse.

Look for similarities from one pattern instance to another. Add what you need this time.

What I know.

   – Similarities: date, time, number, shipping address
   – Add: customer purchase order number, status.

Who I know.

   – Similarities: customer (participant-transaction), order line items
          (transaction–transaction line item)
   – Add: customer contact (participant-transaction), shipment
          (transaction–subsequent transaction).

What I do.

   – Similarities: calculate subtotal, calculate tax, calculate total
   – Add: is fulfilled, rate importance (based upon order date and customer
          priority).

Here's the result (Figure 3–13):

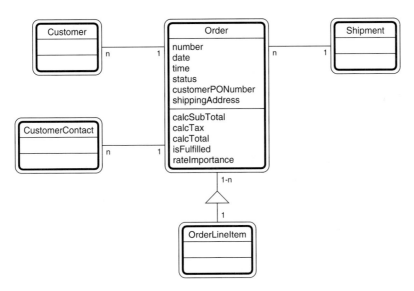

Figure 3–13: Order—for Ollie's Order Center.

Order line item

Previously you worked with this (Figures 3–14 and 15):

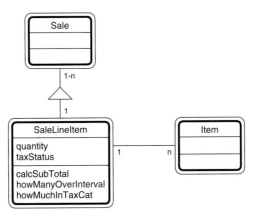

Figure 3–14: Sale Line Item—for Connie's Convenience Store.

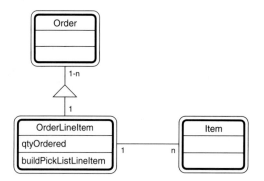

Figure 3–15: Order Line Item—for Wally's Warehouse.

Add responsibilities.
What I know.

 – Similarities: quantity, tax status.

Who I know.

 – Similarities: order (transaction–transaction line item), item (item–line
    item)
 – Add: shipment line item (line item–subsequent line item).

What I do.

 – Add: is fulfilled, calculate subtotal, how much tax for category.

Here's the result (Figure 3–16):

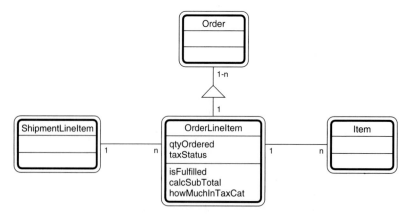

Figure 3–16: Order line item—for Ollie's Order Center.

Item

Take a look at what you've done before (Figures 3–17 and 18):

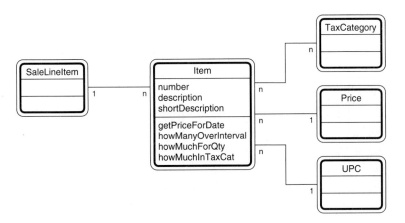

Figure 3–17: Item—for Connie's Convenience Store.

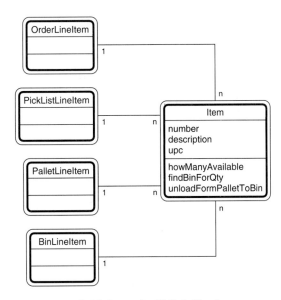

Figure 3–18: Item—for Wally's Warehouse.

Add responsibilities.

What I know.

— Similarities: number, description.

Who I know.

— Similarities: order line item (item–line item), price (item–item description), tax category (item–item description), upc

— Add: shipment line item (item–line item), warehouse line item (container–container line item).

What I do.

— Similarities: get price for date, how much for quantity, how much in tax category.

The result (Figure 3–19):

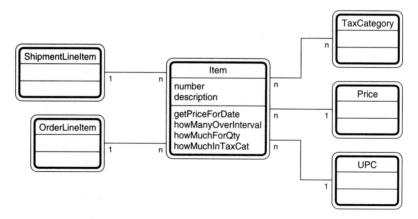

Figure 3–19: Item—for Ollie's Order Center.

Person–order clerk–order–order line item–item

You've taken care of all of these, except for person and order clerk. Now take care of them, too.

Person

Previously, you worked with this (Figure 3–20):

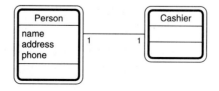

Figure 3–20: Person—for Connie's Convenience Store.

Add responsibilities.
What I know.

   – Similarities: name, address, phone.

Who I know.

   – Add: order clerk (actor-participant), customer contact (actor-participant).

What I do: just the basics.
Here's the result (Figure 3–21):

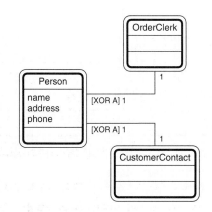

Figure 3–21: Person—for Ollie's Order Center.

Order clerk

Gain reuse insights from analogous classes. Previously, you worked with cashier (Figure 3–22):

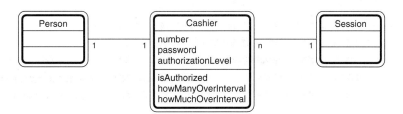

Figure 3–22: Cashier—for Connie's Convenience Store.

By analogy, now consider order clerk.
What I know.

   – Similarities: number (consider that enough, for this application)

Who I know.

   – Similarities: person (actor-participant)
   – Add: orders (participant-transaction).

What I do.

   – Similarities: assess performance over interval, how (money) much over interval, how many (orders) over interval.

The result (Figure 3–23):

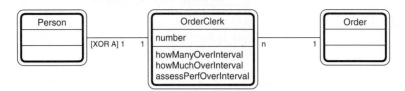

Figure 3–23: Order clerk—for Ollie's Order Center.

Person–customer contact–order–order line item–item

You've taken care of all of these, except for customer contact. Now take care of it, too.

Customer contact

At last! This is an all-new object. You did not have a customer contact for Connie's Convenience Store or Wally's Warehouse.

So what now? Hey, you've already worked out another participant object, one which is an abstraction of a person. Consider its responsibilities, and how it might apply here.

What I know:

– Add: direct phone (direct phone number).

Who I know:

– Similarities: orders (participant-transaction)
– Add: person (actor-participant), order (participant-transaction), customer (group-member).

What I do:

– Similarities: how much (money) over interval? how many (orders) over interval?

Here's the result (Figure 3–24):

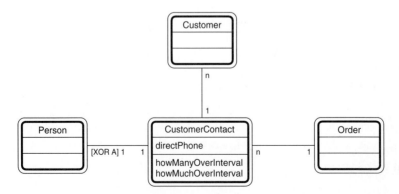

Figure 3–24. Customer contact—for Ollie's Order Center.

Actor–participant–transaction–subsequent transaction–subsequent transaction line item–item
Organization–customer–order–shipment–shipment line item–item

You've taken care of all of these, except for shipment and shipment line item. Now take care of them, too.

Shipment

Add responsibilities.

> What I know: date.
> Who I know: warehouse (participant-transaction), shipment line items
> (transaction–transaction line item), order (transaction–subsequent transaction).
> What I do: just the basics.

Here's the result (Figure 3–25):

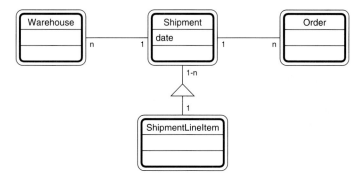

Figure 3–25: Shipment—for Ollie's Order Center.

Shipment line item

Add responsibilities.

> What I know: quantity.
> Who I know: shipment, order line item.
> What I do: just the basics.

Here's the result (Figure 3–26):

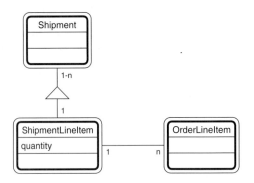

Figure 3–26: Shipment line item—for Ollie's Order Center.

Transaction line item–subsequent transaction line item

Order line item–shipment line item

You've already taken care of these two.

Group-member

Customer–customer contact

You've already taken care of these two.

A customer is a group; each customer contact is a member.

What could a customer do across its collection of customer contacts? It could find the customer contacts who are active within an interval. True. Yet that's not really within scope.

Just leave customer and contact as-is for now.

Actor–participant/group–member/container–container line item–item

Organization–distributor–warehouse–warehouse line item–item

You've already taken care of organization and item. Work out the others.

Distributor

Distributor is something new. You can treat is as a large container, of warehouses, items, order clerks, and customers.

Add responsibilities.

What I know: name.

Who I know: warehouse (group-member), order clerk (group-member), customer (group-member), items (group-member).

What I do. Work this out.

#93. "Question, Calculation, Selection" Strategy	establishing responsibilities / what I do (fundamentals)

- For an object, consider:
    What *questions* can I answer?
    What *calculations* can I do? What ongoing monitoring could I do? What calculations across a collection could I make (letting each worker do its part)?
    What *selections* across a collection could I make (letting each worker do its part)?

First, what questions could it answer for you?

– how many (orders) over interval
– how much (money) over interval.

What calculations could it do for you?

– calculate fill rate over interval
– calculate percent in-stock (orders) over interval.

What kind of selections could it make for you? As a collection of warehouses, given customer, it could ask each warehouse to rate its suitability for that customer (based on proximity, for example).

Add this service to distributor:

– select (best) warehouse for order.

And add this service to warehouse:

– rate suitability for customer.

What kind of searches could it do for you?

– get customer for number
– get item for number.

Add these responsibilities to your model (Figure 3–27):

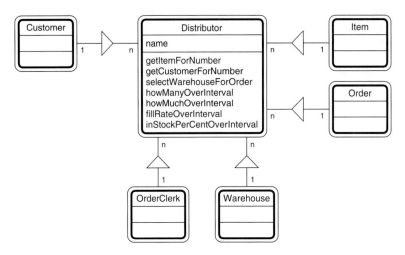

Figure 3–27: Distributor—for Ollie's Order Center.

Warehouse

Use view management, to reuse what you've done before.

You already have this (Figure 3–28):

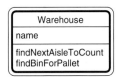

Figure 3–28: Warehouse—for Wally's Warehouse.

Hmmm. Not very helpful here. Oh well, at least you get an attribute out of it.
What I know.

– Reuse: name.

Who I know.

– Add: orders (participant-transaction), warehouse line item
(transaction–transaction line item).

What I do.

– Add: select next order, how many (orders) over interval
– Add: rate suitability for customer (discovered while considering the responsibilities for a distributor).

Here's the result (Figure 3–29):

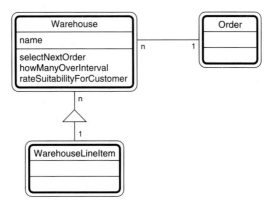

Figure 3–29: Warehouse—for Ollie's Order Center.

Warehouse Line Item

Just another line item, no big deal. Add responsibilities.

What I know: quantity.
Who I know: warehouse (container–container line item), item (item–line item).
What I do: just the basics.

Here's the result (Figure 3–30):

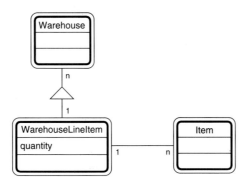

Figure 3–30: Warehouse line item—for Ollie's Order Center.

Progress at this point

All right. Check it out (Figure 3–31):

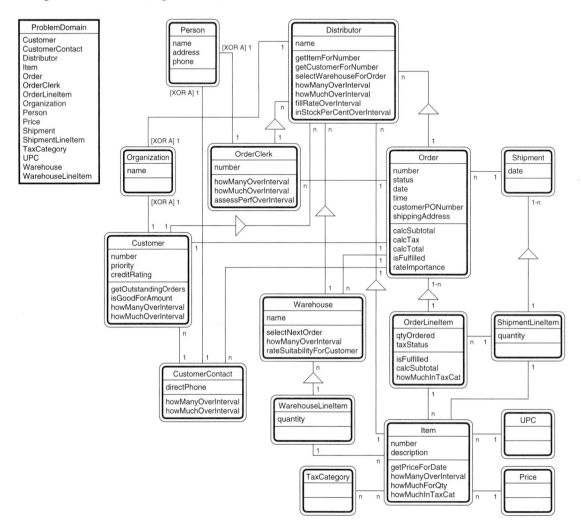

Figure 3–31: Progress at this point.

WORKING OUT PROBLEM-DOMAIN DYNAMICS WITH SCENARIOS

Select one or more problem-domain scenarios

Most of the services are the same or similar to the ones used for the preceding applications.

What might be interesting here?

Looking over the system features, you might choose this scenario: select next order to fill.

Scenario: select next order to fill

Here's the scenario view (Figure 3–32):

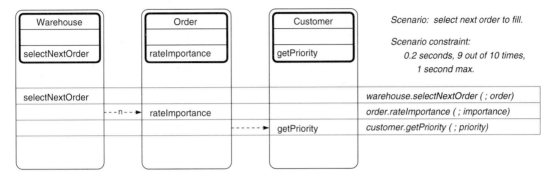

Figure 3–32: The "select next order to fill" scenario view.

An observation

Notice that scenarios don't have to be long and complex to be meaningful!

SELECTING HUMAN-INTERACTION OBJECTS

Finally, you are ready to check out some human-interaction objects.

Select windows

Shift your attention to the windows you need for this system.
    You need some setup windows:

> – customer and customer contact, order clerk, distributor, warehouse and
>   warehouse line item, and item windows.

    You need some "conducting business" windows:

> – warehouse operations window (with the action "select next order to fill")
> – order and order line item window (also known as an order entry window).

Select reports

Reports are just another human-interaction view.
    What kind of reports might you need? Nothing special comes to mind. And that's fine.
    Add human-interaction objects to your model (Figure 3–33):

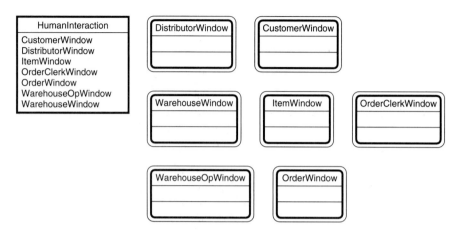

Figure 3–33: Human-interaction objects.

ESTABLISHING HUMAN-INTERACTION RESPONSIBILITIES

Responsibilities for windows

Order entry window

What I know

For an order entry window, you need:

      – search fields for the order:
          customer number
          customer contact name
          order clerk number
          distributor name
      – search fields for each order line item:
          item number (or UPC, if desired)
      – data values for the order:
          customer PO
      – data values for each line item:
          quantity.

Who I know

An order entry window object needs to know:

      – distributor
      – customer
      – customer contact
      – order (to get to order line items and items).

What I do

Here's how.

For a window, the "what I do" are those the window-specific menu actions for that window.

In addition, every window object knows how to display itself. And every window class knows how to create (and initialize) a new object in that class.

Here, all you need to add is:

- add an order
- add an order line item
- total an order
- commit an order

Add the window and its responsibilities to your model (Figure 3–34):

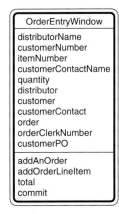

Figure 3–34: An order-entry window object.

WORKING OUT HUMAN-INTERACTION DYNAMICS WITH SCENARIOS
Select human-interaction scenarios

So what is the primary human interaction scenario for an order entry application?

Not surprisingly, it's whatever it takes to enter an order into the system!

For Connie's Convenience Store, you had a similar major scenario: enter a sale into the system.

Similar scenarios? Potential reuse! Good deal.

"Enter an order" scenarios

These scenarios include:

- start order
- add order line item
- total order
- complete order.

Here are the scenario views (Figures 3–35 to 38):

Scenario: start an order

Here is the scenario view:

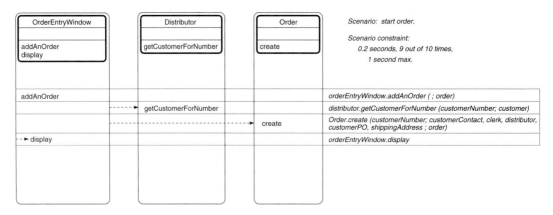

Figure 3–35: The "start order" scenario view.[1]

Scenario: add order line item

Here is the scenario view:

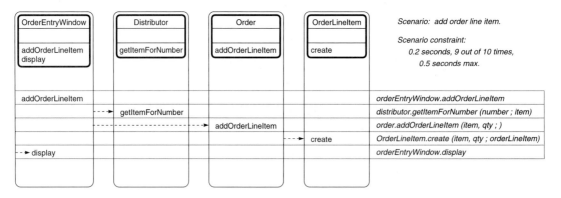

Figure 3–36: The "add order line item" scenario view.

[1]One of the challenges of human-interface development is validating the values before they are officially assigned to problem-domain objects. Ideally, the validation criterion should be encapsulated in the problem-domain objects themselves. In practice, such validation criteria are often placed directly in human-interaction objects—a less than ideal situation when it comes to reuse of problem-domain objects.

Scenario: total order

Here is the scenario view:

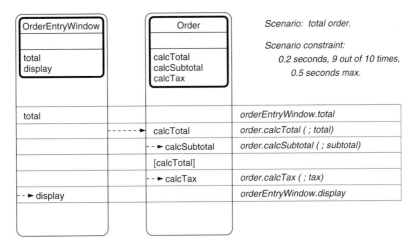

Figure 3–37: The "total order" scenario view.

The detailed calculation interactions are just like the ones you worked out for Connie's Convenience Store (and are not repeated here).

Scenario: complete order

Here is the scenario view.

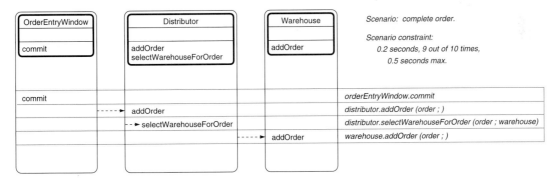

Figure 3–38: The "complete order" scenario view.

SELECTING SYSTEM-INTERACTION OBJECTS
Interaction with other systems

Based upon conversations with Ollie, recorded earlier in this chapter, you know that the interacting systems are:

> – a warehouse system
>> out: orders
>> back: shipments
> – an accounts receivables system
>> out: orders, shipments, and customers.

Add these objects to your model (Figure 3–39):

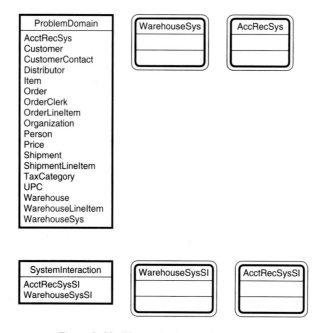

Figure 3–39: Objects for interacting systems.

ESTABLISHING SYSTEM-INTERACTION RESPONSIBILITIES

Warehouse system

The warehouse system actually runs the warehouse and knows the current inventory of each item in the warehouse. It receives orders, to be processed.

What I know: address, operational state.
Who I know: warehouse system SI (the corresponding system interaction object).
What I do:

- send order to warehouse
- receive shipment result from warehouse.

Add these responsibilities (Figure 3–40):

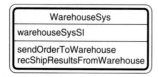

Figure 3–40: Responsibilities for a warehouse system.

Accounts-receivable system

The order-entry system interacts with an accounts-receivable system, giving it what it needs to bill customers, namely, groupings of orders, shipments, and customers.

What I know: address, operational state.
Who I know: accounts receivable system SI (the corresponding system interaction object).
What I do: send order for billing.

Add these responsibilities (Figure 3–41):

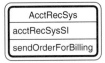

Figure 3–41: Responsibilities for an accounts-receivable system.

WORKING OUT SYSTEM-INTERACTION DYNAMICS WITH SCENARIOS

You could work out a scenario, one that includes a system interaction object.

Scenario: send order to warehouse system

Here is the scenario view (Figure 3–42):

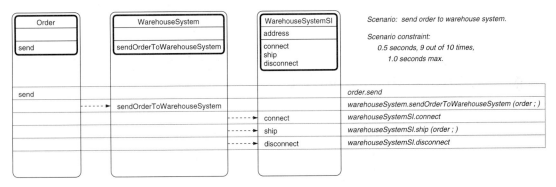

Figure 3–42: The "send order to warehouse system" scenario view.

SELECTING DATA-MANAGEMENT OBJECTS AND RESPONSIBILITIES

The order entry system also needs for some of its objects to be persistent, remembered over time, from one execution of the system to the next.

Here's the approach. If the underlying storage management is not object-oriented, then add a data-management (DM) object for each class with objects that need to be persistent.

Here, simply add these DM objects:

– customer DM
– customer contact DM
– distributor DM

– item DM
– order DM
– order clerk DM
– organization DM
– person DM
– warehouse DM.

What about your warehouse system object and your accounts-receivable system object? You don't really need objects for them (just one object in a class). Kind of boring. Just create them on startup.

Each DM object knows its corresponding PD objects.

Each DM object does the DM basics: add, remove, and search.

Add DM objects and responsibilities to your model (Figure 3–43):

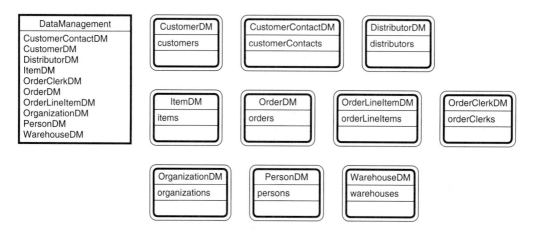

Figure 3–43: Data-management objects and their responsibilities.

WORKING OUT DATA-MANAGEMENT DYNAMICS WITH SCENARIOS

To work out data-management dynamics:

– Begin with a service in an HI component (for "save" and "load"), or
– Begin with a search need from the PD component.

Here, consider a search need from a PD object:

– distributor.getCustomerForNumber
– distributor.getItemForNumber.

Work out the dynamics for interacting with DM objects.

Scenario: get customer for number

Add this scenario.

Note that a customer DM object knows how to use the local file system to find efficiently the customer object for the corresponding customer number.

Here is the scenario view (Figure 3–44):

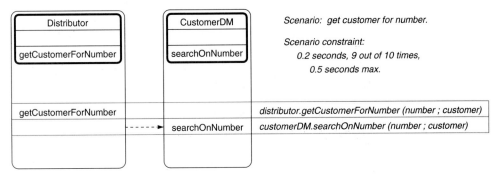

Figure 3–44: The "get customer for number" scenario view.

Scenario: get item for number

Work out this one.

The item DM knows how to use the local file system to efficiently find the item object for the specified item number.

Here is the scenario view (Figure 3–45):

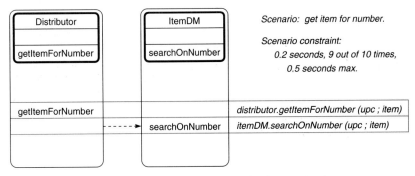

Figure 3–45: The "get item for number" scenario view.

PROGRESS AT THIS POINT

Here's the object model. Along with the scenarios in this chapter, this wraps up your work for Ollie's Order Center (Figures 3–46 to 49).

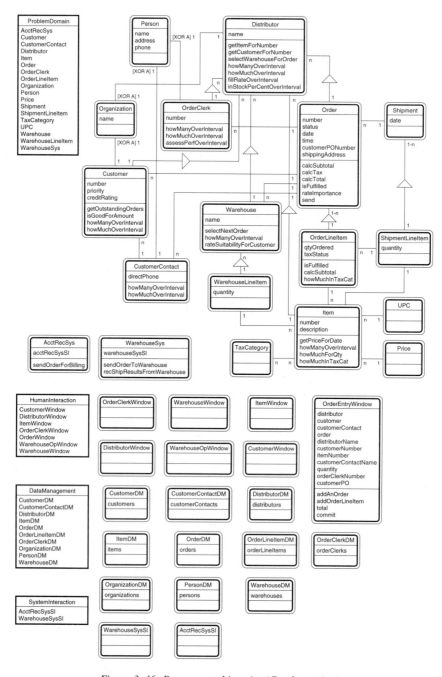

Figure 3–46: Progress at this point (Coad notation).

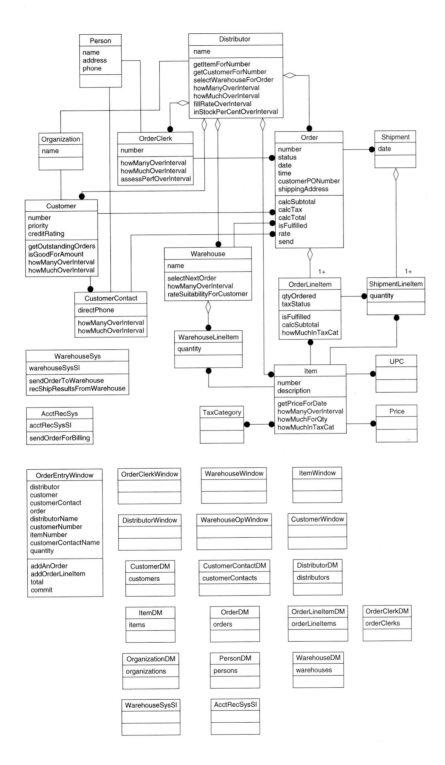

Figure 3–47: Progress at this point (OMT notation).

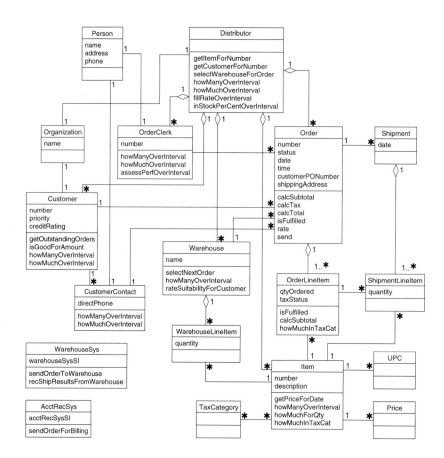

Figure 3–48: Progress at this point (Unified notation).

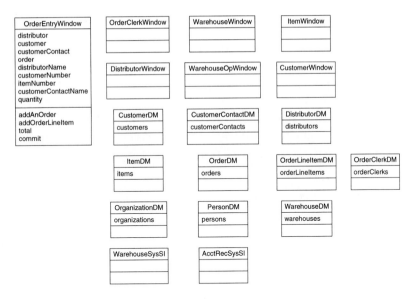

Figure 3–49: Progress at this point (Unified notation, continued).

WRAP-UP

You did it! You built an object model for an order-entry application.

It's important! Nearly every business uses an order-entry application, in one form or another. You can directly relate to (and for some readers, you can directly apply) this object modeling experience.

In this chapter, you learned and applied more strategies and patterns.

In addition, you gained practical, down-to-earth, no-hype understanding of reuse concepts, including pattern reuse and pattern instance reuse.

Excellent!

4

Dani's Diverters (A Soft Real-Time Conveyance Application)

Dani is charged with improving warehouse and loading operations at Wally's Warehouse. Her immediate task is to develop and deliver an automated conveyor system, one that moves totes to the loading docks.

Dani is well versed in automated warehouses, having worked in them and with them for a number of years. The good news: she understands the business. The bad news: she may not have kept up with the rapid technology changes—and the options now available to her.

Welcome to Dani's Diverters!

Figure 4–1: Dani's Diverters.

IDENTIFYING SYSTEM PURPOSE AND FEATURES

Identify purpose: ask a domain expert

(Peter) Okay. Let's start with the basics, just to make sure we're on the same wavelength.

(Dani) We need to develop and deliver an automated conveyor system, one that moves totes to loading docks.

(Peter) What's a tote?

(Dani) A tote is a large plastic container. Pickers put items in them.

#10. "Now and Later" Strategy	identifying purpose and features
• Consider current capabilities—and anticipated future capabilities. • Ask, "How is it done now? How will it be done later, with the new system?" • Look at things that people do to objects now, and consider features you can add (your automated objects might be able to do those actions to themselves).	

(Peter) Okay. A picker loads a tote. What happens next, the way it's done now?

(Dani) The picker carries the tote to whatever loading dock we've assigned that order to.

(Peter) What will happen with the new system?

(Dani) The picker will put the tote on a conveyor. The conveyor will automatically take the tote to the loading dock that we've assigned that order to. Meanwhile, the picker gets another tote and keeps on picking.

(Peter) So, we need to work together to develop an automated system to control the conveyor and somehow route each tote to the loading dock we assign to its order. Right?

(Dani) That'd be cool.

Identify purpose : 25 words or less

(Peter) The purpose of the system, then, is:

> to control the conveyor and route each tote to the loading dock we assign to
> its order.

(Dani) Yes! Rock!

Build a features list

Sketch out a picture. Then use it to help you build a features list.

(Peter) Have you seen how this works in some other warehouse?

(Dani) Yes. In fact, let me show you a diagram of what this kind of system looks like (Figure 4–2):

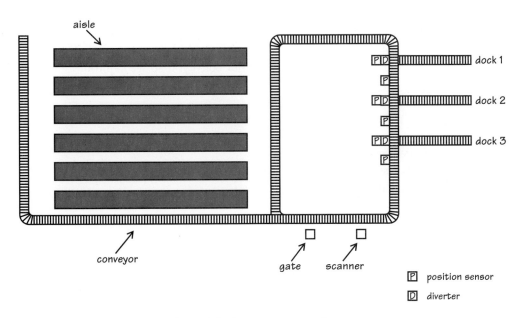

Figure 4–2: Conveyance system layout.

Walk through the diagram

(Peter) Walk me through the diagram, step by step. (Walk this way, talk this way.)

(Dani) What's that? Oh, the diagram. A picker gets an empty tote. He slaps on a bar code label, identifying the order. He fills it with items listed on a pick list. He puts it on a conveyor.

(Peter) Where do bar code labels come from?

(Dani) Didn't your parents teach you about that? Sorry. Bar code labels come from the warehouse system, along with a pick list.

(Peter) Okay. Someone will need to add that to the pick list report. No big deal. What's next?

(Dani) The conveyor moves the tote along to the next section of the conveyor, called the sorter.

(Peter) The sorter?

(Dani) It's the part of the conveyor system that sorts the totes and delivers them to the right loading dock.

The sorter

(Peter) Tell me more about the sorter.

(Dani) The sorter is a conveyor with extra goodies: a gate, a scanner, some position sensors, and some diverters.

(Peter) What does the gate do?

(Dani) The gate does two things for us. It controls the entry of the tote into the sorter.

(Peter) Why is that important?

(Dani) We need the totes to be well-spaced on the sorter conveyor, so we can route accurately.

(Peter) What's the other thing a gate does for you?

(Dani) It stops each tote momentarily, just long enough so the scanner can read it accurately.

(Peter) Let's move on to the next device.

(Dani) The scanner reads the bar code, so we can identify the tote and determine which loading dock it is supposed to go to.

(Peter) What's next?

(Dani) Position sensors detect that a tote is passing by. They just don't tell us which tote is passing by. Diverters push a tote onto a specific spur, heading towards a loading dock.

(Peter) I notice in the diagram that all diverters have corresponding position sensors, yet not all position sensors have corresponding diverters. Is that right?

(Dani) That's right. You can use the extra position sensors to help you make sure that the totes are making reasonable progress.

(Peter) Why does the conveyor go past the last dock?

(Dani) The totes don't always make it down a spur so they need to go around again.

(Peter) Why don't they make it?

(Dani) Lots of reasons. A diverter may miss a box. A diverter may jam. Sometimes we haven't assigned a loading dock to that order just yet. From time to time, say due to a power outage, we need to run all of the totes on the sorter back through another time.

Software rules

Hold on! What's happening here?

Someone is laying out what data acquisition and control devices you should use here—without regard for what the real cost driver is: the software that runs this system.

In two words: software rules!

If you use smarter devices, available at lower and lower costs, you can significantly reduce the complexity of your object model—and favorably impact schedule and cost, during development and maintenance. Here's the strategy:

#12. The "Smarter Devices" Strategy	identifying purpose and features
• Look for opportunities to use smarter devices, simplifying your object model and reducing software development schedule and costs.	
• When building an object model in a field with rapidly changing data acquisition and control technology, be sure to take a systems perspective, spanning both hardware and software.	

Yet, sadly, some hardware weenies and administrative types still participate in pagan hardware worship! This is a real sociological (and political) problem for many software developers.

You see, Dani's not a bad person. She just needs to see how much simpler the software architecture will be, with more capable data acquisition and control devices. Perhaps you can find a way to use a pair of object models, to help her make the right decision about all of this.

Exploring two approaches

(Peter) Dani, I've got some questions for you.

(Dani) Shoot.

(Peter) Each year, we find that we can buy smarter data acquisition and control devices at lower cost. It's incredible. Smarter devices help us reduce software costs. In effect, we transfer workload from software to smart devices.

(Dani) Understood. So what are the questions?

(Peter) Could we consider using scanning diverters? Let me sketch it out on the white board (Figure 4–3):

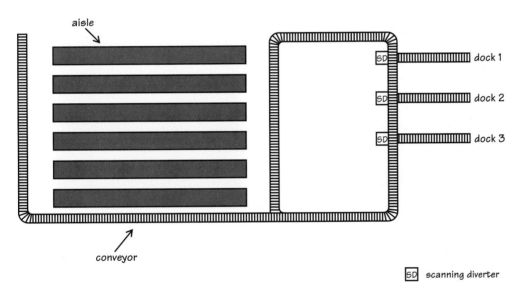

Figure 4–3: Conveyance system layout—using scanning diverters.

(Peter) We could get rid of the gate, the scanner, the position sensors, and the diverters.

(Dani) Let me think about that a bit. Hmmm. Okay, I can see getting rid of the gate —as long we use one or a limited number of standard tote sizes. Yet what about scanning? Can we scan a bar code without a gate momentarily stopping the tote, so we can read it?

(Peter) Sure. The latest scanners can read a bar code even if it's moving, and even if it's at an angle (within reason!). The local grocery store uses them.

(Dani) Won't that drive our costs sky-high?

(Peter) Hardware costs will be somewhat higher. We'll need to get price quotes.

(Dani) So why bother?

(Peter) With smarter devices, we can develop a simpler object model, and that means we can develop (and later maintain) the software at lower cost.

(Dani) I'm not convinced.

(Peter) Fair enough. All I ask is that you let my team build an initial object model for both approaches. Then let's decide.

(Dani) Fair enough. I want to do what's best. Show me.

Help from another system, too

(Peter) We'll need some help from the warehouse system.

(Dani) What's needed?

(Peter) Please ask them to print a bar code with the order number on it. Add a tote number, too—if we need to keep track of the totes in an order.

(Dani) Why would we need to keep track of the totes in an order?

(Peter) So we can find out things like, "For this order, what are its totes?" and "Is this order (all of its totes) now at the loading dock?"

(Dani) Cool.

Finally, a features list

Here's the features list. It's short and to the point:

> – to run conveyor motors (activate, standby, shutdown)
> – to scan and divert a tote to the loading dock that its order is assigned to.

ACTIVITIES, ACTIVITIES, ACTIVITIES

The major activities (not steps!) for building an object model are:

> – identifying purpose and features
> – selecting objects
> – establishing responsibilities
> – working out dynamics with scenarios.

You've identified purpose and features.

With a data acquisition and control system, you may find it helpful to select objects, work out dynamics with scenarios, and then establish responsibilities.

#1. "Four Major Activities, Four Major Components" Strategy   major activities
                                                                        and components

---

• Organize your work around four major activities, within four major components:

• Four major activities:

> Standard: Identify purpose and features, select objects, establish responsibilities, work out dynamics with scenarios.

> Variation 1: You may find it helpful to focus on working out dynamics with scenarios, establishing responsibilities along the way. This is especially suitable for real-time applications.

> Variation 2: You may find it helpful to select transaction, aggregate, and plan objects, then use the corresponding patterns to guide you through selecting additional objects, establishing responsibilities, and working out dynamics with scenarios.

• Four major components:

> Standard: Problem domain, human interaction, data management, system interaction.

> Variation 1: You may find it helpful to begin with human interaction, followed by problem domain, data management, and system interaction. This is especially suitable when your domain experts want to talk in terms of human interaction from the very start.

> Variation 2: You may find it helpful to begin with problem domain and system interaction, followed by human interaction and data management. This is especially suitable for real-time applications, when your domain experts are keenly interested in the data acquisition and control aspects of the system under consideration.

Remember that you are investigating two possibilities:

> – a system with a gate, scanner, position sensors, and diverters
> – a system with scanning diverters.

SELECTING PROBLEM-DOMAIN OBJECTS
Select actors and participants

Actors are either people or organizations (or things that fulfill different missions). Only people are actors in this system. The role played is "picker." Yet does the system under consideration need to know about pickers?

No.

Add picker to the "not this time" component (Figure 4–4):

Figure 4–4: Select actors and roles.

Select places where things come to rest

What are the places where things come to rest in this system?

— tote

— loading dock.

Add these objects (Figure 4–5):

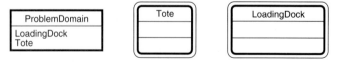

Figure 4–5: Select places where things come to rest.

So far, so good.

Select things

Data acquisition and control devices

Now consider data acquisition and control devices.

#20. "Select Interacting Systems and Devices" Strategy	selecting objects (pattern players)

- Look for other systems, ones that your system is responsible for interacting with.

- (Real-time systems) Look for devices, ones that your system needs for data acquisition and control.

- Add it to the PD component. Example: sensor.

- Add a companion SI class to the system interaction component. Example: sensorSI. (SI objects encapsulate the specific communication needs for interacting with another system or device.)

In the basic system, the devices are:

— gate

— scanner

— position sensor

— diverter.

You also need to include something to run the conveyor belt itself, namely:

— conveyor motor.

Add these objects (Figure 4–6):

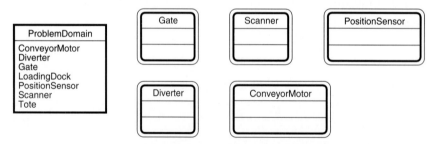

Figure 4–6: Select data acquisition and control devices, for the basic system.

Actually, you need to plan to work with some number of conveyor motors. Usually, conveyors are divided into sections, with separate motors for each. Why? Certain mechanical constraints make this a necessity. Yet there is another reason: workers can keep loading totes and putting them onto the conveyor, even when other parts of the system are down for a while.[1]

In the scanning diverter system, the data acquisition and control devices are:

- scanning diverter
- conveyor motor.

Add these objects (Figure 4–7):

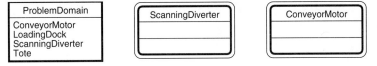

Figure 4–7: Select data acquisition and control devices, for the scanning diverter system.

Tangible things

What is the "tangible thing" in this system? It's a:

- tote.

You already found this one.
Keep moving.

Collection things

What collection things are in the problem domain, ones that might be useful for capturing behavior across a collection?

#21. "Select Collections of Objects" Strategy	selecting objects (pattern players)

• Look at each object as a worker in a collection. Name the collections.
 	
• Look at each object as a collection with workers. Name the workers.
 	
• Examples:
    Collections of participants: company, department, group, organization, squad, team.
    Collections of places: airport, campus, store chain.
    Collections of things: assembly, batch, collection, list, log, queue, pool.	

In the basic system, the collection is:

- conveyor: a collection of a gate, a scanner, position sensors, diverters,
     and conveyor motors.

---

[1]This is important, too. Otherwise, someone might end up having to do the work of that conveyor whenever the system shuts down (as one of the authors did, shoveling hamburger meat all day long many years ago).

Add this object (Figure 4–8):

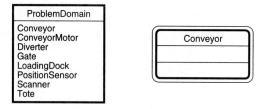

Figure 4–8: Select collection things, for the basic system.

For the scanning diverter system, the collection is:

– conveyor: a collection of scanning diverters and conveyor motors.

Add this object (Figure 4–9):

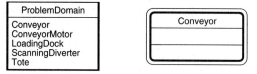

Figure 4–9: Select collection things, for the scanning diverter system.

Transactions

Data acquisition and control systems tend to have fewer transaction objects, compared to business applications like a point-of-sale system or a warehouse system.

In fact, you don't need any for this application.

If this system were responsible for remembering detected events (such as problems, alarm conditions, and the like), then you would need transaction objects in your model.

Associates

An associate is an object that knows about another object it's associated with—directly, without an intervening transaction object.

#18. "Select Associates" Strategy	selecting objects (pattern players)

• Look for associates, objects that need to know each other, yet:
    have no need to capture information or provide services about that association
    have no need for history about that association.
• Most often, this strategy applies to the interaction of objects, whose actual objects are closely related.
• Examples: aileron-gyro; aircraft-runway; building-sensor; driver-vehicle, loading dock–order; order-tote; truck–loading dock.	

An order is an associate.

What are its associates?

– an order knows its totes
– an order knows its loading dock.

Add this object (Figure 4–10):

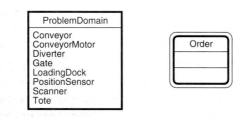

Figure 4–10: Select associates.

APPLYING PATTERNS: ORGANIZE PROBLEM-DOMAIN OBJECTS

Use patterns as templates, to initially organize the objects you've selected.

Associate–other associate

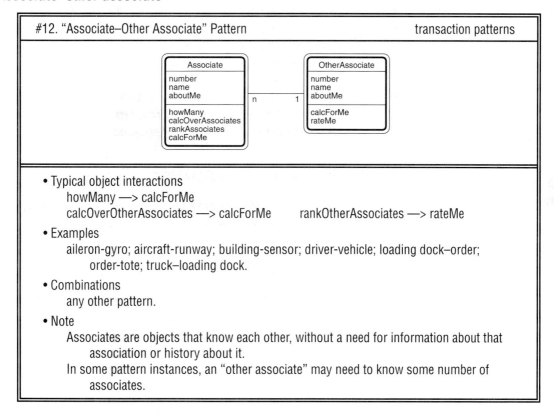

Consider order and its associates:

      – an order and its totes
      – an order and its loading dock.

  For the basic approach, also consider a position sensor and its associates:

      – a position sensor and its (optional) diverter.

And so, add this layout to the basic approach (Figure 4–11):

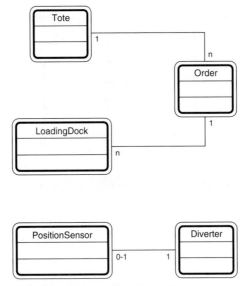

Figure 4–11: Layout, using associate–other associate.

And add this layout to the scanning diverter approach (Figure 4–12):

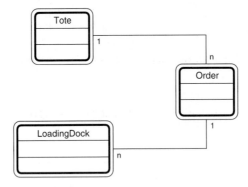

Figure 4–12: Layout, using associate–other associate (for the scanning-diverter approach).

Container-content

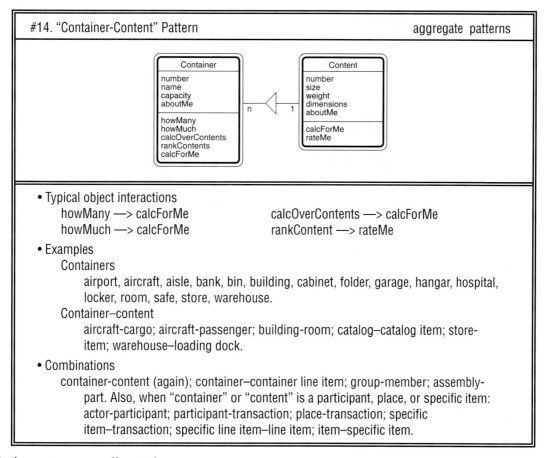

You've got one overall container—a conveyor.

Add whole-part connections to its parts.

For the basic system, that's gate, scanner, position sensors, diverters, and conveyor motors (Figure 4–13):

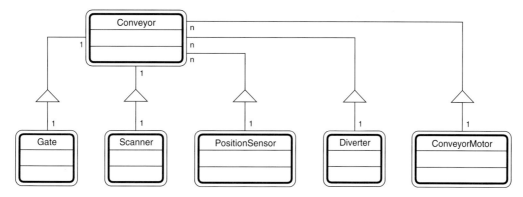

Figure 4–13: Layout, using container-content (for the basic approach).

For the scanning-diverter system, it's scanning diverters and conveyor motors (Figure 4–14):

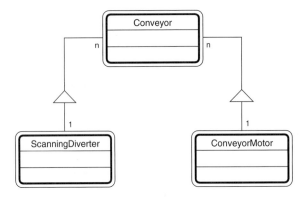

Figure 4–14: Layout, using container-content (for the scanning diverter approach).

Progress at this point

Here's what the two object models look like at this point (Figures 4–15 and 16):

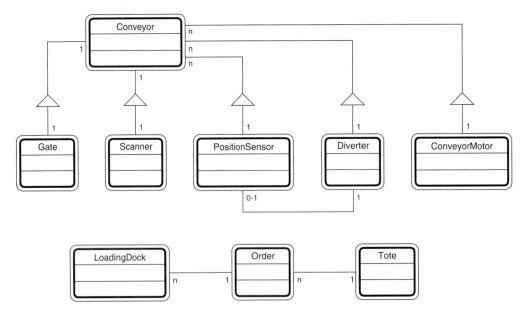

Figure 4–15: Progress at this point, for the basic system.

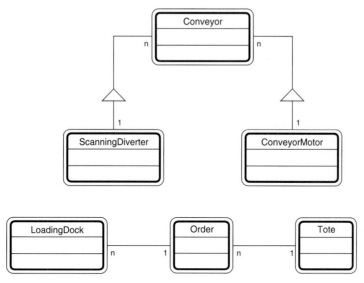

Figure 4–16: Progress at this point, for the scanning diverter approach.

WORKING OUT PROBLEM-DOMAIN DYNAMICS WITH SCENARIOS

Check out the key scenarios, ones that illustrate system features.

Perhaps with this, you'll have enough evidence to get Dani to go with the scanning diverter approach.

The system features list is:

– to run conveyor motors (activate, standby, shutdown)
– to scan and divert totes to the loading dock that its order is assigned to.

Scenario: activate motors

Activating the conveyor motors is going to be about the same, for both approaches.

Put together a scenario view (Figure 4–17):

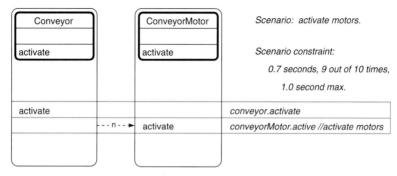

Figure 4–17: The "activate motors" scenario view.

Note that the conveyor object activates some number of motors (some combination of conveyor motors and sorter motors).

Boring! Really. And this scenario does little to help us compare the basic approach versus the scanning diverter approach.

You did discover some new services, though.

Meanwhile, move on to another scenario. Keep looking for more.

"Get a tote to the loading dock" scenarios (the basic approach)

What's involved here?

- detect and release tote
- scan tote
- position sensor detects a tote
- divert, if applicable.

Consider it, working through one scenario at a time.

Scenario: detect and release tote

Here's what happens:

- a gate object monitors for a tote
- an actual tote comes up to a gate
- a gate object notifies the conveyor object
- when it is ready to do so, the conveyor object tells the gate to release.

Here is the scenario view (Figure 4–18):

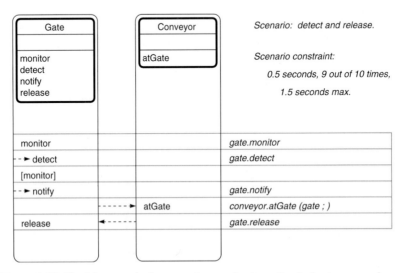

Figure 4–18: The "detect and release tote" scenario view—for the basic approach.

Time for another strategy.

#140. "Object Creation and Deletion" Strategy	working out dynamics with scenarios (consider and challenge)
• Look at scenarios that create (and initialize) and delete the objects you work with. • Ask, "Who is responsible for creating (and initializing) that object? Who is responsible for deleting it?"	

Ask: when does that object get created and initialized, anyway?

Here, these objects are created via setup windows. (Or they could even come from interacting with some other system.) Make a note of this; come back to it a bit later.

Scenario: scan tote

Here's what happens next:

- an actual tote starts rolling
- a scanner object reads the bar code number
- a scanner object asks the conveyor to notify the corresponding tote
- the conveyor object queries its tote, asking if it is the tote that corresponds to the number
- the conveyor object tells the winning tote object to set its time last seen
- the conveyor adds the winning tote object to its collection of scanned totes.

Here is the scenario view (Figure 4–19):

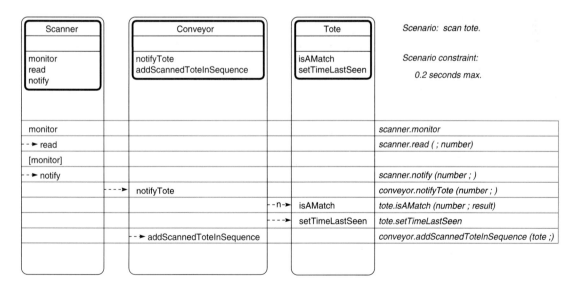

Figure 4–19: The "scan tote" scenario view—for the basic approach.

Notice that a conveyor knows all the totes, so that it can query each one until it finds a match.

Also notice that a conveyor knows all the *scanned* totes, too—so it knows the totes that have already made it past the scanner. Here's why: when a conveyor gets a position report, and needs to figure out the most likely tote that the position report applies to, the conveyor has the added (and needed) benefit of knowing which totes have already passed the scanner (in sequence, too).

Who sets up an order and its totes? Someone does this work—either your system or another system. Let the warehouse system take care of that for you—after all, if it's generating bar code labels, it already knows about orders and totes. The impact? Sounds like you'll need a system interaction object, representing the interface to that other system. Make a note of this; come back to it after you work out which system approach you're going to use (the basic approach vs. the scanning diverter approach).

Scenario: position sensor detects a tote

What's next?

- a position sensor object detects that a tote is there
- a position sensor object asks the conveyor object to update its most likely tote
  - a conveyor object asks each tote to calculate probability that it's at that position
    - a tote object calculates the probability that it is at that position
  - a conveyor objects tells the winning tote to update its position
    - a tote object records that it has reached that position.

Wait! How does a tote object calculate the probability that it is at that position? A tote needs to ask:

- my collection of sensor positions that I've already passed: have I already passed that position?
- order, what's my loading dock?
- dock, is this newly reported position on my path to you?
- based upon the time since I reached my previous position in the sequence, how likely is it that I'm now at this reported position?

Here is the scenario view (Figure 4–20):

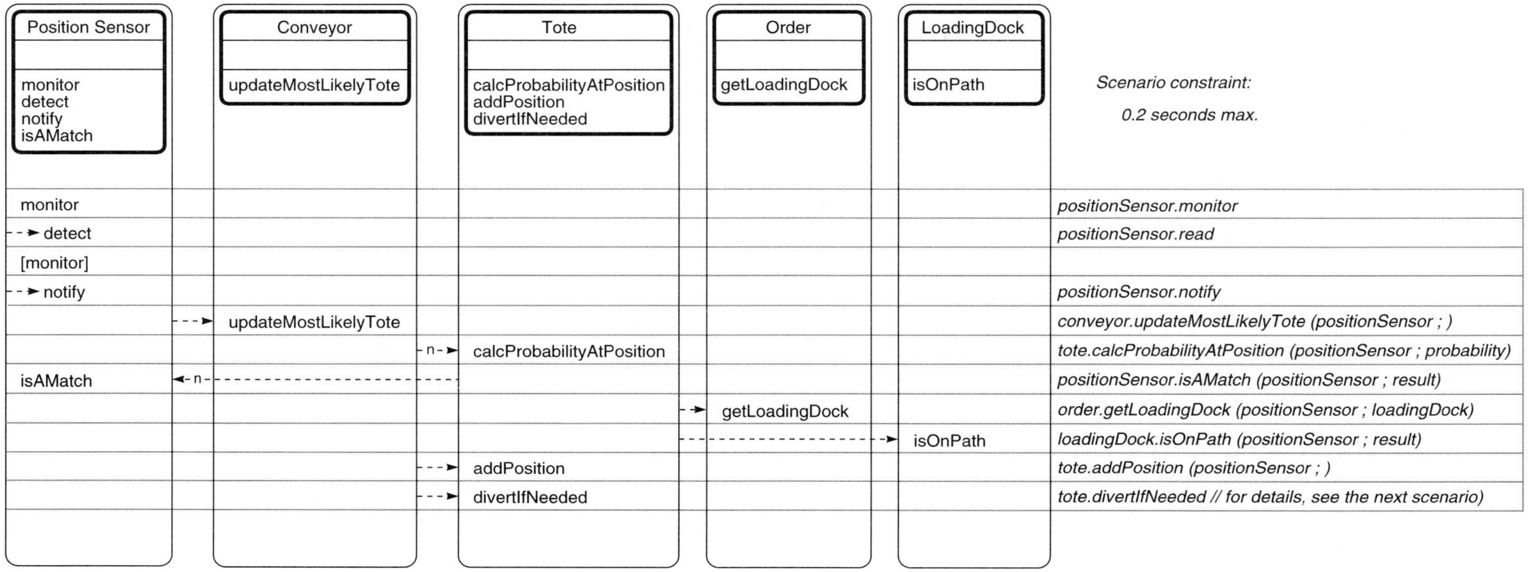

Position Sensor
monitor
detect
notify
isAMatch

Conveyor
updateMostLikelyTote

Tote
calcProbabilityAtPosition
addPosition
divertIfNeeded

Order
getLoadingDock

LoadingDock
isOnPath

monitor
detect
[monitor]
notify
updateMostLikelyTote
isAMatch
calcProbabilityAtPosition
getLoadingDock
isOnPath
addPosition
divertIfNeeded

Scenario constraint:
0.2 seconds max.

positionSensor.monitor
positionSensor.read

positionSensor.notify
conveyor.updateMostLikelyTote (positionSensor ;)
tote.calcProbabilityAtPosition (positionSensor ; probability)
positionSensor.isAMatch (positionSensor ; result)
order.getLoadingDock (positionSensor ; loadingDock)
loadingDock.isOnPath (positionSensor ; result)
tote.addPosition (positionSensor ;)
tote.divertIfNeeded // for details, see the next scenario)

Figure 4-20: The "position sensor detects a tote" scenario view—for the basic approach.

215

What happens if you need a tie-breaker, meaning, you're not sure which tote is the winner? You'd probably just clear the sorter part of the conveyor, rescan, and try again. This could be the focus of another scenario.

It's worth asking the question: how do these objects get created? You need a setup window (or some other system), to create and initialize conveyors, position sensors, diverters (already in your model, soon appearing in a scenario) and loading docks. Make a note of this; track it down a bit later in the chapter.

For now, keep focused on selecting your system approach!

Scenario: divert, if applicable

Finally, it's time to divert.

Here's what happens:

– a tote object asks an order to get its loading dock
  – a tote object asks its loading dock to divert if needed
    – a loading dock object asks itself if that position sensor is a point on the diverter path for that loading dock
    – a loading dock asks the corresponding diverter to divert.

Here is the scenario view (Figure 4–21):

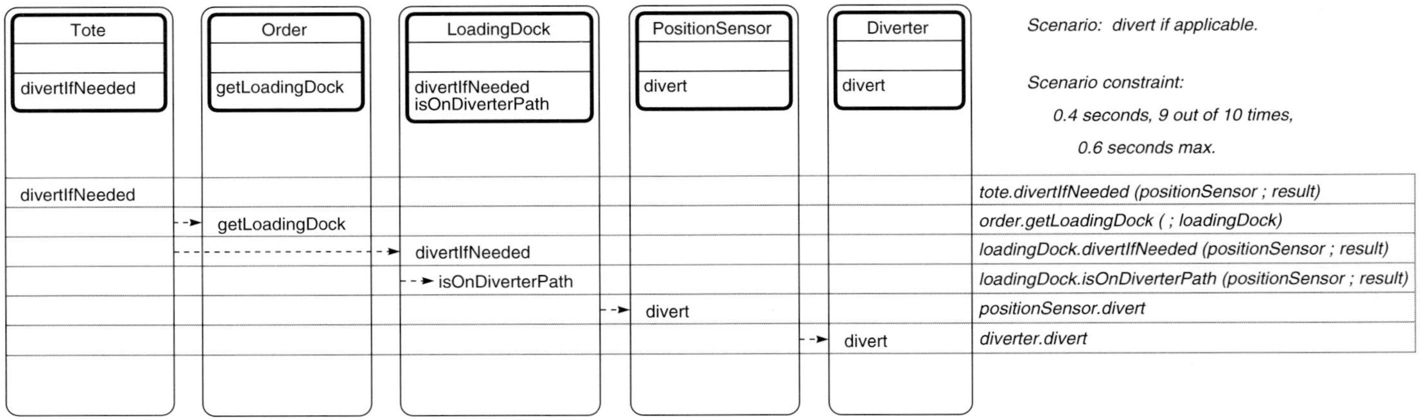

Tote — divertIfNeeded

Order — getLoadingDock

LoadingDock — divertIfNeeded, isOnDiverterPath

PositionSensor — divert

Diverter — divert

Messages:
- divertIfNeeded
- getLoadingDock
- divertIfNeeded
- isOnDiverterPath
- divert
- divert

Scenario: divert if applicable.

Scenario constraint:

0.4 seconds, 9 out of 10 times,

0.6 seconds max.

tote.divertIfNeeded (positionSensor ; result)

order.getLoadingDock (; loadingDock)

loadingDock.divertIfNeeded (positionSensor ; result)

loadingDock.isOnDiverterPath (positionSensor ; result)

positionSensor.divert

diverter.divert

Figure 4–21: The "divert if applicable" scenario view—for the basic approach.

Observations on these scenarios

Good grief!

Someone activates the conveyor. Then three monitor services run concurrently. And so many objects play along.

The good news: you now know how to show Dani just how complex the so-called "basic approach" really is. The bad news: you need more—you need to show what happens with the other approach.

Help is on the way.

An object model update for the basic approach

Update the object model with lessons from the scenarios. Here's the model (Figure 4–22):

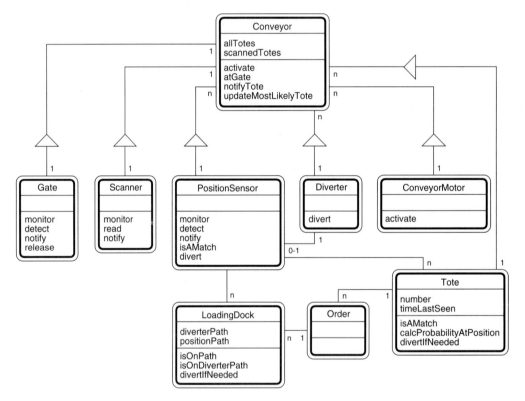

Figure 4–22: An object model update, for the basic approach.

Note that a loading dock object has multiple meanings to its object connections with position sensor objects.

#84. "Object Connection with Multiple Meanings" Strategy	establishing responsibilities / who I know (consider and challenge)

• What if you have an object connection with multiple meanings?
    Add a transaction object, an "event remembered" about each meaning being
      established.
    Or: add attributes to the participating object that needs to know those meanings—
      along with the object connection.	

In the object model, a conveyor has two collections of totes—all totes and scanned totes. In addition, a loading dock has two collections of position sensors—position path and diverter path. Note how such object connections are shown: just one object connection, plus associated attributes, describing the specific collections held.

Consider how much you've accomplished at this point. Just look how many responsibilities come out, when working out dynamics with scenarios.

And please make this observation: for data acquisition and control systems, applying "objects, scenarios, and responsibilities" (again and again, in that order) works out quite well.

"Get a tote to the loading dock" scenario (the scanning-diverter approach)

Sketch out what's involved, when it comes to using the scanning diverter approach:

- an actual tote comes up to a scanning diverter
- a scanning-diverter object scans an actual tote
- a scanning-diverter object knows all of the loading docks it diverts to
- a scanning-diverter object asks each loading-dock object if it wants this tote
  - a loading-dock object asks each order object if it includes this tote
    - an order object asks each tote if it has a matching bar code
- if the scanning diverter gets an answer of "yes," then the scanning diverter diverts the tote.

Here is the scenario view (Figure 4–23):

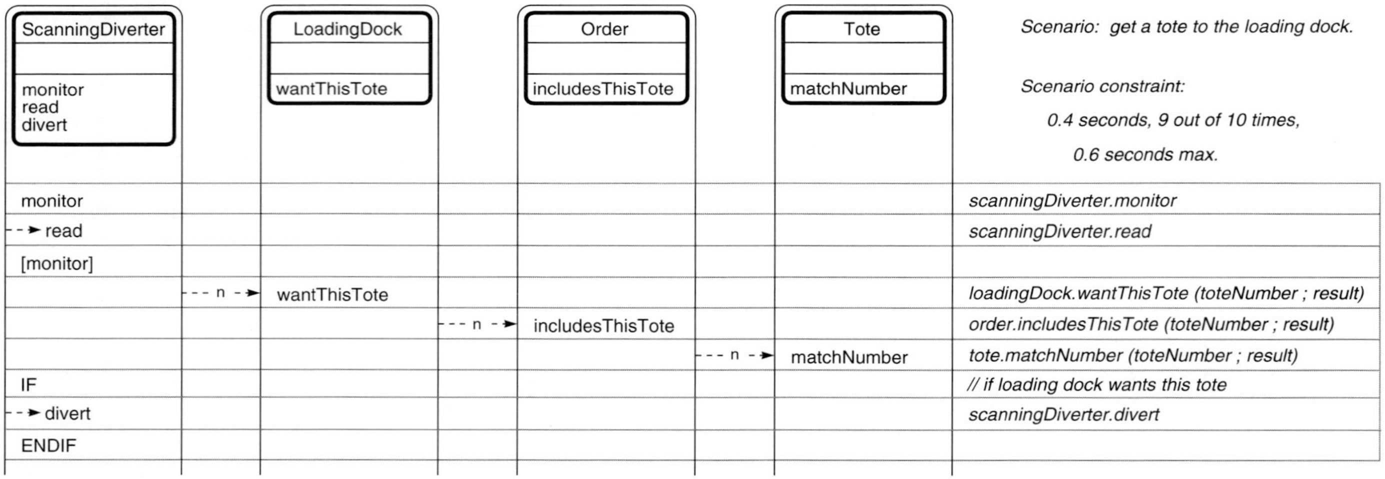

Scenario: get a tote to the loading dock.

Scenario constraint:
0.4 seconds, 9 out of 10 times,
0.6 seconds max.

ScanningDiverter	LoadingDock	Order	Tote
monitor read divert	wantThisTote	includesThisTote	matchNumber

monitor				scanningDiverter.monitor
- ► read				scanningDiverter.read
[monitor]				
	- - n - ► wantThisTote			loadingDock.wantThisTote (toteNumber ; result)
		- - n - ► includesThisTote		order.includesThisTote (toteNumber ; result)
			- - n - ► matchNumber	tote.matchNumber (toteNumber ; result)
IF				// if loading dock wants this tote
- ► divert				scanningDiverter.divert
ENDIF				

Figure 4–23: The "get a tote to the loading dock" scenario view—for the scanning diverter approach.

An object-model update for the scanning-diverter approach

Update the object model with lessons from the scenarios. Here's the model (Figure 4–24):

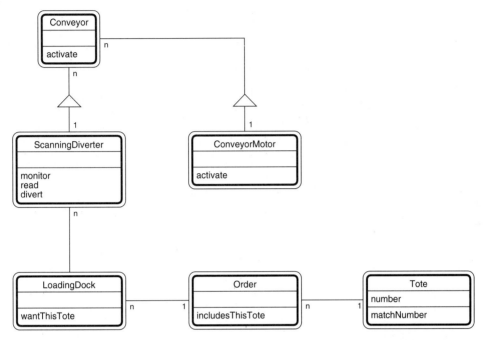

Figure 4–24: An object model update, for the scanning diverter approach.

Just look how many responsibilities come out when working out dynamics with scenarios.

Again, an observation: for data acquisition and control systems, applying "object, scenarios, and responsibilities" (again and again, in that order) works out quite well.

Good show!

Dare to compare

The basic approach vs. the scanning diverter approach?

You have a clear winner! Quick! Call Dani, review the object model, and act out the scenarios.

(A short while later . . .)

(Dani) Okay, okay, okay. You win! And thanks—you've saved us a lot of time and expense.

(Peter) We learned a lot by considering more than one systems approach. Somehow, we all seem to do a better job when we take the time to do this. The result in this case? We ended up with a simpler object model and much simpler scenarios.

The scanning diverter approach wins! That's the approach that you'll work with during the rest of this application chapter.

SELECTING HUMAN INTERACTION OBJECTS

Select setup windows

Do you need any windows?

Logon window

A logon window? You need a logon window only if you need:

- to control access
- to keep track of who does what (accountability)
- or both.

A logon window is not of much help here. Leave it out this time.

System setup

What things must be defined before the system runs?
You'll need to set up the following objects:

- conveyor object
- conveyor-motor objects
- loading-dock objects
- scanning-diverter objects.

Add a "conveyor setup" window—for setting up a conveyor and its many parts.

Activate/monitor/deactivate actions

A conveyor needs these actions: activate, monitor, deactivate.
Add these actions to your conveyor window.
(You could also add a setup service, to open a setup window.)

Select main windows

Assignments

You've got some assignments to make, too:

- order to a loading dock
- totes to an order.

How does this information get into the system?

- A worker enters it in.
- Or another system provides it.

What about this time?

(Peter) Who assigns an order to a loading dock? And totes to an order?

(Dani) Oh, the warehouse system will do that. Our system will take those orders and execute them.

Now you could explore this decision. After all, any human-organization boundary or computing-system boundary is a good place for reengineering opportunities.

Nevertheless, in this example application, accept that assignments are made in the warehouse system, and passed on to you.

So, get new orders from the warehouse system into your system.

Display what's going on in your system:

– Use a conveyor window for that.

Conducting "business"

What kind of windows do you need to conduct "business"?

Here, it's pretty simple.

You need to get orders. Add a "get new orders" menu command, another service, to the conveyor window.

Windows at this point

Here are the windows you've identified at this point (Figure 4–25):

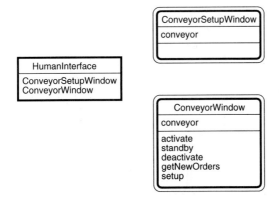

Figure 4–25: Selecting human interaction objects.

SELECTING SYSTEM-INTERACTION OBJECTS

You've already selected problem-domain objects that need some low-level system interaction support, namely:

– conveyor motor
– scanning diverter.

Someone's been yacking about a warehouse system—and had the audacity to give out all sorts of responsibilities, too (to be negotiated with the wonderful owners of that system). At this point, add:

– warehouse system

as a problem-domain object (Figure 4–26):

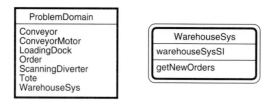

Figure 4–26: A warehouse system object.

Good show. Now add corresponding system interaction objects, to encapsulate low-level communication needs.

Add:

- conveyor motor SI
- scanning diverter SI
- warehouse system SI

as system-interaction objects (Figure 4–27):

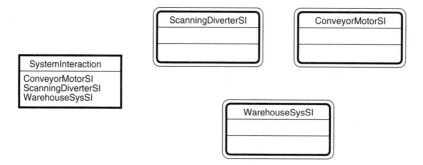

Figure 4–27: Selecting system interaction objects.

SELECTING DATA-MANAGEMENT OBJECTS AND RESPONSIBILITIES

Look for problem-domain classes with objects that must be stored between program invocations.

You don't need data-management objects for this system. Hooray! Just create and initialize the objects you need at system startup.

ESTABLISHING RESPONSIBILITIES

Objects. Scenarios. And now, responsibilities.

By working out dynamics with scenarios, you've already established many key responsibilities.

Now focus on "what I know, who I know, and what I do"—further detailing the responsibilities for the objects in your model.

Add attributes to satisfy these needs:

- "I know—for my use."
- "I know—for display."
- or both.

Add object connections to satisfy these needs:

- "I know others—for my use."
- "I know others—for display."
- or both.

Now work on establishing responsibilities, for:

- places where things come to rest
- things
    data acquisition and control devices
    conveyor motor
    collection things
    associates
- windows
- system interaction objects.

Responsibilities for places where things come to rest

Tote

Work it out.

What I know: number. The "match bar code" service needs this. The "loading status" window needs it, too.

Who I know: order. No service needs this. Yet you do need it to support the query, "Given a tote, tell me its corresponding order." Go ahead and add that a tote knows about one order.

What I do: match number.

Loading dock

Work it out.

What I know: number.

Who I know: order. The "want this tote" service needs to know to whom to send its messages. You also need it to support the query, "Given a loading dock, tell me the orders assigned to it."

Who I know, continued. Oh, you could know scanning diverters, to support the query, "Given a loading dock, tell me the scanning diverter sequence to get to it." That seems a little silly, though. So indicate in your model that a loading dock has no need to know scanning diverters, by not including an object connection constraint for it.

What I do: want this tote?

Responsibilities for things
Data acquisition and control devices

#56. "Establish Interacting System and Device Attributes" Strategy	establishing responsibilities / what I know (pattern players)
• For another system or device, include: number, name, operational state. • For its companion object, in the system interaction component, include: address, password.	

#78. "Establish Interacting System or Device Object Connections" Strategy	establishing responsibilities / who I know (pattern players)
• For an interacting system or device, include an object connection (expressed an attribute) to: its corresponding system interaction (SI) object, one that encapsulates low-level interaction details.	

#98. "Establish Interacting System or Device Services" Strategy	establishing responsibilities / what I do (pattern players)
• For an interacting system or device, include: activate, monitor (maintain), report, deactivate (plus calculate for me, rate me, is <value>). • For an interacting system or device as a collection, include: how many, how much, rank parts, calculate over parts. • Add a corresponding object in the system interaction (SI) component, to isolate specific interaction needs (examples: connect, logon, query, logoff, disconnect).	

Data acquisition and control devices usually need an "operational state" attribute, along with service descriptions that express state-dependent behavior (using keywords precondition, postcondition, trigger, and terminate).

Scanning diverter

Work it out.

What I know: number, operational state.

Who I know: loading dock. The "want this tote" service needs to know to whom to send its messages. You also need it to support the query, "Given a scanning diverter, tell me all the loading docks that use it to get totes to that loading dock."

Who I know: scanning diverter SI, a companion object that encapsulates low-level interaction detail.

What I do: monitor, read, want this tote, and divert.

Conveyor motor

Work it out.

What I know: number, operational state.

Who I know: conveyor motor SI, a companion object that encapsulates low-level interaction detail.

What I do: activate, monitor, deactivate.

Collection things

Now you turn to conveyor.

What I know: number, operational state (the operational state of a conveyor, as a collection of data acquisition and control devices).

Who I know: conveyor motors, scanning diverters.

What I do: activate, monitor, deactivate.

Associates

Consider order.

What I know: number.

Who I know: tote. The "includes this tote" service needs to know to whom to send its messages. You also need it to support the query, "Given an order, tell me all of its totes."

Who I know: loading dock. You need it to support the query, "Given an order, tell me its loading dock."

What I do: the service "includes this tote."

What about the other associates? You've already taken care of both of them—tote and loading dock. Cool.

Responsibilities for windows

Now consider the windows.

Conveyor setup window

Work it out.

What I know: —

Who I know: conveyor (the window can access the objects connected to it, including conveyor motor, scanning diverter, and loading dock).

What I do (special commands): you might include services like adding, deleting, and updating the conveyor configuration and its parts.

Conveyor window

Do it again.

What I know: —

Who I know: conveyor

What I do (special commands): activate, standby, shutdown; get new orders (to tell the warehouse system object to get new orders).

Responsibilities for interacting systems

You've got just one object to take care of here: a warehouse system object.

Warehouse system

Do it again.

> What I know: —
> Who I know: my corresponding "warehouse system SI" object, in the system inter-action component.
> What I do: get new orders.

Responsibilities for system-interaction component objects

You need system interaction (SI) objects, for the warehouse system, conveyor motors, and scanning diverters.

Warehouse system SI

Put together some responsibilities, suitable for this application.

> What I know: address
> Who I know: —
> What I do (low-level, device-specific functions): connect, make request, and dis-connect.

Conveyor motor SI

Do it again.

> What I know: address
> Who I know: —
> What I do: activate, monitor, deactivate.

Scanning diverter SI

Do it again.

> What I know: address
> Who I know: —
> What I do: read value, read status.

Progress at this point

Here's the object model at this point (Figure 4–28):

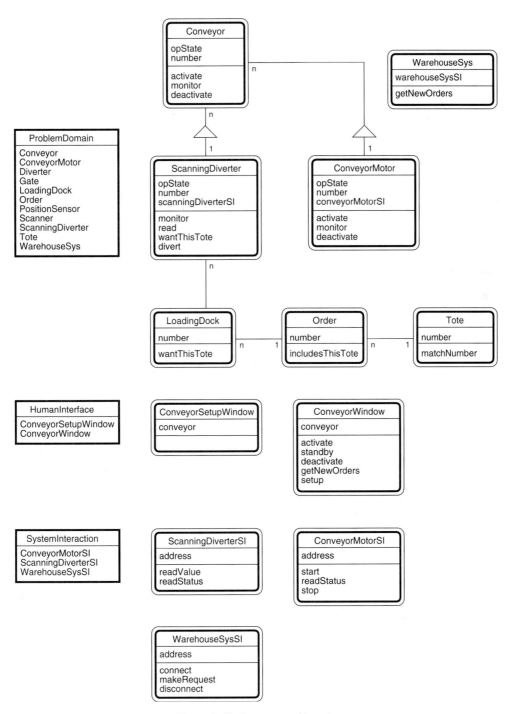

Figure 4–28: Progress at this point.

REAL-TIME SYSTEM CONSIDERATIONS

By now, you may be tempted to feel pretty smug. After all, your object model is coming along just fine. And you've helped Dani decide on a better systems approach. But along comes real-time Randy. And he's coming after you—with his favorite real-time pet peeves.

(Randy) I understand you're working on Dani's conveyor system.
(Peter) Yes.
(Randy) Have you considered the real-time aspects of the system?
(Peter) We've only just begun our work in this area.
(Randy) Good. This would be a good time for me to unload some of my favorite real-time issues.
(Peter) Okay. Then together we can add real-time aspects to the object model.

What makes a system "real-time?"

Often it seems that "real time" is in the eye of the beholder. Many developers who work on engineering systems label their work as "real time."

What are the characteristics of a real-time system?

Timeliness—must be "on time"

Dynamic internal structure—dynamic creation and destruction of software components

Reactiveness—continuously responds to different events in its environment, detected by data acquisition and control devices, or by interacting systems

State-dependency—responds differently, depending upon the state of a system

Concurrency—multiple simultaneous activities can be taking place

Multiple device abstractions—needs abstractions that represent both physical and logical abstractions

Distribution—multiple computing sites.

(an extension of the list presented in the book *Real-Time Object-Oriented Modeling* by Selic, Gullekson, and Ward)

How do you address those core issues?

Timeliness

Timeliness is next to godliness—especially for a real-time system.

Hard real-time systems are so constrained by time that if certain time constraints are not met, then data goes in the bit bucket—there is no time to catch up. Examples: airplane-control software, pacemaker software, radar software.

Soft real-time systems are constrained by time, yet the system is still able to make use of incoming data, even in the event it falls temporarily behind. Examples: flight-data software, satellite data-gathering software.

How can you express timeliness constraints?

#106. "Real Time: Timeliness" Strategy	establishing responsibilities / what I do (real time)

- Timeliness: must be "on time"

- Put performance constraints on your scenarios (on services, too, as needed—although allocating performance constraints to individual services often takes more guesswork than most engineers feel comfortable with).

The most meaningful place for placing time constraints is on specific scenarios.

For example, you can express a performance constraint on a scenario, adding something like this to a scenario view:

> Performance constraint: 50 milliseconds (hard constraint); 40 milliseconds in 999 out of 1,000 test cases.

Note the format. Yes, the hard real-time performance constraint is stated. In addition (and very important), a constraint based upon some number of tests is included, too. This establishes *measurable* criteria for whether this requirement is satisfied.

Where else can you place performance constraints?

A less meaningful (yet at times, necessary) place to put a performance constraint is on a specific service in your model. This is effective only when you are working with an algorithmically intensive service whose performance is critical to the overall real-time system itself. Simply place the constraint in the service description, rather than within a scenario view. The format is the same in each case.

Example: a timeliness constraint on a scenario

Consider the scenario "scan and divert a tote to the loading dock an order is assigned to."

> Add a performance constraint:
>> this scenario
>>> performance constraint: 0.6 seconds (soft constraint); 0.4 seconds in 99 out of 100 test cases; impact: if exceeded, let it keep going until the next pass.

Example: a timeliness constraint on a service

Consider a diverting sensor and its services.

> What performance constraints might apply here?
>> the "read" service
>>> performance constraint:
>>>> 100 milliseconds (soft constraint), 80 milliseconds in 9 out of 10 test cases

Please, don't get carried away, specifying performance constraints on individual services. Remember, performance constraints on scenarios are nearly always more meaningful (and require less engineering judgment, also known as "guessing," concerning what the need really is).

Dynamic internal structure

Dynamic creation and deletion of software components? How is this supported?

#107. "Real Time: Dynamic Internal Structure" Strategy	establishing responsibilities / what I do (real time)

• Dynamic internal structure: dynamic creation and destruction of software components
 	
• How: show dynamic creation and deletion of objects in scenarios.
  Every class knows how to create new objects in that class.
  Every collection knows how to add and remove objects in that collection.
  Every object knows how to delete itself.
  In addition, you can selectively place additional creation and deletion constraints.	

Use scenarios to work out (and describe) system dynamics.
Include dynamic creation and deletion of objects within your scenarios, as needed.
What about creation and deletion itself?

– Every class knows how to create new objects in that class.
– Every collection knows how to add and remove objects in that collection.
– Every object knows how to delete itself.

In addition, you can selectively place additional creation and deletion constraints:

– create
    capacity limit: a limit on the number of objects allowed in that class
– delete
    aging limit: a limit on how long an object is allowed to stick around
        (else it auto-deletes).

For Dani's Diverters, you might add:

  Tote
      delete
          aging limit: delete after 8 hours.

Reactiveness

Reactiveness indicates that the system continuously responds to events.
Every system reacts to events.
Real-time systems respond to events in its environment—things detected by data acquisition and control devices, things detected by an interacting system.

#108. "Real Time: Reactiveness" Strategy	establishing responsibilities / what I do (real time)
• Reactiveness: continuously responds to different events in its environment, detected by data acquisition and control devices, or by interacting systems • Use a specific "maintain" or "monitor" service, for ongoing capabilities. • Use the "activate, monitor, deactivate" triad.	

Objects that correspond to devices or interacting systems usually have:

> – a state attribute: operational state (on, off, standby)
> – some state-dependent services: monitor, standby, shutdown.

The monitor service expresses ongoing behavior needed continuously to respond to events.

The "monitor, standby, and shutdown" triad is very common. The corresponding service descriptions often include the keywords "precondition, trigger, terminate, and postcondition" to accurately portray what the services are all about.

Example

Consider the "monitor" service for a scanning diverter. To a service description, add the corresponding trigger and terminate conditions:

> monitor
>> trigger upon: state = monitor
>> terminate upon: state ≠ monitor.

State-dependency

Objects in a real-time system include state-dependent attributes and services.

#109. "Real Time: State-Dependency" Strategy	establishing responsibilities / what I do (real time)
• State-dependency: responds differently, depending upon the state of a system • Attributes: state, state-dependent, state-independent In its description, include: applicable states. • Services: state-dependent, state-independent In its description, you may need to include: precondition: \<indicate what you assert to be true, before this service can run> postcondition: \<indicate what you assert to be true, before this service can go to completion> trigger condition: \<indicate what state transitions activate this service> terminate condition: \<indicate what state transitions terminate this service> exception: \<indicate object.service to invoke, upon detecting an exception>.	

A state-dependent attribute is one that has meaning only within specific states. A state-dependent service is one that is allowed only within specific states. How is this shown in an object model?

Divide the attribute section into three subsections:

> – state attributes (for example, operational state)
> – state-dependent attributes
> – state-independent attributes.

Divide the services section into two subsections:

> – state-dependent services
> – state-independent services.

In attribute descriptions, include a line with:

Applicable state(s):

In service descriptions, include these lines:

Precondition: <indicate what you assert to be true, before this service can run>

Postcondition: <indicate what you assert to be true, before this service can go to completion>

Trigger: <indicate what state transitions activate this service>

Terminate: <indicate what state transitions terminate this service>.

By the way, real-time objects aren't the only objects which exhibit state-dependent behavior. Any service that applies only at certain times is a state-dependent service. (An example? How about this: an investment account, with premium services that may be invoked only when a specified account value precondition is satisfied.)

Example

Take another look at the scanning diverter.

First, check out its attributes:

scanning diverter
    state attribute: operational state
       values: monitor | standby | off.

Second, go ahead and specify its services. All of these services are state-dependent services.

scanning diverter
  monitor
    trigger upon operational state = monitor
      every 100 milliseconds,
        read (; number)
        gotOne := (number > 0)
        if gotOne then
            loadingDock.wantThisOne (number ; result)
        if result = yes then divert.
    terminate upon state ≠ monitor
  read (; value)
    precondition: state = monitor
    scanningDiverterSI.read (; value)
  divert
    precondition: state = monitor
    scanningDiverterSI.divert
  want this tote
    precondition: state = monitor
    loadingDock.wantThisTote (number ; result)

Concurrency

Objects—at least, conceptually—are multitasking creatures. This means that an object can do more than one thing at a time:

  – receive multiple messages at the same time
  – handle multiple threads of execution internally
  – maintain integrity of internal data (using semaphores and mailboxes as needed).

Now that's encapsulation!

#110. "Real Time: Concurrency" Strategy	establishing responsibilities / what I do (real time)

- Concurrency: multiple simultaneous activities can be taking place.

- Objects can do more than one thing at once — they are multitasking creatures.

- Objects encapsulate real-time tasks.
    Activation / deactivation
        Trigger condition: <request, state change, value change, time lapse>
        Terminate condition: <request, state change, value change, time lapse>
    Communication, coordination
        Communication between objects is by synchronous messaging.
        Communication within objects is by synchronous and asynchronous messaging, as needed.

- Note: this encapsulation is made possible with effective object modeling (not with data objects and controller objects).

Objects for a real-time system must have multitasking capabilities.

Unfortunately, commercially available object-oriented programming languages include syntax for synchronous messaging and limited structures for concurrent programming.[2] Ugh! This means it's the same old story, same old song and dance, my friend: you've got to write services that reach out to the operating system, to support the true nature of objects as multitasking creatures.

For objects with multitasking ability, watch for attributes that you must add access controls to (using semaphores, mailboxes, and the like). Look for services that participate in multiple, potentially concurrent threads of execution. Then look for attribute values used by more than one of those services.

Add access controls for those attributes. Locks, semaphores, mailboxes, gatekeepers, protected records, and critical regions are specific techniques that you can use, so that an object can maintain the integrity of its attribute values.

By the way, concurrency itself is not just a real-time systems issue. Recall Wally's Warehouse. Items can get multiple concurrent requests to provide pick-list line items. Each bin-line item acts as a counter, preventing overpicking, by keeping track of the pick list line items that have already laid claim to some of the items in that bin.

---

[2] Ada 94 is an exception.

Example

Are there any multitasking objects in the system under consideration?

Look for objects that may get requests from multiple senders at the same time. What's the source for asynchronous, competing requests? People, interacting systems, and devices.

As an example, take a closer look at a "warehouse system" object. Periodically, that object gets new orders. Then it needs to send messages:

> – to the tote class, to create and initialize some totes
> – to the order class, to create and initialize an order
> – to a loading dock object, to add an order.

Ah. A loading dock object already exists. It must provide "wants tote" and "add order" services—even at the same time.

At this point, you may want to add some access controls for the loading dock's collection of orders. You could use a variety of access control mechanisms (locks, semaphores, mail boxes, gatekeepers, protected records, critical regions, and the like). The choice depends upon what's available in your environment. An excellent book on access controls and concurrent programming is M. Ben-Ari's *Principles of Concurrent Programming*. It includes the classic access issues, deadlock and starvation, too.

Just remember to encapsulate concurrent programming techniques, right in the objects that need them.

Multiple device abstractions

Objects for data acquisition and control devices need multiple device abstractions.

#111. "Real Time: Multiple Device Abstractions" Strategy	establishing responsibilities / what I do (real time)

• Multiple device abstractions: needs both physical and logical abstractions.
 	
 • Physical abstraction — express with an object in the system interaction component.
 	
 • Logical abstractions — express with:
   –a domain-based object (a problem-domain object)
   –an object which shows "this is how we'll work with it" (a human interaction object)
   –an object which persists from one program invocation to the next (a data management object).	

One abstraction is problem-domain–based. In this abstraction, a data acquisition and control device is modeled as smart enough to do things on its own. Include this kind of object in the problem domain component of an object model.

Three other abstractions capture interaction abstractions with an abstraction that is problem-domain–based.

One interaction abstraction is system-interaction–based. In this abstraction, a data acquisition and control device is modeled as it really is—what's required to support the actual interface to a specific physical device is expressed here.

Another interaction abstraction is data-management–based. In this abstraction, a data acquisition and control device is modeled as a persistent object, one that the object must remember, from one program invocation to the next.

A third interaction abstraction is human-interaction–based. In this abstraction, a data acquisition and control device is modeled as a window or report, so people can work with it effectively.

Example

You've already worked with all three of these interaction abstractions.

For example, consider the application in this chapter. You've worked with:

- warehouse system and warehouse system SI
- conveyor motor and conveyor motor SI
- scanning diverter and scanning diverter SI.

Distribution

#112. "Real Time: Distribution" Strategy	establishing responsibilities / what I do (real time)

• Distribution: multiple computing sites
 	
• Across multiple computing systems
    Use software that supports distributed objects.
    Or do it yourself (inevitable, at least for systems that you must interact with and
        cannot change).
      Allocate objects, not mere functionality.
      Add "pack and ship; receive and route" infrastructure.
• Within an existing system
    Use an object model to understand what's really going on.
    Tag each service with its location; tag each attribute with who is using it.	

Distributing system responsibility across multiple computing systems

You've got two choices.

Choice #1. Use a software package that supports distributed objects.

Choice #2. Do it yourself. Put groups of interacting objects on the same system. Don't break the systems into functional groups; doing so requires too much communication and coordination, and such partitioning is a black hole for critical project resources. In addition, if an object is needed on more than one computing system, then you will need to add system interaction infrastructure to keep attribute values in sync with each other.

Distribution within existing systems

Most distribution within existing systems is "all functioned up."

In the past, developers have built distributed systems based on groupings of functions, not by distributing objects. The impact? When you build an object model of what the system is really trying to do, you'll find that some number of objects have their services spread across multiple computing systems. Bummer.

Here's what to do about it. Use your object model to help you understand what's really going on in the existing system. Examine the objects with services located on different computing systems. Tag each service with the system it resides on. Look at the attributes that each service requires. Tag each attribute with the same tag as the service that uses it (you may find it helpful to categorize the attribute's tags into read and write).

Example

Yes, life is much easier with distributed object support—and no need to interface with systems that are already running.

Few of us have that privilege.

An example of facing this reality: the warehouse system object, in this chapter.

With distributed object support for both systems, you would not need that object. Why? You'd already have access to loading dock objects, order objects, and tote objects—just as if they were residing on your own system.

Without distributed object support for both systems, you need that extra object—and the extra work you did in this chapter.

PROGRESS AT THIS POINT

Here's the object model (Figures 4–29 to 31). Along with the scenarios in this chapter, this wraps up your work for Dani's Diverters.

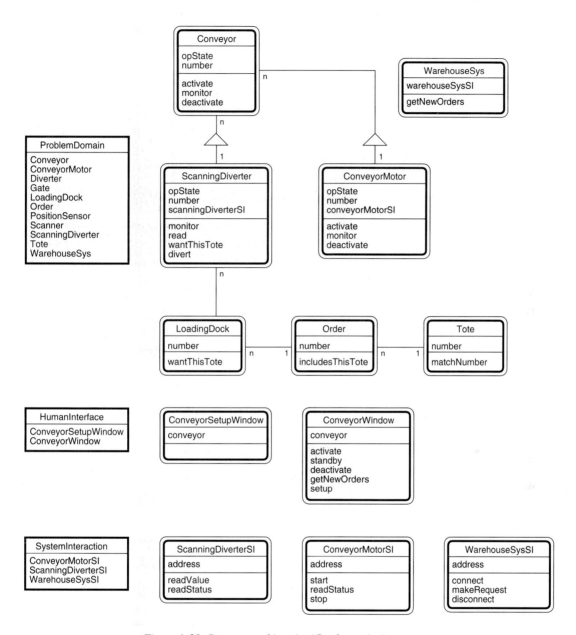

Figure 4–29: Progress at this point (Coad notation).

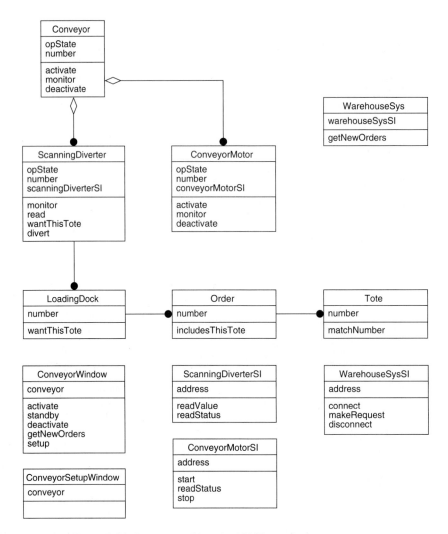

Figure 4–30: Progress at this point (OMT notation).

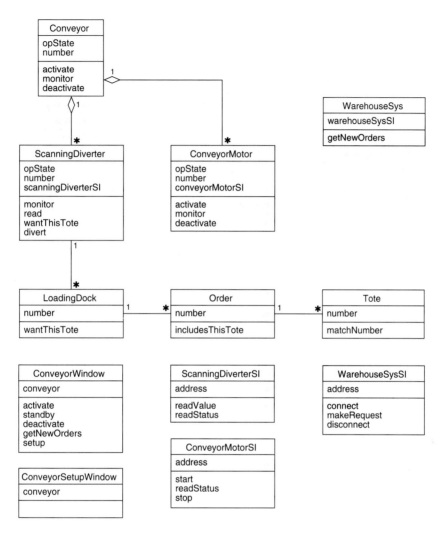

Figure 4–31: Progress at this point (Unified notation).

WRAP-UP

You did it! You built an object model for a conveyance application.

It's important! Nearly every manufacturing and shipping business uses a conveyance application in one form or another. You can directly relate to (and for some readers, you can directly apply) this object modeling experience.

In this chapter, you learned and applied some additional strategies and patterns, especially for real-time applications.

In addition, you experienced using an object model to help you (and your organization) make sensible hardware/software tradeoffs; the number of objects was close enough, yet the scenarios proved that one approach would be far less complex (less costly to build and maintain) than the other approach.

Excellent!

5

Andi's Autopilot
(A Hard Real-Time Control Application)

This chapter explores some additional issues for building object models for real-time systems, including:

- object models for real-time systems: is a centralized controller really needed?
- object models for real-time systems: are separate input and output device groupings really needed?
- object models for data acquisition and control: reduced message traffic, higher cohesion?
- asynchronous messaging: where is it best used? between objects? or within objects?
- real-time tasking: what's the impact on objects?

It's a "hard" real-time system in that the system must, absolutely must, keep up with the data streaming in and respond in a timely fashion. No garbage collection.[1] No hoping to catch up later. The inputs must be processed before more input data comes in. Your system must keep up—or the data just goes into the bit bucket.

Please keep in mind the principles of real-time systems set forth in the previous chapter as you read this one.

By the way: those of you with little or no interest in engineering or real-time systems will still find this chapter interesting and thought-provoking. No kidding. Read on.

Onward!

IDENTIFYING SYSTEM PURPOSE AND FEATURES

Andi owns a small business. Her target market: upgrades for small airplanes that enthusiasts build and fly in.

Listening to her customers, Andi sees a market opportunity for a low-cost autopilot system. She's an entrepreneur. She knows the problem domain. She seeks your expertise and help in getting the new system off the ground (!).

Identify the purpose of the system

Begin with some purpose-setting questions.

(Peter) Okay. So we're going to develop an autopilot system. Let me ask: what does an autopilot system usually do?

---

[1] "Garbage collection" takes on a special meaning in the context of flight-control systems.

(Andi) Fly the airplane! In fact, some autopilots go so far as to take care of all segments of a flight, including:

– the takeoff segment
– the climb segment
– the en route segment
– the approach segment
– the landing segment.

(Peter) That's right. I remember the first time a pilot announced that the landing had just been completed entirely by an autopilot. Somehow, I didn't find it all that reassuring.

(Andi) Yes, I wouldn't like that either. Nevertheless, some airlines use autopilots that way.

(Peter) What about for our system? It's a low-cost version, right?

(Andi) Right. This autopilot system is for the en route segment. It must deliver three capabilities, the key features for this system:

– maintain altitude
– maintain direction
– maintain attitude (orientation relative to the horizon).

(Peter) Okay. Let's see if we can work together to come up with a statement of the purpose of the system, in 25 words or less. How about:

> "To maintain aircraft altitude, direction, and attitude during the en route segment of a flight."

(Andi) Right.

SELECTING OBJECTS

In this chapter, you'll go from PD to HI to DM to SI. In each case, you'll use strategies and patterns to help you:

– select objects
– work out dynamics with scenarios
– establish responsibilities.

Read, read, read

(Peter) I've read up on autopilots, getting ready for this assignment. Here's a bird's-eye view that I got from my children's encyclopedia:

> An automatic pilot for airplanes contains three gyros. The vertical speed gyro (and an altimeter) controls the altitude of the airplane. The attitude gyro keeps it flying level. The directional gyro controls the steering and keeps the airplane flying in the same direction.
>
> The automatic pilot sends signals to the ailerons, the elevators, and the rudder.

Corrective signals are produced when the aircraft moves from its proper course and attitude (position). These signals are voltage displacements which are amplified and sent to servo units, which have motors and hydraulic devices that move the aircraft's controls (adapted from *World Book*, "Automatic Pilot").

An initial discussion

(Peter) Please share with me about what it takes to maintain altitude, direction, and attitude during the en route segment of a flight.

(Andi) It's pretty straightforward. We need to collect information about the status of the airplane:

- current altitude
- current direction
- current attitude (that's orientation, relative to the horizon).

(Andi) Then we make corrections by adjusting the control surfaces of the airplane:

- ailerons
- elevators
- rudder.

(Peter) What about power?

(Andi) Some autopilots do take care of that. Not this time, though. I want to introduce a low-cost version first. Then we can look at add-on options.

(Peter) So who will set the power? The pilot?

(Andi) Yes, the pilot will set the power at a sufficient level. That's his responsibility.

(Peter) How do we know about the status of the airplane? What do those control surfaces do?

(Andi) Let's go for a ride and I will show you.

(Peter) What a great job! Getting paid to go for a ride in an airplane.

A field trip

(Andi) I need to go through my preflight checklist, contact the tower, and taxi to the runway. Let me do that much—and without answering a lot of questions. Then, once we get up in the air, on an en route segment, I'll demonstrate what the autopilot needs to do.

(Peter) Sounds great. I'll let you do your thing.

Takeoff

(Tower) 6-7-Yankee cleared for takeoff.

(Andi) 6-7-Yankee, Roger.

(Andi) Here we go. I'm applying lots of power. We're building up our speed. Okay, now we're just about fast enough. So—I'll pull back on the yoke and—up, up, and away.

(Peter) Wow! This is great. So when are the free drinks served on this flight anyway?

(Andi, grinning) Oh, shut up, Coad.

(Peter) Yeah, yeah, yeah.

Cockpit instruments

(Andi) In a few minutes, we'll be ready for a typical en route segment. Meanwhile, let's walk through the instruments with information that the autopilot will use.

(Peter) Ready.

(Andi) Let me introduce you to these instruments:

– altimeter
– vertical speed indicator
– attitude indicator
– directional gyro.

Check it out (Figure 5–1):

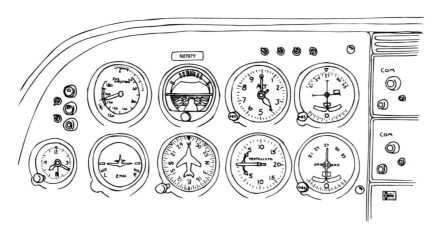

Figure 5–1: Cockpit instruments and cockpit controls pertinent to this application.

Altimeter

(Andi) The altimeter displays the current altitude in feet. (Actually, it works by sensing changes in atmospheric pressure, relative to the calibration point I set while working through my preflight sequence.)

(Peter) Okay. So right now the altitude is 4, like, four thousand feet above sea level.

(Andi) Yes.

About gyros

(Andi) Gyros—fun food, nifty toys, and essential aircraft gear.

(Peter) Ugh!

(Andi) Well, I try. Anyway, gyros spin. When they spin, they want to stay in the same position—techno-nerds call this the "rigidity in space" principle (good taste prohibits me from making any jokes about that).

(Andi, continuing) There are two kinds of gyroscopes—velocity (rate) gyroscopes and displacement gyroscopes. (If you really want to know, velocity gyroscopes take input at a right angle to the spin axis; directional gyroscopes take input aligned with the spin axis.)

(Andi, continuing) Here's another variation. The way the gyro is mounted determines which axis of movement it detects. In fact, some gyros detect movement in two directions (a two-frame gyroscope) or three directions (a three-frame gyroscope).

(Peter) Tell me about axes of movement.

(Andi) An airplane moves in three basic ways:

     – roll, movement around its longitudinal axis
     – pitch, movement around its lateral axis
     – yaw, movement around its vertical axis.

Check it out (Figure 5–2):

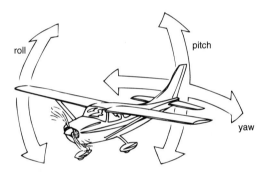

Figure 5–2: Roll, pitch, and yaw.

(Andi, continuing) As the airplane moves, the gyro stays in the same position, relative to the earth. An airplane uses a vertical speed gyro, a velocity gyro, to determine its change rate, up or down. It uses an attitude gyro, a two-frame directional gyro, to detect differences in the airplane's position relative to the horizon.

(Peter) Got it. Tell me more.

Vertical speed indicator

(Andi) You need another instrument, to go along with the altimeter. It's the vertical speed indicator. It tells you the rate of altitude change, reported in feet per minute.

(Peter) Sounds like it uses a velocity gyro to measure change rate.

(Andi) You're catching on. That's right.

(Peter) So certain instruments use one or a combination of these gyros.

(Andi) That exactly right. Good point, too. Each instrument that uses one or more gyros has its own gyro. Why? So if one gyro fails, it affects only one of the instruments.

(Peter) Very good. Please tell me more about the gyro-based instruments.

Attitude indicator

(Andi) That instrument is called attitude indicator. It shows both roll and pitch. So it has two gyros.

(Peter) Both roll and pitch?

(Andi) That's right. An attitude indicator is sometimes called an artificial-horizon indicator. You see, the horizon is all around us, right? To consider the aircraft's position relative to the horizon, roll and pitch are important; yaw has no impact.

(Peter) Got it: the attitude indicator shows the airplane's orientation relative to the horizon.

Directional gyro

(Andi) Here's the directional gyro. It shows what direction the airplane is going in.

(Peter) North, south, east, and west?

(Andi) Yes, like that. Direction is reported in degrees, where 0 degrees is north, and 180 degrees is south. I set it up just before the flight based on the magnetic compass.

Enough instruments

(Peter) That's a lot of instruments. Let me run through them, one more time:

- altimeter: altitude, above sea level
- vertical speed indicator: speed, up or down
- attitude indicator: orientation, relative to the horizon
- directional gyro: direction.

(Peter) By the way, that indicator called "directional gyro" is actually a "directional gyro indicator," right? You don't actually see the gyro, right?

(Andi) You're right about that. In fact, there is another, similar pair: a vertical speed gyro has a corresponding vertical speed indicator.

(Peter) Good. That distinction will be very helpful.

Cockpit controls

(Andi) That takes care of the instruments. They tell you what's going on with the airplane—lots of data. Now let's look at the cockpit controls, the kinds of controls a pilot or an autopilot might use.

(Peter) Let's check it out.

(Andi) A pilot has two main control devices to work with: the yoke (or control wheel) and the rudder pedals.

The yoke

(Andi) The yoke moves forward and backward, and it rotates from side to side. The yoke is connected to control surfaces on the wings and the tail.

(Peter) Okay. Tell me more about the control surfaces.

(Andi) The yoke controls two kinds of control surfaces: ailerons and elevators.

(Peter) So far, so good.

(Andi) The ailerons are hinged sections located on the trailing edge of each wing. When I want to turn the airplane to the right, I turn the yoke to the right. Here's what happens. The left aileron goes down; the right aileron goes up. That makes the left wing go up and the right wing go down. The airplane rolls to the right.

(Andi, continuing) Take a look out the window. Check out those ailerons! Anyway, that's how you can rotate the airplane around its longitudinal axis (called the "roll axis").

(Peter) That's what those surfaces are for. Interesting.

(Andi) The elevators are hinged sections, located on the trailing edge of each horizontal section of the tail. When I want to get the airplane to go up, I pull the yoke back. Here's what happens. The elevators move up. That makes the tail go down. And so the nose goes up, right where I want it to go. That's how you can move the airplane around its lateral axis (called the "pitch axis").

The rudder pedals

(Andi) The rudder pedals are on the floor. A pilot pushes them with his feet.

(Peter) Tell me more.

(Andi) The pedals control the rudder. It's a hinged section on the vertical part of the tail. When I want the airplane to move to the right, I press on the right pedal. Here's what happens. The tail moves to the left. And that means that the nose is moved to the right, where I want it to go. That's how you move the airplane around its vertical axis (called the "yaw axis").

(Peter) Let me play it back to you.

- turn the yoke left and right to move the airplane around its longitudinal (roll) axis
- push and pull the yoke to move the airplane up and down, around its lateral (pitch) axis
- push on the left and right pedals to move the airplane sideways, around its vertical (yaw) axis.

(Andi) Hey, pal. You're starting to sound like a real pilot. Wait a minute. Here's a pair of junior pilot flight wings for you. Wear them proudly.

(Peter) Okay, okay. What a pal! What's next?

Data acquisition and control

(Andi) Now let's put it all together. It takes time to develop some skill at this.

(Peter) Can I give it a try?

(Andi) Sure.

(Andi) Using the cockpit instruments and cockpit controls, make a gentle turn to the right. Here's how. Turn the yoke to the right and press the right pedal a little, too. Meanwhile, be sure to watch your instruments. And, remember to look outside, watching out for other planes in the area.

(Peter) Whew! That's a lot to keep track of.

(Andi) With a little practice, you'll just think about turning right—and do it, taking care of all of those things kind of automatically.

(Peter) You mean I'll be on autopilot?

(Andi) That's the idea.

(Andi, continuing) Take a look at your altimeter.

(Peter) Uh-oh. We're losing altitude.

(Andi) And check out your attitude.

(Peter) I've got a new attitude.

(Peter, continuing) Hey, we're beginning to roll to the left. Good grief.

(Andi, taking over the cockpit controls) It does get a lot easier with practice.

(Peter) I can see how an autopilot might come in handy. Looks like data acquisition and control all right—with the autopilot running the show.

(Andi) Well, in the low-cost version, remember it's doing something a little less ambitious than running the show. The pilot gets the aircraft flying the way he wants it to. Once activated, the autopilot reads the current values and does its best to maintain them. Remember the key features:

> – maintain altitude
> – maintain direction
> – maintain attitude.

(Peter) Okay. Thanks for this field trip. I'll use the visual images and feelings from this trip throughout the project.

(Andi) Robert Mueller Tower, this is 6-7-Yankee.

(Tower) 6-7-Yankee. Go ahead.

(Andi) 6-7-Yankee. Request permission to land.

SELECTING PROBLEM-DOMAIN OBJECTS

Select actors and participants

What are the actors and participants in the problem domain?

Here, the actor is:

> – person.

What is a role that a person plays?

> – pilot.

Do you need to keep track of each pilot? Or answer questions about the pilot? Or assess the pilots' performance? No way.

[Fred and Barney are team members.]

(Fred) Hey, wait a minute. How about an autopilot? Let's add an autopilot. Let's add a new strategy, something like this: select objects that take the place of people and roles.

#48. "No Objects Mimicking What a Human Does" Strategy	selecting objects (consider and challenge)

- Don't let an object mimic what a person does (unless you are building a simulation system). Otherwise, that object will end up as a controller, a function blob.
- Reasons why:
  The controller ends up with functionality that's better done by other objects themselves (lower cohesion for all).
  The controller makes messaging more complicated (higher coupling for all).
  The overly busy controller is harder to develop.
  The overly busy controller is minding everyone else's state-dependent responsibilities.

(Peter) No way! Here's why. When you select objects just to take the place of a person, you end up with a controller. And that's a problem!

  – The controller ends up with functionality that's better done by other objects themselves (lower cohesion for all).
  – The controller makes messaging more complicated (higher coupling for all).
  – The overly busy controller is harder to develop (can you say "data flow diagram?").
  – The overly busy controller is minding everyone else's state-dependent responsibilities (can you say "state transition diagram?").

(Fred) Okay, okay. So, when I'm looking for a targeted analogy, I'm better off looking for metaphors for objects other than people. Otherwise, I'll end up with controllers, every time.

(Peter) You've got it! Keep at it, Fred. You're getting better and better at this.

(Fred) Thanks.

Select places

Again go back and take a look at the objects in the problem domain.

Yes, a number of places come to mind:

  – gates
  – taxiways
  – runways
  – airports
  – flight paths.

Yet, you are building an autopilot for the en route segment only. And it's a low-cost autopilot, too. Remember the purpose of the system?

  "To maintain altitude, direction, and attitude—during the en route segment of a flight."

So all of these places, while interesting and within the problem domain, are not within the responsibilities, not within the scope, of the system under consideration.

Select things

Some things

(Fred) Let's add autopilot object like this (Figure 5–3).

Figure 5–3: An initial object model—round I.

(Peter) Why?

(Fred) It represents this system. And it controls all of the objects in the system.

(Peter) Here's another way to look at it. The system under consideration is represented by the sum of all of the objects in your object model. You don't really need an autopilot object; that would be redundant. The autopilot is already represented by the entire object model that we're building.

(Fred) I never really thought of myself as a control freak—not until today. Thanks for the added insight.

Some interaction things

(Fred) Let's add objects for all the interaction things that you saw on the flight.

(Peter) Okay. What do you have in mind?

(Fred) We could add objects for each instrument:

- altimeter
- vertical speed indicator
- attitude indicator
- directional gyro.

(Peter) Keep going.

(Fred) We could add objects for each control:

- yoke
- rudder pedal.

(Peter) Okay. What else?

(Fred, continuing) Finally, we could add objects for each control surface:

- ailerons
- elevators
- rudder.

(Fred) We can add airplane, too, as a collection of all of these objects—to encapsulate any responsibilities across the collection of objects we're working with.

(Peter) Yes, that uses the assembly-part pattern. Sketch it out and let's take a look at it.

(Fred) Just give me a minute or two to put it together. There. See? It looks something like this (Figure 5–4):

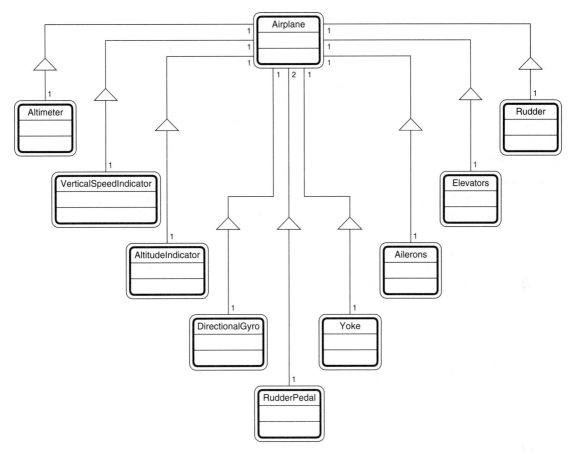

Figure 5–4: An initial object model—round II.

(Fred) Note that "ailerons" and "elevators" are plural. Each object in those classes corresponds to a pair of actual ailerons or elevators.

(Peter) That's a good example of the few times that a plural class name does make sense. Good for you!

(Peter, continuing) Now, let's look at another object-model consideration. Take a close look at the model. What are the problem-domain objects?

(Fred) They all are!

#49. "Alternative Human Interaction" Strategy	selecting objects (consider and challenge)
• Consider what changes if you used a very different human-interaction style (for example, using a heads-up display and voice commands). • Would any of your problem-domain objects change? If so, pay close attention to those objects. Separate presentation from what's really going on in the problem domain. • Examples: vertical-speed indicator (human interaction) and vertical-speed gyro (problem domain), traffic light (human interaction) and traffic lane (problem domain).	

(Peter) Let me ask a different question. Suppose we changed the human interaction—say, with a heads-up display and voice commands. What objects would be affected?

(Fred) Let's see. Hmmm. That would affect a number of objects, including all of the cockpit indicators:

- altimeter
- vertical speed indicator
- attitude indicator
- directional gyro.

It would affect the cockpit control objects, too:

- yoke
- rudder pedal.

(Peter) So what would remain the same, no matter what human-interaction style might be in vogue?

(Fred) Just the opposite—almost. Let's see. Those objects are:

- altimeter
- vertical speed gyro
- attitude gyro
- directional gyro.

(Fred, continuing) Plus the control objects:

- the ailerons
- the elevators
- the rudder.

(Peter) Excellent, Fred. Those objects are indeed problem-domain objects.

(Fred) Oh, I get it. Those objects are the problem-domain objects. The cockpit indicators and cockpit controls are human-interaction devices (Figure 5–5).

(Andi) Right.

(Peter) By George, you've got it. I think you've got it.

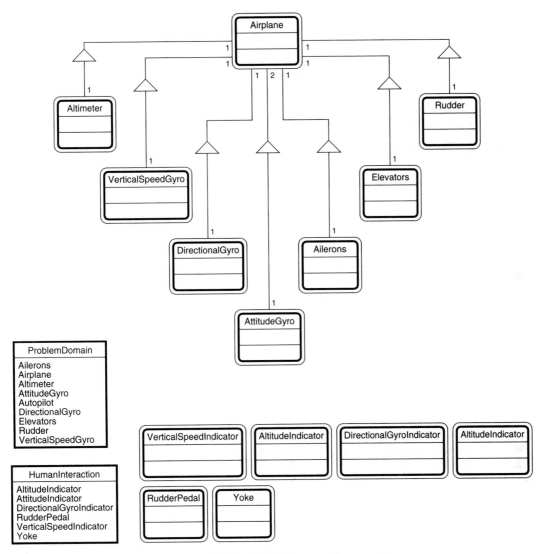

Figure 5–5: An initial object model—round III.

Human-interaction objects and problem-domain objects

Now take a closer look at human-interaction objects and problem-domain objects.

Don't confuse these two kind of objects. That separation of concerns is very important. Here's why:

> – understandability—for all members of the development team (including domain experts)
>
> – increased likelihood of reuse—for domain objects and pattern instances that are free of application-specific human-interaction compromises

This separation is especially important in data acquisition and control applications. Here's why. If you fail to distinguish between human interaction and problem domain, you'll miss out on domain understanding, essential for discovering and adding capabilities that offer real competitive advantages to your application.

Human-interaction objects are wonderful. Just keep in mind that they deliver a view of what's really going on in the problem-domain component. Eventually, you really need to look behind the curtain—and model the domain objects themselves.

Human-interaction objects

Meanwhile, begin by checking out the human-interaction objects. What are the human-interaction devices you discovered during the field trip? Make up some lists.

You've got a number of cockpit indicators:

– altimeter (indicator)
– vertical speed indicator
– attitude indicator
– directional gyro (indicator).

All of these can be modeled with human-interaction objects.

#39. The "Domain Terms and Add-Ons" Strategy	selecting objects (names)
• Use a domain name in the problem domain component. • Use the same name, with a suffix, in the other components. • Examples: customer, customer window, customer DM; altimeter, altimeter indicator, altimeter SI.	

Note the addition of the word "indicator" for two of the human-interaction objects. Why is that necessary? Simply this: in the problem-domain component, stick to the problem-domain vocabulary, even if it's not 100 percent accurate, semantically. That means you've got problem-domain objects called "altimeter" and "directional gyro." So, for the corresponding human-interaction objects, you would use something like "altimeter indicator" and "directional gyro indicator," to make the distinction (without leaving the domain vocabulary).

What other human-interaction devices do you have? Consider the two cockpit controls:

– the yoke
– the rudder pedals.

For human interaction, you've got cockpit indicators and cockpit controls. Yet what are the problem-domain objects, the ones that the human-interaction objects are just a view of?

Data acquisition and control objects

Take a look at the problem-domain objects.

This is a real-time data acquisition and control application.

It's not about people. It's not about places. It's not about human interaction. It *is* about things—data acquisition and control things.

Make a list of the data acquisition and control devices, using your discussions with Andi as a guide. For this system, an airplane is a collection of:

    – data acquisition devices
        – altimeter
        – vertical speed gyro
        – attitude gyro
        – directional gyro.
    – control devices
        – control surfaces
            ailerons, to turn left or right, around the roll
            elevators, to move up or down, around the pitch
            a rudder, to move left or right, around the yaw axis
        – a steering subsystem, to keep the airplane flying in the same direction.

WORKING OUT THE MODEL

Before working on specific responsibilities, work with the dynamics a bit, getting a sense about who is doing what.

Watch out!

What should you be watching out for? Check it out:

#118. "Watch Out for Data Objects and Control Objects" Strategy	establishing responsibilities / what I do (consider and challenge)
• Watch out for grouping by data objects and control objects. • Keep data and the actions on that data — together. • Why: better encapsulation, stronger cohesion, lower coupling, fewer objects, and fewer object interactions.	

#119. "Watch Out for Excessive Behavior" Strategy	establishing responsibilities / what I do (consider and challenge)
• Watch out for objects that interact with nearly all other objects in the model. • Try adjusting responsibilities (what I know, who I know, what I do). • Apply the collection-worker pattern, too.	

An initial look at object interactions

Take a closer look at the object model at this point.

    What's the data acquisition and control loop all about?

    It looks like the airplane object could request inputs from its altimeter, vertical speed sensor, attitude sensor, and directional gyro.

    Then the airplane object could decide what needs to be done and send commands to its control surfaces (ailerons, elevators, and rudder).

But wait a minute. That means the approach looks something like this (Figure 5–6):

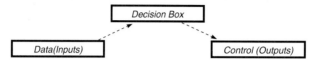

Figure 5–6: Not an object model.

Yuck! Ugh! Barf!

It looks like you've got inputs, a decision-making box, and outputs. Input, process, output. Ugh! What ever happened to encapsulation?

The messaging is troublesome. And so are the groupings of input objects (data) and output objects (control).

There must be a better way.

Exploring some alternatives

System purpose and features (revisited)

The purpose of the system is:

> "To maintain altitude, direction, and attitude—during the en route segment of a flight."

The key features of the system are:

- – maintain altitude
- – maintain direction
- – maintain attitude.

Would collections help out here?

Here's what one team member suggests, at this point.

(Barney) Hey, I've got it. What we need is an object that maintains altitude and an object that maintains course. I don't want to use altimeter and compass, and I don't like using the airplane. If we make the model general enough then we could have the autopilot maintain altitude, direction, and attitude of nearly anything that flies.

(Peter) That's an interesting point.

(Barney) How about an altitude generator and a direction maintainer? No, when I say that out loud, it sounds too much like function blobs to me.

(Peter) Yes, I agree with you. Yet what if you look at system features and the objects that work together to fulfill each feature? That might help you sort out who needs to collaborate with whom.

#26. "Feature, PD Objects, HI Objects" Strategy	selecting objects (model components)

- Tabulate: feature, corresponding problem-domain objects, corresponding human interaction objects.
- Why: identify objects—and sort out who needs to collaborate with whom.

(Barney) Cool. How about looking at it this way:

feature	PD objects	HI objects
maintain altitude	altimeter, elevators	altimeter indicator
maintain direction	directional gyro, ailerons, rudder	directional gyro indicator
maintain attitude	attitude gyro, ailerons, elevators	attitude indicator

(Peter) Let's focus on features and problem-domain objects, for now.

(Barney) Agreed. We don't need a "mega-collection" for all of these objects. Instead, we need three smaller collections, encapsulating responsibility across a collection more closely with the objects that need each other.

(Peter) Yet what do we call these collections?

(Barney) That's the challenge, all right. If we had a domain-based name, that would be great. Yet we don't. I suppose we could use:

- altitude subsystem
- direction subsystem
- attitude subsystem.

(Peter) Yes, well, if we need to go this way, we ought to name these objects as collections. Why? Simply this: to remind all of us that their responsibilities with respect to their parts should be limited to what can be done across a collection of objects. We could use something like this:

- altitude collection
- direction collection
- attitude collection.

Like this (Figure 5–7):

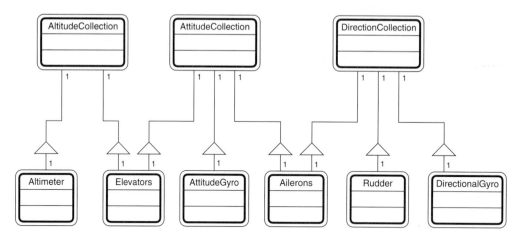

Figure 5–7: An initial object model, round IV.

(Barney) That's okay by me.

(Fred, cutting in) I don't see any reason to add objects that are not domain-based, just for the sake of controlling.

(Peter) A collection of objects encapsulates responsibility across a collection of domain objects. The objects in the collection are domain-based. And the collection objects are domain-based, too. After all, the collection does exist in the domain; it just never got a domain-specific "shorthand" name. So we just call it a "_____ collection" and leave it at that.

(Fred) Okay. I'll buy that. Yet I don't think we need those collections.

(Peter) Fred, you may be right about that. Take a look at that model. Consider what the collection objects really do. Do they do anything across their collection of objects? Not really. So what do they do? The collection objects get input data from one object and pass it on to output objects. Ugh! Why not let those objects work together, without the collection getting in the way?

(Barney) Sounds cool. Let's do it.

Another look

(Fred, continuing) Now I want to talk a bit about potential object interactions. Each data acquisition object—altimeter, vertical speed indicator, attitude indicator, and directional gyro—could run continually, sending data messages to the airplane whenever a change from the current value occurs. Better yet, those objects could report a change once the change is confirmed over some number of readings, notifying the aircraft object.

(Peter) Good. The data acquisition objects get a little smarter than "I read a value and pass it on." You've added some asynchronous behavior. You've added some smarts to "make sure it's really a change" before sending a message to the airplane object. Sounds promising. You may not need an aircraft object, though. Let's keep working on this.

(Fred) I want to point out that some services will need trigger and terminate conditions, namely:

> trigger upon: change in altitude deviation
> terminate upon: adjustment is near-zero.

(Peter) Agreed. Good point, Fred.

Some generalization-specialization, perhaps?

(Fred) One more thing. We could add some generalization-specialization to the model, too:

> – data acquisition
>> altimeter object
>> vertical speed gyro object
>> attitude gyro object
>> directional gyro object
> – control
>> ailerons objects
>> elevators objects
>> rudder object.

(Barney, cutting in) Fred, Fred, Fred. You could specialize most anything based upon "data" and "control"—but coupling and cohesion go down the drain.

(Fred) Gee, Barney, I guess you're right about that one.

(Barney) The point is, use an architecture that keeps data acquisition and corresponding control together—not isolated as separate data and control hierarchies.

A good dose of problem-domain knowledge goes a long way
Get some input from an outside source

Sounds like the team needs some help from an outside source.

Remember the encyclopedia quotation cited at the beginning of this chapter? You've got a vertical speed gyro (and an altimeter). It "controls the altitude of the airplane and keeps it flying level."

Does it really do that? Not literally—after all, a vertical speed gyro is something used in a vertical velocity indicator. It's a data acquisition device, not a control device.

So is the statement incorrect? No way. The statement is correct—it's a figure of speech, bringing added emphasis to the statement.

Domain experts use personification, too. So be it. Use it here and see what happens. Keep this information in mind, too:

feature	objects
maintain altitude	altimeter, vertical speed gyro, elevators
maintain direction	directional gyro, ailerons, rudder
maintain attitude	attitude gyro, ailerons, elevators.

Here it goes.

"The vertical speed gyro (and an altimeter) controls the altitude of the airplane" (Figure 5–8):

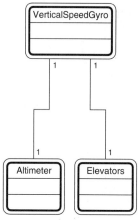

Figure 5–8: The vertical speed gyro, with its associated altimeter, and elevators.

So far, so good.

"The attitude gyro keeps it flying level," says *World Book* (Figure 5–9):

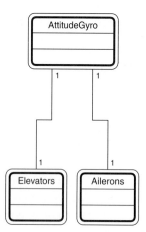

Figure 5–9: The attitude gyro, with its associated ailerons and elevators.

"The directional gyro controls the steering and keeps the airplane flying in the same direction" (Figure 5–10):

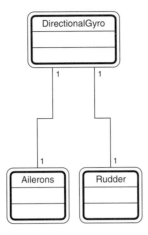

Figure 5–10: The directional gyro, with its associated ailerons and rudder.

The result? It's an object model that looks something like this (Figure 5–11):

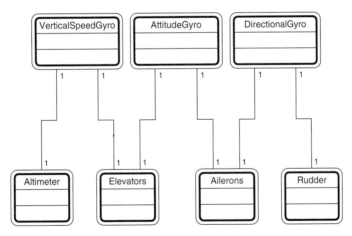

Figure 5–11: An initial object model, round V.

Work it out with the team

(Peter) So what do you think about this, Barney?

(Barney) I like it. Consider the possibilities. Each gyro object looks for a change in value. It notifies its corresponding control objects, directly.

(Peter) Directly connect data acquisition objects and control objects? Great idea.

(Barney) If the desired altitude or direction is not met within a certain time interval, the respective data-acquisition object could change its operational state. A human-interaction object could pick up that change in operational state and report it.

(Barney, continuing) We need some coordinated action. An elevator's object needs reports from an altimeter and a vertical speed gyro, so it can adjust itself. A rudder object needs reports from the directional gyro. An aileron object needs reports from the directional gyro, too.

(Peter) Excellent point.

(Fred) How about something like this:

    airplane
        elevators
            altimeter
            vertical speed gyro
            attitude gyro
        rudder
            directional gyro
        ailerons
            attitude gyro
            directional gyro.

How about this (Figure 5–12)?

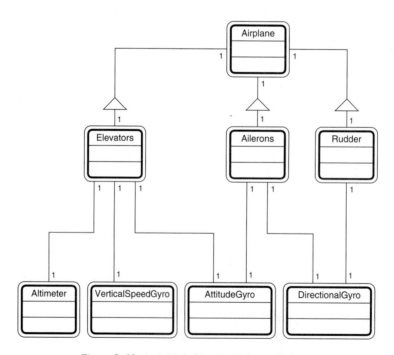

Figure 5–12: An initial object model, round VI.

(Fred, continuing) On command (say, from a human-interaction object), an airplane object can activate the elevators, rudder, and ailerons objects. In turn, they can activate their respective devices.

(Barney) All right, then. I could go with that. Could we fine-tune it a little bit? How about something like this:

> airplane—activates its parts
> > elevators—adjusts, based on reports
> > > altimeter—gets, compares, and reports: altitude value
> > > vertical speed gyro—gets, compares, and reports: altitude change rate
> > > attitude gyro—gets, compares, and reports: pitch value and pitch change rate
> > rudder—adjusts, based on reports
> > > directional gyro—gets, compares, and reports: direction value and direction change rate
> > ailerons—adjusts, based on reports
> > > attitude gyro—gets, compares, and reports: roll value and roll change rate
> > > directional gyro—gets, compares, and reports: direction value and direction change rate.

(Barney, continuing) Each data-acquisition object needs to know its respective control-device objects, so it send reports to it. Right now, each control-device object doesn't need to know the airplane object; it sends no reports to it (although it might as we develop this model further; that's why I'm still showing all the connection constraints, for now).

(Barney, continuing) Hey, I've got a question for the domain expert. Why is change rate important, anyway?

(Andi) You need the change rate so you can speed up the rate of change, then slow that rate of change down as you get closer and closer to a desired value.

(Andi, continuing) I'm amazed. I really understand the model—that's a welcome change. And I'm happy with what we've accomplished, together.

(Fred) Me too. The airplane has its parts. The control surface objects move themselves. The device objects report problems. "Yabba-dabba-doo!"

A shortcut

There is a shortcut for all of this.

You need not go through so many object-model rounds to get there. All you need is this strategy:

#141. "Responsive Data Acquisition and Control Objects" Strategy	working out dynamics with scenarios (consider and challenge)

- If data acquisition and control are done by one actual object, then model them with one object.

- Otherwise:
  For each control object:
      Add a collection of data acquisition objects.
      The control object takes care of itself — and behavior across the collection.
  For each data acquisition object:
      Each data acquisition object takes care of itself, as much it can do with what it knows (for example, reading values and detecting something from those values).

Cool.

WORKING OUT PROBLEM-DOMAIN DYNAMICS WITH SCENARIOS

Overview

Now you have a model and some ideas on how the interaction might work.

Now work out the scenarios in detail to make sure it can really work.

Begin by telling an airplane object to activate itself. That will kick off some important and interesting scenarios, including:

> airplane—activate autopilot
> elevators—maintain altitude
> altimeter—activate altitude deviation monitoring
> altimeter—monitor altitude deviation
> elevators—monitor updates.

And, at some time later, a final scenario called:

> airplane—deactivate autopilot.

A more detailed overview

Take a closer look at what happens.

Someone tells the airplane object to activate.

The airplane object tells its elevators, ailerons, and rudder objects to activate. The elevators object is the most interesting and complex.

Consider the elevators object and one of its data-acquisition objects, an altimeter object.

What happens when someone tells an "elevators" object to activate?

The elevators object initializes and activates itself.

- The elevators object initializes its altitude deviation to zero.
- The elevators object asks each of its data-acquisition objects to activate itself.
- The elevators object activates a task, to monitor for updates.

The elevators object tells its altimeter object to activate itself.

  – The altimeter object reads an initial value.
  – The altimeter object activates a monitoring task.

On receiving a new value, the elevators object does something about it.

  – The elevators object wakes up.
  – The elevators object calculates whatever adjustments it needs to make.
  – The elevators object moves the actual elevators accordingly.

At some time later, someone tells the airplane object to deactivate.

  – The airplane object tells its elevators object to deactivate.
  – The elevators object deactivates itself, stopping the task it encapsulates.
  – The elevators object tells its parts, for example, its altimeter, to deactivate.
  – The altimeter object deactivates itself, stopping the task it encapsulates.

End of story.

Oh so simple.

Objects encapsulate whatever tasks are needed. Very cool.

Now, with this overview in mind, continue with the scenarios for the elevators object and one of its data acquisition objects, an altimeter object.

Scenario: airplane—activate autopilot.

Sketch out what the scenario is all about:

  – Someone (for example, a human-interaction object) sends a message to
      an aircraft object, telling it to activate the autopilot.
  – The airplane object then asks:
    – the elevators object to activate altitude maintenance
    – the rudder object to activate heading maintenance
    – the ailerons object to activate heading maintenance.

Here is the scenario view (Figure 5–13):

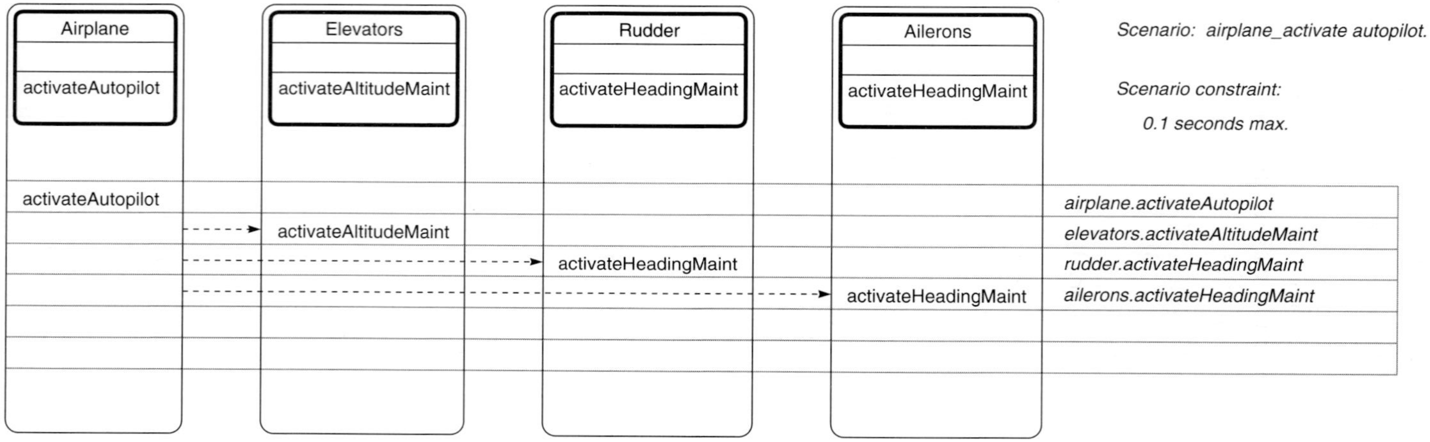

Figure 5–13: The "airplane—activate autopilot" scenario.

Scenario: elevators—maintain altitude

Sketch out what happens:

- Someone (an airplane object) tells the elevators object to maintain altitude.
- The elevators object initializes itself, getting initial values for its use.
  It asks its vertical speed gyro object to read the altitude change rate.
  It asks the attitude gyro object to read the pitch angle.
- The elevators object activates itself.
  It asks the altimeter object to activate its altitude deviation monitoring.
  It asks the vertical speed gyro to activate its altitude change rate monitoring.
  It asks the attitude gyro to activate its pitch angle deviation monitoring.
- Finally, the elevators object activates a task, monitor updates.

Here is the scenario view (Figure 5–14):

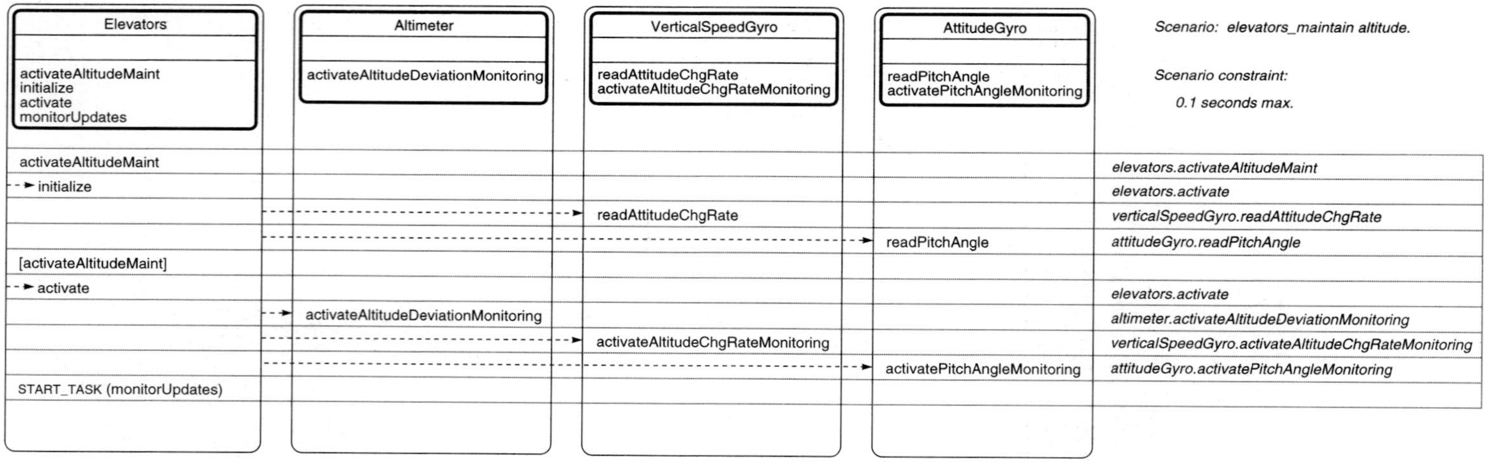

Figure 5–14: The "elevators—maintain altitude" scenario.

You've selected objects. You're working out dynamics with scenarios. Keep on the lookout for responsibilities along the way.

Consider the elevators object. It's a device object; it needs to know its operational state. Based on this scenario, it also knows its:

- altitude deviation
- altitude change rate
- pitch angle.

A side point: if you needed to keep track of some number of values over time, you could:

- just make the attribute plural, and allow for some number of recent values
- apply the device-log-log entry pattern, to log each reading or to log each correction (something you might add for testing the autopilot).

Continue. Who does the elevators object know? It knows its altimeter, its vertical speed gyro, and its attitude gyro (the elevators object knows to whom to send its messages).

What does the elevators object do? Based upon this scenario, it does the following:

- maintain altitude
- initialize
- activate
- monitor reports (which, inside the object, one finds out is a real-time task).

You've also identified services for the data acquisition objects, too. Cool.

So what's next?

Investigate the interaction between the elevators object and its altimeter object.

(The elevators object interacts with the vertical speed gyro object and with the attitude gyro in a similar fashion.)

But first, a couple of observations follow, before you continue with the regularly scheduled program.

An observation on data objects, function objects, and controller objects

Data objects, function objects, and controller objects fail to encapsulate real-time tasks.

If you settled for an object model with so-called data objects, function objects, and controller objects, then your real-time tasks would be all over the place. A task would need to work across many objects to get its job done. High coupling, weak cohesion, low understandability, increased implementation difficulty. Yuck!

Oh, but perhaps there is a silver lining to all of this. The benefit? Oh, why, the model is so very complex. Oooooh. What a wonderful thing for techno-bureaucrats. ("We're not worthy; we're not worthy.")

Nuts! If an architecture is so complex that only a few elite ones on the team understand it, then those elite ones have yet to exert the time, effort, and talent necessary to develop an effective object model.

There is great beauty in simplicity, brevity, and clarity. Even (indeed, especially) in real-time systems.

An observation on objects and encapsulating real-time tasks

An object encapsulates responsibilities, including whatever tasks it needs to get its job done. Think about what this means.

An object can do more than one thing at once. An object is a multitasking creature. Hmmm. That's just like any living object. Cool.

The impact?

First, it means that all multitasking considerations are encapsulated within objects. The complexities of a real-time task—initialization, ongoing behavior, interrupt mechanisms, intertask communication and coordination details—are encapsulated. Yes! (Just consider how much time your team usually spends working out these complexities, and you'll see just how important this encapsulation really is. Even in real-time tasking, effective communication is a must.)

Second, messaging between objects remains like any other messaging between objects. So, when you send a message to an object, you just send it a message (after all, that really is none of your business!).

Just send it a message. You get an immediate acknowledgment that the message was received. As needed, that object may later send you a subsequent message with the result. If someone comes up with an "asynchronous message" between objects, you can rest assured that one or more function blobs are lurking nearby. Apply the "what I do" strategies and come up with a more effective object model, one which delivers on the promise of encapsulation (even for real-time considerations).

Okay, so what if you have one hundred data-acquisition devices? You probably don't want a hundred tasks; the context switch time might be a real problem. So the question is: where would you put a task across a collection of objects? In a collection object! It could be a zone or some other sensor collection. Each object in that class could contain some number of sensor objects. And that zone object would encapsulate the task that works across its collection of sensors.

A very important point

The complexities of asynchronous behavior—including asynchronous messages—are encapsulated.

There is no need for a special "task icon" or "task management component."

There is no need for an "asynchronous message" notation.

Why?

Because all real-time tasking issues are encapsulated within the respective objects.

Yes, to achieve this encapsulation of tasks, you must first develop an effective object model. That's what the strategies and patterns are all about.

Very cool.

Scenario: altimeter—activate altitude-deviation monitoring

How does it work? Sketch it out:

   – Someone asks an altimeter object to activate altitude monitoring.
   – The altimeter object sets its initial deviation to zero.
   – The altimeter object activates a task to monitor altitude.

Here is the scenario view (Figure 5–15):

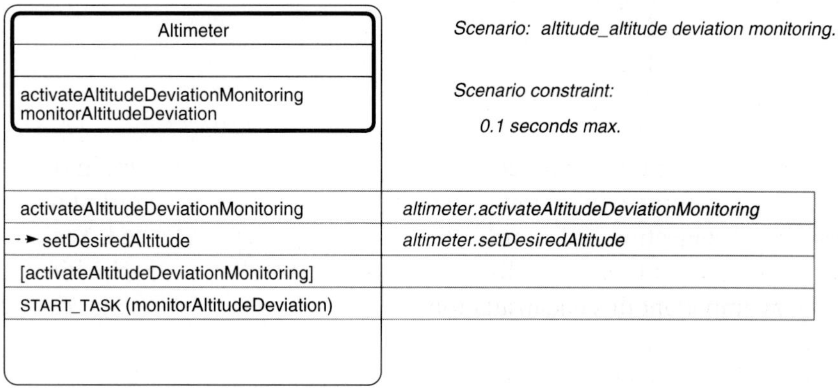

Altimeter		Scenario: altitude_altitude deviation monitoring.
activateAltitudeDeviationMonitoring monitorAltitudeDeviation		Scenario constraint: 0.1 seconds max.
activateAltitudeDeviationMonitoring	altimeter.activateAltitudeDeviationMonitoring	
- -►setDesiredAltitude	altimeter.setDesiredAltitude	
[activateAltitudeDeviationMonitoring]		
START_TASK (monitorAltitudeDeviation)		

Figure 5–15: The "altimeter—activate altitude deviation monitoring" scenario.

Some new responsibilities? An altimeter knows its:
- desired altitude.

And an altimeter object provides the following services:
- monitor altitude deviation
- report altitude deviation.

Note that you could add a service within altimeter, to set its initial deviation to zero. Don't show such intraobject accessor services in a scenario view. Leave such details to service descriptions.

Next up: how does the altitude deviation reporting work?

Scenario: altimeter—monitor altitude deviation

How does this one work? Periodically, the altimeter object:
- reads the value
- calculates a deviation
- checks to see if the deviation is reportable
    (that is to say, the deviation is at or above a threshold *and*
    it's different from the last report, by more than a minimum difference
    value)
- reports the new altitude deviation to the elevators object.

Here's the scenario view (Figure 5–16):

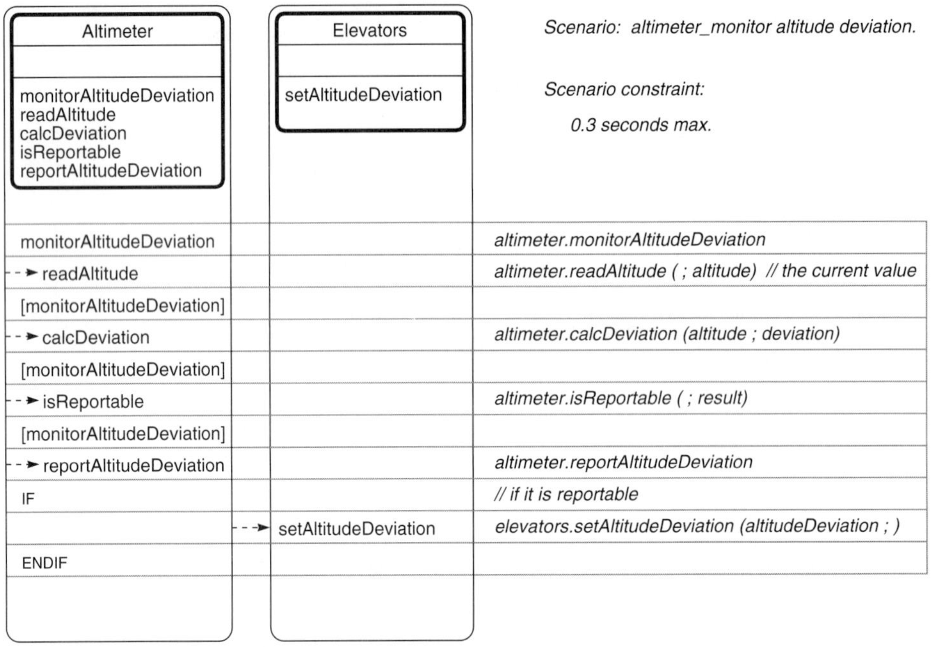

Altimeter	Elevators	
monitorAltitudeDeviation readAltitude calcDeviation isReportable reportAltitudeDeviation	setAltitudeDeviation	*Scenario: altimeter_monitor altitude deviation.* *Scenario constraint:* *0.3 seconds max.*
monitorAltitudeDeviation		*altimeter.monitorAltitudeDeviation*
- -► readAltitude		*altimeter.readAltitude (; altitude) // the current value*
[monitorAltitudeDeviation]		
- -► calcDeviation		*altimeter.calcDeviation (altitude ; deviation)*
[monitorAltitudeDeviation]		
- -► isReportable		*altimeter.isReportable (; result)*
[monitorAltitudeDeviation]		
- -► reportAltitudeDeviation		*altimeter.reportAltitudeDeviation*
IF		*// if it is reportable*
	- -► setAltitudeDeviation	*elevators.setAltitudeDeviation (altitudeDeviation ;)*
ENDIF		

Figure 5–16: The "altimeter—monitor altitude deviation" scenario.

Check out those added services! As you work out scenarios, you're also working out responsibilities along the way.

Note that an altimeter object needs an attribute, its altitude deviation, so it can know when it has changed.

What's next? Consider what the elevators object does when it gets a new altitude deviation value.

Scenario: elevators—monitor updates

Sketch out how the elevators object gets this done:

> – The "maintain altitude" service triggers itself upon the receipt of a new
>> report from one of its data acquisition objects.
> – That service:
>> calculates the correct elevator movement based on the reports
>> sends control signals to the actual elevators.

Here's the scenario view (Figure 5–17):

Elevators	Scenario: *elevators_monitor updates.*
monitorUpdates calcAdjustment move sleepIfCloseEnough	Scenario constraint: *0.2 seconds max.*
monitorUpdates	*elevators.monitorUpdates // trigger upon: change in altitude deviation*
- - ► calcAdjustment	*elevators.calcAdjustment (; adjustment)*
[monitorUpdates]	
- - ► move	*elevators.move (adjustment ;)*
[monitorUpdates]	
- - ► sleepIfCloseEnough	*elevators.sleepIfCloseEnough (adjustment ;) // terminate when adjustment is zero +- some noise level*

Figure 5–17: The "elevators—monitor updates" scenario.

Some notes on services that include trigger and terminate conditions
How to model it

For each service with trigger and terminate conditions, just make that service a separate task.

How to implement a trigger condition

Using a programming language with tasking (Ada) or any other programming language teamed up with operating system calls, you can set up the task so it waits for the triggering event to occur.

In this example, the elevators object "monitor reports" task waits until it receives a new report from one of its data-acquisition objects.

The elevators object has attributes for the reported values, such as altitude deviation. The service that sets that report could signal a semaphore. Or the attributes themselves could be a protected type of some kind that has access queuing.

You could use whatever synchronization mechanism your heart desires—and your technology supports—including a semaphore wait/signal mechanism, critical region, mailbox, or a rendezvous—just as long as you can suspend the task until another new report arrives.

How to implement a terminate condition

This is easier.

Check an applicable attribute. In this example, the condition is:

    – terminate when adjustment is zero ± some noise level.

When the terminate condition is satisfied, the service stops (for example, it exits, quits, or goes to sleep).

Scenario: airplane—deactivate autopilot

Here's what this scenario is all about:

> – Someone (for example, a human-interaction object) sends a message to an aircraft object, telling it to deactivate the autopilot.
> – The airplane object asks:
>> the elevators object to deactivate altitude maintenance
>> the rudder object to deactivate heading maintenance
>> the ailerons object to deactivate heading maintenance.

Put together a scenario view (Figure 5–18):

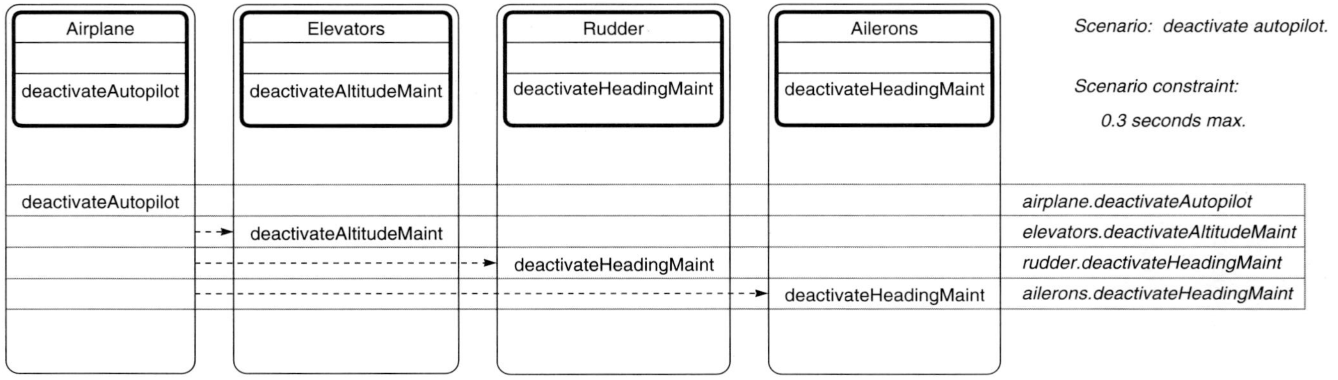

Figure 5–18: The "airplane—deactivate autopilot" scenario.

Scenario: elevators—deactivate altitude maintenance

Here's what the scenario is all about:

- The airplane object tells its elevators object to deactivate.
- The elevators object deactivates itself, stopping the task it encapsulates.
- The elevators object tells its parts (its altimeter, vertical speed gyros, and altitude gyros) to deactivate.
- The altimeter object deactivates itself, stopping the task it encapsulates.
- The vertical-speed-gyro object deactivates itself, stopping the task it encapsulates.
- The altitude-gyro object deactivates itself, stopping the task it encapsulates.

Put together a scenario view (Figure 5–19):

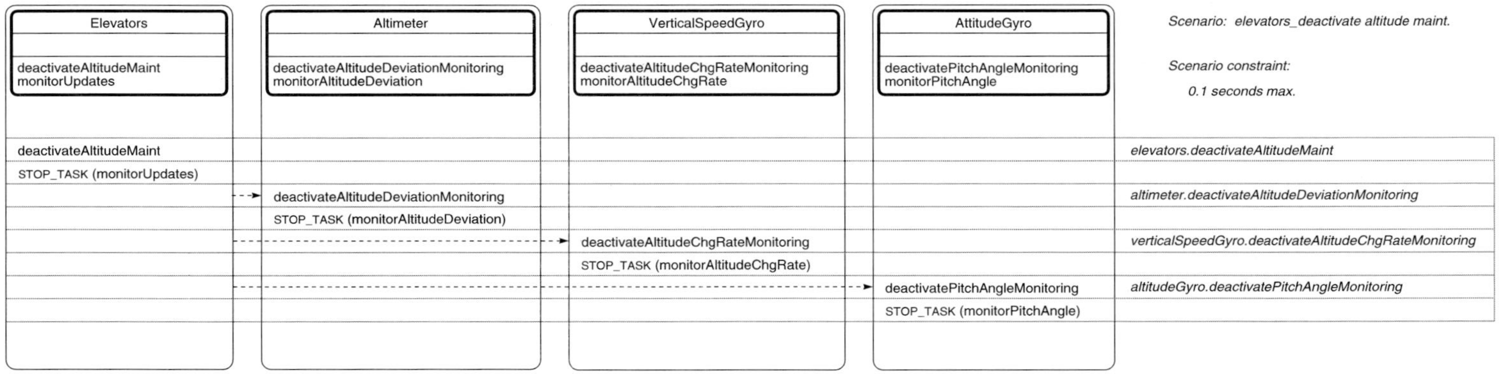

Figure 5–19: The "elevators—deactivate altitude maintenance" scenario.

Elevators
deactivateAltitudeMaint monitorUpdates

deactivateAltitudeMaint
STOP_TASK (monitorUpdates)

Altimeter
deactivateAltitudeDeviationMonitoring monitorAltitudeDeviation

deactivateAltitudeDeviationMonitoring
STOP_TASK (monitorAltitudeDeviation)

VerticalSpeedGyro
deactivateAltitudeChgRateMonitoring monitorAltitudeChgRate

deactivateAltitudeChgRateMonitoring
STOP_TASK (monitorAltitudeChgRate)

AttitudeGyro
deactivatePitchAngleMonitoring monitorPitchAngle

deactivatePitchAngleMonitoring
STOP_TASK (monitorPitchAngle)

Scenario: elevators_ deactivate altitude maint.

Scenario constraint:
0.1 seconds max.

elevators.deactivateAltitudeMaint

altimeter. deactivateAltitudeDeviationMonitoring

verticalSpeedGyro. deactivateAltitudeChgRateMonitoring

altitudeGyro. deactivatePitchAngleMonitoring

Adding responsibilities to your object model

You've worked out the scenarios for the elevators and the corresponding data-acquisition devices. The scenarios for ailerons and rudders are simpler variations on them.

As you've worked out dynamics with scenarios, you've also established responsibilities along the way. Good show!

By analogy, take the responsibilities for the elevators objects and its data-acquisition objects—and extend them to the rest of your object model.

Here's the result (Figure 5–20):

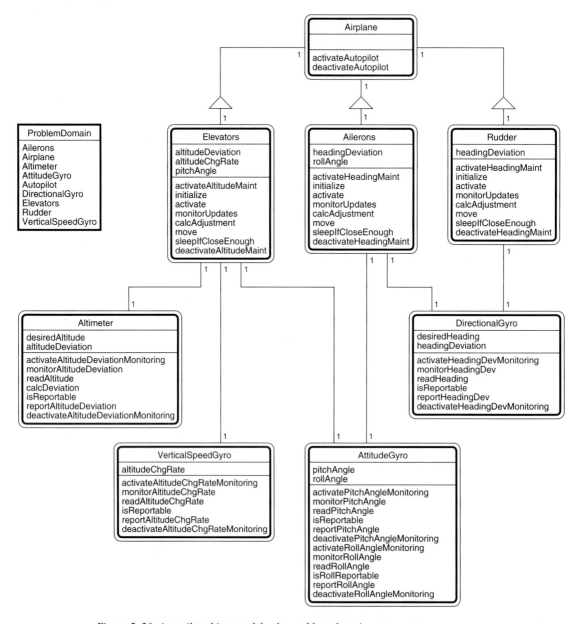

Figure 5–20: Autopilot object model—the problem-domain component.

SELECTING HUMAN-INTERACTION OBJECTS

Select windows

Earlier, you sketched out a number of human-interaction objects, spanning the cockpit instruments and controls that pertain to flying an airplane on autopilot.

The question at this point is: what human-interaction objects do you need for the autopilot system?

Well, it's a lot less glamorous than you might have initially envisioned. (After all, the character "Otto Pilot" in the movie *Airplane* had a most interesting human-interaction approach.)

It's just one window! It's simply the:

– autopilot window.

You need it so a pilot can activate and deactivate the autopilot.
Check it out.

ESTABLISHING HUMAN-INTERACTION RESPONSIBILITIES

Responsibilities for windows

Establish responsibilities for an autopilot window.

> What I know: —
> Who I know: airplane
> What I do: activate, deactivate.

Add an autopilot window to your object model (Figure 5–21):

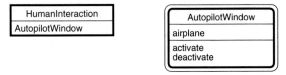

Figure 5–21: Human-interaction objects and responsibilities.

WORKING OUT HUMAN-INTERACTION DYNAMICS WITH SCENARIOS

Yes, there is one simple scenario. Just do it.

Scenario: activate autopilot

Easy. Here's the scenario view (Figure 5–22):

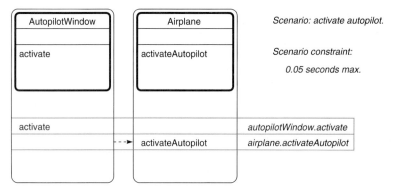

Figure 5–22: The "activate autopilot" scenario.

SELECTING DATA-MANAGEMENT OBJECTS

This application doesn't need any data-management objects.

You can create and initialize all objects at startup.

No big deal.

Actually, you could add some DM objects to handle configuration values, yet that seems out-of-place for this real-time application.

SELECTING SYSTEM-INTERACTION OBJECTS

Add a system-interaction object for each data acquisition and control device that you need to interface with.

Add SI objects for each data acquisition object in the PD component:

data acquisition PD object	data acquisition SI object
altimeter	altimeter SI
vertical speed gyro	vertical speed gyro SI
attitude gyro	attitude speed gyro SI.

Now add SI objects for each control device object in the PD component:

data acquisition PD object	data acquisition SI object
ailerons	ailerons SI
elevators	elevators SI
rudder	rudder SI.

ESTABLISHING SYSTEM-INTERACTION RESPONSIBILITIES

PD and SI pairs: who does what?

You've got pairs of problem-domain objects and system interaction objects:

altimeter—and altimeter SI

vertical speed indicator—and vertical speed indicator SI

attitude gyro—and attitude gyro SI

ailerons—and ailerons SI

rudder—and rudder SI

elevators—and elevators SI.

Who does what?

Each SI object encapsulates low-level interaction details (port number, the bits to sample and latch a value, and the like).

What about data conversion? Who does that?

Let problem-domain objects deal with problem-domain units, not physical units. Why? Decreased dependence on a specific system interaction device. Increased likelihood of reuse.

At times, for performance reasons, you may choose to let the problem domain object work with raw data. That's fine; just realize the tradeoff you are making: faster performance, in exchange for less resiliency to change, for both the current application and for future applications.

For this application, the SI objects convert raw data to problem-domain units. Hence, add the services:

for an altimeter: convert raw data to feet

for a vertical speed gyro: convert raw data to feet per second

for an attitude gyro: convert raw pitch to degrees, convert raw roll to degrees.

Add the SI objects to your model (Figure 5–23):

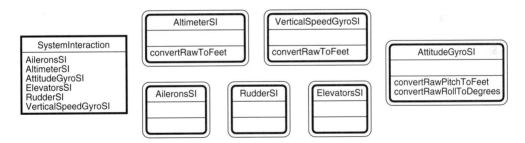

Figure 5–23: System-interaction objects and responsibilities.

WORKING OUT SYSTEM-INTERACTION DYNAMICS WITH SCENARIOS

Scenario: altimeter—monitor altitude

How do our objects for the instruments work? They need to be able to report whatever they watch at any time. They know how to interface the electronics for the instrument. So they continuously monitor the electronics and update the attribute for what they are watching.

Write up a scenario view, including both a problem-domain object and its corresponding system-interaction object (Figure 5–24):

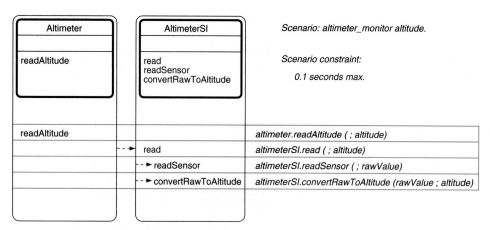

Figure 5–24: The "altimeter—monitor altitude" scenario.

The other PD and SI objects for this application interact in this same basic way.

PROGRESS AT THIS POINT

Here's the object model (Figures 5–25 to 27). Along with the scenarios in this chapter, this wraps up your work for Andi's Autopilot.

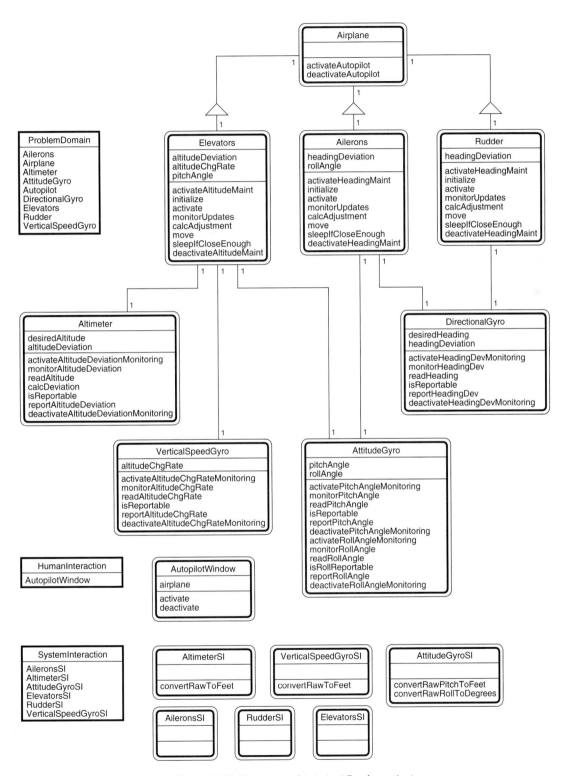

Figure 5–25: Progress at this point (Coad notation).

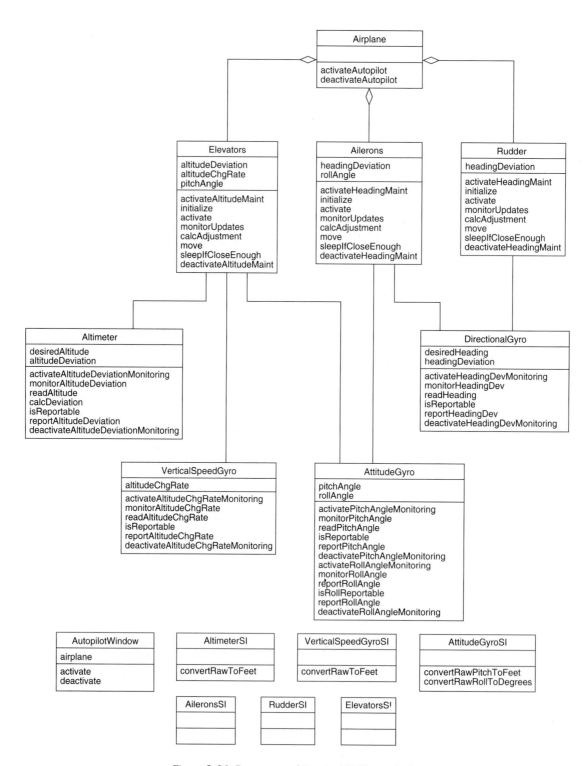

Figure 5–26: Progress at this point (OMT notation).

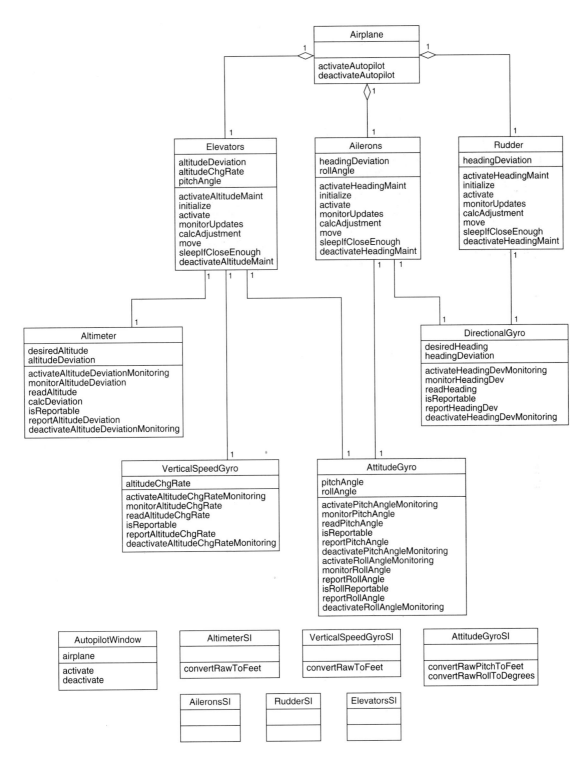

Figure 5–27: Progress at this point (Unified notation).

WRAP-UP

You did it! You built an object model for a data acquisition and control application.

It's important! Nearly every health care and engineering system business uses a data-acquisition and control application, in one form or another. You can directly relate to (and for some readers, you can directly apply) this object-modeling experience.

In this chapter, you learned and applied some additional strategies and patterns, especially for real-time applications.

You've seen how to build an effective object model, rather than have one overly complex central controller doing all the work.

You've also experienced another important lesson: it's a good idea not to fall in love with the first object model you sketch out. It's okay to take an initial object model and replace it with a better one. Allow yourself the privilege of doing so (and you'll end up with even better results).

Excellent!

6

All Five Applications, At High Speed

A wealth of material has been written on design, color, ornament, art history, and every technique imaginable, but little of it comes to grips with the principles of pattern structure. Authors bend over backward to explain the design of beautiful "units," but rarely do they explain the design of beautiful "yardage," the repetition of units.

—Richard M. Proctor, *Principles of Pattern Design*

The recognition of natural patterns is at the heart of both scientific and artistic exploration.

Our buildings, our symphonies, our fabrics, our societies—all declare patterns.

Once you begin to see these patterns, don't be surprised if your view . . . undergoes a subtle shift. . . . Everywhere I looked, I found basic patterns repeating.

—Pat Murphy, *By Nature's Design*

THE POWER OF PATTERNS

This chapter presents all five applications—from Chapters 1 to 5—at high speed. Why? To present how to build initial object models completely with patterns (ready for subsequent refinement with strategies).

It seems that everyone needs to go through the process of learning, applying, and gaining understanding of the fundamentals in a field. One begins with strategies, then adds some patterns along the way. One needs that experiential basis really to see and experience the profound impact of building initial object models completely with patterns (ready for subsequent refinement, using strategies).

At this point, you've got some of that experiential background. Get ready for an exciting time!

In this chapter, you'll build object models for the problem-domain component— and for all five applications. Other considerations, including using strategies and scenarios to refine the model, won't be repeated here. (So don't expect these models to match the ones in Chapters 1 to 5 in every way!)

This chapter exposes how to build object models at the world-class level. You'll build these object models with greater ease than you might have ever thought possible. Enjoy!

PATTERNS, SUPPORTED BY STRATEGIES

Finally, once you have applied strategies and patterns, patterns take on some added impact: patterns tie together selecting objects, establishing responsibilities, and working out scenarios.

Patterns come to center stage.

Patterns are repetitive forms that occur again and again. Use them to your advantage in building effective object models.

#1. "Four Major Activities, Four Major Components" Strategy	major activities and components

- Organize your work around four major activities, within four major components:

- Four major activities:

  Standard: Identify purpose and features, select objects, establish responsibilities, work out dynamics with scenarios.

  Variation 1: You may find it helpful to focus on working out dynamics with scenarios, establishing responsibilities along the way. This is especially suitable for real-time applications.

  Variation 2: You may find it helpful to select transaction, aggregate, and plan objects, then use the corresponding patterns to guide you through selecting additional objects, establishing responsibilities, and working out dynamics with scenarios.

- Four major components:

  Standard: Problem domain, human interaction, data management, system interaction.

  Variation 1: You may find it helpful to begin with human interaction, followed by problem domain, data management, and system interaction. This is especially suitable when your domain experts want to talk in terms of human interaction from the very start.

  Variation 2: You may find it helpful to begin with problem domain and system interaction, followed by human interaction, data management. This is especially suitable for real-time applications, when your domain experts are keenly interested in the data acquisition and control aspects of the system under consideration.

Here's the approach:

- Select transactions, aggregates (containers, groups, assemblies), and devices.
- Apply transaction patterns.
- Apply aggregate patterns.
- Apply device patterns.
- Apply interaction patterns.

Patterns provide a framework, a memorable template, for the strategies you've come to know and appreciate.

Patterns are not a substitute for strategies.

Patterns are a visual summary of the many strategies recorded in this work.

As you will see in this chapter, once understood and properly applied, patterns give you large "building blocks" for snapping together an object model.

Strategies are the key to establishing the details within a model. As you'll see in this chapter, you can only get so far with patterns. You need strategies, too. The combination is awesome.

Onward, with patterns!

CONNIE'S CONVENIENCE STORE (A POINT-OF-SALE APPLICATION)

Select transaction objects and aggregate objects

Begin by selecting transaction objects and aggregate objects.

What are the transactions? For conducting the business, the transactions are sale and payment. For performance assessment, another transaction is session.

What are the aggregates (containers, groups, assemblies)? The aggregate objects are store (a container) and register (an assembly).

So far, so good.

Select objects, using transaction patterns as a guide

Apply transaction patterns, using these transactions: sale, payment, and session.

Look for a pattern—or a combination of patterns—that might apply here.

Select players for these transaction patterns:

- participant-transaction
- place-transaction
- specific item–transaction

- transaction–transaction line item
- transaction–subsequent transaction

- actor-participant
- item–line item
- transaction line item–subsequent transaction line item
- associate–other associate.

Work on the transactions in time sequence, that is to say, in the order you would normally work with them. In this case, work on session, then sale, then payment.

Session

Here you go.

> Using the transaction patterns as a guide, select objects for your system.
> Apply participant-transaction.
>
>> The participant is a cashier.
>> The transaction is a session.
>
> Apply specific item–transaction.
>
>> The specific item is a register.
>> The transaction is a session.
>
> Apply transaction–transaction line item.
>
>> The transaction is a session.
>> The transaction line item? No, this is not needed here. A session is a session; it doesn't have any line items.
>
> Apply transaction–subsequent transaction.
>
>> The transaction is a session.
>> The subsequent transaction is a sale.
>
> Apply actor-participant.
>
>> The actor is a person.
>> The participant is a cashier.
>
> Here's the result:
>
>> – person-cashier-session-sale
>> – register-session.

Sale

Now consider sale, another transaction.

> Apply participant-transaction.
>
>> The participant? A cashier? Well, yes, indirectly. Actually what you have here is:
>>
>>> cashier is a participant in a session.
>>> session is a transaction; a sale is a subsequent transaction.
>>
>> Another participant? A customer participates in a sale. Yet you have no way to know about individual customers. So don't include this participant in the object model. (Yes, strategies and patterns do go hand in hand.)
>> This pattern does not apply here.
>
> Apply transaction–transaction line item.
>
>> The transaction is a sale.
>> The transaction line item is a sale line item.
>
> Apply transaction–subsequent transaction.
>
>> The transaction is a sale.
>> The subsequent transaction is a payment.

Apply actor-participant. It's the same as before:

>   The actor is a person.
>   The participant is a cashier.

Apply item–line item.

>   The transaction line item is a sale line item.
>   The item? Why, it's an item.

A store is the place where the sales happen. A store object can assess itself, answering questions like "how many (sales) over interval?" and "how much (money) over interval?"

Apply place-transaction.

>   The place is a store.
>   The transaction is a sale.

Here's the result:

>   – person-cashier-session-sale-payment.
>   – sale–sale line item–item.
>   – store-sale.

Payment

Move on to the next transaction, payment.

>   Apply transaction–subsequent transaction.

>>   The transaction is a sale.
>>   The subsequent transaction is a payment.

>   Apply transaction–transaction line item.

>>   The transaction is a payment.
>>   The transaction line item? No, this is not needed here. A payment is a payment; it doesn't have any parts.

Here's the result—nothing new:

>   – sale-payment.

Results, using transaction patterns

Here are the results:

>   – person-cashier-session-sale-payment
>   – sale–sale line item–item.

Here's that part of the object model (Figure 6–1):

Patterns

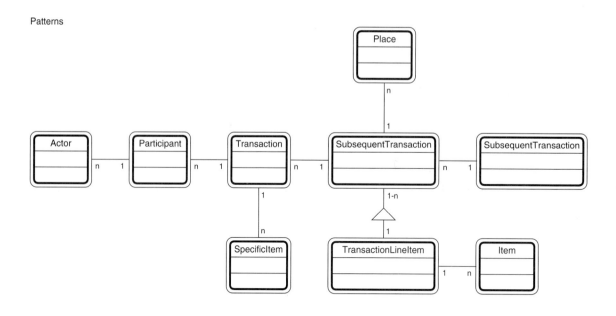

Pattern Instances

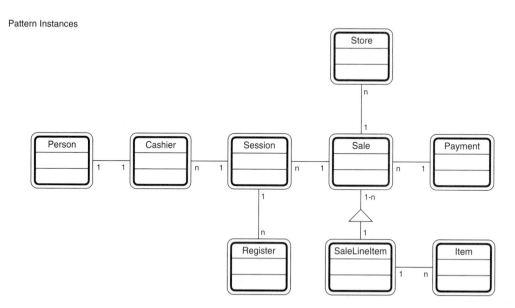

Figure 6–1: Selecting objects, using transaction patterns as a guide.

Cool. Very cool.

Select objects, using aggregate patterns as a guide

Apply aggregate patterns, using these aggregates: store (a container) and register (an assembly).

Select players for these aggregate patterns:

  – container-content
  – group-member
  – assembly-part
  – container–container line item.

Store

Here you go again.

Using the aggregate patterns (specifically, container patterns) as a guide, select objects for your system.

Apply container-content.

  The container is a store.
  The content is an item.

Apply container-content.

  The container is a store.
  The content is a register.

Apply container-content.

  The container is a store.
  The content is a cashier.

Now apply container–container line item.

  The container is a store.
  The container line item? No. (You'd need a container line item only if you were responsible for keeping track of the inventory in the store. See Wally's Warehouse for an example.)

Here's the result:

  – store–cashier, item, register, sale.

Register

It's time for another round.

  Apply assembly-part.

    The assembly is a register.
    The part is a cash drawer.

  Here's the result:

    – register–cash drawer.

Results, using aggregate patterns

Here are the results:

  – store–cashier, item, register
  – register–cash drawer.

Here's that part of the object model (Figure 6–2):

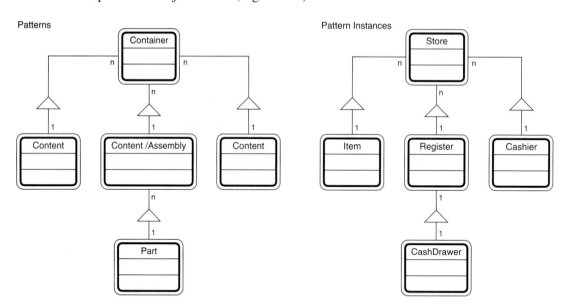

Figure 6–2: Selecting objects, using aggregate patterns as a guide.

Establish initial responsibilities, using transaction patterns as a guide

The players in a pattern have stereotypical responsibilities.

You can use those stereotypical responsibilities as a guide to establishing responsibilities.

How? Look at each stereotypical responsibility. If it applies this time, add it. If something similar applies this time, add it. Then consider the collection-worker aspect of the pattern, looking for responsibilities across the collection that might apply to the player you are working on.

The point: use stereotypical responsibilities as a guide in establishing the responsibilities within a specific instance of a pattern.

Back to Connie's. Using stereotypical responsibilities as a guide, add initial responsibilities to the model. Begin with the transaction patterns—and what you've discovered so far:

      – person-cashier-session-sale-payment
      – sale–sale line item–item.

Person-cashier-session-sale-payment
Person

The pattern player that corresponds to "person" is "actor" (Figure 6–3):

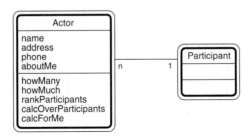

Figure 6–3: Actor, from actor-participant.

Establish initial responsibilities for person:

> What I know: name, address, phone.
> Who I know: cashier (participant).
> What I do: just the basics.

Add responsibilities (Figure 6–4):

Figure 6–4: Person, for Connie's.

Cashier

A pattern player may participate in more than one pattern. Such a pattern player has stereotypical responsibilities from each pattern it participates in.

For example, for participant-transaction and transaction-transaction line item, the transaction has stereotypical responsibilities from both patterns it participates in.

Again and again in the figures that follow, you'll see an overlapping pattern player, followed by its usage in a specific situation.

What about cashier? The pattern players that correspond to "cashier" are "participant" and "content" (Figure 6–5):

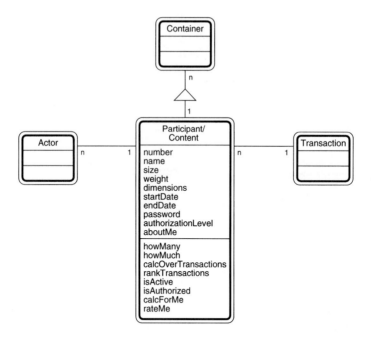

Figure 6–5: A combination of participant and content, from actor-participant AND from participant-transaction AND container-content.

Establish initial responsibilities for cashier:

> What I know: number, password, authorization level.
> Who I know: person (actor), session (transaction), store (container).
> What I do: how many over interval, how much over interval, is authorized, verify password.

Add responsibilities (Figure 6–6):

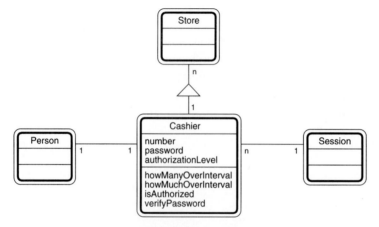

Figure 6–6: Cashier, for Connie's.

Session

The pattern player that corresponds to "session" is "transaction" (Figure 6–7):

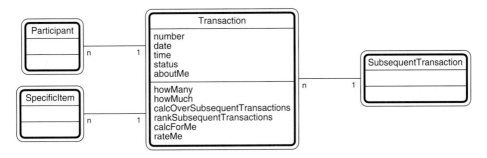

Figure 6–7: Transaction, from participant-transaction AND specific item–transaction AND transaction–subsequent transaction.

Establish initial responsibilities for session:

> What I know: start date, start time, end date, end time.
> Who I know: cashier (participant), register (specific item), sale (subsequent transaction).
> What I do: how many over interval, how much over interval.

Add responsibilities (Figure 6–8):

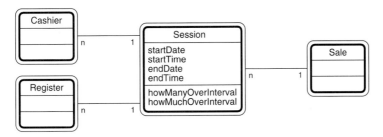

Figure 6–8: Session, for Connie's.

Sale

The pattern players that correspond to "sale" are "transaction" and "subsequent transaction" (Figure 6–9):

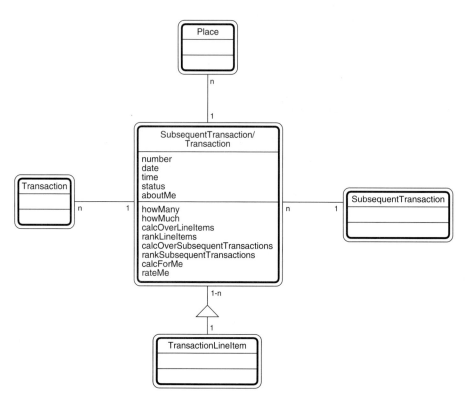

Figure 6–9: A combination of transaction and subsequent transaction, from transaction–transaction line item AND transaction–subsequent transaction AND place-transaction.

Establish initial responsibilities for sale:

What I know: date, time.

Who I know: sale line item (transaction line item), session (transaction), payment (a subsequent transaction), store (place).

What I do: how many over interval, how much over interval, calculate subtotal, calculate discount, calculate tax, calculate total.

Add responsibilities (Figure 6–10):

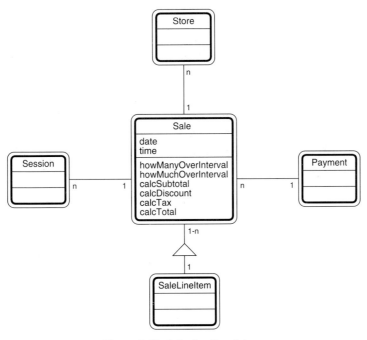

Figure 6–10: Sale, for Connie's.

Payment

The pattern player that corresponds to "payment" is "subsequent transaction" (Figure 6–11):

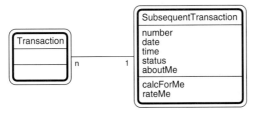

Figure 6–11: Subsequent transaction, from transaction–subsequent transaction.

Establish initial responsibilities for payment:

> What I know: amount.
> Who I know: sale (transaction).
> What I do: just the basics (one could use the "what I do" strategies, to develop this further).

Add responsibilities (Figure 6–12):

Figure 6–12: Payment, for Connie's.

Sale–sale line item–item

You've already taken care of sale. Now work on sale line item and item.

Sale line item

The pattern players that correspond to "sale line item" are "transaction line item" and "line item" (Figure 6–13):

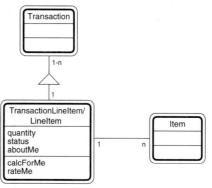

Figure 6–13: A combination of transaction line item and line item, from transaction–transaction line item AND item–line item.

Establish initial responsibilities for sale line item:

> What I know: quantity.
> Who I know: sale (transaction), item (item).
> What I do: how many over interval, how much over interval, calculate subtotal.

Add responsibilities (Figure 6–14):

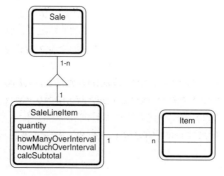

Figure 6–14: Sale line item, for Connie's.

Item

The pattern players that correspond to "item" are "content" and "item" (Figure 6–15):

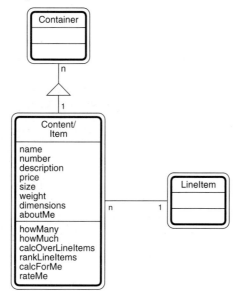

Figure 6–15: A combination of content and item, from item–line item AND container-content.

Establish initial responsibilities for item in this application:

> What I know: number, description, price.
> Who I know: sale line item (line item), store (container).
> What I do: how much for quantity.

Add responsibilities (Figure 6–16):

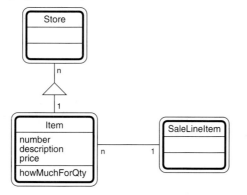

Figure 6–16: Item, for Connie's.

Note that item might have an attribute called price. Or, as you saw in Chapter 1, price could become a separate class in your model. The key? Apply a strategy: as soon as you see that an attribute value varies over time, and you need a record of those values, you know it's time to add another class to your model. The point? Patterns help you lay out an object model and its stereotypical responsibilities; strategies help you work out the details.

Establish initial responsibilities, using aggregate patterns as a guide

Using stereotypical responsibilities as a guide, add initial responsibilities to these pattern instances:

- store–cashier, item, register
- store-sale
- register–cash drawer.

Store–cashier, item, register

Store

The pattern players that correspond to "store" are "place" and "container" (Figure 6–17):

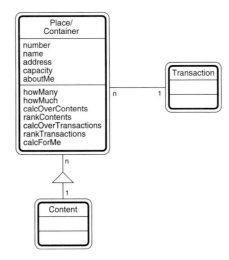

Figure 6–17: A combination of place and container, from place-transaction AND container-content.

Establish initial responsibilities for store:

> What I know: name.
>
> Who I know: cashier (content), item (content), register (content), sale (transaction).
>
> What I do: just the basics (use "what I do" strategies to develop this further).

Add responsibilities (Figure 6–18):

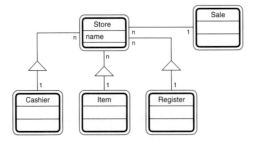

Figure 6–18: Store, for Connie's.

Cashier, item, register, sale

You have already taken care of these objects. There is nothing new to add, at this point. Onward!

Register-cash drawer
Register

The pattern players that correspond to "register" are "content," "assembly," and "specific item" (Figure 6–19):

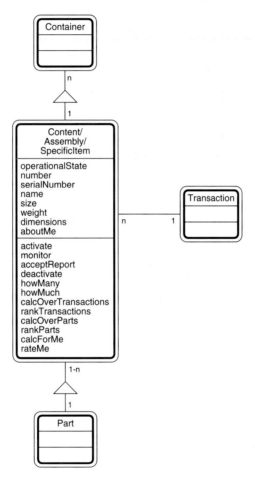

Figure 6–19: A combination of content, assembly, and specific item, from assembly-part AND container-content AND specific item–transaction.

Establish initial responsibilities:

> What I know: number.
>
> Who I know: cash drawer (part), store (container), session (transaction).
>
> What I do: how much over interval (you saw this earlier, because a register knows its corresponding sales).

Add responsibilities (Figure 6–20) for register:

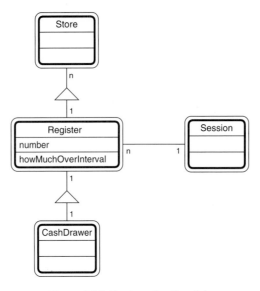

Figure 6–20: Register, for Connie's.

Cash Drawer

The pattern player that corresponds to "cash drawer" is "part" (Figure 6–21):

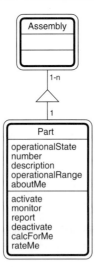

Figure 6–21: Part, from assembly-part.

Using the assembly-part pattern, establish initial responsibilities:

    What I know: operational state, position, balance.
    Who I know: register (assembly).
    What I do: open.

Add responsibilities (Figure 6–22) for cash drawer:

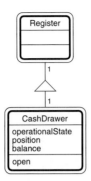

Figure 6–22: Cash drawer, for Connie's.

Progress so far

Patterns don't get you all the way there, it's true.

Yet patterns do provide templates for building better object models, including stereotypical responsibilities

Check it out (Figures 6-23 to 25).

In a word: awesome!

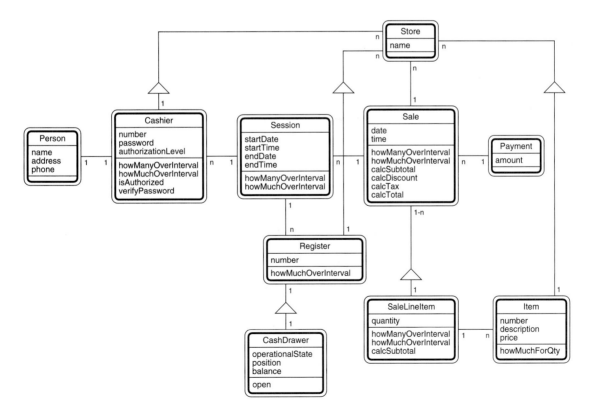

Figure 6–23: Connie's, all from patterns (Coad notation).

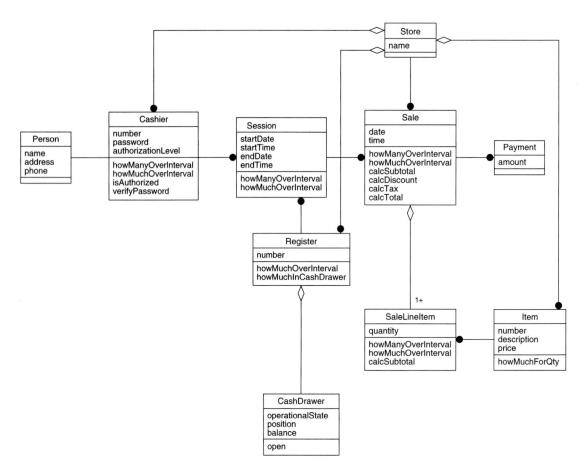

Figure 6–24: Connie's, all from patterns (OMT notation).

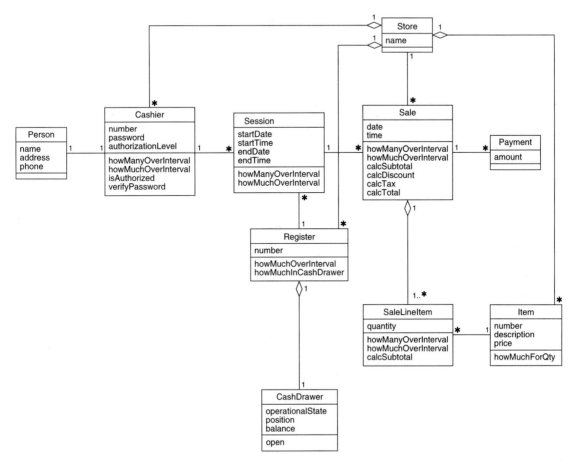

Figure 6–25: Connie's, all from patterns (Unified notation).

WALLY'S WAREHOUSE (A WAREHOUSE APPLICATION)

Select transaction objects and aggregate objects

Begin by selecting transactions and aggregates.

What are the transactions? The transaction objects are order and pick list.

What are the aggregates (containers, groups, assemblies)? The aggregate objects are warehouse, aisle, bin, and pallet—all containers.

So far, so good.

Select objects, using transaction patterns as a guide

Apply transaction patterns, using these two transactions: order and pick list.

Look for a pattern—or a combination of patterns—that might apply here.

Select players for these transaction patterns:

- participant-transaction
- place-transaction
- specific item–transaction

- transaction–transaction line item
- transaction–subsequent transaction

- actor-participant
- item–line item
- transaction line item–subsequent transaction line item
- associate–other associate.

Work on the transactions in time sequence, that is to say, in the order you would normally work with them. In this case, work on order, then pick list.

Order

Here you go.

Using the transaction patterns as a guide, select objects for your system.

Apply participant-transaction.

The participant is a customer.
The transaction is an order.

Apply specific item–transaction.

The specific item is a loading dock.
The transaction is an order.

Apply transaction–transaction line item.

The transaction is an order.
The transaction line item is an order line item.

Apply item–line item.

The item is an item.
The line item is an order line item.

Apply actor-participant.

The actor is an organization.
The participant is a customer.

Here's the result:

- organization–customer–order–order line item–item
- order–loading dock.

Pick list

Now consider pick, another transaction.

Using the transaction patterns as a guide, select objects for your system.

Apply transaction–transaction line item.

The transaction is a pick list.
The transaction line item is a pick list line item.

Apply item–line item.

The item is an item.
The line item is a pick list line item.

Apply transaction–subsequent transaction.

The transaction is an order.
The subsequent transaction is a pick list.

Apply transaction line item–subsequent transaction line item.

The transaction line item is an order line item.
The subsequent transaction line item is a pick list line item.

Here are the results:

– pick list–pick list line item–item
– order–pick list
– order line item–pick list line item.

Results, using transaction patterns

Here are the results:

– organization–customer–order–order line item–item
– loading dock–order
– pick list–pick list line item–item
– order–pick list
– order line item–pick list line item.

Check it out (Figure 6–26):

Patterns

Pattern Instances

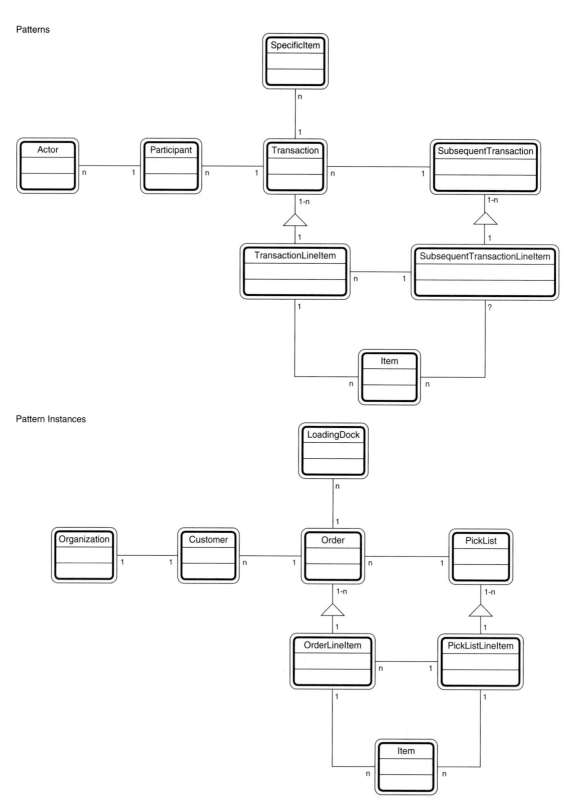

Figure 6–26: Selecting objects, using transaction patterns as a guide.

Select objects, using aggregate patterns as a guide

Apply aggregate patterns, using these containers: warehouse, aisle, bin, and pallet.

Select players for these aggregate patterns:

- container-content
- group-member
- assembly-part
- container–container line item.

Warehouse

Here you go again.

Using aggregate patterns (specifically, container patterns) as a guide, select objects for your system.

Apply container-content.

The container is a warehouse.
The content is a loading dock.

Apply container-content.

The container is a warehouse.
The content is an aisle.

Apply container-content.

The container is a warehouse.
The content is a pallet.

Here are the results:

- warehouse–loading dock
- warehouse-aisle
- warehouse-pallet.

Aisle

Here you go again.

Apply container-content.

The container is an aisle.
The content is a bin.

Here is the result:

- aisle-bin.

Bin

Here you go again.

A bin is the smallest container, in the sequence of warehouse to aisle to bin. For a container without subcontainers, apply container–container line item.

The container is a bin.
The container line item is a bin line item.

You've got some line items. Try using a transaction pattern, item–line item; it's a very likely combination.

> The item is an item.
> The line item is a bin line item.

Here is the result:

> – bin–bin line item–item.

Pallet

Here you go again.

A container without subcontainers is a pallet. One more time, apply container–container line item.

> The container is a pallet.
> The content is a pallet line item.

You've got some line items. Try using a transaction pattern, item–line item; it's a very likely combination.

> The item is an item.
> The line item is a pallet line item.

Here is the result:

> – pallet–pallet line item–item.

Results, using aggregate patterns

Here are the results:

> – warehouse–loading dock
> – warehouse–aisle–bin–bin line item–item
> – warehouse–pallet–pallet line item–item.

Check it out (Figure 6–27).

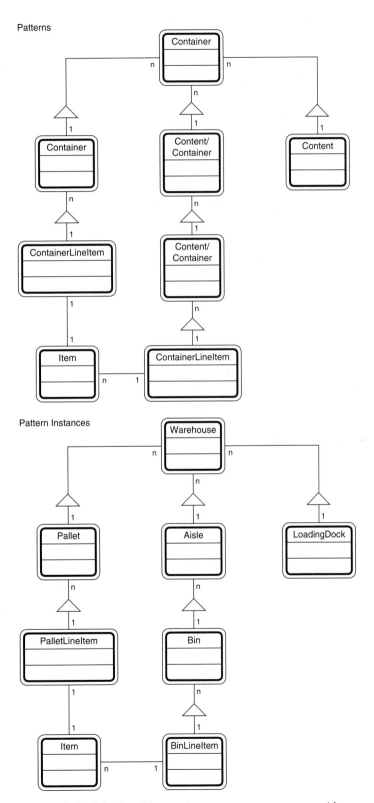

Figure 6–27: Selecting objects, using aggregate patterns as a guide.

Establish initial responsibilities, with transaction patterns

Using stereotypical responsibilities as a guide, add initial responsibilities to the model.

Begin with the transaction patterns—and the pattern instances you've already identified:

- organization–customer–order–order line item
- loading dock–order
- pick list–pick list line item–item
- order line item–pick list line item.

Organization–customer–order–order line item–item

Organization

The pattern player that corresponds to "organization" is "actor" (Figure 6–28):

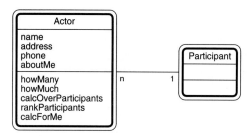

Figure 6–28: Actor, from actor-participant.

Establish initial responsibilities for organization:

What I know: name.
Who I know: customer (participant).
What I do: just the basics.

Add responsibilities (Figure 6–29):

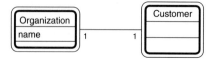

Figure 6–29: Organization, for Wally's.

Customer

The pattern player that corresponds to "customer" is "participant" (Figure 6–30):

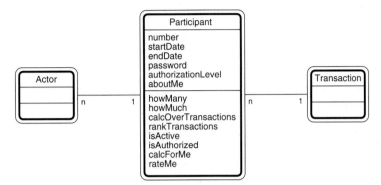

Figure 6–30: Participant, from actor-participant AND participant-transaction.

Establish initial responsibilities for customer:

What I know: number, address.
Who I know: organization (actor), order (transaction).
What I do: just the basics.

Add responsibilities (Figure 6–31):

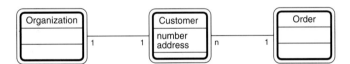

Figure 6–31: Customer, for Wally's.

Order

The pattern player for "order" is "transaction" (Figure 6–32):

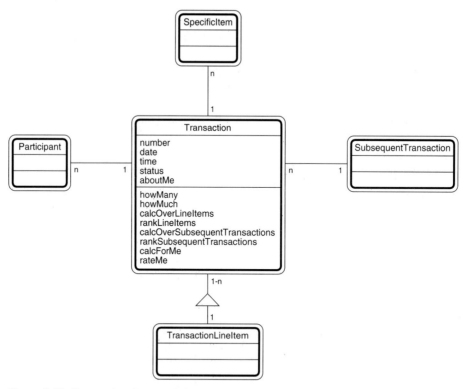

*Figure 6–32: Transaction, from participant-transaction AND specific item–transaction
AND transaction–transaction line item AND transaction–subsequent transaction.*

Establish initial responsibilities for transaction:

    What I know: number, shipping date, shipping address.
    Who I know: customer (participant), loading dock (specific item), order
        line item (transaction line item), pick list (subsequent transaction).
    What I do: build pick list.

Add responsibilities (Figure 6–33):

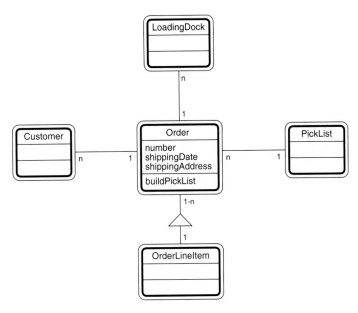

Figure 6–33: Order, for Wally's.

Order line item

The pattern players that correspond to "order line item" are "transaction line item" and "line item" (Figure 6–34):

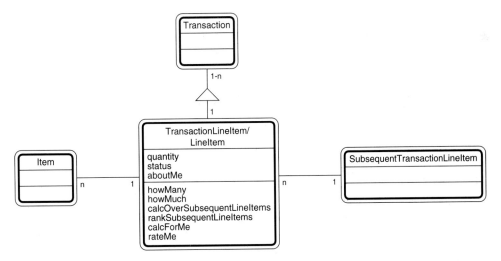

Figure 6–34: A combination of transaction line item and line item, from transaction–transaction line item AND item–line item AND transaction line item–subsequent transaction line item.

Establish initial responsibilities for order line item:

> What I know: quantity.
>
> Who I know: order (transaction), item (item), pick list line item (subsequent transaction line item).
>
> What I do: just the basics.

Add responsibilities (Figure 6–35):

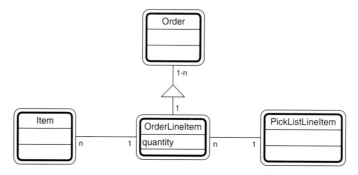

Figure 6–35: Order line item, for Wally's.

Item

The pattern player that corresponds to "item" is simply "item" (Figure 6–36):

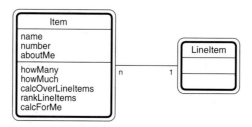

Figure 6–36: Item, from item–line item.

Establish initial responsibilities for item, in this application:

> What I know: number, description.
>
> Who I know: order line item (line item), pick list line item (line item), pallet line item (line item).
>
> What I do: the basics.

Add responsibilities (Figure 6–37):

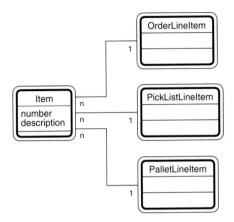

Figure 6–37: Item, for Wally's.

Loading dock-order
Loading dock

The pattern players that correspond to "loading dock" are "content" and "specific item" (Figure 6–38):

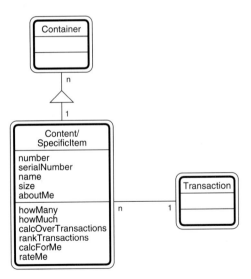

Figure 6–38: A combination of content and specific item, from specific item–transaction AND container-content.

Establish initial responsibilities for loading dock:

What I know: number.
Who I know: order (transaction), warehouse (container).
What I do: the basics.

Add responsibilities (Figure 6–39):

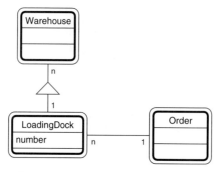

Figure 6–39: Loading dock, for Wally's.

Order

You've already taken care of this one.

Pick list–pick list line item–item
Pick list

The pattern players that correspond to "pick list" are "transaction" and "subsequent transaction" (Figure 6–40):

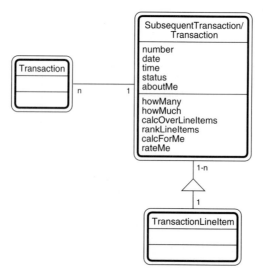

Figure 6–40: A combination of transaction and subsequent transaction, from transaction–transaction line item AND transaction–subsequent transaction.

Establish initial responsibilities for pick list:

> What I know: date.
> Who I know: order (transaction), pick list line item (transaction line item).
> What I do: the basics.

Add responsibilities (Figure 6–41):

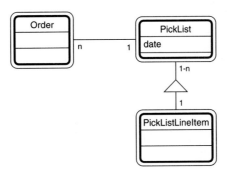

Figure 6–41: Pick list, for Wally's.

Pick list line item

The pattern players that correspond to "pick list line item" are "transaction line item," "subsequent transaction line item," and "line item." (Figure 6–42):

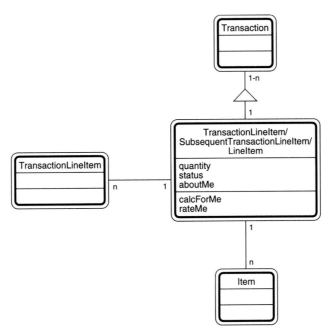

Figure 6–42: A combination of transaction line item, subsequent transaction line item, and line item, from transaction–transaction line item AND transaction line item–subsequent transaction line item AND item–line item.

Establish initial responsibilities for pick list line item:

　　What I know: quantity needed, quantity picked.
　　Who I know: pick list (transaction), order line item (line item), item (item).
　　What I do: the basics.

Add responsibilities (Figure 6–43):

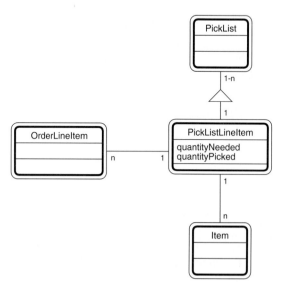

Figure 6–43: Pick list line item, for Wally's.

Item

You've already taken care of this one.

Order line item–pick list line item

You've already taken care of both of these.
　　That's it, for transaction patterns.

Establish initial responsibilities, with aggregate patterns

Using stereotypical responsibilities as a guide, add initial responsibilities to these pattern instances:

　　　　– warehouse–loading dock
　　　　– warehouse–aisle–bin–bin line item–item
　　　　– warehouse–pallet–pallet line item–item.

Warehouse–loading dock
Warehouse

The pattern player that corresponds to "warehouse" is "container" (Figure 6–44):

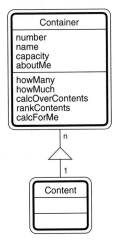

Figure 6–44: Container, from container-content.

Establish initial responsibilities for warehouse:

> What I know: name.
> Who I know: pallet (content), aisle (content), loading dock (content).
> What I do: find bin for pallet.

Add responsibilities (Figure 6–45):

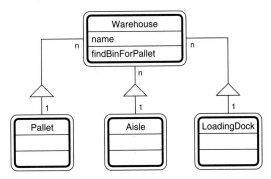

Figure 6–45: Warehouse, for Wally's.

Loading dock

You've already taken care of this one.

Warehouse–aisle–bin–bin line item–item
Aisle

The pattern players that correspond to "aisle" are a combination of "content" and "container" (Figure 6–46):

Figure 6–46: A combination of content and container, from container-content.

Establish initial responsibilities for aisle:

    What I know: number.
    Who I know: warehouse (container), bin (content).
    What I do: find bin for pallet.

Add responsibilities (Figure 6–47):

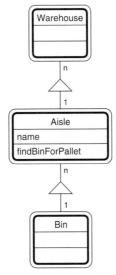

Figure 6–47: Aisle, for Wally's.

Bin

The pattern players that correspond to "bin" are "content" and "container" (Figure 6–48):

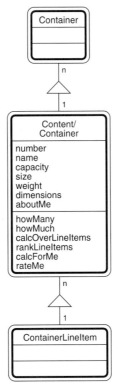

Figure 6–48: A combination of content and container, from container-content AND container–container line item.

Establish initial responsibilities for bin:

> What I know: number.
> Who I know: aisle (container), bin line item (container line item).
> What I do: is empty, is available for pallet.

Add responsibilities (Figure 6–49):

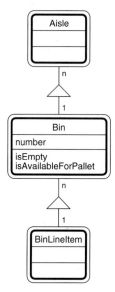

Figure 6–49: Bin, for Wally's.

Bin line item

The pattern players that corrrespond to "bin line item" are "container line item" and "line item" (Figure 6–50):

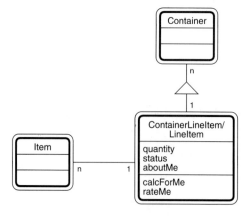

Figure 6–50: A combination of container line item and line item, from container–container line item AND item–line item.

Establish initial responsibilities for bin line item:

> What I know: quantity.
> Who I know: bin (container), item (item).
> What I do: decrement quantity.

Add responsibilities (Figure 6–51):

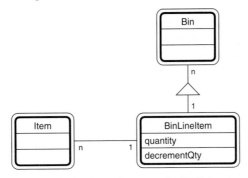

Figure 6–51: Bin line item, for Wally's.

Item

You've already taken care of this one.

Warehouse–pallet–pallet line item–item
Pallet

The pattern players that corrrespond to "pallet" are "content" and "container" (Figure 6–52):

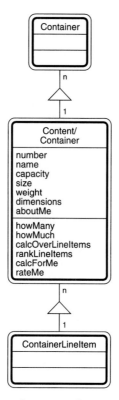

Figure 6–52: A combination of content and container, from container-content AND container–container line item.

Establish initial responsibilities for pallet:

What I know: number.
Who I know: warehouse (container), pallet line item (container line item).
What I do: the basics.

Add responsibilities (Figure 6–53):

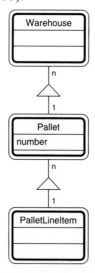

Figure 6–53: Pallet, for Wally's.

Pallet line item

The pattern players that correspond to "pattern line item" are "container line item" and "line item" (Figure 6–54):

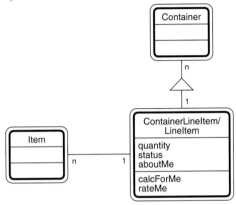

Figure 6–54: A combination of container line item and line item, from container–container line item AND item–line item.

Establish initial responsibilities to pallet line item:

> What I know: quantity
> Who I know: pallet (container), item (item).
> What I do: the basics.

Add responsibilities (Figure 6–55):

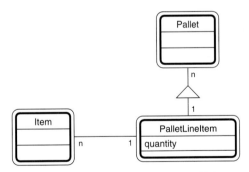

Figure 6–55: Pallet line item, for Wally's.

Progress so far

Patterns don't get you all the way there, it's true.

Yet patterns do provide templates for building better object models, including stereotypical responsibilities.

Check it out (Figures 6–56 to 58).

In a word: awesome!

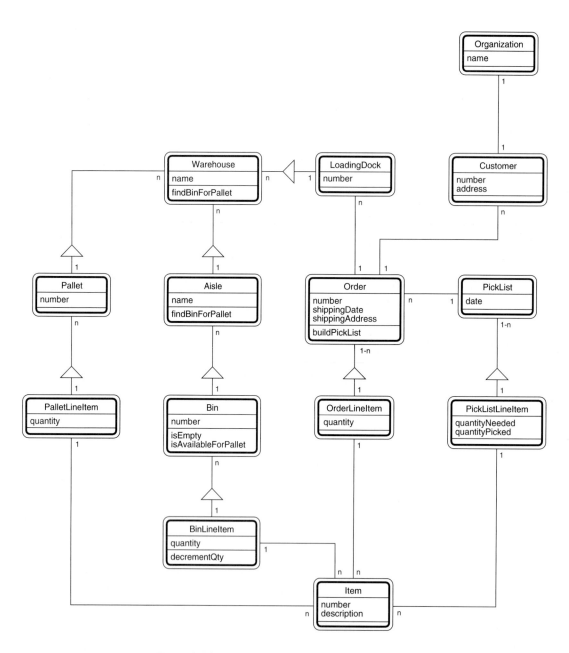

Figure 6–56: Wally's, all from patterns (Coad notation).

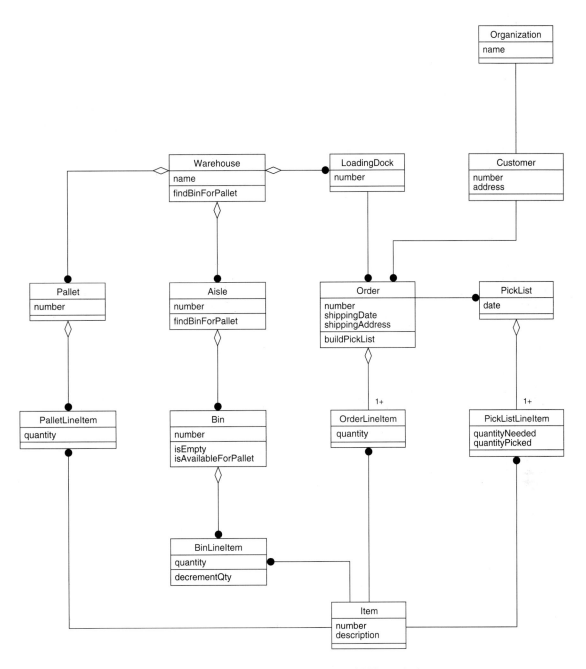

Figure 6–57: Wally's, all from patterns (OMT notation).

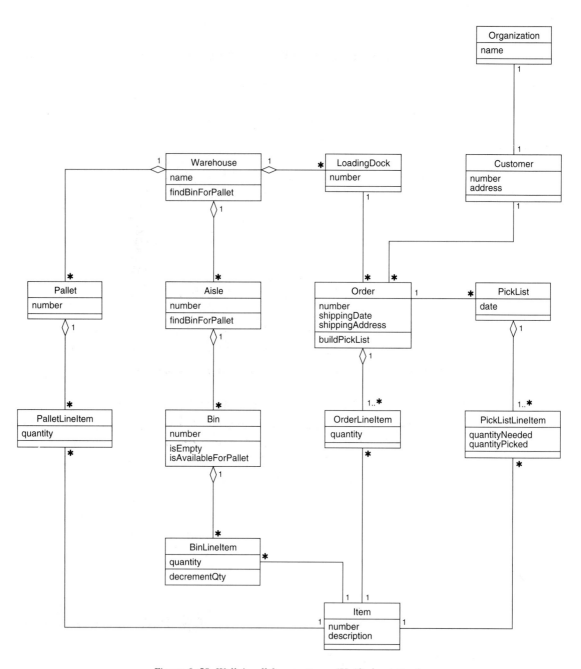

Figure 6–58: Wally's, all from patterns (Unified notation).

OLLIE'S ORDER CENTER (AN ORDER ENTRY APPLICATION)

Select transaction objects and aggregate objects

Begin by selecting transactions and aggregates.

What are the transactions? The transaction objects are order and shipment.

What are the aggregates (containers, groups, assemblies)? The aggregate objects are distributor (a group) and warehouse (a container).

So far, so good.

Select objects, using transaction patterns as a guide

Apply transaction patterns, using these two transactions: order and shipment.

Look for a pattern—or a combination of patterns—that might apply here.

Select players for these transaction patterns:

- participant-transaction
- place-transaction
- specific item–transaction

- transaction–transaction line item
- transaction–subsequent transaction

- actor-participant
- item–line item
- transaction line item–subsequent transaction line item
- associate–other associate.

Work on the transactions in time sequence, that is to say, in the order you would normally work with them. In this case, work on order, then shipment.

Order

Here you go.

Using the transaction patterns as a guide, select objects for your system.

Apply participant-transaction.

The participant is a customer.
The transaction is an order.

Apply participant-transaction.

The participant is a customer contact.
The transaction is an order.

Apply participant-transaction.

The participant is an order clerk.
The transaction is an order.

Apply specific item–transaction.

> The specific item is a warehouse.
> The transaction is an order.

Apply transaction–transaction line item.

> The transaction is an order.
> The transaction line item is an order line item.

Apply item–line item.

> The item is an item.
> The line item is an order line item.

Apply actor-participant.

> The actor is an organization.
> The participant is a customer.

Apply actor-participant.

> The actor is a person.
> The participant is a customer contact.

Apply actor-participant.

> The actor is a person.
> The participant is an order clerk.

Apply associate–other associate.

> The associate is a customer.
> The other associate is a customer contact.

Here are the results:

> – organization–customer–order–order line item–item
> – person–customer contact–order
> – person–order clerk–order
> – warehouse–order
> – customer–customer contact.

Shipment

Now consider shipment, another transaction.

> Using the transaction patterns as a guide, select objects for your system.
> Apply transaction–transaction line item.

>> The transaction is a shipment.
>> The transaction line item is a shipment line item.

Apply item–line item.

>The item is an item.
>The line item is a shipment line item.

Apply transaction–subsequent transaction.

>The transaction is an order.
>The subsequent transaction is a shipment.

Apply transaction line item–subsequent transaction line item.

>The transaction line item is an order line item.
>The subsequent transaction line item is a shipment line item.

Here are the results:

>– shipment–shipment line item–item
>– order-shipment
>– order line item–shipment line item.

Results, using transaction patterns

Here are the results:

>– organization–customer–order–order line item–item
>– organization–customer contact–order
>– person–order clerk–order
>– warehouse-order
>– customer–customer contact
>– shipment–shipment line item–item
>– order-shipment
>– order line item–shipment line item.

Check it out (Figure 6–59).

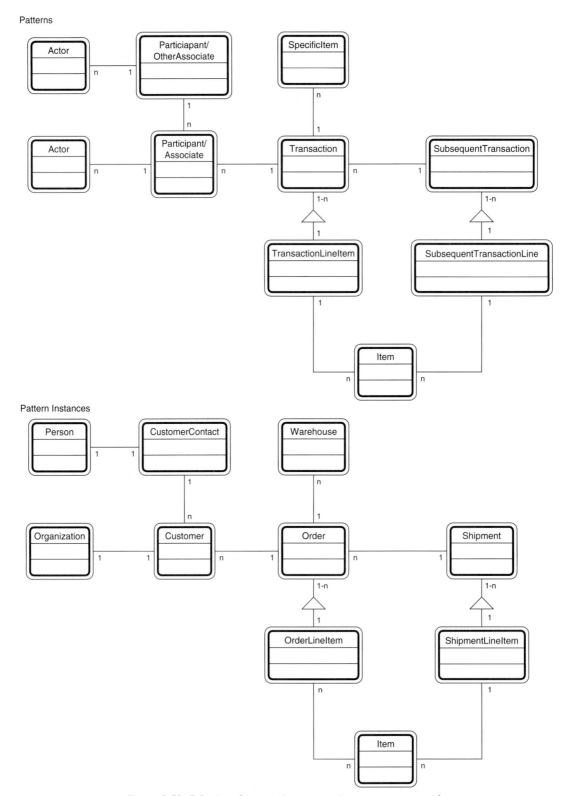

Figure 6–59: Selecting objects, using transaction patterns as a guide.

Select objects, using aggregate patterns as a guide

Apply aggregate patterns, using distributor (group) and warehouse (container).

Select players for these aggregate patterns:

- container-content
- group-member
- assembly-part
- container–container line item.

Distributor

Here you go again.

Using aggregate patterns as a guide, select objects for your system.

Apply group-member.

The group is a distributor.
The member is a warehouse.

Apply group-member.

The group is a distributor.
The member is a customer.

Apply group-member.

The group is a distributor.
The member is an order clerk.

Apply group-member.

The group is a distributor.
The member is an order.

Apply group-member.

The group is a distributor.
The member is an item.

Here is the result:

- distributor-warehouse
- distributor-customer
- distributor–order clerk
- distributor-order
- distributor-item.

Warehouse

Here you go again.

A warehouse is the smallest container in this problem domain. For a container without subcontainers, apply container–container line item.

The container is a warehouse.
The container line item is a warehouse line item.

You've got some line items. Try using a transaction pattern, item–line item; it's a very likely combination.

The item is an item.
The line item is a warehouse line item.

Here is the result:

– warehouse–warehouse line item–item.

Order Clerk

Now use actor-participant for the participant you found.

– person–order clerk

Results, using aggregate patterns

Here are the results:

– distributor-warehouse
– distributor-customer
– distributor–order clerk
– distributor-order
– distributor-item
– warehouse–warehouse line item–item
– person–order clerk.

Check it out (Figure 6–60).

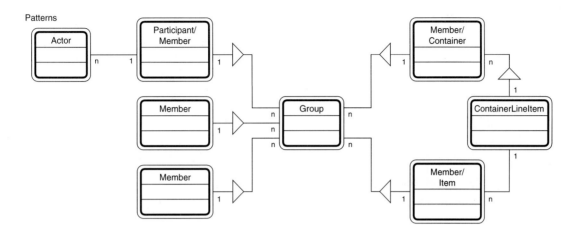

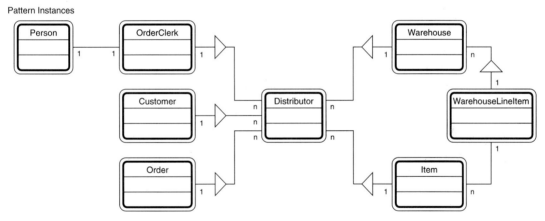

Figure 6–60: Selecting objects, using aggregate patterns as a guide.

Establish initial responsibilities, with transaction patterns

Using stereotypical responsibilities as a guide, add initial responsibilities to the model.

Begin with the transaction patterns—and the pattern instances you've already identified:

- organization–customer–order–order line item–item
- person–customer contact–order
- person–order clerk–order
- warehouse-order
- customer–customer contact
- shipment–shipment line item–item
- order-shipment
- order line item–shipment line item.

Organization–customer–order–order line item–item

This entire "pattern of patterns" instance occurred back at Wally's.

This should be a snap.

Organization

The pattern player that corresponds to "organization" is "actor" (Figure 6–61):

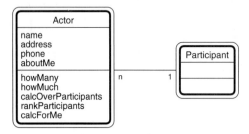

Figure 6–61: Actor, from actor-participant.

Establish initial responsibilities for organization:

What I know: name.

Who I know: customer (participant), distributor (participant).

What I do: just the basics.

Add responsibilities (Figure 6–62):

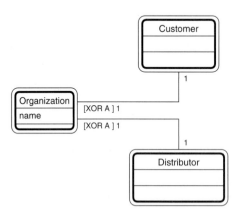

Figure 6–62: Organization, for Ollie's.

Customer

The pattern players that correspond to "customer" are "participant," "member," and "associate" (Figure 6–63):

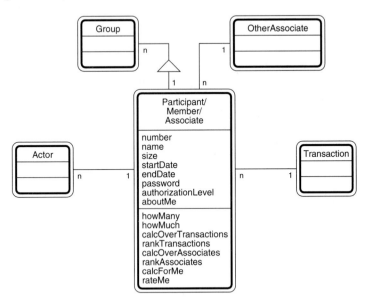

Figure 6–63: A combination of participant, member, and associate, from actor-participant AND participant-transaction AND group-member AND associate–other associate.

Establish initial responsibilities for customer:

> What I know: number, priority, credit rating.
> Who I know: organization (actor), order (transaction), distributor (group), customer contact (other associate).
> What I do: how many (orders) over interval, how much (money) over interval, is good for amount.

Add responsibilities (Figure 6–64):

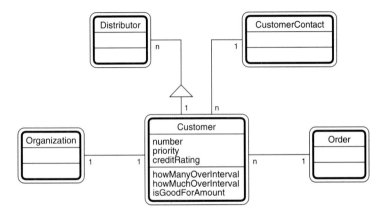

Figure 6–64: Customer, for Ollie's.

Order

The pattern players that correspond to "order" are "transaction" and "member" (Figure 6–65):

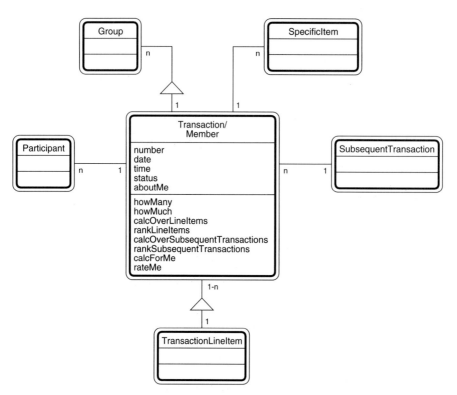

Figure 6–65: A combination of transaction and member, from participant-transaction AND specific item–transaction AND transaction–transaction line item AND transaction–subsequent transactionAND group-member.

Establish initial responsibilities for order:

> What I know: number, date, time, customer PO number.
>
> Who I know: customer (participant), customer contact (participant), order clerk (participant), warehouse (specific item), order line item (transaction line item), shipment (subsequent transaction), distributor (group).
>
> What I do: calculate subtotal, calculate tax, calculate total, is fulfilled.

Add responsibilities (Figure 6–66):

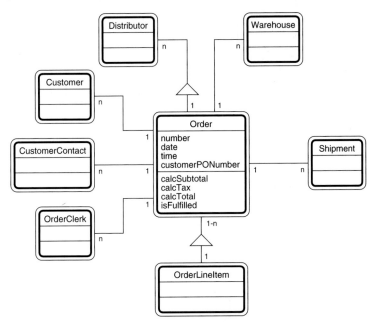

Figure 6–66: Order, for Ollie's.

Order line item

The pattern players that correspond to "order line item" are "transaction line item" and "line item" (Figure 6–67):

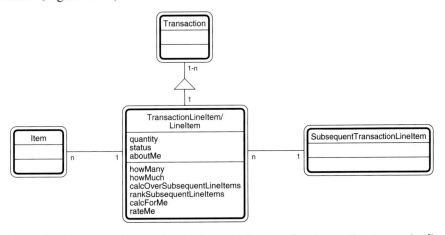

Figure 6–67: A combination of transaction line item and line item, from transaction–transaction line item AND item–line item AND transaction line item–subsequent transaction line item.

Establish initial responsibilities for order line item:

   What I know: quantity.
   Who I know: order (transaction), item (item), shipment line item (subse-
      quent transaction line item).
   What I do: is fulfilled.

Add responsibilities (Figure 6–68):

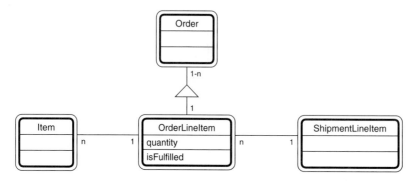

Figure 6–68: Order line item, for Ollie's.

Item

The pattern players that correspond to "item" are "member" and "item" (Figure 6–69):

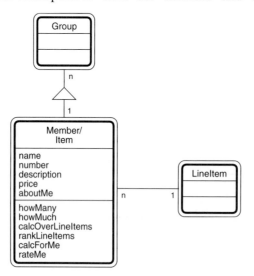

Figure 6–69: A combination of member and item, from item–line item AND group-member.

Establish initial responsibilities for item:

   What I know: number, description.
   Who I know: order line item (line item), shipment line item (line item),
      warehouse line item (line item), distributor (group).
   What I do: how much for quantity.

Add responsibilities (Figure 6–70):

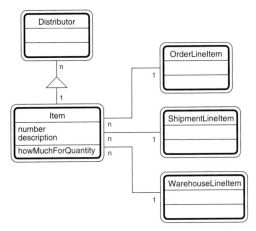

Figure 6–70: Item, for Ollie's.

Person–customer contact–order
Person

The pattern player that corresponds to "person" is "actor" (Figure 6–71):

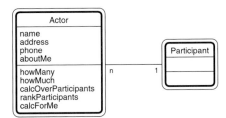

Figure 6–71: Actor, from actor-participant.

Establish initial responsibilities for person:

> What I know: name, address, phone.
> Who I know: customer contact (participant), order clerk (participant).
> What I do: just the basics.

Add responsibilities (Figure 6–72):

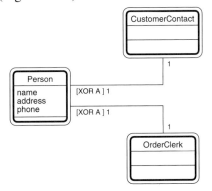

Figure 6–72: Person, for Ollie's.

Customer contact

The pattern players that correspond to "customer contact" are "participant" and "other associate" (Figure 6–73):

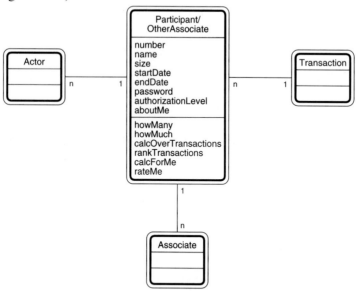

Figure 6–73: A combination of participant and other associate, from actor-participant AND participant-transaction AND associate–other associate.

Establish initial responsibilities for customer contact:

What I know: direct phone.
Who I know: person (actor), order (transaction), customer (associate).
What I do: how many over interval, how much over interval.

Add responsibilities (Figure 6–74):

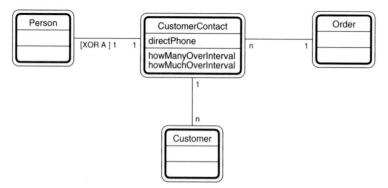

Figure 6–74: Customer contact, for Ollie's.

Order

You've already taken care of this one.

Person–order clerk–order
Person

You've already taken care of this one.

Order clerk

The pattern players that correspond to "order clerk" are "participant" and "member" (Figure 6–75):

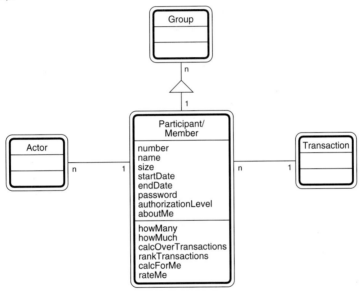

Figure 6–75: A combination of participant and member, from actor-participant AND participant-transaction AND group-member.

Establish initial responsibilities for order clerk:

> What I know: number.
>
> Who I know: person (actor), order (transaction), distributor (group).
>
> What I do: how many (sales) over interval, how much (money) over interval, assess performance over interval.

Add responsibilities (Figure 6–76):

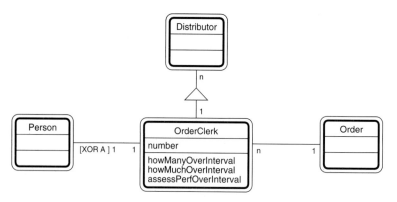

Figure 6–76: Order clerk, for Ollie's.

Order

You've already taken care of this one.

Warehouse-order
Warehouse

The pattern players that correspond to "warehouse" are "member," "specific item," and "container." (Figure 6–77):

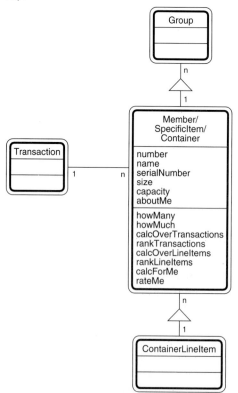

Figure 6–77: A combination of member, specific item, and container, from group-member AND specific item–transaction AND container–container line item.

Establish initial responsibilities for warehouse:

> What I know: name.
> Who I know: order (transaction), warehouse line item (container line item), distributor (group).
> What I do: how many (orders) over interval.

Add responsibilities (Figure 6–78):

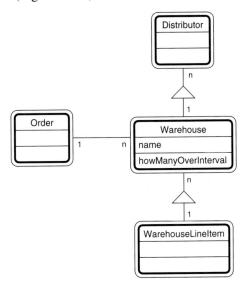

Figure 6–78: Warehouse, for Ollie's.

Order

You've already taken care of this one.

Customer–customer contact

You've already taken care of both of these.

Shipment–shipment line item–item
Shipment

The pattern player that corresponds to "shipment" is "subsequent transaction" (Figure 6–79):

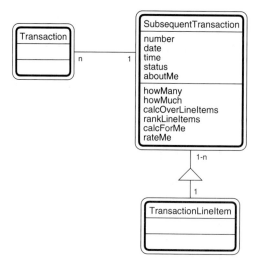

Figure 6–79: Subsequent transaction, from transaction–subsequent transaction
AND transaction–transaction line item.

Establish initial responsibilities for shipment:

> What I know: date.
> Who I know: order (transaction), shipment line item (transaction line item).
> What I do: the basics.

Add responsibilities (Figure 6–80):

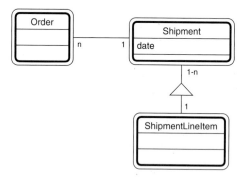

Figure 6–80. Shipment, for Ollie's.

Shipment line item

The pattern players that correspond to "shipment line item" are "subsequent transaction line item" and "line item" (Figure 6–81):

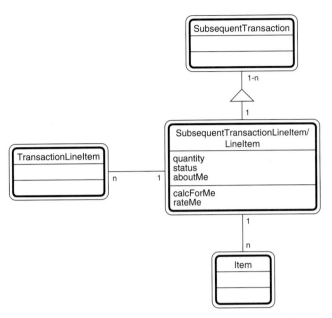

Figure 6–81: A combination of subsequent transaction line item and line item, from transaction–transaction line item AND transaction line item–subsequent transaction line item AND item–line item.

Establish initial responsibilities for shipment line item:

>What I know: quantity.
>Who I know: shipment (subsequent transaction), order line item (transaction line item), item (item).
>What I do: is fulfilled.

Add responsibilities (Figure 6–82):

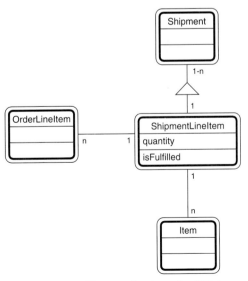

Figure 6–82: Shipment line item, for Ollie's.

Item

You've already taken care of this one.

Order-shipment

You've already taken care of both of these.

Order line item–shipment line item

You've already taken care of both of these.

Establish initial responsibilities, with aggregate patterns

Using stereotypical responsibilities as a guide, add initial responsibilities to these pattern instances:

> – distributor-warehouse
> – distributor-customer
> – distributor–order clerk
> – distributor-order
> – distributor-item
> – warehouse–warehouse line item–item.

Distributor-warehouse
Warehouse

You've already taken care of this one.

Distributor

The pattern player that corrresponds to "distributor" is "group" (Figure 6–83):

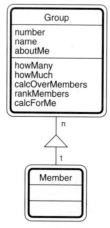

Figure 6–83: Group, from group-member.

Establish initial responsibilities for distributor:

What I know: name.

Who I know: order clerk (member), customer (member), warehouse (member), order (member), item (member).

What I do: how many (orders) over interval, how much (money) over interval.

Add responsibilities (Figure 6–84):

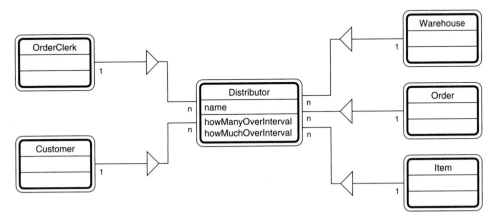

Figure 6–84: Distributor, for Ollie's.

Distributor-customer

You've already taken care of both of these.

Distributor–order clerk

You've already taken care of both of these.

Distributor-order

You've already taken care of both of these.

Distributor-item

You've already taken care of both of these.

Warehouse–warehouse line item–item
Warehouse

You've already taken care of this one.

Warehouse line item

The pattern players that correspond to "warehouse line item" are "container line item" and "line item" (Figure 6–85):

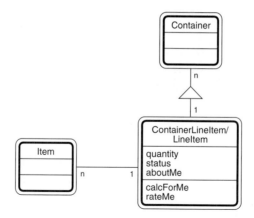

Figure 6–85: A combination of container line item and line item, from container–container line item AND item–line item.

Establish initial responsibilities for warehouse line item:

> What I know: quantity.
> Who I know: warehouse (container), item (item).
> What I do: the basics.

Add responsibilities (Figure 6–86):

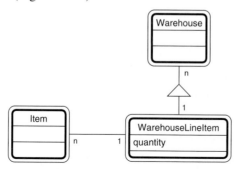

Figure 6–86: Warehouse line item, for Ollie's.

Item

You've already taken care of this one.

Progress so far

Patterns don't get you all the way there, it's true.

Yet patterns do provide templates for building better object models, including stereotypical responsibilities.

Check it out (Figures 6–87 to 89).

In a word: awesome!

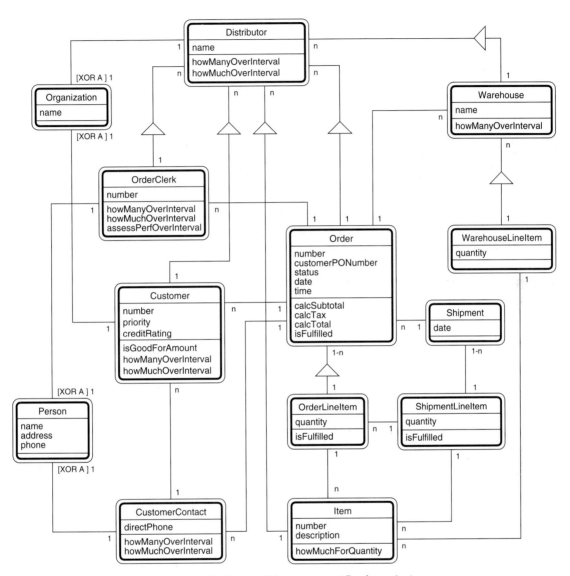

Figure 6–87: Ollie's, all from patterns (Coad notation).

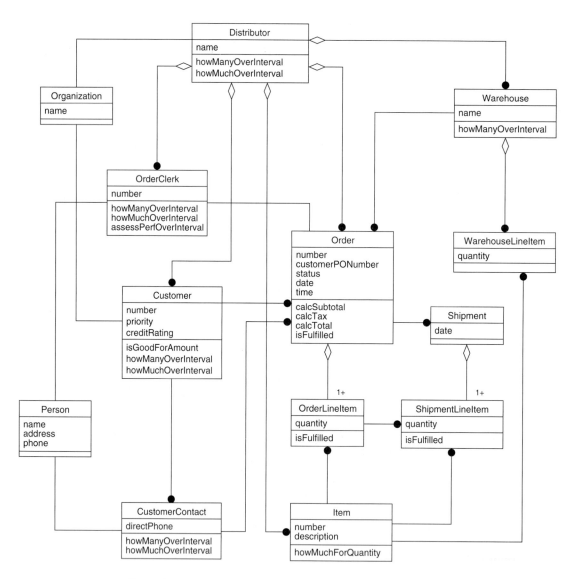

Figure 6–88: Ollie's, all from patterns (OMT notation).

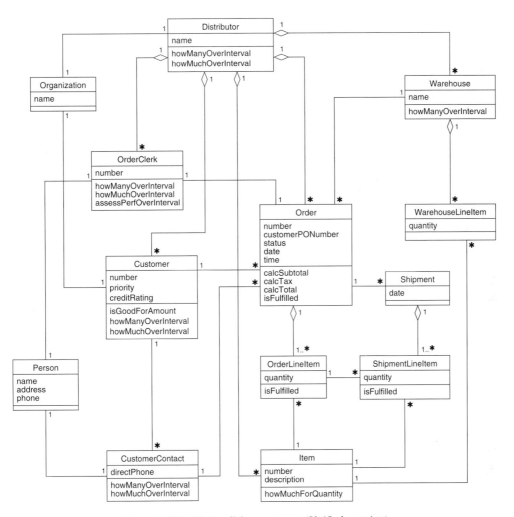

Figure 6–89: Ollie's, all from patterns (Unified notation).

DANI'S DIVERTERS (A SOFT REAL-TIME APPLICATION)

Select device objects, aggregate objects, and transaction objects

Data acquisition and control? Follow this path: devices, then aggregates, then transactions.

What are the devices? The device objects are conveyor motor and scanning diverter.

What are the aggregates (containers, groups, assemblies)? The aggregate object is conveyor (an assembly).

What are the transactions? The transaction object is an order object.

So far, so good.

Select objects, using aggregate patterns as a guide

Apply aggregate patterns.

Select players for these aggregate patterns:

– container-content
– group-member
– assembly-part
– container–container line item.

Conveyor

Here you go again.

Using aggregate patterns as a guide, select objects for your system.
Apply assembly-part.

The assembly is a conveyor.
The part is a conveyor motor.

Apply assembly-part.

The assembly is a conveyor.
The part is a scanning diverter.

Results, using aggregate patterns

Here are the results:

– conveyor–conveyor motor
– conveyor–scanning diverter.

Check it out (Figure 6–90):

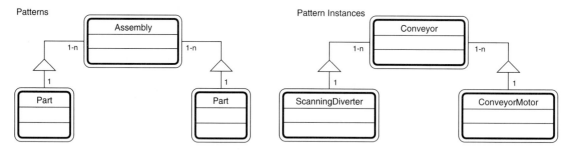

Figure 6–90: Selecting objects, using aggregate patterns as a guide.

Select objects, using transaction patterns as a guide

Apply transaction patterns, using this transaction: order.

Look for a pattern—or a combination of patterns—that might apply here.
Select players for these transaction patterns:

– participant-transaction
– place-transaction
– specific item–transaction

– transaction–transaction line item
– transaction–subsequent transaction

– actor-participant

– item–line item
– transaction line item–subsequent transaction line item
– associate–other associate.

The only transaction object is an order.

For this system an order has no participants, line items, subsequent transactions.

Looking down the list, the only pattern that might apply is associate–other associate. Go for it.

Apply associate–other associate.

> The associate is an order.
> The other associate is a tote.

Apply associate–other associate.

> The associate is a loading dock.
> The other associate is an order.

Again, apply associate–other associate.

> The associate is a scanning diverter.
> The other associate is a loading dock.

Results, using transaction patterns

Here are the results:

> – order-tote.
> – loading dock–order
> – scanning diverter–loading dock.

Check it out (Figure 6–91):

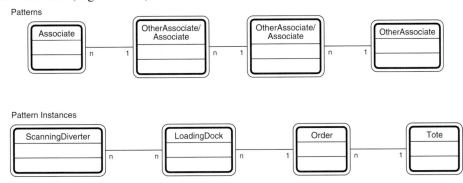

Figure 6–91: Selecting objects, using transaction patterns as a guide.

In some pattern instances, an "other associate" may need to know some number of associates (rather than just one associate, which is the more common case). That's the case for a loading dock and its corresponding scanning diverters.

Establish initial responsibilities, with aggregate patterns

Using stereotypical responsibilities as a guide, add initial responsibilities to the model:

> – conveyor–conveyor motor
> – conveyor–scanning diverter.

Conveyor-conveyor motor
Conveyor

The pattern player that corresponds to "conveyor" is "assembly" (Figure 6–92):

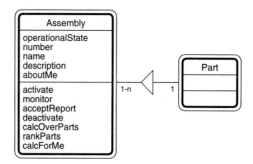

Figure 6–92: Assembly, from assembly-part.

Establish initial responsibilities for conveyor:

What I know: operational state, number.
Who I know: conveyor motor (part), scanning diverter (part).
What I do: activate, monitor, deactivate.

Add responsibilities (Figure 6–93):

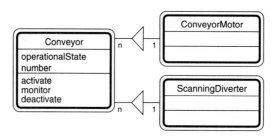

Figure 6–93: Conveyor, for Dani's.

Conveyor motor

The pattern player that corresponds to "conveyor motor" is "part" (Figure 6–94):

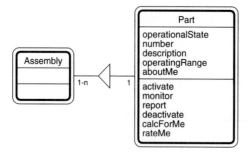

Figure 6–94: Part, from assembly-part.

Establish initial responsibilities for conveyor:

> What I know: operational state, number.
> Who I know: conveyor (assembly).
> What I do: activate, monitor, deactivate.

Add responsibilities (Figure 6–95):

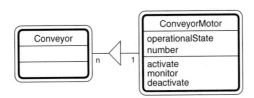

Figure 6–95: Conveyor motor, for Dani's.

Conveyor–scanning diverter
Conveyor

You've already taken care of this one.

Scanning diverter

The pattern players that correspond to "scanning diverter" are "part" and "associate" (Figure 6–96):

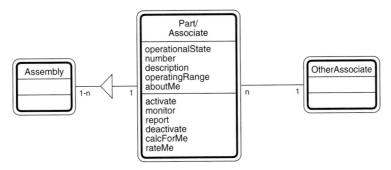

Figure 6–96: Part, from assembly-part.

Establish initial responsibilities for scanning diverter:

> What I know: operational state, number.
> Who I know: conveyor (assembly), loading dock (other associate).
> What I do: activate, monitor, deactivate.

Add responsibilities (Figure 6–97):

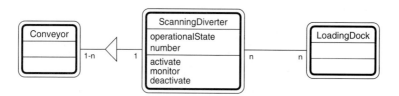

Figure 6–97: Scanning diverter, for Dani's.

Establish initial responsibilities, with transaction patterns

Using stereotypical responsibilities as a guide, add initial responsibilities to these pattern instances:

  – scanning diverter–loading dock
  – loading dock–order
  – order-tote.

These are all instances of the associate–other associate pattern.(Figure 6–98):

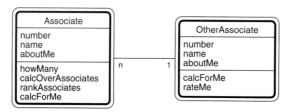

Figure 6–98: Associate–other associate.

Consider the pattern instances, one-by-one.

Scanning diverter–loading dock
Scanning diverter

You've already taken care of this one.

Loading dock

Establish initial responsibilities for loading dock:

  What I know: number.
  Who I know: scanning diverter (associate), order (other associate).
  What I do: want this tote.

Add responsibilities (Figure 6–99):

Figure 6–99: Loading dock, for Dani's.

Loading dock–order
Loading dock

You've already taken care of this one.

Order

Establish initial responsibilities for order:

> What I know: number.
> Who I know: loading dock (associate), tote (other associate).
> What I do: include this tote.

Add responsibilities (Figure 6–100):

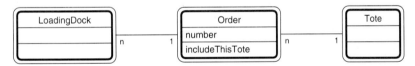

Figure 6–100. Order, for Dani's.

Order-tote
Order

You've already taken care of this one.

Tote

Establish initial responsibilities for tote:

> What I know: number.
> Who I know: order (associate).
> What I do: match number.

Add responsibilities (Figure 6–101):

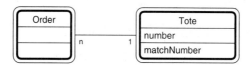

Figure 6–101. Tote, for Dani's.

Progress so far

Patterns don't get you all the way there, it's true.

Yet patterns do provide templates for building better object models, including stereotypical responsibilities.

Check it out (Figures 6–102 to 104).

In a word: awesome!

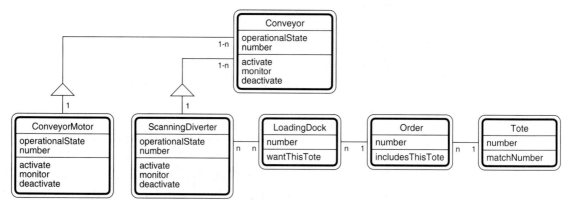

Figure 6–102: Dani's, all from patterns (Coad notation).

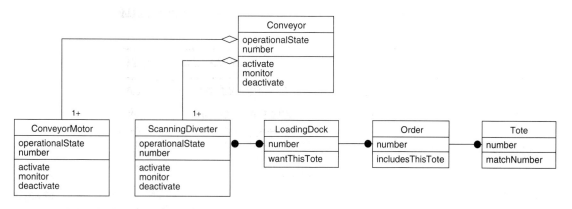

Figure 6–103: Dani's, all from patterns (OMT notation).

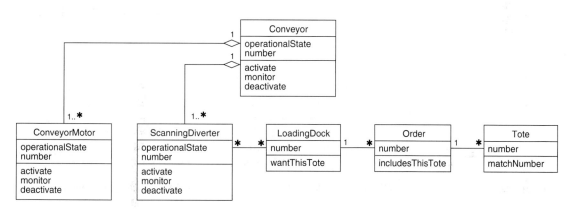

Figure 6–104: Dani's, all from patterns (Unified notation).

ANDI'S AUTOPILOT (A HARD REAL-TIME APPLICATION)

Select device objects, aggregate objects, and transaction objects

Data acquisition and control? Follow this path: devices, then aggregates, then transactions.

What are the devices? The control devices and their corresponding data-acquisition devices are:

control device	data-acquisition devices
elevator	altimeter (altitude sensor), vertical speed gyro, attitude gyro
ailerons	directional gyro, attitude gyro
rudder	directional gyro.

What are the aggregates (containers, groups, assemblies)? The aggregate object is aircraft (assembly).

What are the transactions? None, this time. Yet you may find some use for associate–other associate, along the way.

So far, so good.

Select objects, using aggregate patterns as a guide

Apply aggregate patterns.

Select players for these aggregate patterns:

- container-content
- group-member
- assembly-part
- container–container line item.

Airplane

Here you go again.

Using aggregate patterns as a guide, select objects for your system.

Apply assembly-part.

The assembly is an airplane.

The parts are its ailerons, elevators, and rudder.

By naming a class "ailerons," you indicate that each object in the class corresponds to ailerons (more than one). The same is true with "elevators."

Results, using aggregate patterns

Here is the result:

- airplane–ailerons, elevators, rudder.

Add objects to your model (Figure 6–105):

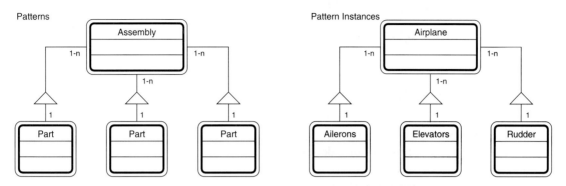

Figure 6–105: Selecting objects, using aggregate patterns as a guide.

Select objects, using transaction patterns as a guide

Apply transaction patterns.

> Mainly, see what you can do with associate–other associate.

Airplane

Here you go again.

> Using associate–other associate as a guide, select objects for your system.
> Apply associate–other associate.

>> The associate is the ailerons object.
>> The other associates are a directional gyro and attitude gyro.

> Apply associate–other associate.

>> The associate is the elevators object.
>> The other associates are an altimeter, a vertical speed gyro, and an attitude gyro.

> Again, apply associate–other associate.

>> The associate is the rudder object.
>> The other associate is a directional gyro.

Results, using transaction patterns

Here are the results:

> – ailerons–directional gyro, attitude gyro
> – elevators–altimeter, vertical speed gyro, attitude gyro
> – rudder–directional gyro.

> Add objects to your model (Figure 6–106):

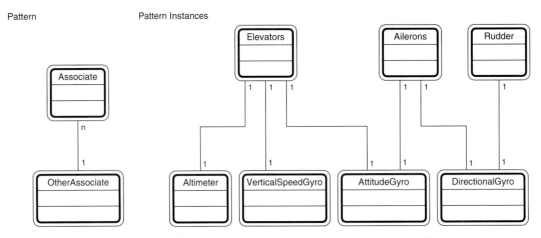

Figure 6–106: Selecting objects, using transaction patterns as a guide.

Establish initial responsibilities, with aggregate patterns

Using stereotypical responsibilities as a guide, add initial responsibilities to these pattern instances:

> – airplane–ailerons, elevators, rudder.

Airplane–ailerons, elevators, rudder
Airplane

The pattern player that corresponds to "airplane" is "assembly" (Figure 6–107):

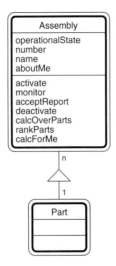

Figure 6–107: Assembly, from assembly-part.

Establish initial responsibilities for airplane:

> What I know: operational state.
> Who I know: elevators (part), ailerons (part), rudder (part).
> What I do: activate autopilot, monitor autopilot, deactivate autopilot.

Add responsibilities (Figure 6–108):

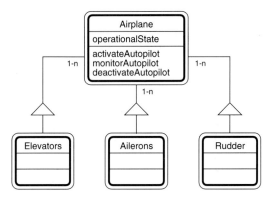

Figure 6–108: Airplane, for Andi's.

Ailerons

The pattern players that correspond to "ailerons" are "part" and "associate" (Figure 6–109):

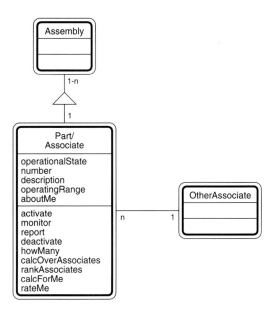

Figure 6–109: A combination of part and associate, from assembly-part AND associate–other associate.

Establish initial responsibilities for ailerons:

> What I know: operational state.
> Who I know: airplane (assembly), directional gyro (other associate), attitude gyro (other associate).

What I do: activate maintain heading, maintain heading, deactivate maintain heading.

Add responsibilities (Figure 6–110):

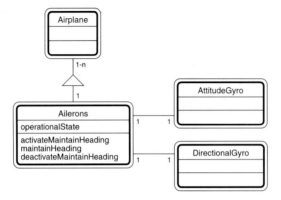

Figure 6–110: Ailerons, for Andi's.

Elevators

The pattern players that correspond to "elevators" are the same as before—"part" and "other associate" (Figure 6–109).

Establish initial responsibilities for elevators:

What I know: operational state.

Who I know: airplane (assembly), altimeter (other associate), vertical speed gyro (other associate), attitude gyro (other associate).

What I do: activate maintain altitude, maintain altitude, deactivate maintain altitude.

Add responsibilities (Figure 6–111):

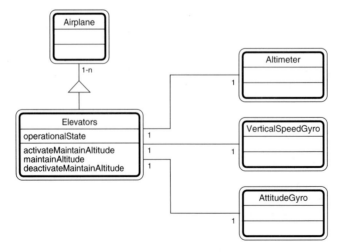

Figure 6–111: Elevators, for Andi's.

Rudder

The pattern players that correspond to "rudder" are the same as before—"part" and "other associate" (Figure 6–109).

Establish initial responsibilities for rudder:

What I know: operational state.
Who I know: airplane (assembly), directional gyro (associate).
What I do: activate maintain heading, maintain heading, deactivate maintain heading.

Add responsibilities (Figure 6–112):

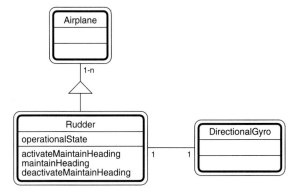

Figure 6–112: Elevators, for Andi's.

Establish initial responsibilities, with transaction patterns

Using stereotypical responsibilities as a guide, add initial responsibilities to these pattern instances:

– ailerons–directional gyro, attitude gyro
– elevators–altimeter, vertical-speed gyro, attitude gyro
– rudder–directional gyro.

They are all instances of the associate–other associate pattern (Figure 6-113):

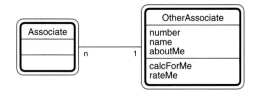

Figure 6–113: Other associate, from associate–other associate.

Ailerons–directional gyro, attitude gyro
Ailerons

You've already taken care of this one.

Directional gyro

Establish initial responsibilities for directional gyro:

What I know: operational state.

Who I know: ailerons (associate), rudder (associate).

What I do: activate heading deviation monitoring, monitor heading deviation, deactivate heading deviation monitoring.

Add responsibilities (Figure 6–114):

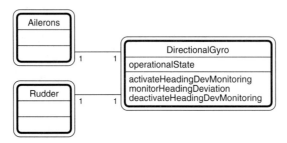

Figure 6–114: Directional gyro, for Andi's.

Attitude gyro

Establish initial responsibilities for attitude gyro:

What I know: operational state.

Who I know: ailerons (associate), elevators (associate).

What I do: activate roll angle monitoring, monitor roll angle, deactivate roll angle monitoring; activate pitch angle monitoring, monitor pitch angle, deactivate pitch angle monitoring.

Add responsibilities (Figure 6–115):

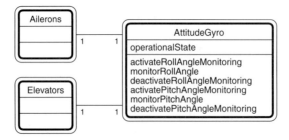

Figure 6–115: Atitude gyro, for Andi's.

Elevators–altimeter, vertical-speed gyro, attitude gyro
Elevators

You've already taken care of this one.

Altimeter

Establish initial responsibilities for altimeter:

> What I know: operational state.
> Who I know: elevators (associate).
> What I do: activate altitude deviation monitoring, monitor altitude deviation, deactivate altitude deviation monitoring.

Add responsibilities (Figure 6–116):

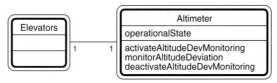

Figure 6–116: Altimeter, for Andi's.

Vertical-speed gyro

Establish initial responsibilities for vertical-speed gyro:

> What I know: operational state.
> Who I know: elevators (associate).
> What I do: activate altitude change rate monitoring, monitor altitude change, deactivate altitude change rate monitoring.

Add responsibilities (Figure 6–117):

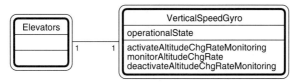

Figure 6–117: Vertical-speed gyro, for Andi's.

Attitude gyro

You've already taken care of this one.

Rudder–directional gyro

You've already taken care of these two.

Progress so far

Patterns don't get you all the way there, it's true.

Yet patterns do provide templates for building better object models, including stereotypical responsibilities.

Check it out (Figures 6–118 to 120).

In a word: awesome!

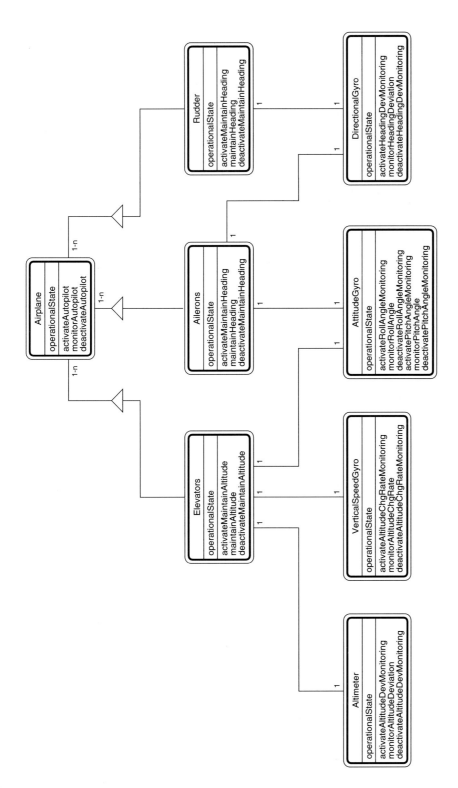

Figure 6–118: Andi's, all from patterns (Coad notation).

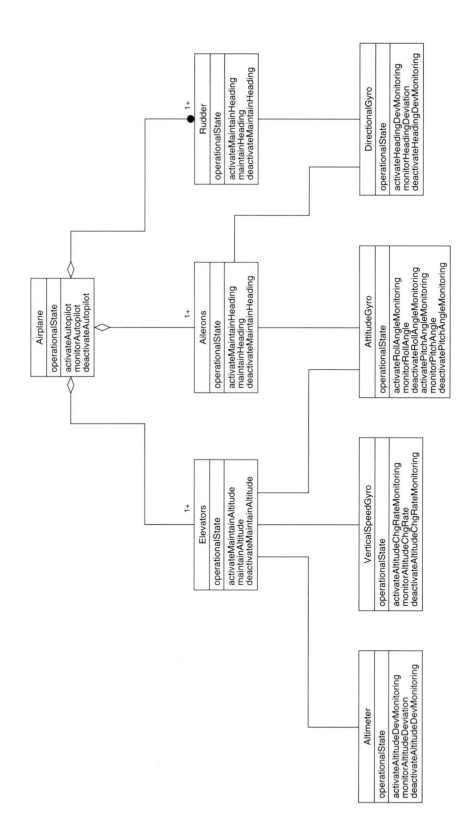

Figure 6–119: Andi's, all from patterns (OMT notation).

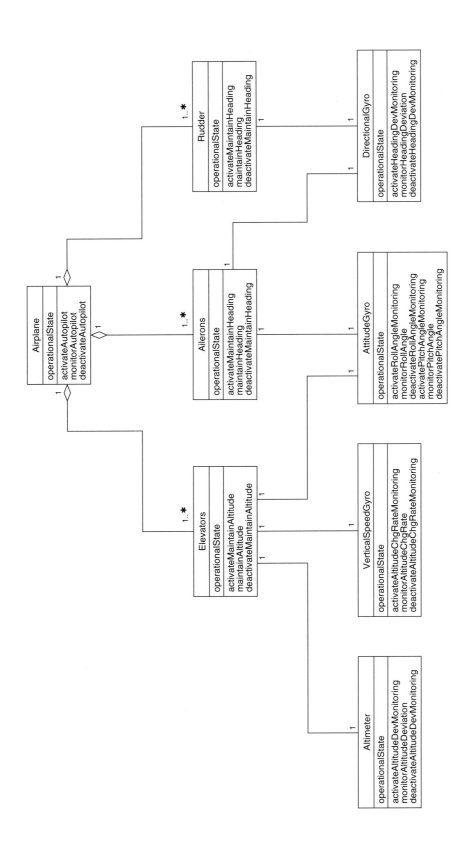

Figure 6—120: Andi's, all from patterns (Unified notation).

379

WRAP-UP

You did it! You built initial object models for five applications—at high speed.

It's important! You see, strategies come first; it takes talent, time, and practice to learn a new skill. Patterns come later. Patterns embody a right-brain summary and context for so many of the left-brain strategies. In any field of human endeavor, at the world-class level, people work intuitively, using patterns.

That's why strategies and patterns are so important.

That's why this chapter is so important: so you can experience and gain some insights as to what it's like to build object models with patterns, intuitively, at the world-class level.

Excellent!

CONGRATULATIONS!

Congratulations on working through all six application chapters. Way to go!

You've applied strategies and patterns again and again, in a variety of problem domains.

The next chapter is a strategy and patterns summary. You'll find all of the strategies and patterns from the application chapters, as well as some new ones, to help out along the way.

Enjoy!

7

Strategies and Patterns Handbook

While the preface discusses the definition of both "strategy" and "pattern," this chapter presents a handbook of strategies and patterns, ready-to-apply practical advice for building effective object models. These strategies and patterns span these major categories:

- Strategies for building object models
  - Activities and components
  - Identifying system purpose and features
  - Selecting objects
  - Establishing responsibilities
  - Working out dynamics with scenarios
  - Discovering new strategies and patterns
- Patterns for building object models
  - Fundamental pattern
  - Transaction patterns
  - Aggregate patterns
  - Plan patterns
  - Interaction patterns.

This is a practical, how-to guide for building better objects models. It features 177 strategies and 31 patterns. Each strategy is a nugget of how-to advice. Each pattern is a template you can use for snapping together an overall object model.

This handbook now includes 29 new strategies, above and beyond those included in the first printings of this book. You can recognize a new strategy by its number: new strategy numbers have an alpha suffix (for example, strategy 80a).

To download the most recent hypertext version of this handbook, visit http://www.oi.com. On CompuServe: GO CASE, file stpthlp.zip.

STRATEGIES FOR BUILDING OBJECT MODELS

A strategy is a plan of action intended to accomplish a specific objective. This major section presents strategies. It begins with an overall strategy.

- Guiding the effort with major activities and components.

Next, it presents the four major activities of building effective object models:

- Identifying system purpose and features
- Selecting objects
- Establishing responsibilities
- Working out dynamics with scenarios.

Finally, it presents some discovery strategies:

- Discovering new strategies and patterns.

Please note that strategies are presented in single-border boxes (patterns are presented in double-border boxes).

Guiding the effort with major activities and components

When building object models, what's a reasonable path to take?

You can approach object models using one or a combination of suggested paths.

Each path consists of activities, not steps.

An activity is something you can do at any time, whenever it makes technical or sociological sense to do so.

In contrast, a step is something you must do and must follow, in a prescribed sequence. (May God help you if you think about something before it's time to do the corresponding step. Step advocates love to see others go marching down the hallways, just like the tower guards in the *Wizard of Oz*, crying "Oh-ee-oh. Yo—ho.")

The purpose of these strategies is to present some common paths, reasonable ways of organizing your activities.

Please recognize that with objects, using one model from concept to code, you should plan, schedule, and deliver frequent, tangible, working results. Indeed, all milestones should be based upon frequent, tangible, working results, not merely the completion of an activity (or step—yuck).

#1. "Four Major Activities, Four Major Components" Strategy   major activities and components

- Organize your work around four major activities, within four major components:

- Four major activities:

   Standard: Identify purpose and features, select objects, establish responsibilities, work out dynamics with scenarios.

   Variation 1: You may find it helpful to focus on working out dynamics with scenarios, establishing responsibilities along the way. This is especially suitable for real-time applications.

   Variation 2: You may find it helpful to select transaction, aggregate, and plan objects, then use the corresponding patterns to guide you through selecting additional objects, establishing responsibilities, and working out dynamics with scenarios.

- Four major components:

   Standard: Problem domain, human interaction, data management, system interaction.

   Variation 1: You may find it helpful to begin with human interaction, followed by problem domain, data management, and system interaction. This is especially suitable when your domain experts want to talk in terms of human interaction from the very start.

   Variation 2: You may find it helpful to begin with problem domain and system interaction, followed by human interaction and data management. This is especially suitable for real-time applications, when your domain experts are keenly interested in the data acquisition and control aspects of the system under consideration.

#1a. "Build an Initial Object Model, then Proceed
    Feature-by-Feature" Strategy   activities and model components

---

- Here is a very helpful path for building object models.

- Identify purpose and features.

    Purpose statement. Prioritized list of features.

- Build an initial object model, working with domain experts.

    Select initial objects (using strategies; include participants, transactions, places, items, specific items).

    Establish initial responsibilities (using strategy #86 and the stereotypical responsibilities expressed by object-model patterns).

- Work out dynamics with scenarios, feature-by-feature.

    a. Develop a scenario view for the feature.

    b. Add objects and responsibilities that you need for the scenario.

#1b. "Use Feature Milestones" Strategy   activities and model components

---

- Use your prioritized features list to plan, build, and measure.

- Early in the development effort, use your prioritized features list day-by-day, while developing an initial object model and scenario views (one scenario view for each feature).

- For the rest of the development effort, use your prioritized features list to plan, build, and measure what you produce — namely, the frequent, tangible, working results.

- Some notes:

    How frequent is "frequent"?
    Each week, each month, or each quarter — depends upon the size of the project and the amount of added effort required tomake working results available to others.

- Why use features milestones — and measure features completed, using frequent, tangible, working results?

In two words: risk reduction.

- How do you estimate percent completion?

    Take the features list, assign a weight to each feature (based upon level of difficulty, relative number of lines of code, and level of skill of the person who will do the work), and then make your estimates.
    Your estimates will improve over time, as you deliver more and more tangible results along the way.

#1c. "Take Multiple Paths" Strategy   activities and model components

---

- For each outcome, consider multiple paths for reaching that goal. Travel down one of those paths. When your progress sly "sneaker net:" such interaction is outside the scope of your object model; no SI object needed for this.

#1d. "Invest an Hour" Strategy   activities and model components

---

- Rather than philosophize endlessly, invest an hour in each of several different ways of modeling a particularly challenging area. Compare your results — and decide which way to go (based upon actual results, rather than the outcome of a multiweek debate).

#1e. "Consider the Domain First; Artifacts After   activities and model components
**   That" Strategy**

- Build an object model with a domain expert first. Then add in content that you can extract from artifacts (existing data models, source code, whatever).

- Reason why: you need the benefit of the former (fresh insights, new ideas) to help you grapple with the latter (what to include, what to exclude).

#1f. "Extract Useful Content From An Existing   activities and model components
**   Data Model" Strategy**

- Yes, it can be done.

- Best practice: build an initial object model with a domain expert first. Then use that model to help you filter out the classes and attributes (in previous data model) that are no longer needed. Why: the added domain understanding will help you do a better job leaving unneeded things behind, rather than dragging everything from the past along with you once again.

- For the entities:

  List them. Delete correlation tables. Delete (or revise) names that do not fit the problem domain vocabulary (words that a domain expert uses and understands). Collapse supertypes-subtypes that do not express domain-based generalization-specialization.

- Then, when you work on attributes:

  List them. Delete (or revise) names that do not fit the problem domain vocabulary (words that a domain expert uses and understands). Delete flags, indicators, sequence numbers, and unique keys — nearly all of which are simply leftover implementation.

Identifying system purpose and features

A purpose is an overall desired result, the aim of one's actions. Features are specific capabilities for the system under consideration.

This section presents "purpose and features" strategies.

#2. "System Purpose" Strategy	identifying purpose and features

- Develop an overall purpose statement in 25 words or less. Why this system? Why now?
- Keep the overall goal, the critical success factor, always before you.
- "To support, to help, to facilitate, . . ."

#3. "Field Trips, Pictures, and Examples" Strategy	identifying purpose and features

- Work with domain experts, ones well-versed in the business.
- Ask for a guided tour; ask for a picture; ask for lots of examples.

#3a. "Multiple Learning Sources" Strategy	identifying purpose and features

- Read about it; try out software for it; listen to domain experts!

#3b. "Build A Glossary" Strategy	identifying purpose and features

- Are you finding that people use terms differently? Perhaps using different words to convey the same meaning? Or giving different meanings to the same word? Not a surprise!
- Recommendation: build a glossary using a three-column spreadsheet (term, dictionary definition, project definition).

#4. "Identify Major Sources of Stress" Strategy	identifying purpose and features

- Ask people about the most pressing problems that they face each day. "What stresses you out the most? What frightens you the most? What's the worst thing that could happen to you while your boss is watching?"
- Look for ways to eliminate or reduce the impact of those problems.

#5. "Develop a Features List" Strategy	identifying purpose and features

- Build a list of features.
- Think through each feature: the feature, who it's for, and why it's important.
- Use qualifiers to narrow the scope of the purpose and features statements.
- Prioritize your features list.
- Use the features list for planning and building frequent, tangible, working results.

#6. "Four Kinds of Features" Strategy	identifying purpose and features

- Be certain to include features that cover the following:
  1. Log important information.   3. Analyze business results.
  2. Conduct business.   4. Interact with other systems.

#6a. "Add Features, Inspired by Patterns" Strategy	identifying purpose and features

- Add features inspired by the stereotypical responsibilities of a participant (in pattern #3, Participant-Transaction), transaction (in pattern #6, Transaction-Transaction Line Item), and place (in pattern #4, Place-Transaction).
- Examples: assess the performance of a participant (how many, how much), calculate the total of a transaction, assess the performance of a place (how many, how much).

#6b. "Organize and Prioritize Features" Strategy | identifying purpose and features

- Organize the features into "feature categories" (also known as "use cases").

    Example: maintaining employee info; assigning employees; assessing employee performance

- Prioritize the features.

    Identify the prioritization criteria. For example: normal sequence of business usage; greatest risk; customer interest; management interest; ease of implementation.

#7. "Calculation Results and Decision Points" Strategy | identifying purpose and features

- Add features that deliver calculation results. Add features that support decision points.

#8. "Best and Worst Features" Strategy | identifying purpose and features

- Ask users:

    What are the best features of the current system? Of competitive systems?
    What are the worst problems of the current system? Of competitive systems?
    What are the unneeded features of the current system? Of competitive systems?

#9. "Top 10" Strategy | identifying purpose and features

- Build a list of features.

- When you face an abundance of features (or classes, attributes, services), go after the top 10.

- Why: avoid being overwhelmed by a sea of low-level details.

#10. "Now and Later" Strategy | identifying purpose and features

- Consider current capabilities—and anticipated future capabilities.

- Ask, "How is it done now? How will it be done later, with the new system?"

- Look at things that people do to objects now, and consider features you can add (your automated objects might be able to do those actions to themselves).

#11. "Reengineer on the Boundaries" Strategy	identifying purpose and features
• Look at each organization or automated system boundary. • Look for duplicate efforts on each side of such a boundary. • Model the capability one time—and encourage some reengineering improvements for the organization.	

#12. The "Smarter Devices" Strategy	identifying purpose and features
• Look for opportunities to use smarter devices, simplifying your object model and reducing software development schedule and costs. • When building an object model in a field with rapidly changing data acquisition and control technology, be sure to take a systems perspective, spanning both hardware and software.	

Selecting objects

An object is a person, place, or thing. (A class is a description applies to each of some number of objects.)

In this section, you'll find "selecting objects" strategies, presented in these categories:

  – pattern players
  – model components
  – kinds of objects
  – analogies
  – reuse
  – names
  – what to consider and challenge.

Selecting objects — pattern players

#13. "Select Actors" Strategy	selecting objects (pattern players)
• Look for actors: people and organizations that act as participants within the system under consideration. • Examples: person, organization (agency, company, corporation, foundation).	

#14. "Select Participants" Strategy   selecting objects (pattern players)

- Analyze how each actor participates, in ways that might be of interest to the system under consideration.

- Why. Each actor participates in one or more ways through time. It's the same actor, just different ways of participating. People talk about wearing "different hats" during the day. That's exactly what such participation is all about.

- Examples: agent, applicant, buyer, cashier, clerk, client, civilian, customer, dealer, delegate, distributor, donor, employee, investor, manufacturer, member, officer, official, order clerk, owner, participant, policy holder, professional, prospect, recipient, retailer, sales clerk, sales rep, shipper, student, subscriber, supervisor, supplier, suspect, teacher, wholesaler, worker.

#15. "Select Places" Strategy   selecting objects (pattern players)

- Look for places where things come to rest, places that contain other objects.

- Examples: airport, assembly-line, bank, clinic, depot, garage, geographic entity, hangar, hospital, manufacturing site, plant, region, sales outlet, service center, shelf, station, store, warehouse, zone.

#16. "Select Tangible Things" Strategy   selecting objects (pattern players)

- Look for tangible objects, ones used in the problem domain.

- Take a walk through the business. Select objects from the tangible ones around you.

- Examples: account, cash box, cash drawer, item, plan, procedure, product, schedule, scheduled event.

#17. "Select Transactions" Strategy · selecting objects (pattern players)

- Look for transactions, "events remembered," events that the system must remember through time. A transaction is a moment in time (for example, a sale) or an interval of time (for example, a rental).

- Look for an entry in a historical record or log, an entry that must be maintained. Why? To answer questions or to perform assessments.

- Examples: agreement, assignment, authorization, contract, delivery, deposit, incident, inquiry, order, payment, problem report, purchase, refund, registration, rental, reservation, sale, shift, shipment, subscription, time charge, title, withdrawal.

- Note: Nearly all transactions consist of a number of transaction line items.

- Note: Where do these transactions come from? The possibilities are:
  A window (the event logged is based upon human interaction at some point in time)
  Another object, monitoring for a significant event, then logging that such an event
      occurred
  Another system, one that your system can interact with regarding events it logs.

#18. "Select Associates" Strategy · selecting objects (pattern players)

- Look for associates, objects that need to know each other, yet:
  have no need to capture information or provide services about that association
  have no need for history about that association.

- Most often, this strategy applies to the interaction of objects, whose actual objects are closely related.

- Examples: aileron-gyro; aircraft-runway; building-sensor; driver-vehicle, loading dock–order; order-tote; truck–loading dock.

#19. "Select Items and Specific Items" Strategy · selecting objects (pattern players)

- Look for items, descriptive objects with values that apply to some number of specific items and actions that apply across those specific items.

- Examples: aircraft–specific aircraft, loan description–specific loan, job description–specific job, video description–videotape, price category item–specific item, tax category item–specific item.

#19a. "Separate Definition from Usage" Strategy   selecting objects (pattern players)

- When you need to define something (standard parts of a plan, standard parts of a schedule, standard descriptions of a product) and then use it in some way (a specific plan, a specific schedule for today, a specific thing you are putting together) — include both description classes (each object is like a catalog entry) and usage classes (each object keeps track of things that are happening this special time) in your object model.

- This is an example of pattern #9 "Item - Specific Item," repeatedly applied.

#20. "Select Interacting Systems and Devices" Strategy   selecting objects (pattern players)

- Look for other systems, ones that your system is responsible for interacting with.

- (Real-time systems) Look for devices, ones that your system needs for data acquisition and control.

- Add it to the PD component. Example: sensor.

- Add a companion SI class to the system interaction component. Example: sensorSI. (SI objects encapsulate the specific communication needs for interacting with another system or device.)

#20a. "Add Outbound/Inbound Request" Strategy   selecting objects (pattern players)

- Yes, add both PD and SI objects, separating logical and physical system interaction needs.

- For the PD side, add an OutboundRequest object (to keep track of a sending object and the request number — so you can handle an outbound asynchronous request correctly).

- Also for the PD side, add an InboundRequest object (to parse and route inbound a command from another systems — and keep track of to whom to return the results of the request.)

#21. "Select Collections of Objects" Strategy   selecting objects (pattern players)

- Look at each object as a worker in a collection. Name the collections.

- Look at each object as a collection with workers. Name the workers.

- Examples:
  Collections of participants: company, department, group, organization, squad, team.
  Collections of places: airport, campus, store chain.
  Collections of things: assembly, batch, collection, list, log, queue, pool.

#22. "Select Container Objects" Strategy   selecting objects (pattern players)

- Use a domain-based container, one that holds other objects.

- Examples: airport, aircraft, aisle, bank, bin, building, cabinet, folder, garage, hangar, hospital, locker, room, safe, store, warehouse.

#23. "Select a Collection" Strategy   selecting objects (pattern players)

- What if you need a collection of objects, yet such a collection has no special name?
  Add a collection, using a plural form of the worker name. Example: authorization systems.
  Add a collection, using the worker name, followed by the word "collection" or "server." Example: authorization server.

#24. "Select the Smallest Applicable Collection" Strategy   selecting objects (pattern players)

- Use the smallest domain collection within the system's responsibility, to express responsibility across that collection—expressing appropriate scope.

- Examples: bin, aisle, warehouse; city, county, state, country; team, department, organization, company, industry.

Selecting objects — model components

#25. "Object-Model Components as a Guide" Strategy   selecting objects (model components)

- Use object-model components as a working outline for organizing your search for objects.

- PD: problem domain HI: human interaction
  DM: data management SI: system interaction (and NT: not this time).

#26. "Feature, PD Objects, HI Objects" Strategy   selecting objects (model components)

- Tabulate: feature, corresponding problem-domain objects, corresponding human interaction objects.

- Why: identify objects—and sort out who needs to collaborate with whom.

#27. "Select Windows: A First Cut" Strategy   selecting objects (model components)

- Add windows for each problem-domain object that you are working with.

- If an object has line items, model both with a single window.

#28. "Select Logon Window" Strategy   selecting objects (model components)

- Add a logon window—if the system needs to know who is using the system, for access control and accountability.

- Examples: cashier logon window, customer logon window, order clerk logon window—or simply a logon window.

#29. "Select Setup Windows" Strategy   selecting objects (model components)

- Add system setup windows.
  Create and initialize the objects you need, to get the system ready to go.
  Add system administration services for adding users and privileges.

- Add activate and deactivate actions.
  Do this for whatever human interaction might be needed for activating or deactivating an interacting system or device.
  Put the actions with a window that knows objects that can carry those actions out.

- Note: Don't include data entry "nuts and bolts," such as screen, monitor keyboard, mouse, mag-stripe reader, and the like.

#30. "Select Core Windows" Strategy   selecting objects (model components)

- Consider who (audience) needs what (content), and why (purpose).

- Add "conducting business" windows.
  Include transaction windows. Examples: sale window, session window, payment window.

- Add "analyzing business results" windows.

- Consider combination windows, when content is closely related in time.
  Examples: a transaction and its line items; a sale and payment window.

#30a. "Select HI Windows for PD Transactions" Strategy   selecting objects (model components)

- For each PD transaction object:

  add an HI list window and an HI detail window.
  Example: Registration (PD); RegistrationsWindow (HI),
        RegistrationDetailWindow (HI).

#31. "Select Reports" Strategy   selecting objects (model components)

- Put together key summaries and specialized outputs, meeting specific legal or business needs.

- Look carefully at who (audience) needs what (content), and why (purpose).

- Don't include every ad hoc query that someone might eventually ask; don't include outdated batch reports.

#32. "Select Data Management Objects" Strategy   selecting objects (model components)

- Add a DM object for each problem-domain class of objects that you want to be persistent—stored between program invocations.

- Why: use data management (DM) objects to encapsulate search and storage mechanisms across all of the objects within a problem-domain class.

- Examples: cashier DM, sale DM, sale line item DM, item DM.

#33. "Select Interacting Systems or Devices" Strategy   selecting objects
(model components)

- Select it.
    Look for other systems and pieces of equipment that your system must interact with.
    Look for interacting systems; look for devices needing data acquisition and control.
        (Skip display or printing "nuts and bolts.")

- Examples: aileron, avionics system, controller, diverter, elevator, radar, rudder, sensor, scanner.

- Model it.
    With a problem-domain object, and
    With a corresponding system-interaction (SI) object, encapsulating low-level
        communication detail.

Selecting objects — kinds of objects

#34. "Select Kinds of Objects" Strategy   selecting objects (kinds of objects)

- Use generalization-specialization (gen-spec) to find additional classes.
    Look at each class as a generalization. Name its specializations, ones that fit with
        system objectives.
    Look at each specialization. Name its generalizations, ones that fit within system
        objectives.

- Use gen-spec for domain-based reuse within an application; use configuration
  management for reuse across multiple applications, even multiple problem domains.

- Use gen-spec to show domain-based "what's the same, what's different," within an
  application.

- Examples: equipment, kinds of equipment; participants, kinds of participants;
  transactions, kinds of transactions.

#34a. "Fits within a Specialization Class — Forever"   selecting objects (kinds of objects)
       Strategy

- Use generalization-specialization (gen-spec) whenever you can classify an object as being
  within a specialization class — and you know that it will stay in that class.

- Otherwise, use pattern #3 "Actor-Participant" instead (referred to as "composition,"
  instead of "inheritance").

Selecting objects — analogies

#35. "Select Corresponding Objects from Analogous Systems" Strategy	selecting objects (analogies)
• Look for a system with an analogous purpose. • Examine its objects, looking for ones that might correspond by analogy to objects you need in your system. • Add the corresponding objects (grammatically, called "metaphors") to your object model.	

Selecting objects — reuse

#36. "Select and Reuse an Analogous Class" Strategy	selecting objects (reuse)
• Look for a class that might apply. • Consider synonyms. • Consider a more general name, using "is a kind of." • Consider metaphors (corresponding objects) within analogous systems (a system that has an analogous purpose). • Caution: Watch out for metaphors based on what people are doing. Focus on what people act on instead, letting those objects do those things to themselves. (Reason why: do otherwise, and you'll end up with controller objects and data objects, resulting in weaker cohesion and higher coupling.)	

#37. "Select and Reuse a Group of Interacting Objects" Strategy	selecting objects (reuse)
• Reuse another instance of a pattern as is. • Reuse an instance of a pattern, specializing in one or more of its classes. • Reuse a pattern, by analogy.	

Selecting objects — names

| #38. "Use the Domain Vocabulary" Strategy | selecting objects (names) |

- Use the domain vocabulary.

- Encourage domain experts to eliminate names of things that aren't their own.

- Don't put words in your domain expert's mouth.

- Don't change the vocabulary unless the domain expert feels the need to do so.

- Don't change the domain vocabulary—unless your domain experts choose to change their own vocabulary.

| #39. The "Domain Terms and Add-Ons" Strategy | selecting objects (names) |

- Use a domain name in the problem domain component.

- Use the same name, with a suffix, in the other components.

- Examples: customer, customer window, customer DM; altimeter, altimeter indicator, altimeter SI.

| #40. "Always Look for a Better Class Name" Strategy | selecting objects (names) |

- Look for a better class name.
    Consider synonyms.
    Consider a more general name, using "is a kind of."
    Consider metaphors (corresponding objects) within analogous systems (a system that
        has an analogous purpose).

| #41. "Consistent Class Name Format" Strategy | selecting objects (names) |

- Use a name that describes an object in a class (usually that means a singular name).

- If an object is a collection, use a singular domain name; the plural of its parts; or the part name plus "collection" or "server."

- In an object model, begin each class name with an uppercase letter (begin all other names with a lowercase letter).

Selecting objects — what to consider and challenge

#42. "System Responsibility" Strategy	selecting objects (consider and challenge)

- Is the object something that your system is responsible to know or do anything about?
- If not, put it in the "not this time" model component.

#43. "Duplicate Responsibilities" Strategy	selecting objects (consider and challenge)

- Is this object just a duplication of another object? Are the names different, yet identical responsibilities?
- Such duplications arise over time in large organizations and on large systems.
- When this happens, seek a common name (get help from dictionaries, a thesaurus, and domain-specific books and articles).

#44. "Reengineer with Objects" Strategy	selecting objects (consider and challenge)

- Look for objects (and repeating instances of a pattern) that are likely to have the same responsibilities—and actually reflect an organizational boundary or previous system boundary.
- Model the objects once—for a simpler object model. Make recommendations for reengineering the organization, too.

#45. "Useful Questions" Strategy	selecting objects (consider and challenge)

- What useful questions could you ask this object, if you include it in your object model?
- Examples: How many over interval? How much over interval? How good are you?

#46. "More Than a Report" Strategy	selecting objects (consider and challenge)

- Is that report simply a human interaction object, just a view of problem-domain values and calculation results? Or does it embody something about which the system needs to know and do something through time?
- Add to your object model, when your system is responsible for both producing and remembering the content expressed in that report.

#47. "Way to Know" Strategy　　　　　　　selecting objects (consider and challenge)

- You need a way to know each object—and its attribute values.

- If you have no way to know an object, either find a way to know about it or put the object in the "not this time" model component.

- Example: customer. You must have a way to know about customer objects; otherwise, put customer in the "not this time" model component.

#48. "No Objects Mimicking What a Human Does" Strategy　　　selecting objects
　　　　　　　　　　　　　　　　　　　　　　　　　　　　(consider and challenge)

- Don't let an object mimic what a person does (unless you are building a simulation system). Otherwise, that object will end up as a controller, a function blob.

- Reasons why:
    The controller ends up with functionality that's better done by other objects
        themselves (lower cohesion for all).
    The controller makes messaging more complicated (higher coupling for all).
    The overly busy controller is harder to develop.
    The overly busy controller is minding everyone else's state-dependent responsibilities.

#49. "Alternative Human Interaction" Strategy　　　selecting objects (consider and challenge)

- Consider what changes if you used a very different human-interaction style (for example, using a heads-up display and voice commands).

- Would any of your problem-domain objects change? If so, pay close attention to those objects. Separate presentation from what's really going on in the problem domain.

- Examples: vertical-speed indicator (human interaction) and vertical-speed gyro (problem domain), traffic light (human interaction) and traffic lane (problem domain).

Establishing responsibilities / what I know

Attributes represent "what I know."

　　In this section, you'll find "what I know" strategies, presented in these categories:
　　　　– fundamentals
　　　　– pattern players
　　　　– model components (HI)
　　　　– descriptions
　　　　– what to consider and challenge.

Fundamentals (what I know)

#50. "Select Attributes from Actual Ones" Strategy	establishing responsibilities / what I know (fundamentals)
• This is an aspect of a software object coming to life: "I know selective things that describe the actual object that I'm an abstraction of." • Select the attributes for your software objects, taken from the abundance of the attributes that could be used to describe a corresponding actual (real-world) object. • Consider attributes from a broad-sweeping perspective; then work your way into the specific ones you need. Look at attributes in general, in this domain, and ultimately just within this system's responsibilities.	

#51. "Establish Usual Attributes" Strategy	establishing responsibilities / what I know (fundamentals)
• Include the attributes that come to mind when you first think about the object. • Criteria: the system needs to know a given attribute value; the system has some way to get that value. • Examples: number, name, address, date, time, operational state, phone, status, threshold, type.	

Pattern players (what I know)

#52. "Establish Actor and Participant Attributes" Strategy	establishing responsibilities / what I know (pattern players)
• For actor, consider: name, address, phone. • For participants, include: number, date and time (perhaps an ending date and time), password, authorization level.	

#53. "Establish Place Attributes" Strategy	establishing responsibilities / what I know (pattern players)
• For location, include: number, name, address (perhaps latitude, longitude, altitude).	

#54. "Establish Transaction Attributes" Strategy	establishing responsibilities / what I know (pattern players)

- For transactions, include: number, date, time, status.
- For line items, include: quantity (if it knows an item, rather than a specific item), status.

#54a. "Transaction Times" Strategy	establishing responsibilities / what I know

- A transaction object corresponds to a moment in time (e.g., sale) or an interval of time (e.g., rental).
- A moment in time (dateTime, dateTimeOfBirth, dateTimeOfManufacture, effectiveDateTime, plannedDateTime, actualDateTime)
- An interval of time (interval, effectiveInterval, dateTime + duration)
- An interval of time, expressed as a start/stop combination (dateTimeStart, dateTimeEnd; dateTimeIn, dateTimeOut; dateTimeOut, dateTimeBack; effectiveDateTime, expirationDateTime). Fine detail: the second attribute in these pairs belongs in a transaction line item, when different values may apply to each line item.

#54b. "An Attribute? Or Something More?" Strategy	establishing responsibilities / what I know

- Is a person's hobby (or hobbies) just an attribute? Or something more?
- Value. Just need a current value, based upon an enumeration of values? Add an attribute. Describe the enumeration of values in text. Example: Hobbyist, with a "hobbies" attribute.
- Standard Catalog Description. Need standard catalog descriptions you can choose from? Add a "standard catalog description" class with whatever descriptive attributes you need. Each "standard catalog description" object captures attribute values which may apply again and again. Example: Hobbyist — Hobby (attributes: type, name, description).
- History. Need history? Add a transaction object, to remember intervals of activity. Example: Hobbyist — HobbyActivity — Hobby.

#55. "Establish Item and Specific Item Attributes" Strategy	establishing responsibilities / what I know (pattern players)

- For items, include: name, description, dimensions, size, universal product code (UPC), weight.
- For specific items, include: serial number, purchase date. (It might know a custom value, while an item might know a default value.)

#56. "Establish Interacting System and Device Attributes" Strategy	establishing responsibilities / what I know (pattern players)
• For another system or device, include: number, name, operational state. • For its companion object, in the system interaction component, include: address, password.	

Model components — HI (what I know)

#57. "Establish Window or Report Attributes" Strategy	establishing responsibilities / what I know (model components)
• For windows or reports, include: search fields, data entry fields, or both.	

Descriptions (what I know)

#58. "Describe Attributes with a Template" Strategy	establishing responsibilities / what I know (descriptions)

• Describe each attribute, using a template as your guide.
    description
    legal values (range; limit; enumeration of values)
    unit of measure
    data type
    tolerance
    required (yes or no)
    get/set constraints
    how to get a default value from another source, in the event a custom value is
        not known
    applicable states (for state-dependent attributes)
    traceability codes (to a requesting document, if any).	

#59. "Describe Real-Time Attributes" Strategy	establishing responsibilities / what I know (descriptions)

• For real-time, categorize each attribute as: state, state-dependent, or state-independent.
 	
• Examples:
    state attributes: status, operational state
    state-dependent attributes: value, reading
    state-independent attributes: name, serial number.	

What to consider and challenge (what I know)

In this section, you'll find "what I know (consider and challenge)" strategies, presented in these categories:

- values
- gen-spec with attributes
- names.

What to consider and challenge (what I know): values

#60. "Closely Related Values as One" Strategy	establishing responsibilities / what I know (consider and challenge)
• A collection of closely related values, commonly referred to as one? • Use one attribute (e.g., name) and describe its parts in text. • Example: name. In the description for that attribute, include something like "name consists of title, first name, middle initial, last name (and if applicable, maiden name.)"	

#61. "Yes/No Attribute" Strategy	establishing responsibilities / what I know (consider and challenge)

• Attribute has values "yes or no?"
    The attribute name itself may be a value for some other attribute name
    Example: taxable (yes or no); change to tax status (taxable, tax-exempt, resale).
    Why bother: added detail now, added ease of change in the future.	

#62. "Values Over Time" Strategy | establishing responsibilities / what I know (consider and challenge)

- An attribute value that varies over time, and you need to know that variation?

- Add an additional object, with an effective date and value.

- Example: item and its price. If you need to keep track of multiple prices, applicable over different time periods, then add price objects, ones that know effective date and price, and do things like "is applicable for date" and "get price."

#62a. "You? Me? Or Something Between Us?" Strategy | establishing responsibilities / what I know (consider and challenge)

- For each attribute, ask:

  Does it describe me? (If so, add it to the corresponding class.)
  Does it describe an object I know? (If so, add it to that other corresponding class.)
  Does it describe something in-between us? (If so, add a transaction object in between, and add the attribute to that class.)

- Example:

  Consider a "user."
  Q. Does "password" describe a user?
  A. Yes, in a single-system context.
     Looks like this: User, with a password attribute
     No, in a multisystem context. In this case, a "password" describes neither a user nor a system. Instead, it describes something in-between them, a transaction object called something like "Access Authorization."
     Looks like this: User — Access Authorization — System

#63. "Embedded Meaning in a Number" Strategy | establishing responsibilities / what I know (consider and challenge)

- Attribute is a number, with encoded meanings?

- Add an attribute for each meaning.

- Most often, include a number attribute, too (a sequence number, no longer a source of encoded meaning).

#64. "Attribute with Repeating Values" Strategy	establishing responsibilities / what I know (consider and challenge)

- An attribute that may have a number of values?

- Add a new class to your model. Add an object connection. Look for additional attributes that may apply.
    - Add a new class, even if it has only one attribute for now.
    - Why: make the most of problem-domain partitioning; pave the way for accommodating future change gracefully.
- Example: Item with the attribute UPCs. Add a UPC class. Add an object connection between an item and its UPCs.

#65. "Attribute Value Granularity" Strategy	establishing responsibilities / what I know (consider and challenge)

- Check the granularity for each attribute that applies across a collection:
    - Does the same value apply across the entire collection?
    - If not, move the attribute to the worker class, so each object in the collection can have its own value.
- Example: rental (checkout date and time), rental line item (return date and time).

#66. "Calculable Result" Strategy	establishing responsibilities / what I know (consider and challenge)

- An attribute for holding a calculable result? At first, don't show it in the object model.

- At some point, you may want to add the attribute. Here's how:
    - Add an explicit "get <attribute>" service for it.
        - Specify that service so it:
            - checks for an attribute value—and returns it, if it has one
            - otherwise, invokes a calculate service, saves the result, and returns the result to the sender.
    - Add an explicit "calculate <attribute>" service, too—so you can tell the object to do the calculation you want it to do.

What to consider and challenge: gen-spec with attributes (what I know)

#67. "Common Attributes" Strategy	establishing responsibilities / what I know (consider and challenge)

- Classes with common attributes?

- If the attributes have the same name and meaning, and if you can find a generalization-specialization that makes good sense, then add a generalization class and factor out the commonality.

#67a. "Collapse Whole-Part When Same Attributes Apply" Strategy	establishing responsibilities / what I know (consider and challenge)

- When you find a whole-part — and the same attributes apply to the whole and the part:

Collapse the whole and part into "class with objects" symbol.
    Add a whole-part object connection to that one symbol.
    Add "super" and "sub" attributes, showing that each object knows the objects above it
        and below it.
    Why: Fewer symbols. Less redundancy. And more resilient to change.
    Example: Company - Division - Section - Team Collapse to "Organization" or
        "OrgUnit."

#68. "Partially Applicable Attribute" Strategy	establishing responsibilities / what I know (consider and challenge)

- Attribute that applies only to certain objects in a class?

- Do you have an attribute which applies only to certain kinds of objects?

- Do you have an attribute that may have the value "not applicable"?

- If so, factor out the specialized attribute into a specialization class.

#69. "No Attributes" Strategy | establishing responsibilities / what I know (consider and challenge)

- An object with no attributes? When this happens, one of two things is going on.
  - Either it's a narrow "need to know" and just one object in that class.
    - Check: there really is just one object in that class.
    - Check: attributes really could apply, yet all potential attributes are outside of the system's responsibilities.
    - Fine!
  - Or it's got object connections (an attribute, show graphically). That's fine!
  - Or it's a nasty "function blob," with services better done by other objects themselves.
    - Centralized control is troublesome; here's why:
      - It fails to use problem domain classes to partition both attributes and services.
      - Encapsulation goes down (higher coupling and weaker cohesion).
    - Here's what to do about it.
      - Get rid of the "function blob."
      - Applying the "what I do" strategies as a guide, put each service in the object that the old function blob was acting on.

What to consider and challenge (what I know): names

#70. "Embedded Value in an Attribute Name" Strategy | establishing responsibilities / what I know (consider and challenge)

- Attribute name includes the name of another object?

- Add that object to your model. Let that object know its own attribute(s).

- Note: an object connection, expressed textually rather than graphically, names another object (as it should).

#71. "Type Attribute" Strategy	establishing responsibilities / what I know (consider and challenge)

- Attribute expressing type, kind, or category?

- If it's needed solely for display or report, that's fine.

- If it's a redundant expression of what gen-spec already portrays, get rid of it (it's not needed).

- If it's needed to decide what to do in a service, use gen-spec so that each object can just do its thing—without needing to determine "what kind am I?" before taking appropriate action. Why: take advantage of an opportunity to apply polymorphism—and, as a result, increase resiliency to change.

Establishing responsibilities / who I know

Object connections represent "who I know."

In this section, you'll find "who I know" strategies, presented in these categories:
- fundamentals
- pattern players
- model components (HI, DM)
- what to consider and challenge.

Fundamentals (who I know)

#72. "Establish Objects I Know" Strategy	establishing responsibilities / who I know (fundamentals)

- This is an aspect of a software object coming to life: "I know other objects, ones that are related to the actual object that I'm an abstraction of."

- Select connecting objects to satisfy these two purposes:
  To directly know "to whom to send a message" (within one or more scenarios).
  To answer a query about objects that are directly related to it.

#73. "Show Who I Know" Strategy   establishing responsibilities / who I know (fundamentals)

- Show "who I know" graphically, with an object connection.

  Include constraints, placed next to each object being constrained: 1   0-1   n   1-n
       <blank>   ordered n   [XOR A] 1   [OR B] 2   [C] ordered n   all

  "n" is the same thing as "0-n" (it's just easier to write it as "n").
  A <blank> constraint indicates that an object has no need to know the other objects
       (this may occur, notably for a part in an aggregate).
  ordered n   an ordered collection of some number of connections
  [XOR A] 1   indicates an exclusive or, pertaining to all object connections labeled
       with the same tag (in this example the tag is "A"). Place whatever constraint
       applies to the right of the brackets, e.g., [XOR A] 1.
  [OR B] 2   two connections, selected from the connections labeled "B".
  [C] ordered n   an ordered collection of some number of connections (any connection
       from that object that is labeled "C").

- Or show "who I know" textually, with an attribute.

  Use this format whenever an object connection spans across model components — or
       any other time that an object connection would be cumbersome, visually.
  For a textual representation, use this format:
       "<class name, beginning with a lowercase letter>"
       Make it singular or plural, reflecting the number of objects that the object may
         know.

#73a. "Whole-Part and Existence Dependency: Two Distinct Issues" Strategy   establishing responsibilities / who I know (fundamentals)

- Whole-part object connections express: assembly-part or container-content or group-member.

- Existence dependency shows: one object depends upon another, else it cannot exist.
  Show existence dependency with an object connection constraint of 1 or more.

These are two distinct issues. Whole-part does not imply existence dependency; the
connection constraints of any object connection express existence dependency (if any).

Pattern players (who I know)

#74. "Establish Actor and Participant Object Connections" Strategy   establishing responsibilities / who I know (pattern players)

- For an actor, include an object connection to: its participants.

- For a participant, include an object connection to: its actor, its transactions.

#75. "Establish Place Object Connections" Strategy	establishing responsibilities / who I know (pattern players)

- For a location, include object connections to objects which come to rest at a location . . . or are contained by a location.

- For a location, include object connections to transaction objects, to show that location's participation in that transaction.

#76. "Establish Transaction Object Connections" Strategy	establishing responsibilities / who I know (pattern players)

- For a transaction, include object connections to: participants, transaction line items, a companion transaction, one that occurs at the same moment in time.

- For a transaction line item, include object connections to: the transaction, a companion "item description" object, a subsequent transaction line item.

#77. "Establish Item and Specific Item Object Connections" Strategy	establishing responsibilities / who I know (pattern players)

- For an item, include object connections to: specific item, transaction line item (if specific item is not needed in the model), container line item (if specific item is not needed in the model).

- For a specific item, include object connections to: item, transaction line item, container line item.

#78. "Establish Interacting System or Device Object Connections" Strategy	establishing responsibilities / who I know (pattern players)

- For an interacting system or device, include an object connection (expressed an attribute) to: its corresponding system interaction (SI) object, one that encapsulates low-level interaction details.

Model components — HI, DM (who I know)

#79. "Establish Window or Report Object Connections" Strategy	establishing responsibilities / who I know (model components)
• For a window or report, include an object connection (expressed as an attribute) to: the contents of the window, the objects it knows directly, to get the content it needs to do its job (note that a window can use those objects to get to other objects, indirectly).	

#79a. "Establish HI-PD Object Connections"	establishing responsibilities / who I know (model components)

• For a window, show "who I know" in text:
    (a) A problem-domain container, to ask for a list
    (b) An object (or objects) selected from a list
• For a PD object who needs to notify a window:
 	
Inherit the attribute "subscribers" and the service "publish" — from a PDObject class — and notify your subscribers when a change occurs (up to each subscriber to decide what to do from there).	

#80. "Establish Data Management Object Connections" Strategy	establishing responsibilities / who I know (model components)
• For a data management object, include an object connection (expressed as an attribute) to the problem-domain objects (all of the objects in some problem-domain class) that it is responsible for.	

#80a. "ABC" Strategy	establishing responsibilities / who I know (consider and challenge)
• Consider: A — B — C • Do you need an object connection between A and C? Yes, if an A and C can exist without a B, and you need to know that mapping even when a B is not present. No, otherwise.	

#80b. "Double 1's" Strategy   establishing responsibilities / who I know
(consider and challenge)

- For object connections that have double 1's:

  ———————

  1   1

should you combine the participating objects?

- Reason to combine: fewer symbols, fewer object interactions to deal with, easier to understand. This approach recognizes that effective communication is a must. Recommendation: follow this approach, unless the benefits listed below justify the added complexity.

- Reason to keep apart: finer-grained partitioning, more resiliency to change.

#80c. "Double n's" Strategy   establishing responsibilities / who I know
(consider and challenge)

- For object connections that have double n's:

  ——————— or ——————- or ———————-
  n   n   n   1-n   1-n   1-n

check and see if a transaction object belongs in-between them.

- Example:

Owner-Vehicle could become Owner-Purchase-Vehicle.

- The point here is not to obliterate double n's, but rather to use the occasion to look for a missing transaction object.

#80d. "Relationships Between Objects in the Same Class" Strategy   establishing responsibilities / who I know
(consider and challenge)

- At times, one object in a class needs to know other objects in a class.

- One choice: add an object connection — and an attribute, naming that connection. Works well if you don't need to know anything else about that relationship, or its history over time.

- Another choice: add and connect another object, one that further describes what's going on between those objects. This could even be abstracted into a new pattern, called "Thing - Thing Relationship."

What to consider and challenge (who I know)

#81. "Common Object Connection" Strategy	establishing responsibilities / who I know (consider and challenge)
• Common object connection? Add a generalization class, if it is indeed a generalization.	

#82. "Uncommon Object Connection" Strategy	establishing responsibilities / who I know (consider and challenge)
• Object connection that applies only to certain objects in a class? Connect to objects in a specialization class, instead.	

#83. "One Object with Special Meaning" Strategy	establishing responsibilities / who I know (consider and challenge)
• Many potential object connections, with one that is "the current one" or some other special meaning? • Add an attribute like "current <connecting class name>."	

#84. "Object Connection with Multiple Meanings" Strategy	establishing responsibilities / who I know (consider and challenge)

• What if you have an object connection with multiple meanings?
    Add a transaction object, an "event remembered" about each meaning being established.
    Or: add attributes to the participating object that needs to know those meanings— along with the object connection.	

#85. "An Object with No Connections" Strategy	establishing responsibilities / who I know (consider and challenge)
• An object with no object connections? 　　Consider who it needs to know to answer queries. Anything needed? 　　Consider who it needs to know to get its services done. Anything needed? 　　Otherwise, it's okay (from a different domain, yet part of the system's responsibilities).	

Establishing responsibilities / what I do

Services represent "what I do."

In this section, you'll find "what I do" strategies, presented in these categories:
  – fundamentals
  – pattern players
  – model components (HI, DM)
  – where to put a service
  – real time
  – message traffic
  – descriptions
  – what to consider and challenge.

Fundamentals (what I do)

#86. "Do It Myself" Strategy	establishing responsibilities / what I do (fundamentals)
• This is an aspect of a software object coming to life: "I do those things that are normally done to the actual object that I'm an abstraction of."	
• Here's why. "Doing it myself" encapsulates attributes with the services that work on those attributes. That results in lower coupling and stronger cohesion.	
• If you are building a simulation system, then a software object will mimic what an actual object does. In most systems, this is not so. Software objects do those things that the system is responsible to do with regard to that object.	

#87. "Put Services with the Attributes They Work On" Strategy	establishing responsibilities / what I do (fundamentals)
• Put the services with the attributes they work on.	
• The result? Sensor objects that monitor themselves, customer objects that qualify themselves, target objects that destroy themselves.	
• Why: better encapsulation, stronger cohesion, lower coupling, increased likelihood of reuse.	

#88. "Why, Why, Why" Strategy	establishing responsibilities / what I do (fundamentals)

- Add value by asking "why, why, why?"
    Why, why, does the system need this object anyway?
    What useful questions can it answer? What useful actions can it perform?
    What is done to an actual object, something that this object could do itself?

#89. "Basic Services" Strategy	establishing responsibilities / what I do (fundamentals)

- The basic service, done by all, are not shown in an object model, except within specific scenario views that might use them.

- The basics: get, set; add (a connecting object), remove (a connecting object); create (something a class does) and initialize, delete.

- Note: attributes are private, by convention. In scenarios, use "get <attribute name>" and "set <attribute name>" services to access attribute values.

- The basic DM services—for data management objects—are: search, load, and save.

#90. "Service as a Question" Strategy	establishing responsibilities / what I do (fundamentals)

- Ask: what questions can an object answer?

- Some good starting words to choose from: has, how many, how much, includes, is.

- Why: stronger encapsulation, better partitioning of services; fewer objects that are mere data holders.

#91. "Service as a Verb" Strategy	establishing responsibilities / what I do (fundamentals)

- Some good service name verbs to choose from:
    activate (initialize, initiate, open, start)
    answer (reply, respond)
    assess (appraise, assay, evaluate, value)
    calculate (compute, count, estimate, rate, tally)
    deactivate (close, end, shut down, terminate)
    determine (decide, figure out, observe, resolve)
    find (get, look for, pinpoint)
    measure (bound, gauge, limit)
    monitor (conduct, direct, manage, observe, operate, supervise, watch)
    qualify (characterize, differentiate, discriminate, distinguish, mark)
    select (choose, cull, elect, opt for, pick).
- Append "over interval" for services that apply to different time intervals.

#92. "What Can I Do for You" Strategy	establishing responsibilities / what I do (fundamentals)

- Ask, "What can I do for you, based on what I know?"

- Ask, "What can I do for you, based on whom I know?"

#93. "Question, Calculation, Selection" Strategy	establishing responsibilities / what I do (fundamentals)

- For an object, consider:
    What *questions* can I answer?
    What *calculations* can I do? What ongoing monitoring could I do? What calculations
        across a collection could I make (letting each worker do its part)?
    What *selections* across a collection could I make (letting each worker do its part)?

Pattern players (what I do)

#94. "Establish Actor and Participant Services" Strategy	establishing responsibilities / what I do (pattern players)

- For an actor or participant, include: calculate for me, rate me, is <value>.
- For an actor as a collection, include: how many, how much, rank participants, calculate over participants (plus services to enforce business rules across that collection).

- For a participant as a collection, include: how many, how much, rank transactions, calculate over transactions (plus services to enforce business rules across that collection).

#95. "Establish Place Services" Strategy	establishing responsibilities / what I do (pattern players)

- For a place, include: calculate for me, rate me, is <value>.

- For a place as a collection, include: how many, how much, rank transactions, rank contents, rank container line items, calculate over transactions, calculate over contents, calculate over container line items (plus services to enforce business rules across that collection).

#96. "Establish Transaction Services" Strategy	establishing responsibilities / what I do (pattern players)

- For a transaction, include: calculate for me, rate me, is <value>.

- For a transaction as a collection, include: how many, how much, rank transaction line items, rank subsequent transactions, calculate over transaction line items, calculate over subsequent transactions (plus services to enforce business rules across that collection).

- For line items, include: calculate for me, rate me.

#97. "Establish Item & Specific Item Services" Strategy	establishing responsibilities / what I do (pattern players)

- For an item or a specific item, include: calculate for me, rate me, is <value>.

- For an item as a collection, include: how many, how much, rank, calculate over specific items (plus services to enforce business rules across that collection).

- For a specific item as a collection, include: how many, how much, rank line items, calculate over line items, (plus services to enforce business rules across that collection).

#98. "Establish Interacting System or Device Services" Strategy	establishing responsibilities / what I do (pattern players)

- For an interacting system or device, include: activate, monitor (maintain), report, deactivate (plus calculate for me, rate me, is <value>).

- For an interacting system or device as a collection, include: how many, how much, rank parts, calculate over parts.

- Add a corresponding object in the system interaction (SI) component, to isolate specific interaction needs (examples: connect, logon, query, logoff, disconnect).

Model components—HI, DM (what I do)

#99. "Establish Window or Report 'What I Do'" Strategy	establishing responsibilities / what I do (model component)

- For a window or report: include the actions for that window, actions that can be carried out by an object that window knows.

- Add action-initiating services. Let the PD objects do all the real work. (Why: so you can charge the HI objects and not lose application smarts.)

- Examples: activate, commit, delete, initiate, log, total, save, send, terminate.

#100. "Establish Data Management Services" Strategy	establishing responsibilities / what I do (model component)

- For data management objects, include these services: search, save, load.

#100a. "Add System Interaction (SI) Responsibilities" Strategy	establishing responsibilities / what I do (model component)

- Include a "logical" representation, expressing the role the other system plays, in the problem domain component. Typical services: actions that name the desired result. Example: AuthorizationSystem, with an "authorize" service.

- Include a "physical" representation, expressing the interaction details, in the SI component. Typical services: logon, connect, exchange, disconnect, logoff. Example: AuthorizationSystemSI, with "logon, sendRequest, receiveResponse, logoff" services.

- Consider various activation paths, too.

On demand by a user: HI to PD to SI. On demand from another system: SI to PD to SI. On a schedule: PD to SI. Or by "sneaker net:" such interaction is outside the scope of your object model; no SI object needed for this.

Where to put a service (what I do)

#101. "Placing Services" Strategy	establishing responsibilities / what I do (where to put)

- Use the key principles for placing a service.
  - act on something in the domain -> the object does it itself
  - collection-worker pattern
    - collection object works on its own attributes
    - collection object asks workers to do something useful (rarely just "get a value for me")
  - encapsulation (more than a value holder; it acts upon what it knows)
  - generally useful in subsequent reuse
  - messaging simplicity (more understandable, more efficient).

#102. "Service across a Collection" Strategy	establishing responsibilities / what I do (where to put)

- Service across a collection of objects?
  - Add a service to a collection object, an object that knows and does things across that collection.
  - Let each worker within a collection do its fair share—as much as it can, based upon what it knows.
- Be sure the collection does just those things that apply across a collection; makes its workers do as much work as they know enough to accomplish.
- Across its workers: enforce business rules that may apply to its participation.

#103. "Service in the Smallest Applicable Container" Strategy	establishing responsibilities / what I do (where to put)

- Begin with a problem-domain object.
- Identify the smallest problem-domain collection that it's a part of.
- Add the "service across a collection" to that object.
- Does the collection include all of the objects you need to work with?
  - If yes, you're done.
  - If not, do it again, letting the collection be the problem-domain object for the next pass.

#104. "Worker in a Collection" Strategy | establishing responsibilities / what I do (where to put)

- Service in a worker object? Let it do something of value!
    Answer a question.
    Calculate. Calculate a result, given input parameters.
    Get a custom value OR a default value for objects in that collection (which would require sending a message from the worker to its collection object).
- In other words, add some value—endeavor to let each object be more than just a data holder.

#105. "Programmable Action" Strategy | establishing responsibilities / what I do (where to put)

- Service which is actually a programmable action?
    Add an attribute called something like "programmable action."
    Add a service called something like "execute action."

Real-time (what I do)

#106. "Real Time: Timeliness" Strategy | establishing responsibilities / what I do (real time)

- Timeliness: must be "on time"

- Put performance constraints on your scenarios (on services, too, as needed—although allocating performance constraints to individual services often takes more guesswork than most engineers feel comfortable with).

#107. "Real Time: Dynamic Internal Structure" Strategy | establishing responsibilities / what I do (real time)

- Dynamic internal structure: dynamic creation and destruction of software components

- How: show dynamic creation and deletion of objects in scenarios.
    Every class knows how to create new objects in that class.
    Every collection knows how to add and remove objects in that collection.
    Every object knows how to delete itself.
    In addition, you can selectively place additional creation and deletion constraints.

#108. "Real Time: Reactiveness" Strategy — establishing responsibilities / what I do (real time)

- Reactiveness: continuously responds to different events in its environment, detected by data acquisition and control devices, or by interacting systems

- Use a specific "maintain" or "monitor" service, for ongoing capabilities.

- Use the "activate, monitor, deactivate" triad.

#109. "Real Time: State-Dependency" Strategy — establishing responsibilities / what I do (real time)

- State-dependency: responds differently, depending upon the state of a system

- Attributes: state, state-dependent, state-independent
    In its description, include: applicable states.

- Services: state-dependent, state-independent
    In its description, you may need to include:
        precondition: <indicate what you assert to be true, before this service can run>
        postcondition: <indicate what you assert to be true, before this service can go to
            completion>
        trigger condition: <indicate what state transitions activate this service>
        terminate condition: <indicate what state transitions terminate this service>
        exception: <indicate object.service to invoke, upon detecting an exception>.

#110. "Real Time: Concurrency" Strategy — establishing responsibilities / what I do (real time)

- Concurrency: multiple simultaneous activities can be taking place.

- Objects can do more than one thing at once — they are multitasking creatures.

- Objects encapsulate real-time tasks.
    Activation / deactivation
        Trigger condition: <request, state change, value change, time lapse>
        Terminate condition: <request, state change, value change, time lapse>
    Communication, coordination
        Communication between objects is by synchronous messaging.
        Communication within objects is by synchronous and asynchronous messaging,
            as needed.

- Note: this encapsulation is made possible with effective object modeling (not with data objects and controller objects).

#111. "Real Time: Multiple Device Abstractions" Strategy	establishing responsibilities / what I do (real time)

- Multiple device abstractions: needs both physical and logical abstractions.

- Physical abstraction — express with an object in the system interaction component.

- Logical abstractions — express with:
    - a domain-based object (a problem-domain object)
    - an object which shows "this is how we'll work with it" (a human interaction object)
    - an object which persists from one program invocation to the next (a data management object).

#112. "Real Time: Distribution" Strategy	establishing responsibilities / what I do (real time)

- Distribution: multiple computing sites

- Across multiple computing systems
    Use software that supports distributed objects.
    Or do it yourself (inevitable, at least for systems that you must interact with and cannot change).
        Allocate objects, not mere functionality.
        Add "pack and ship; receive and route" infrastructure.
- Within an existing system
    Use an object model to understand what's really going on.
    Tag each service with its location; tag each attribute with who is using it.

Message traffic (what I do)

#113. "Batch Up Immediate Results" Strategy	establishing responsibilities / what I do (message traffic)

- Excess message traffic can make an object model harder to understand and harder to implement, too.

- Here's what to do about it:

    "Batch up" immediate results. Add attributes that hold intermediate results, to reduce message traffic. In effect, you are moving a repeated calculation "outside of the (iteration) loop." A classic example: adding a "total" attribute along with a "calcTotal" service.

#114. "Traveling Object" Strategy	establishing responsibilities / what I do (message traffic)
• Pass an object (or object ID) as a parameter, allowing it to travel along a series of message sends. At the end of the series, the last object can send the result directly to the originator (a short cut, rather than waiting for all the message sends to work back to the originator. (The caller–dispatcher–caller-back pattern is a good example of this.)	

#115. "Sender, Intermediary, Receiver" Strategy	establishing responsibilities / what I do (message traffic)
• To loosely couple a sender, use a "pass-through" intermediary. • To simplify an intermediary, use a "lookup" intermediary. • (Refer to the "sender-pass through-receiver" and "sender-lookup-receiver" patterns.)	

Descriptions (what I do)

#116. "Describe Services with a Template" Strategy	establishing responsibilities / what I do (descriptions)
• Describe each service, using a template as your guide. 　input, output parameters 　description (including pseudo-code or actual code, detailing the algorithm to be 　　applied) 　traceability codes to preceding documentation, if any 　visibility: public, protected, private.	

#117. "Describe Real-Time Services" Strategy	establishing responsibilities / what I do (descriptions)
• For each state-dependent service, specify: 　precondition <condition(s) for activation> 　postcondition <condition(s) for termination> 　trigger condition <request, state change, value change, time lapse> 　terminate condition <request, state change, value change, time lapse> 　exception action <object.service to invoke, upon detecting an exception> 　performance constraints (in addition to scenario performance constraints, when 　　needed).	

What to consider and challenge (what I do)

In this section, you'll find "what I do (consider and challenge)" strategies, presented in these categories:
- responsibilities
- gen-spec with services
- names.

What to consider and challenge (what I do): responsibilities

#118. "Watch Out for Data Objects and Control Objects" Strategy	establishing responsibilities / what I do (consider and challenge)
• Watch out for grouping by data objects and control objects. • Keep data and the actions on that data — together. • Why: better encapsulation, stronger cohesion, lower coupling, fewer objects, and fewer object interactions.	

#119. "Watch Out for Excessive Behavior" Strategy	establishing responsibilities / what I do (consider and challenge)
• Watch out for objects that interact with nearly all other objects in the model. • Try adjusting responsibilities (what I know, who I know, what I do). • Apply the collection-worker pattern, too.	

#119a. "Watch Out for 'Workaholic - Data Holder'" Strategy	establishing responsibilities / what I do (consider and challenge)
• "Workaholic - Data Holder" is a pattern that points to trouble. The workaholic makes all the decisions and does all of the work. The data holder just holds values — and provides "gets" and "sets" for working with those values. • Corrective action: instead of asking the data holder for a value, ask it a question or ask it to calculate a result, based upon what it knows, who it knows, and arguments you might pass to it. Then reduce the workaholic's workload, accordingly.	

What to consider and challenge (what I do): gen-spec with services

#120. "Common Services" Strategy	establishing responsibilities / what I do (consider and challenge)

- Classes with common services?
  If the services have the same name and meaning, and if you can find a generalization-specialization that makes good sense, then add a generalization class and factor out whatever commonality you discovered.

  If the service name is the same, yet the details of the service are different, then show the service name in both the generalization and the specialization.

#121. "Partially Applicable Service" Strategy	establishing responsibilities / what I do (consider and challenge)

- Do you have a service that applies only to certain objects in a class?

- Do you have a service that applies only to certain kinds of objects?

- Do you have a service which tests for what kind it is, and then acts accordingly?

- If so, factor out the specialized service into a specialization class.

#122. "Meaningful Gen-Spec" Strategy	establishing responsibilities / what I do (consider and challenge)

- What if "specialization is a kind of generalization" doesn't make sense? Get rid of that gen-spec.

- Insist upon domain-based generalization-specialization, for understandability and greater likelihood of factoring which facilitates reuse.

- Exception: generalization class is from another team, insufficiently factored out, yet you must use it as-is. In that case, mark aspects of a new specialization with "does not apply."
  Precede an inherited but unneeded attribute name with an "x."
  Precede an inherited but unneeded object connection (expressed in text) with an "x."
  Precede an inherited but unneeded service name with an "x."

#123. "Specialization Redundancies" Strategy	establishing responsibilities / what I do (consider and challenge)

- An entire specialization level with an attribute or service name repeated throughout?
  If there is a variation in the descriptions behind the repeated name, that's fine.
  Yet if the attribute or service is indeed the same for each specialization, move it to a generalization.

#124. "No Level of Empty Specializations" Strategy	establishing responsibilities / what I do (consider and challenge)

- An entire level of specializations — without attributes, object connections, or services?

- What's happened: a graphical enumeration of values (not a very efficient representation of an enumeration of values).

- What to do: replace all of those empty specializations with an attribute in the generalization class, plus a description that includes an enumeration of values.

#125. "Abundant Specializations" Strategy	establishing responsibilities / what I do (consider and challenge)

- Where to begin?
  Divide and conquer: model a simple one; model a complex one.
  Model an initial gen-spec, showing "what's the same, what's different."
  Then work on additional specializations, based upon "what I know, who I know, what I do."
- An incredible number of specializations, and you aren't sure which to apply?
  Consider the system's responsibilities.
  Model generalization-specialization based upon what the system knows and does regarding its specializations.
  Use gen-spec to capture similarity and differences in system responsibility (not as a classification system of all classification systems).
- Lots of specializations, resulting from multiple inheritance?
  Use the actor-participant pattern, to express an actor and the many ways it acts as a participant.
  Example: person (actor) and participant (customer, cashier, head cashier, order clerk).

What to consider and challenge (what I do): names

#126. "Class Name in a Service Name" Strategy	establishing responsibilities / what I do (consider and challenge)

- Service name includes the name of another class?
  Let the objects in that class provide that service — or at least let them help out in a meaningful way.

Working out dynamics with scenarios

A scenario is a sequence of object interactions, demonstrating the object interactions for delivering a specific feature of the system under consideration.

Use scenarios to work out model dynamics, discovering additional responsibilities and scenarios.

Developers test against classes and scenarios; an independent test organization uses scenarios for its testing, too.

#127. "Select Key Scenarios" Strategy   working out dynamics with scenarios

- Work out and demonstrate the satisfaction of a system feature.
  Include scenarios that get you to work through the object interactions that are required to deliver a feature of the system under consideration.
  Consider using subscenarios, to make a scenario easier to work with and easier to understand.
- Stretch the model, examining it for completeness.
  Include scenarios that really stretch your object model; use them to check out the overall completeness of your model.
- Examine key object interactions within your model.
  Include scenarios that let you investigate dynamics for important services in your model.

#128. "Where to Begin a Scenario" Strategy   working out dynamics with scenarios

- Begin with a PD object's service, an HI object's service, or an SI object's service.

#129. "Act It Out" Strategy   working out dynamics with scenarios

- Act out the interactions.
  Each person plays a role.
  Each object does its job—no more, no less.
    "What I know; who I know; what I do."
    "I know enough; I have the arguments I need; I know to whom to send messages; and I send messages to other objects, to get work done on my behalf."
- Discover and refine both objects and responsibilities, all along the way.

- Check it out.
  Look at what arguments each object needs to know enough to get its job done.
  Look at who creates and who eventually deletes the objects.
  Look at objects that dominate the overall functionality; apply patterns to help you better distribute responsibility.
  Look at objects that ask other objects for values, yet insist on doing all of the work; again, apply patterns to help you better distribute responsibility.

#130. "Two-Pass Scenario Development" Strategy   working out dynamics / with scenarios

- Once you have an initial object model in place, use a two-pass approach to developing scenarios.

- Why: this two-pass strategy supports making an explicit decision regarding how much detail you need or want in a specific scenario.

- First pass: work out a scenario using the objects in your model, adding no new objects (or very few new objects).

- Second pass (when you need additional understanding of dynamics and the additional detail that goes with it): consider each participating service; look for what other objects it needs to call upon, to get that service accomplished. Add objects, responsibilities, and interactions, as needed.

Description (scenarios)

#131. "Describe Scenarios with a Scenario View" Strategy   working out dynamics with scenarios

- Describe each scenario with a scenario view. A scenario view portrays:
      recognizer
      end-to-end performance constraint (as needed)
      a time-ordered sequence of:
            sender and sending service
            receiver and receiving service (with arguments).

- For starting and stopping a real-time task, use:
      START_TASK (service name) and STOP_TASK (service name).

What to consider and challenge (scenarios)

#132. "Don't Ask 'What Kind?'" Strategy   working out dynamics with scenarios (consider and challenge)

- Don't ask "What kind of object are you?"—and then follow-up with a second message, telling that object what you want it to do.

- Instead, specialize the classes of those objects, so an object already knows what kind it is. Then send one message and let that object do its thing.

#132a. "More Than 'Get A Value'" Strategy	working out dynamics with scenarios (consider and challenge)

- Don't send "get value" without first considering:

    What question do I really want answered?
    What calculation result do I need?
    Can I pass an argument to that object and have it do something useful for me?
- Why: this strategy helps you distribute both attributes and services, using problem-domain classes as a more stable, more understandable organizational framework.

#133. "Search then Interact" Strategy	working out dynamics with scenarios (consider and challenge)

- If you need to traverse multiple object connections in search for an object you want to interact with:
    –search for it
    –then interact with it.
- Reason: simpler objects in between.

#134. "Act, Rather than Poll" Strategy	working out dynamics with scenarios (consider and challenge)

- For each object that recognizes that something needs to be done, let it initiate that work.
- Don't let a manager poll that object, asking for a status change. Reason: no need for that extra managing activity (adds complexity, weakens encapsulation).

#135. "Get Values Only When You Need Them" Strategy	working out dynamics with scenarios (consider and challenge)

- Pass an object as a parameter. Get values from that object only at the point you are ready to use those values.
- Why: better encapsulation; better localization of interface details.

#136. "Take Extra Work Out of the Loop" Strategy	working out dynamics with scenarios (consider and challenge)

- Check each loop within a scenario. Pull work outside of a loop, whenever you can.
- Why: easier to understand (and ultimately, better performance).

#137. "Consistent Object Model and Scenario Views" Strategy	working out dynamics with scenarios (consider and challenge)

- Services in a scenario view should correspond with services in the object model.
  Note: some services in a scenario view are not normally shown in a object model, namely: get, set, add, remove, delete, and create.

- An object in a scenario view needs to know 'to whom to send a message" — either directly (an object connection in an object model) or indirectly (passed as a parameter to a specific service).

#138. "Reduce Interactions" Strategy	working out dynamics with scenarios (consider and challenge)

- Look at interactions that require a lot of messaging—or interactions that require going through many "middle men" to get what you want done, done.

- Consider adding object connections to reduce traffic—and simplify your model.

- Consider the cost: the extra overhead of establishing and maintaining additional object connections.

#139. "Reduce Cascading Messages" Strategy	working out dynamics with scenarios (consider and chalenge)

- If you send a message to to an object, and it sends a message to its collection of objects, whose objects in turn sends a message to its collection of objects: send the message directly to the last object in the cascading message sequence (you might need to add another object connection, so you know to whom to send the message).

- Why: fewer messages makes it easier to understand (and more effecient to implement, too).

- (If the object connections continually change, check out the dynamics of those object connections with scenarios. Then, apply this strategy only if you can keep the object connections in-sync. Sometimes, a few extra object interactions might be simpler after all.)

#139a. "Watch Out For Double Dipping" working out dynamics with scenarios
(consider and challenge)

- Watch out for this shape:

  —-n—->
  —-n—->

- Likely problem:

  —-n—-> qualify
  —-n—-> do the qualified action

- Better approach:

  —-n—-> do it (qualify myself — and if qualified, take action)

- In this way, an object, once it qualifies itself, simply carries out the appropriate action.

  Benefits: reduced object interactions; simpler interface (1 service, rather than 2); stronger cohesion (from decreased distance between recognition and action); better overall performance.

- Related strategy: #132 "Don't Ask 'What Kind'"

#140. "Object Creation and Deletion" Strategy working out dynamics with scenarios
(consider and challenge)

- Look at scenarios that create (and initialize) and delete the objects you work with.

- Ask, "Who is responsible for creating (and initializing) that object? Who is responsible for deleting it?"

#141. "Responsive Data Acquisition
and Control Objects" Strategy working out dynamics with
scenarios (consider and challenge)

- If data acquisition and control are done by one actual object, then model them with one object.

- Otherwise:
  For each control object:
  Add a collection of data acquisition objects.
  The control object takes care of itself — and behavior across the collection.
  For each data acquisition object:
  Each data acquisition object takes care of itself, as much it can do with what it knows (for example, reading values and detecting something from those values).

Discovering new strategies and patterns

This section presents strategies for discovering new strategies and patterns.

#142. "Discovering New Strategies" Strategy	discovery (strategies)

- Introspectively look at each small step you take in building some part of an object model. What advice could you give to others, so they could get that same task accomplished (in fewer steps, in less time, with more regularity)?

- Introspectively consider each correction you make to your model. What advice could you offer to help others avoid that same pitfall in the future?

#143. "Refining Strategies" Strategy	discovery (strategies)

- Describe what you did — your strategy.

- Apply it several more times (in multiple problem domains, if possible).

- Name it. Categorize it.

- Share it with others — and learn from their response.

#144. "Describing Strategies" Strategy	discovery (strategies)

- Include the following:
    - name (the immediate goal) and category
    - the strategy itself—using practical, "how to" words
    - examples

#145. "Discovering New Patterns" Strategy	discovery (patterns)

- Look at each pair, triple, quadruple (etc.) grouping of interacting objects.

- Generalize the names of each player.

- Relate it, by analogy, to other domains. See if it can be used again and again.

#146. "Naming New Patterns" Strategy	discovery (patterns)

- Look for a name that gives a clue about the players in the interaction, suggesting what these interacting objects stereotypically know and do.

- Name the pattern in honor of the players in the pattern.
    Consider synonyms.
    Consider a more general name, using "is a kind of."
    Consider metaphors (corresponding objects) within analogous systems (a system that has an analogous purpose).

#147. "Refining Patterns" Strategy	discovery (patterns)

- Describe it — your pattern.

- Apply it several times (in multiple problem domains, if possible).

- Categorize it: transactions, aggregate, device, interaction, combination — or some other category.

- Share it with others — and learn from their response.

#148. "Describing Patterns" Strategy	discovery (patterns)

- Include the following:
    name (the players, with analogy-provoking names) and category
    the pattern itself—an object-model template
        include stereotypical responsibilities for the pattern players
            common, specific responsibilities
            a few more general responsibilities
                (to encourage readers to think about the responsibilities in broader
                    terms, too)
    typical object interactions
    examples
    combinations.

PATTERNS FOR BUILDING OBJECT MODELS

An object-model pattern is a grouping of objects with stereotypical responsibilities and scenario interactions.

This major section presents patterns organized into various pattern families. First you'll encounter the:
    – Fundamental pattern
Then:
    – Transaction patterns
    – Aggregate patterns
    – Plan patterns
    – Interaction patterns.

Please note that patterns are presented in double-border boxes (strategies are presented in single-border boxes).

The fundamental pattern

This pattern is the fundamental object-model pattern. It's the template that all other patterns follow.

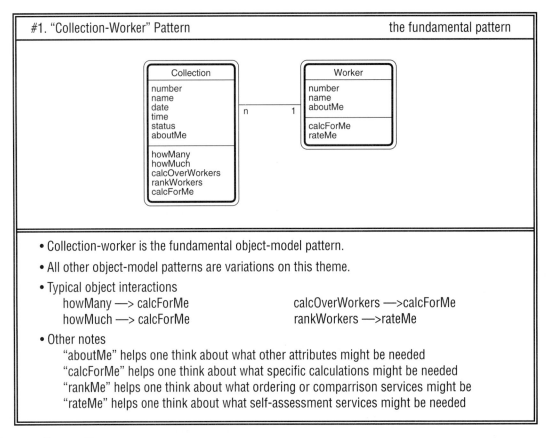

#1. "Collection-Worker" Pattern — the fundamental pattern

- Collection-worker is the fundamental object-model pattern.
- All other object-model patterns are variations on this theme.
- Typical object interactions
  - howMany —> calcForMe   calcOverWorkers —>calcForMe
  - howMuch —> calcForMe   rankWorkers —>rateMe
- Other notes
  - "aboutMe" helps one think about what other attributes might be needed
  - "calcForMe" helps one think about what specific calculations might be needed
  - "rankMe" helps one think about what ordering or comparrison services might be
  - "rateMe" helps one think about what self-assessment services might be needed

Transaction patterns

Transaction patterns are those patterns that have a transaction player — or have players that commonly play with a transaction player.

The transaction patterns are:

- actor-participant

- participant-transaction
- place-transaction
- specific item–transaction

- transaction–transaction line item
- transaction–subsequent transaction
- transaction line item–subsequent transaction line item

- item–line item
- specific item–line item
- item–specific item
- associate–other associate
- specific item–hierarchical item.

Here's an overview of transaction patterns, illustrating how they can interconnect with one another:

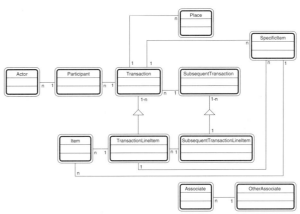

Figure 7–1: An overview of transaction patterns.

#2. "Actor-Participant" Pattern   transaction patterns

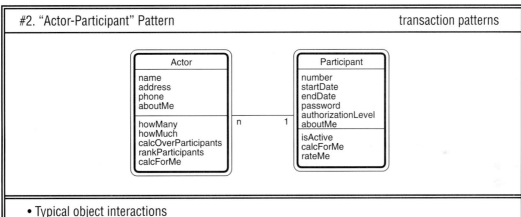

- Typical object interactions

    howMany —> calcForMe   rankParticipants —> rateMe

    howMuch —> calcForMe   getName< — getName

    calcOverParticipants —> calcForMe   getAddress <— getAddress

- Examples

    Actor: person, organization (agency, company, corporation, foundation)

    Participant: agent, applicant, buyer, cashier, clerk, client, civilian, customer, dealer, delegate, distributor, donor, employee, investor, manufacturer, member, officer, official, order clerk, owner, participant, policy holder, professional, prospect, recipient, retailer, sales clerk, sales rep, shipper, student, subscriber, supervisor, supplier, suspect, teacher, wholesaler, worker

    Additional examples: anything used for different missions, such as aircraft-civilian mission, aircraft-military mission.

- Combinations

    participant-transaction; actor-participant, again (for example, customer–gold customer, for a customer who may participate as a gold customer, at least while he qualifies).

#3. "Participant-Transaction" Pattern   transaction patterns

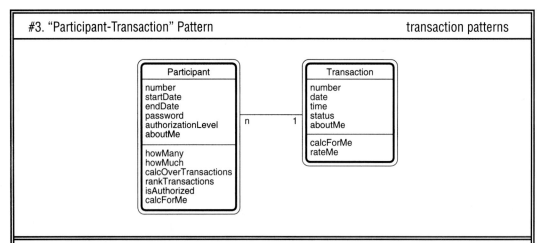

- Typical object interactions
    howMany —> calcForMe   calcOverTransactions —> calcForMe
    howMuch —> calcForMe   rankTransactions —> rateMe
- Examples
    Participant: agent, applicant, buyer, cashier, clerk, client, civilian, customer, dealer,
        delegate, distributor, donor, employee, investor, manufacturer, member, officer,
        official, order clerk, owner, participant, policy holder, professional, prospect,
        recipient, retailer, sales clerk, sales rep, shipper, student, subscriber,
        supervisor, supplier, suspect, teacher, wholesaler, worker.
    Transaction: agreement, assignment, authorization, contract, delivery, deposit,
        incident, inquiry, order, payment, problem, report, purchase, refund, registration,
        rental, reservation, sale, shift, shipment, subscription, time charge, title,
        withdrawal.

- Combinations
    actor-participant; participant-transaction; place-transaction; specific item–
        transaction; transaction–transaction line item; transaction–subsequent
        transaction.

#4. "Place-Transaction" Pattern   transaction patterns

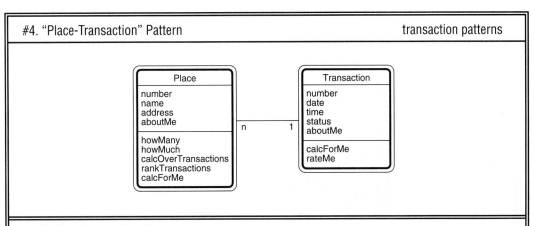

- Typical object interactions
  - howMany —> calcForMe
  - howMuch —> calcForMe
  - calcOverTransactions —> calcForMe
  - rankTransactions —> rateMe
- Examples
  - Place: airport, assembly-line, airport, bank, clinic, depot, garage, geographic entity, hangar, hospital, manufacturing site, plant, region, sales outlet, service center, shelf, station, store, warehouse, zone.
  - Transaction: agreement, assignment, authorization, contract, delivery, deposit, incident, inquiry, order, payment, problem, report, purchase, refund, registration, rental, reservation, sale, shift, shipment, subscription, time charge, title, withdrawal.
- Combinations
  - participant-transaction; specific item–transaction; transaction–transaction line item; transaction–subsequent transaction. Also, using "place" as a container: container-content; container–container line item.

#5. "Specific Item–Transaction" Pattern   transaction patterns

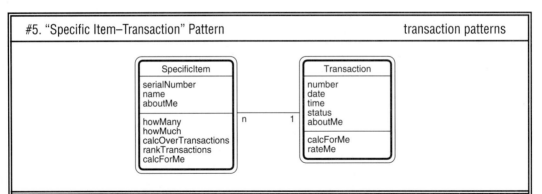

• Typical object interactions

    howMany —> calcForMe   calcOverTransactions —>calcForMe
    howMuch —> calcForMe   rankTransactions —> rateMe

• Examples

    Specific item: specific aircraft, specific container, specific ship, specific register,
        specific vehicle.
    Transaction: agreement, assignment, authorization, contract, delivery, deposit,
        incident, inquiry, order, payment, problem, report, purchase, refund, registration,
        rental, reservation, sale, shift, shipment, subscription, time charge, title,
        withdrawal.

• Combinations

    participant-transaction; place-transaction; specific item–transaction;
        transaction–transaction line item; transaction–subsequent transaction. Also, using
        "specific item" as a container: container-content; container–container line item.

#6. "Transaction–Transaction Line Item" Pattern   transaction patterns

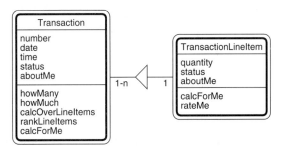

- Typical object interactions
  - howManyOverInterval —> calcForMe   calcOverLineItems —> calcForMe
  - howMuchOverInterval —> calcForMe   rankLineItems —> rateMe
- Examples
  - Transaction: agreement, assignment, authorization, contract, delivery, deposit, incident, inquiry, order, payment, problem, report, purchase, refund, registration, rental, reservation, sale, shift, shipment, subscription, time charge, title, withdrawal.
  - Transaction–transaction line item: deposit–deposit line item; order–order line item; payment–payment line item; rental–rental line item; sale–sale line item; shipment–shipment line item; withdrawal–withdrawal line item.

- Combinations
  - participant-transaction; place-transaction; specific item–transaction; transaction–subsequent transaction; transaction line item–subsequent transaction line item; item–line item; specific item–line item.

#7. "Transaction–Subsequent Transaction" Pattern   transaction patterns

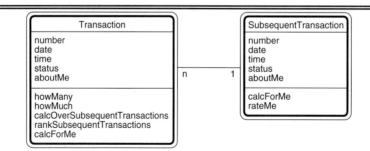

- Typical object interactions

  howMany —> calcForMe   calcOverSubsequentTransactions —> calcForMe

  howMuch —> calcForMe   rankSubsequentTransactions —> rateMe

- Examples

  Transaction: agreement, assignment, authorization, contract, delivery, deposit, incident, inquiry, order, payment, problem, report, purchase, refund, registration, rental, reservation, sale, shift, shipment, subscription, time charge, title, withdrawal.

  Transaction–subsequent transaction: application-issue; intermediate result–final result; order-shipment; purchase-payment; reservation-sale; traffic citation–payment.

- Combinations

  participant-transaction; place-transaction; specific item–transaction; transaction–transaction line item.

- Notes

  Work out transactions in time sequence (the order they usually occur in).

  If subsequent transaction and its line item objects correspond 1-to-1 with transaction and its line item objects, combine them.

#8. "Transaction Line Item–Subsequent Transaction Line Item" Pattern   transaction patterns

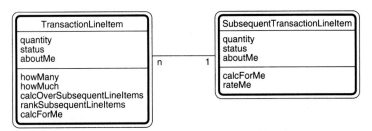

- Typical object interactions
  - howMany —> calcForMe
  - howMuch —> calcForMe
  - calcOverSubsequentLineItems —> calcForMe
  - rankTransactions —> rateMe
- Examples
  - Transaction line items: agreement, assignment, authorization, contract, delivery, deposit, incident, inquiry, order, payment, problem report, purchase, refund, registration, rental, reservation, sale, shift, shipment, subscription, time charge, title, withdrawal.
  - Transaction line item–subsequent transaction line item: order line item–shipment line item; reservation line item–rental line item; shipment line item–delivery line item.

- Combinations
  - transaction–transaction line item; item–line item; specific item–line item.

#9. "Item–Line Item" Pattern   transaction patterns

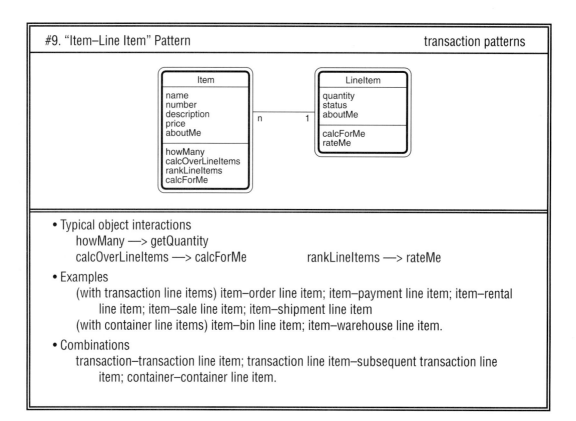

- Typical object interactions
    howMany —> getQuantity
    calcOverLineItems —> calcForMe   rankLineItems —> rateMe
- Examples
    (with transaction line items) item–order line item; item–payment line item; item–rental
        line item; item–sale line item; item–shipment line item
    (with container line items) item–bin line item; item–warehouse line item.
- Combinations
    transaction–transaction line item; transaction line item–subsequent transaction line
        item; container–container line item.

#10. "Specific Item–Line Item" Pattern   transaction patterns

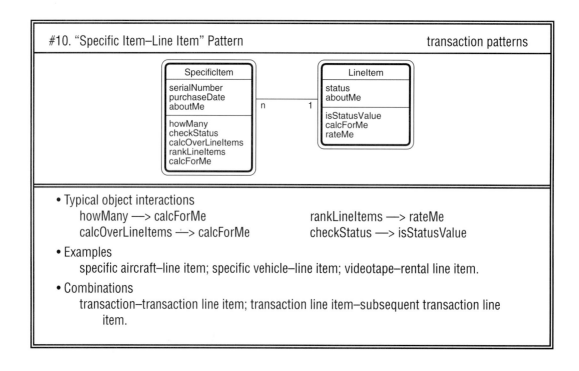

- Typical object interactions
    howMany —> calcForMe   rankLineItems —> rateMe
    calcOverLineItems —> calcForMe   checkStatus —> isStatusValue
- Examples
    specific aircraft–line item; specific vehicle–line item; videotape–rental line item.
- Combinations
    transaction–transaction line item; transaction line item–subsequent transaction line
        item.

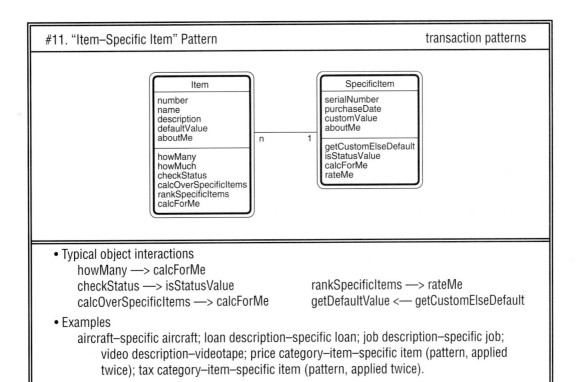

#11. "Item–Specific Item" Pattern   transaction patterns

- Typical object interactions
    - howMany —> calcForMe
    - checkStatus —> isStatusValue   rankSpecificItems —> rateMe
    - calcOverSpecificItems —> calcForMe   getDefaultValue <— getCustomElseDefault

- Examples
    - aircraft–specific aircraft; loan description–specific loan; job description–specific job; video description–videotape; price category–item–specific item (pattern, applied twice); tax category–item–specific item (pattern, applied twice).

- Combinations
    - specific item–transaction; item–line item.

#12. "Associate–Other Associate" Pattern   transaction patterns

```
        ┌─────────────────┐              ┌─────────────────┐
        │    Associate    │              │  OtherAssociate │
        ├─────────────────┤              ├─────────────────┤
        │ number          │              │ number          │
        │ name            │  n        1  │ name            │
        │ aboutMe         │──────────────│ aboutMe         │
        ├─────────────────┤              ├─────────────────┤
        │ howMany         │              │ calcForMe       │
        │ calcOverAssociates│            │ rateMe          │
        │ rankAssociates  │              └─────────────────┘
        │ calcForMe       │
        └─────────────────┘
```

- Typical object interactions
    howMany —> calcForMe
    calcOverOtherAssociates —> calcForMe   rankOtherAssociates —> rateMe

- Examples
    aileron-gyro; aircraft-runway; building-sensor; driver-vehicle; loading dock–order;
        order-tote; truck–loading dock.

- Combinations
    any other pattern.

- Note
    Associates are objects that know each other, without a need for information about that
        association or history about it.
    In some pattern instances, an "other associate" may need to know some number of
        associates.

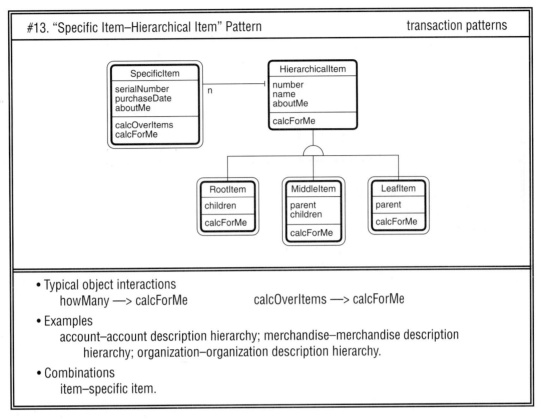

Aggregate patterns

The aggregate patterns are:

     – container-content
     – container–container line item
     – group-member
     – assembly-part
     – compound part–part
     – packet–packet component.

These patterns interconnect with other patterns, sometimes with the help of the "associate–other associate" transaction pattern.

Here's an overview of aggregate patterns:

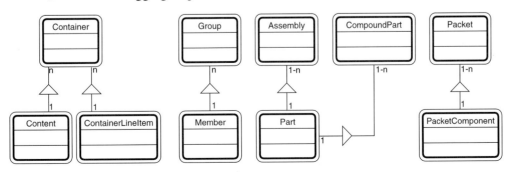

Figure 7–2: An overview of aggregate patterns.

#14. "Container-Content" Pattern   aggregate patterns

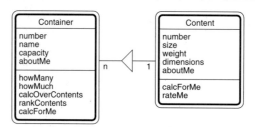

- Typical object interactions

    howMany —> calcForMe   calcOverContents —> calcForMe
    howMuch —> calcForMe   rankContent —> rateMe

- Examples

    Containers

    airport, aircraft, aisle, bank, bin, building, cabinet, folder, garage, hangar, hospital, locker, room, safe, store, warehouse.

    Container–content

    aircraft-cargo; aircraft-passenger; building-room; catalog–catalog item; store-item; warehouse–loading dock.

- Combinations

    container-content (again); container–container line item; group-member; assembly-part. Also, when "container" or "content" is a participant, place, or specific item: actor-participant; participant-transaction; place-transaction; specific item–transaction; specific item–line item; item–specific item.

#15. "Container–Container Line Item" Pattern   aggregate patterns

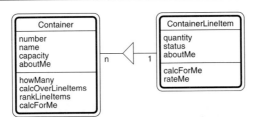

- Typical object interactions
    howMany —> calcForMe
    calcOverLineItems —> calcForMe   rankLineItems —> rateMe

- Examples
    aircraft–aircraft line item; bin–bin line item; warehouse–warehouse line item.

- Combinations
    item–line item; specific item–line item. Also, when "container" is a participant, place,
    or specific item: actor-participant; participant-transaction; place-transaction; specific
    item–transaction; item–specific item.

- Note
    When working with containers within containers, apply this pattern to the smallest
    container in that domain, within your system's responsibilities.

#16. "Group-Member" Pattern   aggregate patterns

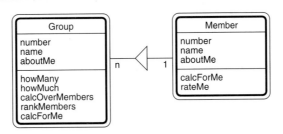

- Typical object interactions
    howMany —> calcForMe
    calcOverMembers —> calcForMe   rankMembers —> rateMe

- Examples
    company-employee; team–team member.

- Combinations
    group-member (again); container-content; assembly-part. Also, when "group" or
    "member" is a participant, place, or specific item:actor-participant; participant-
    transaction; place-transaction; specific item–transaction; specific item–line item;
    item–specific item.

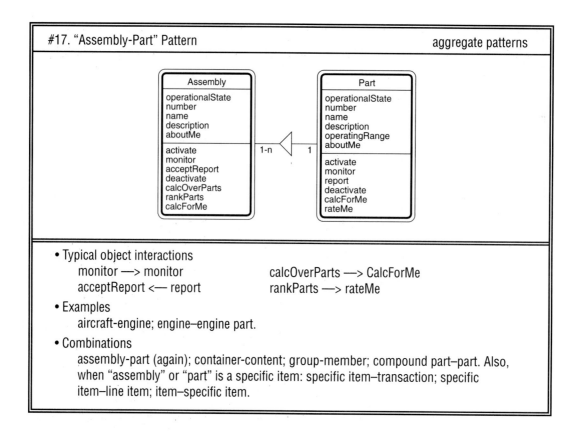

#17. "Assembly-Part" Pattern — aggregate patterns

- Typical object interactions

  monitor —> monitor   calcOverParts —> CalcForMe

  acceptReport <— report   rankParts —> rateMe

- Examples

  aircraft-engine; engine–engine part.

- Combinations

  assembly-part (again); container-content; group-member; compound part–part. Also, when "assembly" or "part" is a specific item: specific item–transaction; specific item–line item; item–specific item.

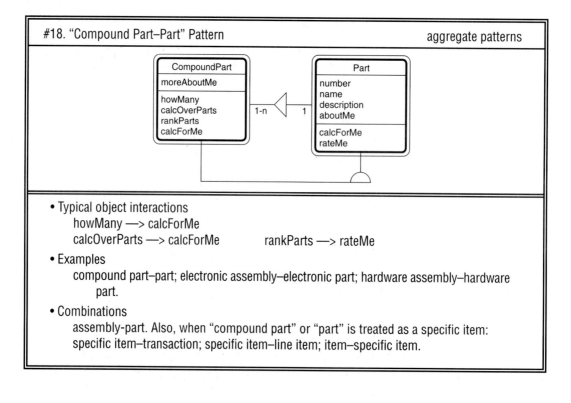

#18. "Compound Part–Part" Pattern — aggregate patterns

- Typical object interactions

  howMany —> calcForMe

  calcOverParts —> calcForMe   rankParts —> rateMe

- Examples

  compound part–part; electronic assembly–electronic part; hardware assembly–hardware part.

- Combinations

  assembly-part. Also, when "compound part" or "part" is treated as a specific item: specific item–transaction; specific item–line item; item–specific item.

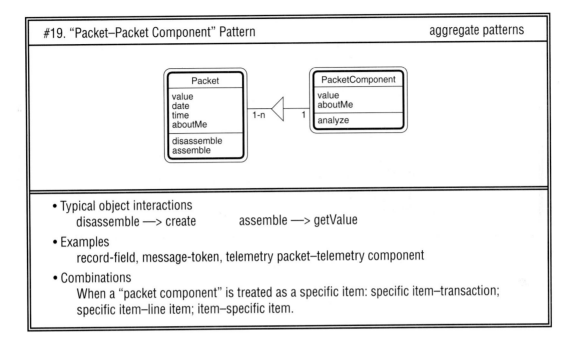

Plan patterns

The plan patterns are:

    – plan-step
    – plan–plan execution
    – plan execution–step execution
    – step–step execution
    – plan–plan version.

Here's an overview of the plan patterns:

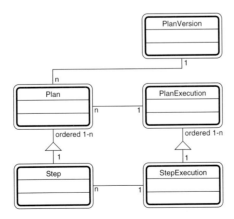

Figure 7–3: An overview of plan patterns.

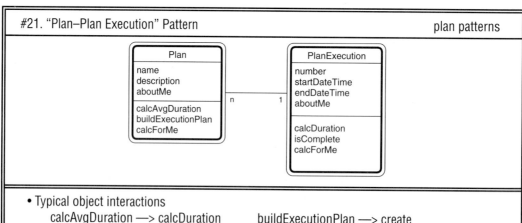

#20. "Plan-Step" Pattern   plan patterns

Plan		Step
name description aboutMe	1-n ◁ 1	description estimatedDuration neededResource aboutMe
estimateDuration gatherNeededResources calcOverSteps rankSteps calcForMe		calcForMe rateMe

- Typical object interactions
     estimateEstDuration —> getEstimatedDuration
     gatherNeededResources —> getNeededResources
     calcOverSteps —> calcForMe
     rankSteps —> rateMe
- Examples
     Plans
          Project plan, battle plan, cooking recipe, batch job, procedure
     Plan-step
          Project plan–task, battle plan–tactical steps, recipe–recipe steps, job–job step,
               procedure–procedure step
- Combinations
     plan–plan execution, step–step execution, plan–plan version.

#21. "Plan–Plan Execution" Pattern   plan patterns

Plan		PlanExecution
name description aboutMe	n 1	number startDateTime endDateTime aboutMe
calcAvgDuration buildExecutionPlan calcForMe		calcDuration isComplete calcForMe

- Typical object interactions
     calcAvgDuration —> calcDuration   buildExecutionPlan —> create
- Examples
     battle plan–battle execution, recipe–recipe execution, job–job execution,
          procedure–procedure execution.
- Combinations
     plan-step, plan execution–step execution, plan–plan version.
- Note
     This is an actual execution of a plan at a date and time. Use this pattern when a plan
          may be executed several times. (If the plan is executed only once, the
          responsibilities for plan execution could be added to a plan.)

#22. "Step–Step Execution" Pattern   plan patterns

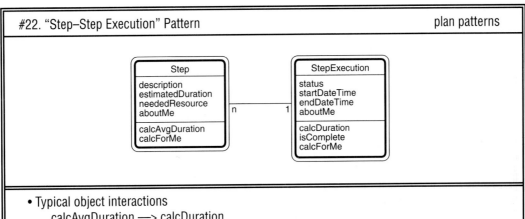

- Typical object interactions
    calcAvgDuration —> calcDuration

- Examples
    tactic–tactic execution, recipe step–recipe step execution, job step–job step execution, procedure step–procedure step execution.

- Combinations
    plan–step, plan execution–step execution.

#23. "Plan Execution–Step Execution" Pattern   plan patterns

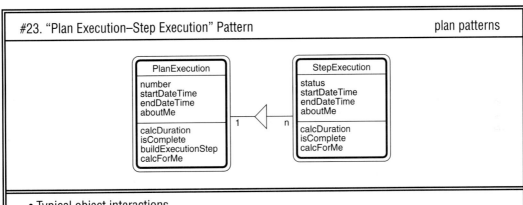

- Typical object interactions
    calcDuration —> calcDuration
    isComplete —> isComplete   buildExecutionStep —> create

- Examples
    battle execution–tactics execution, recipe execution–recipe step execution, job execution–job step execution, procedure execution–procedure step execution

- Combinations
    plan-step, plan–plan execution.

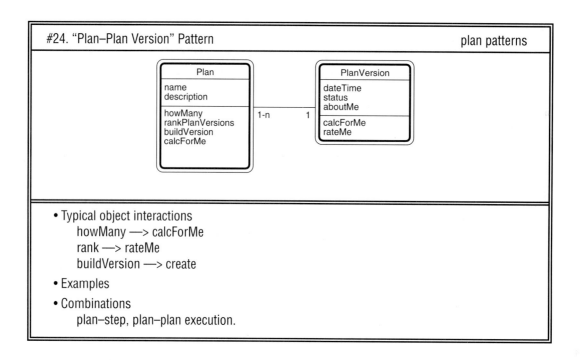

- Typical object interactions
     howMany —> calcForMe
     rank —> rateMe
     buildVersion —> create
- Examples
- Combinations
     plan–step, plan–plan execution.

Interaction patterns

Interaction patterns are patterns of how objects work with each other. Overlay these patterns on players in other patterns.

The interaction patterns are:
- peer-peer
- proxy–specific item
- publisher-subscriber
- sender–pass through–receiver
- sender-lookup-receiver
- caller–dispatcher–caller back
- gatekeeper-request-resource.

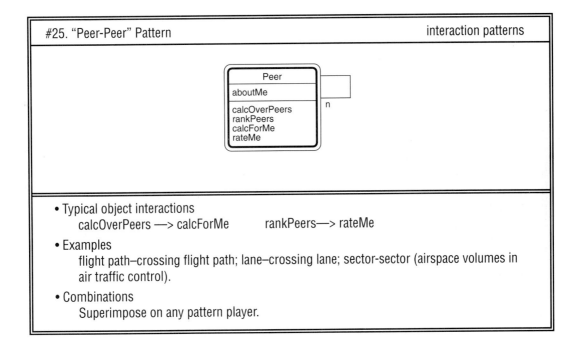

#25. "Peer-Peer" Pattern   interaction patterns

- Typical object interactions
    calcOverPeers —> calcForMe   rankPeers—> rateMe

- Examples
    flight path–crossing flight path; lane–crossing lane; sector-sector (airspace volumes in air traffic control).

- Combinations
    Superimpose on any pattern player.

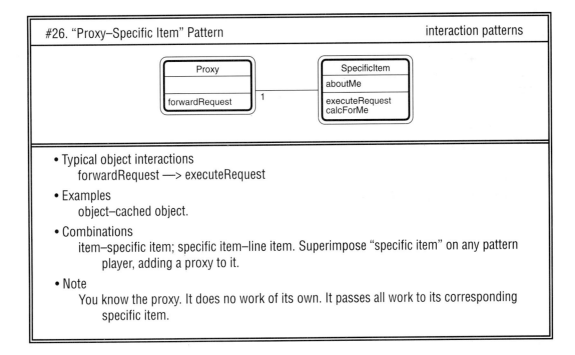

#26. "Proxy–Specific Item" Pattern   interaction patterns

- Typical object interactions
    forwardRequest —> executeRequest

- Examples
    object–cached object.

- Combinations
    item–specific item; specific item–line item. Superimpose "specific item" on any pattern player, adding a proxy to it.

- Note
    You know the proxy. It does no work of its own. It passes all work to its corresponding specific item.

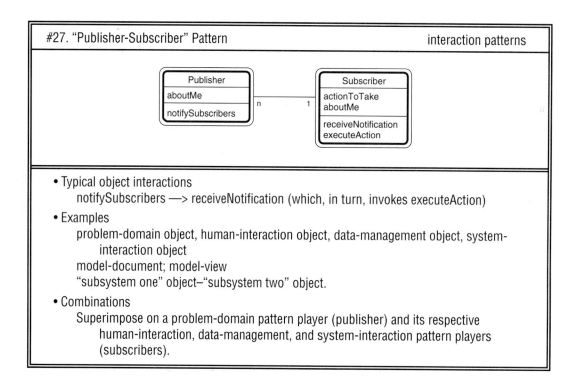

#27. "Publisher-Subscriber" Pattern   interaction patterns

- Typical object interactions
    notifySubscribers —> receiveNotification (which, in turn, invokes executeAction)
- Examples
    problem-domain object, human-interaction object, data-management object, system-
        interaction object
    model-document; model-view
    "subsystem one" object–"subsystem two" object.
- Combinations
    Superimpose on a problem-domain pattern player (publisher) and its respective
        human-interaction, data-management, and system-interaction pattern players
        (subscribers).

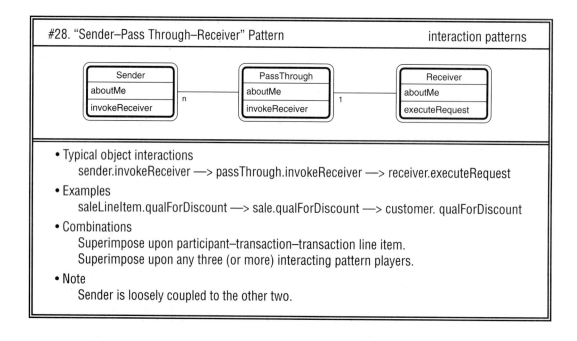

#28. "Sender–Pass Through–Receiver" Pattern   interaction patterns

- Typical object interactions
    sender.invokeReceiver —> passThrough.invokeReceiver —> receiver.executeRequest
- Examples
    saleLineItem.qualForDiscount —> sale.qualForDiscount —> customer. qualForDiscount
- Combinations
    Superimpose upon participant–transaction–transaction line item.
    Superimpose upon any three (or more) interacting pattern players.
- Note
    Sender is loosely coupled to the other two.

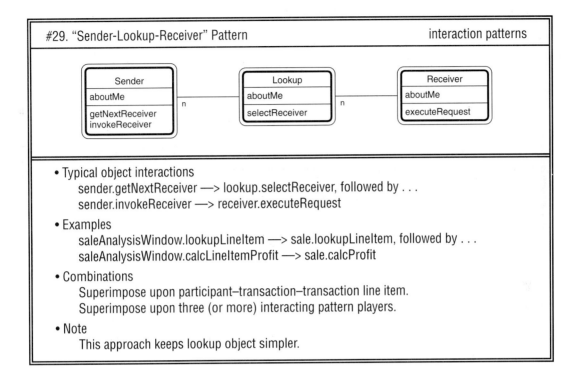

#29. "Sender-Lookup-Receiver" Pattern   interaction patterns

- Typical object interactions
    sender.getNextReceiver —> lookup.selectReceiver, followed by . . .
    sender.invokeReceiver —> receiver.executeRequest
- Examples
    saleAnalysisWindow.lookupLineItem —> sale.lookupLineItem, followed by . . .
    saleAnalysisWindow.calcLineItemProfit —> sale.calcProfit
- Combinations
    Superimpose upon participant–transaction–transaction line item.
    Superimpose upon three (or more) interacting pattern players.
- Note
    This approach keeps lookup object simpler.

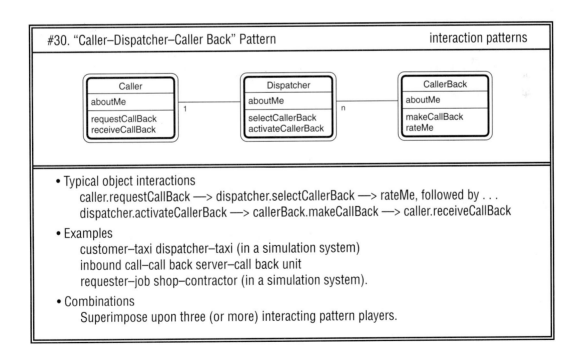

#30. "Caller–Dispatcher–Caller Back" Pattern   interaction patterns

- Typical object interactions
    caller.requestCallBack —> dispatcher.selectCallerBack —> rateMe, followed by . . .
    dispatcher.activateCallerBack —> callerBack.makeCallBack —> caller.receiveCallBack
- Examples
    customer–taxi dispatcher–taxi (in a simulation system)
    inbound call–call back server–call back unit
    requester–job shop–contractor (in a simulation system).
- Combinations
    Superimpose upon three (or more) interacting pattern players.

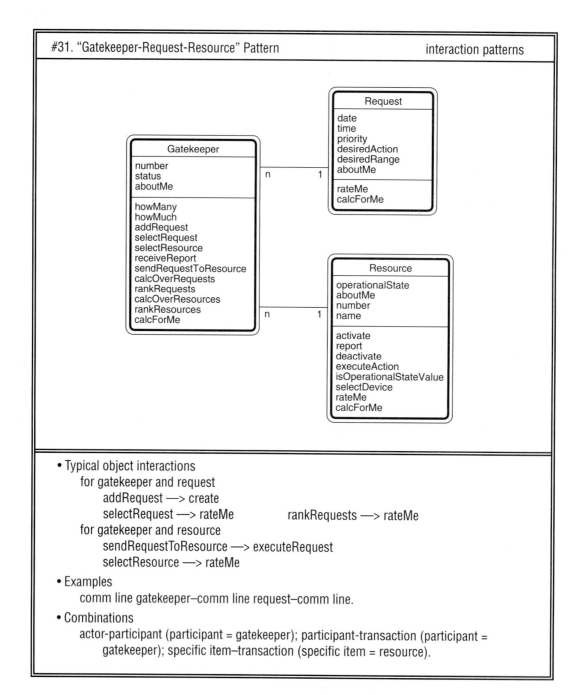

#31. "Gatekeeper-Request-Resource" Pattern   interaction patterns

Request
- date
- time
- priority
- desiredAction
- desiredRange
- aboutMe

- rateMe
- calcForMe

Gatekeeper
- number
- status
- aboutMe

- howMany
- howMuch
- addRequest
- selectRequest
- selectResource
- receiveReport
- sendRequestToResource
- calcOverRequests
- rankRequests
- calcOverResources
- rankResources
- calcForMe

Resource
- operationalState
- aboutMe
- number
- name

- activate
- report
- deactivate
- executeAction
- isOperationalStateValue
- selectDevice
- rateMe
- calcForMe

- Typical object interactions
    - for gatekeeper and request
        - addRequest —> create
        - selectRequest —> rateMe   rankRequests —> rateMe
    - for gatekeeper and resource
        - sendRequestToResource —> executeRequest
        - selectResource —> rateMe

- Examples
    - comm line gatekeeper–comm line request–comm line.

- Combinations
    - actor-participant (participant = gatekeeper); participant-transaction (participant = gatekeeper); specific item–transaction (specific item = resource).

Epilog

A friend and colleague, Roland Racko, inspired us to write this epilog.

THE COAD METHOD—SOME CLOSING REMARKS

What is the Coad method all about?

It's about simplicity, clarity, and brevity (effective communication is a must).

It's about producing frequent, tangible, working results.

It's about one integrated model, from concept to code.

Most importantly, it's about empowering people and helping developers achieve a greater level of creativity and innovation.

STRATEGIES FOR DISCOVERING YOUR OWN STRATEGIES AND PATTERNS

We close this book by sharing with you the strategies for discovering new strategies and patterns.

Why do we share these strategies with you?

– To encourage you to explore, carefully consider, and discover new strategies and patterns of your own.
– To ask you to send in strategies and patterns that you discover, for inclusion in—and recognition in—updates of this work.

And so, here are the discovery strategies:

#142. "Discovering New Strategies" Strategy	discovery (strategies)
• Introspectively look at each small step you take in building some part of an object model. What advice could you give to others, so they could get that same task accomplished (in fewer steps, in less time, with more regularity)? • Introspectively consider each correction you make to your model. What advice could you offer to help others avoid that same pitfall in the future?	

#143. "Refining Strategies" Strategy	discovery (strategies)
• Describe what you did—your strategy. • Apply it several more times (in multiple problem domains, if possible). • Name it. Categorize it. • Share it with others—and learn from their response.	

#144. "Describing Strategies" Strategy   discovery (strategies)

- Include the following:
    - name (the immediate goal) and category
    - the strategy itself—using practical, "how to" words
    - examples

#145. "Discovering New Patterns" Strategy   discovery (patterns)

- Look at each pair, triple, quadruple (etc.) grouping of interacting objects.

- Generalize the names of each player.

- Relate it, by analogy, to other domains. See if it can be used again and again.

#146. "Naming New Patterns" Strategy   discovery (patterns)

- Look for a name that gives a clue about the players in the interaction, suggesting what these interacting objects stereotypically know and do.

- Name the pattern in honor of the players in the pattern.
  Consider synonyms.
  Consider a more general name, using "is a kind of."
  Consider metaphors (corresponding objects) within analogous systems (a system that has an analogous purpose).

#147. "Refining Patterns" Strategy   discovery (patterns)

- Describe it — your pattern.

- Apply it several times (in multiple problem domains, if possible).

- Categorize it: transactions, aggregate, device, interaction, combination — or some other category.

- Share it with others — and learn from their response.

#148. "Describing Patterns" Strategy   discovery (patterns)

- Include the following:
        name (the players, with analogy-provoking names) and category
        the pattern itself—an object-model template
                include stereotypical responsibilities for the pattern players
                        common, specific responsibilities
                        a few more general responsibilities
                                (to encourage readers to think about the responsibilities in broader
                                        terms, too)
        typical object interactions
        examples

        combinations.

Thank you for reading. Have an excellent time building object models! We wish you great success.

Peter Coad
Object International, Inc., Raleigh, NC USA
coad@oi.com   http://www.oi.com
PGP fingerprint:
3D BA 3B DD 57 B6 04 EB
B7 30 9D 06 A1 E1 05 50

David North
Applied Intelligence Group, Oklahoma City OK USA
dnorth@aig.com

Mark Mayfield
Austin TX USA
mlm@oi.com
PGP fingerprint:
B1 CB BE 43 1E 74 22 57
08 AF 7E CE 5B DA A5 3B

Appendix A
Notation

This appendix is a concise summary of the Coad notation.

It covers:

– the symbols
– the connections
– a business example
– a real-time example
– scenario views
– object-model components
– other notations, not included (and why).

CRITICAL SUCCESS FACTORS

What are the critical success factors of a notation? An effective notation is:

– easy to learn, easy to remember, easy to use (even on the back of an envelope or on a white board)
– embodies simplicity, clarity, and brevity (effective communication is a must)
– supports the planning, development, and delivery of frequent, tangible, working results
– consists of one multifaceted model, from concept to code
– facilitate creativity and innovation (what object methods are all about, anyway).

THE SYMBOLS

The notation includes two symbols.

The class-with-objects symbol

The most commonly used icon is a class-with-objects symbol (Figure A–1):

Figure A–1: A class with objects.

The bold, inner-rounded rectangle represents a class (a class is a description which applies to each of some number of objects).

The outer rounded rectangle represents one or some number of objects in a class. Within this symbol:

- the class name goes in the upper section (name begins with an uppercase letter)
- the attribute names go in the center section (name begins with a lower case letter)
- the service names go in the bottom section (name begins with a lower case letter).[1]

Connecting to this symbol:

- a generalization-specialization (gen-spec) structure connects from one class (inner rounded rectangle) to another
- an object connection connects from one object to another (with the object connection constraint place next to the object so constrained)
- within a scenario view, a message goes from sending object to receiving object (or a class, when invoking a "create" service).

The class symbol

The second one is a "class" symbol—a class without directly corresponding objects, useful only as a generalization in a generalization-specialization (gen-spec) structure (Figure A–2):

Figure A–2: A class without directly corresponding objects.

---

[1] What about the ordering of attributes and services? Order attributes only if you find it helpful in being more thorough while building an object model, or more effective in communicating your object-model results.

The patterns follow this ordering approach:
attributes:
operationalState, number, name, address, date, time, status, aboutMe
services:
activate, monitor, deactivate (or similar)
how many, how much, rank, is <whatever, across a collection>
calcForMe, rate, is <whatever, for me>.

Alternatively, you may choose to list your attributes and services using one of these approaches:
- alphabetical order
- state, state-dependent, and state-independent attributes; state-dependent and state-inde pendent services (with each section organized alphabetically; for the state-dependent sections, perhaps in a common sequence over time)
- no particular order at all!

Within this symbol:

- the class name goes in the upper section
- the attribute names go in the center section
- the service names go in the bottom section.

Connecting to this symbol:

- a generalization-specialization (gen-spec) structure connects from one class (inner rounded rectangle) to another
- an object connection connects from one object to another (with the object connection constraint place next to the object so constrained)—so the object connection is shown slightly offset from the bold rounded rectangle (the object connection is inherited by its specialization classes).

Attribute and service descriptions

Attribute and service descriptions communicate fine details in an object model. For attribute descriptions, use the templates described in strategies #58 and #59. For service descriptions, use the templates described in strategies #116 and #117.

THE CONNECTIONS

Connections between classes

The connection between classes is a gen-spec structure (Figure A–3):

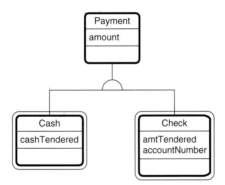

Figure A–3: a gen-spec structure, portraying a generalization class (payment) and its specialization (cash, check).

The semicircle is an umbrella, spanning the "is a kind of" specializations.

Note that this connection is directional, so you are free to place the participating classes wherever you want them.

You may use a class or "class with objects" symbol as a generalization. The bottom-most specializations must be "class with object" symbols.

Connections between objects

The connections between objects is an object connection.

The connecting line

An object connection is a line, from one object to another object.

If an object connection connects to a class symbol, to be inherited by all of its specialization object, then the connection appears just slightly offset from the class symbol.

The meaning of the line

An object connection usually carries the meaning of "participates in" or "is associated with."

Some object connections carry a much stronger meaning, whole-part (also called aggregation). Whole-part has three basic shades of meaning: container-content, group-member, and assembly-part. A whole-part object connection gets an added annotation: a triangle on the line, pointing to the whole object.

The object connection constraints

Object connections have connection constraints.

A connection constraint appears next to each object being constrained.

Nearly always, you need to constrain each object participating in an object connection. Why?

   – an object connection shows the need to maintain "to whom to send a message"
   – an object connection shows the need to maintain knowledge of another object, to support whatever queries might be made of it.

Occasionally, notably in real-time systems, you may need to constrain just one side of an object connection:

   – one object needs to know another, to know "to whom to send a message"
   – no basic querying support is necessary.

Object connection constraints follow these conventions:

   – Include constraints, placed next to each object being constrained:
        1   0-1   n   1-n   <blank>   ordered   n   [XOR A] 1   [OR B] 2
        [C] ordered n   all
   – "n" is the same thing as "0-n" (it's just easier to write it as "n").
   – A <blank> constraint indicates that an object has no need to know the other objects (this may occur, notably for part in an aggregate).
   – *Ordered n*   an ordered collection of some number of connections

   – *[XOR A] 1* indicates an exclusive or, pertaining to all object connections labeled with the same tag (in this example the tag is "A"). Place whatever constraint applies to the right of the brackets, e.g., [XOR A] 1.
   – *[OR B] 2*   two connections, selected from the connections labeled "B".

   – *[C] ordered n* an ordered collection of some number of connections (any connection from that object that is labeled "C").

An alternative representation

At times, an abundance of connecting lines between an abundance of objects can really get out-of-hand.

There is an alternative representation. Use attributes, instead. Here are some guidelines:

Use this format whenever an object connection spans across model components or any other time that an object connection would be cumbersome, visually.

For a textual representation, use this format:

"<class name, beginning with a lowercase letter>"

Make it singular or plural, reflecting the number of objects that the object may know.

A BUSINESS EXAMPLE

Here's an example (Figure A–4):

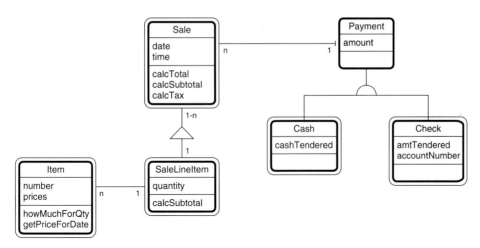

Figure A–4: A connection example.

Here are some notes on the connections in this model:

   – connections between classes

      – gen-spec (generalization-specialization) connections

         the cash and check classes are specializations, a kind of, payment class

   – connections between objects

      – object connections

         a sale knows some number of cash payments, check payments, or both

         a cash payment or check payment knows its sale

         a sale line item knows its item

         an item knows some number of sale line items.

– whole-part object connections
  a sale is a group of one up to some number of sale line items
     (the parts of the sale).
  a sale knows its sale line items; a sale line item knows its sale.

A REAL-TIME EXAMPLE

Here's a real-time data acquisition and control example (Figure A–5):

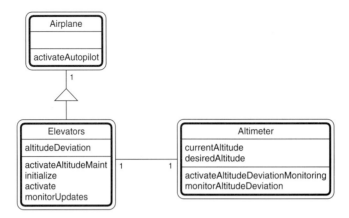

Figure A–5: Another connection example.

Here are some notes on the connections in this model:
- connections between classes
  - none
- connections between objects
  - object connections
    - an elevators object knows its altimeter object
    - an altimeter object knows its elevators object (to report back to it, over time)
  - whole-part object connections
    - an aircraft is an assembly; the elevators object (an object that is re sponsible for a pair of elevators) is its part
    - an aircraft object knows its elevators objects; an elevators object has no need to know its airplane object.

SCENARIO VIEWS

A scenario view is simply a view on an object model, called out to portray a specific scenario, a time-ordered sequence of object interactions, to fulfill a specific need.

In a scenario view, the object part of a class-with-objects symbol grows down the screen (or page) (Figure A–6).

A scenario view shows:

    – the objects participating in the scenario (across the top of the view)

followed by a time sequence (going down the page) with the following:

       – sending service, a message arrow, a receiving service, and arguments
       – sending service, a message arrow, a receiving service, and arguments
       – sending service, a message arrow, a receiving service, and arguments.

Please note that there is a leveling of detail here. Scenario views fully expose the object interactions. Service descriptions present the details of a specific service.

Sale	SaleLineItem	Item	
calcTotal calcSubtotal calcTax	calcSubtotal	howMuchForQty getPriceForDate	Scenario: sale – calculate total. Scenario constraint: 0.1 seconds, 9 out of 10 times, 0.5 seconds max.
calcTotal				*sale.calcTotal (; total)*
- - ► calcSubtotal				*sale.calcSubtotal (; subtotal)*
	- - n - - ► calcSubtotal			*saleLineItem.calcSubtotal (; subtotal)*
		- - - - - ► howMuchForQty		*item.howMuchForQty (qty, date ; amt)*
		- - ► getPriceForDate		*item.getPriceForDate (date ; price)*
[calcTotal]				
IF				*// if taxable*
- - ► calcTax				*sale.calcTax (; totalTax)*
ENDIF				

Figure A–6. The "sale—calculate total" scenario.

Here's how to read it:

A sale object is told to calculate its total.

The "calcTotal" service invokes the "calcSubtotal" service.

The "calcSubtotal" sends a "calcSubtotal" message to a sale line item object (and it may do this a number of times).

A sale line item is told to calculate its subtotal.

The "calcSubtotal" service sends a "howMuchForQty" message to an item object, giving it a quantity and a date.

An item object is told to calculate its amount for quantity. The "howMuchForQty" service invokes the "getPriceForDate" service, giving it a date. The "getPriceForDate" service returns a price. The "howMuchForQty" returns an amount.

The "calcSubtotal" service returns a subtotal.

The "calcSubtotal" service returns "subtotal."

If taxable, the "calcTotal" service invokes the "calcTax" service. The "calcTax" service returns "totalTax."

The "calcTotal" service returns "total."

Here are some scenario view conventions and notes:

- The recognizing object and service is in the leftmost column.
- A message arrow points from a sender service (the service that precedes the tail of a message arrow) to a receiver service (the message arrow head points to it).
- If a message is sent to a collection of objects in another class, label the message with an "n".
- Within an object symbol, when you need a control structure, choose from the following:

    IF / ELSE / ENDIF

    WHILE / ENDWHILE

    DO / ENDDO

    CASE / ENDCASE

    START_TASK / STOP_TASK.

- For real-time tasking, use:

    START_TASK (<service>) starts the service as a new task

    STOP_TASK (<service>) stops the service running as a task.

- To get or set an attribute, or add or remove an object connection, use this format:

    get <attribute name> (; <attribute name>)

        for example, getName (; name)

    set <attribute name> (<attribute name> ;)

        for example, setName (name ;)

    add <the corresponding class name> (<object> ;)

        for example, addSale (rental ;)

    remove <the corresponding class name> (<object> ;)

        for example, removeSale (rental ;)

- When more than one object of a class participates in a scenario, it's often helpful to represent both objects with separate columns in a scenario view (along with the role each one plays, in parentheses). Why? Doing this makes it easier to work out, express, and communicate the object interactions.
- In the right-hand column:
    - name the scenario
    - constrain the scenario, as needed
    - list each invoked service, with its arguments

        <object name>.<service name> (<inputs> ; <outputs>)

    - for a create service, use this format:

        <class name>.<service name> (<inputs> ; <object name>)

            for example, Sale.create (rental line items ; rental)

Here's a real-time example (Figure A–7):

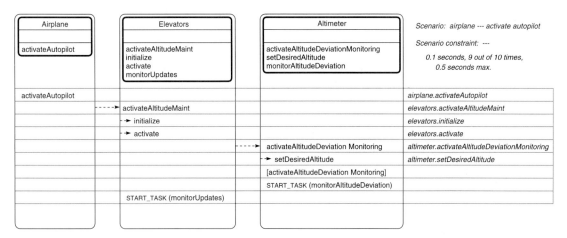

Airplane	Elevators	Altimeter	
activateAutopilot	activateAltitudeMaint initialize activate monitorUpdates	activateAltitudeDeviationMonitoring setDesiredAltitude monitorAltitudeDeviation	
activateAutopilot			airplane.activateAutopilot
	activateAltitudeMaint		elevators.activateAltitudeMaint
	initialize		elevators.initialize
	activate		elevators.activate
		activateAltitudeDeviation Monitoring	altimeter.activateAltitudeDeviationMonitoring
		setDesiredAltitude	altimeter.setDesiredAltitude
		[activateAltitudeDeviation Monitoring]	
		START_TASK (monitorAltitudeDeviation)	
	START_TASK (monitorUpdates)		

Scenario: airplane --- activate autopilot

Scenario constraint: ---

0.1 seconds, 9 out of 10 times,
0.5 seconds max.

Figure A–7: The "airplane—activate autopilot."

OBJECT-MODEL COMPONENTS

So what kind of partitioning works well within an object model?

Use these model components:

- problem domain (PD)
(classes relating to the business at hand)
- human interaction (HI)
(windows and reports)
- data management (DM)
(object servers)
- system interaction (SI)
(other systems)
- "not this time" (NT)
(outside of scope for this system).

Each class fits into just one of these model components.

Why use model components (Figure A–8)? To partition the classes into meaningful, loosely coupled subsets. Here's how it works:

- The PD component has little knowledge about the other components. The PD component broadcasts changes to the other components; it's up to the other components to decide what to do about such changes.
- The HI component interacts with the PD component for whatever content is needed for human interaction.
- The DM component interacts with the HI component, whenever a "save" or "load" is selected from the HI component.
- The SI component interacts with the PD component for whatever content is needed for system interaction.

By organizing classes this way, you facilitate simpler modeling this time (within each model component).

You also increase the likelihood of reuse next time. Why? Here's an example. Next time, you might want to reuse certain problem-domain classes, even though you may choose to work with different human interaction classes.

What's the alternative? Smash the model components together. But then the overall model is harder to understand; and in the future, unless you choose the same problem domain, human interaction, data management, and task management approach, reuse is very unlikely. Ouch!

So, use model components. Use them as an overall outline, a guide for selecting objects. And use them to keep your classes well organized, for understanding and for reuse.

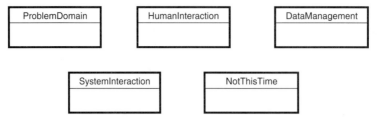

Figure A–8: Object-model components.

The object-model component name (or abbreviation) goes in the upper half of the rectangle. The class names in that component go in the lower half of the rectangle.

Note the "not this time" object-model component. It's a bucket on the side, to portray what's not in the system this time.

OTHER NOTATIONS, NOT INCLUDED (AND WHY)

Many times, people ask why we don't use one notation or another.

Here's the story, covering:

    – class, state, and function diagrams
    – data flow diagrams
    – state-transition diagrams
    – separate analysis and design notations
    – subjects (subsystem) notations
    – symbols without end.

Class, state, and function diagrams

Class, state, and function diagrams?

Can you say "entity-relationship, state-transition, and data-flow"?

Good grief!

A paradigm is a set of rules and guidelines for problem solving. A new paradigm makes old problems go away. A new paradigm greatly simplifies what one did before. A new paradigm levels the playing field (those with experience in the older paradigm have little advantage over others, at the onset of a new paradigm).

Object-oriented development is a paradigm change.

Class, state, and function diagrams? To suggest such a multimodel triad is to miss out entirely on paradigm change. Things don't get simpler. Instead, they get more complex (and justified in the name of rigor and discipline).

Yuck!

Data-flow diagrams

If a service is so complex that you need a data-flow diagram to describe it, you've got a partitioning problem, for sure.

Go back and select some additional objects. Then apply the "establishing responsibilities / what I do (where to put)" strategies.

State transition diagrams

State transition diagrams are a kludge from the past.

Looking for a way to market structured techniques to the real-time community, someone came up with the idea to use control data-flow diagrams and state diagrams—to manage what the bubbles on a data flow diagram were doing. Talk about the antithesis of encapsulation! It's no wonder that state diagrams—even more elaborate, hierarchical ones—couldn't keep up.

Encapsulate state-dependency within an object (or an object which is responsible for a collection objects).

State-dependency means that an object responds differently depending on its state. Regarding attributes services, please note:

  – Attributes: state, state-dependent, state-independent
      In its description, include: applicable states.
  – Services: state-dependent, state-independent
      In its description, include:
          precondition: <indicate what you assert to be true, before this service can run>
          postcondition: <indicate what you assert to be true, before this service can go to completion>
          trigger: <indicate what state transitions activate this service>
          terminate: <indicate what state transitions terminate this service>.

Separate analysis and design notations

Separate analysis and design models?

Yuck!

Yes, you need to separate concerns—problem domain, human interaction, system interaction, data management.

No, you don't need to divide them into separate models.

Why is this important? You need to be free to consider both analysis and design matters as they come up, right when they come up. Moreover, with objects, you can deliver frequent, tangible, working results; separate models will keep you from doing that effectively.

Subject (subsystem) notations

Subjects, subsystems, and comparable notations are rudimentary tools for view management.

Extensive and flexible view management is far better.

In a given view, include only those objects you are interested in:

– the objects and interactions in a scenario
– the objects in a subject area
– the objects to be developed and delivered as a subsystem.

In each case, use view management to present exactly what is needed, when you need it (the whole story, yet nothing more).

Symbols without end

For many years, we have resisted the temptation to add an abundance of symbols.

And we continue to do so, even now.

Why?

Once you open that Pandora's box, there is no end to added symbols.

Object models get harder and harder to read. Effective communication grinds to a halt.

What's the question abundant-symbol advocates forget to ask? It's "What medium best expresses nitty-gritty detail—graphics or text?"

The answer is—text! Such detail is best portrayed in text. You can even use programming-language syntax itself (it's just a small amount of syntax, something everyone on the team can easily relate to and use, without referring to a "notation guidebook" to figure out what's needed).

How can you see the results graphically, without symbols. That's easy. Annotate in text. Then use view management, based upon that text (for example to see public, protected, private, or whatever combination you might choose).

WRAP-UP

That's it! You've got it—a complete summary of the Coad notation, covering:

– the symbols
– the connections
– a business example
– a real-time example
– scenario views
– object-model components
– other notations, not included (and why).

Enjoy.

Appendix B
Patterns In Other Fields

Patterns are a significant part of human experience. To gain insights into the many facets of patterns, consider these selected quotations:

> The speech of man is like embroidered tapestries, since like them this too has to be extended in order to display its *patterns*, but when it is rolled up it conceals and distorts them.
>
> —Themistocles (c. 528–462 B.C.)
> from Plutarch's *Lives*

[selected excerpts]

Figures of delight, drawn after you, you *pattern* of all those;

By the *pattern* of mine own thoughts I cut the purity out of his;

Their memory shall as a *pattern* or a measure live;

So we could find some *pattern* of our shame;

A *pattern*, a precedent and lively warrant for me to perform the like;

Beauty's *pattern* to succeeding men;

Pattern in himself to know;

He is one of the *patterns* of love;

A *pattern* to all princes;

I will be the *pattern* of all patience;

This *pattern* of the worn-out age pawned honest looks;

Knew the *patterns* of his foul beguiling;

A *pattern* of celestial peace;

The *patterns* that by God and by French fathers had twenty years been made;

Behold this *pattern* of thy butcheries;

Thou cunningnest *pattern* of excelling nature;

Let mine own judgment *pattern* out my death;

Which is more than history can *pattern*;

Patterned by thy fault, foul sin may say;

Such a place, *patterned* by that the poet here describes.

—William Shakespeare, (1564–1616)
Various Works

[selected excerpts]

According to all that I shew thee, [after] the *pattern* of the tabernacle, and the *pattern* of all the instruments thereof, even so shall ye make [it].

Make [them] [many objects] after their *pattern*, which was shewed thee in the mount;

According unto the *pattern* which the Lord had shewed Moses, so he made the candlestick;

Behold the *pattern* of the altar of the Lord...it [is] a witness between us and you;

An altar...and the *pattern* of it, according to all the workmanship thereof;

David gave to Solomon his son the *pattern* of the porch, and of the houses thereof;

The *pattern* of all that he had by the spirit, of the courts of the house of the Lord;

The *pattern* of the chariot of the cherubims...and covered the ark of the covenant of the Lord;

The Lord made me understand in writing by [his] hand upon me, [even] all the works of this *pattern*;

Thou son of man, shew the house to the house of Israel...and let them measure the *pattern*;

Howbeit for this cause I [Paul] obtained mercy, that in me first Jesus Christ might shew forth all longsuffering, for a *pattern* to them which should hereafter believe on him to life everlasting;

Shewing thyself a *pattern* of good works: in doctrine [shewing] un-corruptness, gravity, sincerity;

Thou make all things according to the *pattern* shewed to thee in the mount;

[It was] therefore necessary that the *patterns* of things in the heavens should be purified.

—*The Bible*, Authorized Version,
(1611)

The power to guess the unseen from the seen, to trace the implications of things, to judge the whole piece by the *pattern*, the condition of feeling in life in general so completely that you are well on your way to knowing any particular corner of it—this cluster of gifts may almost be said to constitute experience. . . . If experience consists of impressions, it may be said that impressions *are* experience.

—Henry James
The Art of Fiction (1888)

Law accepts as the *pattern* of its justice the morality of the community whose conduct it assumes to regulate.

[On a collection of legal conclusions, made over time] ...the time must come when we shall do prudently to look them [ad hoc conclusions] over, and see whether they make a *pattern* or a medley of scraps and patches.

Benjamin N. Cardozo
The Paradoxes of Legal Science,
(1928)

[On copyrights] Upon any work, and especially upon a play, a great number of *patterns* of increasing generality will fit equally well, as more and more of the incident is left out...

Learned Hand
Nichols v. Universal Pictures Corp.,
(1930)

Art is the imposing of a *pattern* on experience, and our aesthetic enjoyment in recognition of the *pattern*.

—Alfred North Whitehead
Dialogues (1953)

A mathematician, like a painter or a poet, is a maker of patterns. If his *patterns* are more permanent than theirs, it is because they are made with ideas.

—Godfrey Harold Hardy
A Mathematician's Apology (1940)

Physics tries to discover the *pattern* of events which controls the phenomena we observe. But we can never know what this *pattern* means or how it originates; and even if some superior intelligence were to tell us, we should find the explanation unintelligible.

—Sir James Hopwood Jeans
Physics and Philosophy (1942)

Home is where one starts from. As we grow older

The world becomes stranger, the *pattern* more complicated

Of dead and living. Not the intense moment

Isolated, with no before and after,

But a lifetime burning in every moment

And not the lifetime of one man only

But of old stones that cannot be deciphered.

—T.S. Eliot
Four Quartets (1940)

About *patterns*, philosophers and psychologists have been strangely silent; yet most interesting phenomena are almost certainly *patterned*. . . . *Patterns* seem to be precisely the wholes that are more than the sum of the parts. . . . We find *patterns* . . . not only in visual and other sensory stimuli but also in language and other symbols, in assessments and diagnoses and, in general, in descriptions of any complex domain.

—Leonard Uhr
Pattern Recognition (1966)

"*Pattern*" can apply to the plans for a product rather than to the creations made from its specifications. The word often suggests blueprints or templates to be followed in constructing the product. More generally, the word indicates the design or configuration that something takes in actuality. But the word can also refer to the perfect representative of a type, or to any example thought worthy of emulation.

—An excerpt from *Use the Right Word*, (1966)

A wealth of material has been written on design, color, ornament, art history, and every technique imaginable, but little of it comes to grips with the principles of *pattern* structure. Authors bend over backwards to explain the design of beautiful "units," but rarely do they explain the design of beautiful "yardage," the repetition of units.

—Richard M. Proctor
Principles of Pattern Design (1970)

The mind is a *pattern* making system. The mind creates *patterns* out of the environment and then recognizes and uses such *patterns*. This is the basis of its effectiveness.

The *pattern* using system is a very efficient way for handling information. Once established the *patterns* form a sort of code. The advantage of a code system is that instead of having to collect all the information one collects just enough to identify the code *pattern* which is then called forth even as library books on a particular subject are called forth by a catalogue code number.

But inseparable from the great usefulness of a *patterning* system are certain limitations. In such a system it is easy to combine old *patterns* or add to them but it is extremely difficult to restructure them, for the *pattern*s control attention. Creativity . . . involves restructuring .. . .

with emphasis on the escape from restricting *patterns*. Lateral thinking involves restructuring, escape, and the provocation of new *patterns*.

To bring *patterns* up to date . . . one needs a new mechanism for insight restructuring [lateral thinking].

—Edward de Bono
Lateral Thinking (1970)

Like a painter or a poet, a mathematician is a maker of *patterns*; but the special characteristics of mathematical *patterns* are that they are more likely to be permanent because they are made with ideas.

As a young child, he was fascinated by the intricate *patterns* in an Oriental rug. The resulting visual picture seemed to produce a "melody" with relations among the various parts resonating with one another.

It is the ability to relate a perceived *pattern* to past *patterns*, and to envelop the present position into the overall game plan, that is the true sign of talent at chess.

—Howard Gardner
Frames of Mind (1983)

[On racketeering] Indeed, in common parlance two of anything do not generally form a *pattern*... It is this factor of continuity plus relationship which combines to produce a *pattern*.

—Byron R. White
Sedima S.P.R.L. v. IMREX Co.,
(1985)

Physicist Peter A. Carruthers, asked about his methods of research, said, "I have a very pictorial way of thinking." For Carruthers, the organizing *patterns* in a particular set of problems may take time to emerge, like an image on photographic film. "At some point," he says, "you suddenly see what's going on."

—Betty Edwards
Drawing on the Artist Within (1986)

Individual *patterns* are . . . the bricks from which we must build our thoughts.

There seems to be something special in the first time we see a *pattern*.

Creativity includes the ability to take a range of *subpatterns*, perhaps from areas not previously linked, and see a new *pattern*. That *pattern* had repeated unnoticed in the past or can be made to repeat in the future.

[Summary] Viewed as a whole, these ideas result in a system model of the brain as a modulated *pattern* extraction hierarchy. . . . The justification of the system model is threefold. First, it can be mapped into current brain physiology. Second, it can provide convincing descriptions of neurological phenomena. . . . Third, some experimentally verifiable predictions derived from the model can be made.

—L. Andrew Coward
Pattern Thinking (1990)

Once is an instance. Twice may be an accident. But three or more makes a *pattern*. We rely on *patterns*, and we also cherish and admire them.

—Diane Ackerman
By Nature's Design (1993)

The recognition of natural *patterns* is at the heart of both scientific and artistic exploration. Our buildings, our symphonies, our fabrics, our societies—all declare *patterns*. Artists and scientists alike make it possible for people to appreciate *patterns* they were either unable to distinguish or which they had learned to ignore in order to cope with the complexity of their daily lives. Once you begin to see these *patterns*, don't be surprised if your view. . . undergoes a subtle shift. . . . Everywhere I looked, I found basic *patterns* repeating.

—Pat Murphy
By Nature's Design (1993)

Appendix C
Data Management

This appendix presents some additional content on data management (DM) objects, including:

- DM objects: what, when, why
- PD (problem domain) and DM objects
- HI (human interaction) and DM objects
- details on DM objects
- implementation notes.

DM OBJECTS: WHAT, WHEN, WHY

What DM objects know and do

DM objects are an important part of an object model.

Consider what each DM object knows and does.

Each DM object knows all of the objects in a corresponding PD class. For example, a cashierDM object knows about all of the cashier objects.

Each DM object knows how to search. You can ask it to find objects that you need.

Each DM object knows how to load and save. It loads object information from the storage devices, creating and initializing objects in main memory. It saves objects, converting them into a specific the storage format.

Each DM object may cache interim results, during the time period when an interacting system is unavailable. For example, the DM objects on a client may cache interim results, even though its server may be down for a while.

When to use DM objects

When should you consider using DM objects?

Use DM objects whenever you:

- need persistent PD objects
- need to search and retrieve persistent PD objects, or
- need to work with something other than an object-oriented data-management system.

Why DM objects are important

Okay, so why bother with DM objects?

What are the key motivations behind all of this?

A DM object isolates data-management complexities from the rest of the application. It interacts with local data-management facilities and storage devices. When necessary, it interacts with an object that represents another system, to find objects located on an interacting system.

A DM object encapsulates how to store and retrieve objects from whatever storage mechanism is to be used, whether flat file, indexed, relational, or object-oriented.

A DM object encapsulates where data comes from (encapsulating both the location and number of sources involved).

PD AND DM OBJECTS

What about PD objects and DM objects?

When you need persistent PD objects, or when you have a PD object that needs someone to search across some number of persistent objects, then add a corresponding DM object.

A PD object interacts with its corresponding DM object during object creation.

A PD object may ask other DM objects to support search actions across large collections of objects that the PD object knows.

Use PD-DM interaction sparingly—low coupling, strong cohesion, and a separation of concerns. Let PD objects support each other for most of their needs.

HI AND PD OBJECTS

Now, what about HI objects and PD objects?

Most of the time, an HI object gets all the support it needs directly from a PD object. Here's how an HI object interacts with a PD object:

- To create a new object, an HI object sends a "create" message to its corresponding PD class (the new PD object registers itself with its DM object).
- To search a collection of objects, an HI object sends a "search" message to the PD object that holds that collection (in turn, the PD object asks the corresponding DM object to do the search).

At times, HI objects need to work directly with DM objects. How does an HI object interact with a DM object?

- To search a collection of objects, when no PD collection is available, an HI object sends a search message to the DM object responsible for collection of objects that the HI object needs.
- To start, rollback, or commit a database transaction (a controlled set of database updates which may span over updates to several different objects), an HI object sends messages to the DM objects responsible for the corresponding collections of objects that the HI object needs to work with.

DETAILS ON DM OBJECTS

The objects that are a part of data management are:
- the DM objects
- the DM server object
- the persistent PD objects.

The other objects, special kinds of objects often used in data management, are:

- proxy objects
- replicant objects.

Check them out.

The DM objects

Purpose

Each DM object serves one specific class of PD objects, providing:

- persistent storage for a single class
- isolation from data storage mechanisms
- one place to put indexes, search mechanisms, and the like
- buffering of objects already loaded from a data source
- initiating load or save for objects related to one being loaded or saved
- making the object connections to other objects.

What you need in a DM object largely depends upon what your application needs and what data management technology you have available.

Responsibilities

Consider the responsibilities for each DM object.

What I know:

- indexes, dictionaries, btrees
- information for converting an object from and to other formats (row, record, and the like).

Who I know:

- the class being served
- the collection of all objects in the class being served
- related object servers.

What I do:

- search
    return single object
    return collection objects
    search by multiple types of criteria
    maintain multiple indexes
- save
    save in persistent store
- delete
    delete from persistent store
- zap
    remove from memory
- load all
    load all objects from persistent store

– convert

convert object to row or record

convert row or record to object

– do

does work over the collection using the support from the data management services.

When does a DM object participate in scenarios?

– when a PD object needs support for saving, loading, and searching (and some other PD object can't take care of it)

– when an HI object needs support for saving, loading, and searching across a collection of objects that no PD object holds.

The "DM object server" object
Purpose

There is one, just one, "DM object server" object within a system.

Its purpose is:

– to create DM objects for each supported class

– to maintain a collection of DM objects

– to provide a single point of access to get a DM object for a specific class.

Responsibilities

Consider the responsibilities for the "DM object server" object.

Who I know:

– next available unique object ID

Who I know:

– all object servers

What I do:

– get DM object for class

– provide commitment control for all objects transactions (start, rollback, commit)

– get next object ID.

Participation in scenarios

When does the "DM object server" object participate in scenarios?

– when a PD object or an HI object needs to know what the DM object for a given class is

– when a PD object or an HI object needs support for commitment control (start, rollback, commit).

The persistent PD objects
Purpose

A persistent PD object interacts with the DM object responsible for the objects in that PD class.

Responsibilities

Consider the responsibilities for each persistent PD object.

What I know:

– object ID.

Who I know:

– DM object
– change log.

What I do to support persistence (in addition to the other service I provide):

– create (something a class does)

notify the DM object about the new object

– save

save to persistent store

– refresh

undo all changes or read back from persistent store

– delete

remove from persistent store

– zap

remove from main memory

– set, add

extend these basic services with an update to the change log.

Participation in scenarios

When does a persistent PD object interact with DM objects (or the DM server object) in a scenario?

It participates that way when it needs support for saving, loading, and searching (and some other PD object can't take care of it).

Proxy objects
Purpose

A proxy is an object which represents another object.

With distributed or client-server architectures, use proxy objects to provide:

– a local view of an object
– access to an object that is outside of your address space.

IBM's System Object Model (SOM) and Distributed System Object Model (DSOM) implementations and several object database management systems (ODBMS) all use proxy objects.

Note that a proxy is a player in a pattern, the proxy-specific item pattern.

Responsibilities

Consider the responsibilities for a proxy object.

What I know: —.

Who I know:

– an object that it is a proxy for.

What I do:

- receive a message from sender
- relay a message remote object
- return whatever the result is.

Participation in scenarios

A proxy object participates in any scenarios on a local system, just as if the proxy were the real thing.

Replicant objects
Purpose

A replicant is an object which is a complete replication of another object.

With a distributed architecture, use replicant objects to provide:

- access to remote objects
- a local copy of an object.

IBM's SOM and DSOM implementations and several ODBMS all use replicant objects.

Responsibilities

Consider the responsibilities for a replicant object.

What I know: —.

Who I know:

- the object that it's a replicant of.

What I do:

- all services of the object it is a replicant of
- maintains data integrity with other copies of the object on other systems.

Participation in scenarios

A replicant object participates in any scenarios on a local system, as a complete substitute for the object it replicates.

IMPLEMENTATION NOTES

This section presents notes for implementing a DM object architecture.

Using a DM object architecture with an ODBMS
Notes on persistence

DM objects may not be required with an ODBMS. Here are some implementation notes on persistence:

- create
  - create, just like for any other object

– create (continued)
  – a class of persistent objects inherits its persistence capabilities
  – persistence is part of each PD object.
– save
  – usually handled automatically by ODBMS
  – uses transactions and uses commitment control
– load
  – usually handled automatically by ODBMS
  – done when there is a reference
  – uses some rules to determine how many levels of object connections to
      bring into memory.

Notes on searching

Here are some implementation notes on searching:

– indexing
– need DM object to hold indexes
– provides some collection objects that work well
      (for example, dictionaries, ordered collections, btree)
– provides search services.

Notes on the impact of client-server

Here are some implementation notes on the impact of client-server:

– requires very little or no change to implement
– usually returns proxy or replicant to local environment
– does allow for some of the real service work to be done on the server
– need to add concerns about multiuser access for concurrency
– communications support provided by the database
– requires an object-oriented environment on the server.

Using a DM object architecture with an RDBMS
Notes on persistence

Here are some implementation notes on persistence:

– create
  – create, just as for any other object
  – no persistence implied
  – a class of objects needing DM support inherits whatever DM capabili-
      ties it needs.
– save
  – usually handled manually
  – done when there is a specific request to a DM object (or to the DM
      server object)
  – requires conversion to rows in one or more tables
  – use transactions and commitment control supplied by RDBMS
  – must add some way to rollback objects (no automated way to do that).
      load

- usually handled manually
- done when there is a specific request to DM object (or to the DM server object)
- requires SQL requests
- reconstruct objects from rows in one or more tables.

Notes on searching

Here are some implementation notes on searching:

- create SQL request
- use RDBMS search
- need some way to convert rows from one or more tables to objects
- need some way to handle multiple row return.

Notes on the impact of client-server

Here are some implementation notes on the impact of client-server:

- requires very little or no change to implement
- need to add concerns about multiuser access for concurrency
- just moves the SQL communication to a remote system
- communications support provided by the database
- doesn't need an object-oriented environment on the server.

SOM and DSOM

SOM and DSOM, at least in their implementations at the time of this writing, do not provide persistence.

What SOM and DSOM (and other object request brokers) do provide is object-oriented communication to objects on another system, one which may support persistent objects.

Notes on persistence

Here are some implementation notes on persistence:

-create
- done by making a request to object server on the system where you want the object created
- a class of remote objects inherits its capabilities for knowing and being remote
- persistence is provided by the system that an object was created on, using whatever data-management capabilities are available (RDBMS or ODBMS).
- save
- usually based upon the plan for the selected persistence mechanism
- any required communication for saving is done to the object server or the object (the local system needs proxies for both).

  – load
      – usually based upon the plan for the selected persistence mechanism
      – any required communication for loading is done to the object server or
          the object (the local system needs proxies for both).

Notes on searching

Here are some implementation notes on searching:

  – search request
      – request is made to the object server on the system that contains the object.
  – indexes
      – need a DM object to hold indexes, located on the system that contains
          the object.

Notes on the impact of client-server

Here are some implementation notes on the impact of client-server:

  – need to decide what objects will reside on what machine
  – need to make requests of the object server on the machine that contains
      the objects
  – use proxies to automatically route messages to the real object on another
      system (makes the object appear local)
  – use replicants to provide a local copy of an object (so if connections are
      lost the system can still operate; keeps changes in-sync automatically,
      even upon system failure and restart)
  – allows for some real work to be done on the remote system
  – communications support provided by SOM and DSOM
  – allows the persistence to be provide on a remote machine, using whatever
      persistence mechanism is available on that remote machine.
  – requires an object-oriented environment on multiple machines.

WRAP-UP

That's it for this appendix—providing additional content on data management.

Appendix D
The Executive Decision To Adopt Object Technology

Sooner or later, you've got to answer the question for yourself: why should I adopt object technology?

And some time after that, you've got to answer the question for others: why should our organization adopt object technology?

Here are some answers that may prove helpful to you, spanning:

– significant improvements with object technology
– why executives adopt object technology
– how to get started with object technology.

SIGNIFICANT IMPROVEMENTS WITH OBJECT TECHNOLOGY

Object technology offers significant improvements in these areas:

– one model, from concept to code
– frequent, tangible, working results
– multifaceted reuse
– suitability for embracing new technology.

One model, from problem domain to code

One significant improvement with object technology is the ability to use one model, from problem domain to code

An example? A cashier object is: (1) in the problem domain, (2) in an object model, and (3) in the corresponding application code itself. The attributes of a cashier object are (1) in the problem domain, and (3) in the code itself. Finally, the actions done to a cashier object (for example, assess performance over interval) are (1) in the problem domain, (2) in an object model, and (3) in the code itself.

An object model packages results using what *Encyclopaedia Britannica* calls "methods of organization that pervade all of people's thinking:" objects, whole-part, and classification (classes and distinguishing between them). An object is a person, place, or thing—for example, a specific corner grocery store. Whole-part is a relation between objects, expressing assembly-part, container-content, or group-member—for example, a store and its items. A class is a description, one that applies to each of some number of objects—for example, a class called store, with some number of objects in that class. You could think of "object-oriented" as a technical name for a very human way of thinking about things.

So what is the key impact of "one model, from problem domain to code?" Developers can stay in touch with their users (a very good thing, indeed!). In addition: using one model makes the approach easier to learn and easier to apply; the entire development team uses a common graphics-and-text language, facilitating better communication within the team; and the noise and loss of content problems from multi-model approaches is finally overcome.

After all, effective communication is a must—for all players: developers (object modelers and programmers), domain experts, managers, and stakeholders (those who pay for the system, those who will use the system, those who will maintain the system).

Perhaps the most profound (yet most often overlooked) impact is the one that it makes on any organization whose developers are still somewhat leery of analysis and design. Yet no doubt about it: that's the majority of software developers today. With one model, from concept to code, developers can "sketch out" part of their designs in text (in code), and then see the overall object model visually (with tools that are now available, suitable for working back and forth, again and again, between object model and code).

Another profound impact is upon maintenance, where the majority of development costs really occur. With one model, you can embody all object model results in code, using language syntax to encapsulate an object (cashier), its attributes (password, authorization level), and its services (assess performance over interval). Project results that are not expressible within a given language syntax can be captured by tools that generate coded comments, writing textual parts of an object model into the code itself, too. Why is this so important? Simply this: you can generate object models, high-level documents, and detailed documents all from the code itself. Documents that are always accurate, always up-to-date with the code itself, are unheard of, outside of this approach.

And so, one significant improvement with object technology is the ability to use one model, from problem domain to code.

Frequent, tangible, working results

Oh yes. We've all heard the terms "incremental delivery" and "evolutionary development." Those words have been around for a long time.

The missing technology piece has always been an organizational framework that could withstand multiple passes through analysis, design, and programming.

Functions cannot do that; after all, functions are the most likely to change with each pass (that's why so may of us bear the scars of so-called incremental delivery from the past).

Data entities cannot do that; data without function leaves much of the story untold.

The key is using problem-domain classes as an outline, an organizational framework, that remains stable over many iterations. Object technology makes this possible.

Systems built around problem-domain classes tend to be more stable over time, compared to those built around functions (most likely to change) or data (still changing more often than domain classes).

What's the impact? You hold your development team accountable for producing frequent, tangible, working results.

What does this mean?

You can plan with milestones of object models and working results.

You can measure progress based on object models and working results (rather than basing it on the weight of the documentation).

You can make continual estimates on time-to-completion and cost-to-completion based on working results (not on "trust me, trust me, trust me").

You have the option of shipping early, to meet marketplace demand—because you always have working results in hand.

You can get better feedback, sooner.

Your team will stay more focused, building object models as a means to an end (no more analysis and design that become so self-indulgent that with "rigor" and "discipline" those results become an end in themselves).

Your team members will experience working results sooner—something very exciting and encouraging for all developers.

The bottom line: frequent visibility, measurability, accountability. It's the no-BS approach to managing software development. Who could ask for anything more?

Multifaceted reuse

Reuse, reuse, reuse.

Objects facilitate reuse, at many levels.

Keep in mind that understandability is a prerequisite to reuse.

Your team will gain reuse advantages along different dimensions.

Class reuse. A team may reuse a class (a description that applies to each of some number of objects) as-is.

Class reuse with inheritance. A team may reuse a class, by adding to it in some way. Inheritance is a mechanism that makes such reuse easy to do (without having to copy-and-paste some code).

Component reuse. A team many reuse a component, an interacting collection of objects that provide some needed capability.

Pattern reuse. A team may reuse a pattern (a template of interacting objects with stereotypical responsibilities, an example of an effective portion of an object model, one that may be applied again and again, by analogy).

Object model reuse. A team may reuse all or part of an object model from another project, within the same problem domain.

Problem domain reuse. A team, having benefited from building object models in the same or similar problem domain, may reuse that problem domain understanding on another project.

The impact of reuse? Reduced time, reduced cost, increased quality—and competitive advantage for the team.

Reasonable expectations? Expect the same schedule and cost for the first project and a savings of 10 to 30 percent on subsequent projects.

Keep your expectations modest. There is no silver bullet.

Suitability for embracing new technologies

Object technology offers a significant advantage for embracing new technologies.

Graphical User Interfaces (GUIs) are next-to-impossible to build without object technology (objects like window, pull-down menu, button, and the like make a lot of sense).

Client-server and other forms of distributed computing mandate objects, just as soon as one want to distribute data and the functions that work on that data. Objects provide the encapsulation that's an essential ingredient for building such systems.

WHY EXECUTIVES ADOPT OBJECT TECHNOLOGY

Object technology does indeed deliver some significant improvements.

Indeed, those improvements set the foundation for the reasons why executives adopt object technology. The key reasons are:

- reduced risk
- reduced time-to-market
- justified cost.

Reduced risk

Now wait a minute.

New technology means increased risk, doesn't it? Why, there's added training and tools to consider. And we've got to gain some experience with the technology.

All very true.

Yet remember that objects are no longer on the "bleeding edge" of technology. Thousands and thousands of developers now use object technology—in every industry you could imagine.

It's not so scary any more.

You do have the added risk of increased startup costs—workshops, tools, and practice.

Yet you get reduced overall development risk. Check it out.

Remember the last time you managed a two-year project, and the end of the two years was in sight? What did you feel like? What did the uncertainty feel like?

High risk? Here it is: accepting piles of documentation and listening to "trust me, trust me, trust me" until you meet and pass the delivery date.

Reduced risk? Planning, measuring, estimating, and troubleshooting—using object models you (yes you) can understand *and* get frequent, tangible, working results. You get regular visibility into what's really happening on your project. You see what's really happening, what works, and what doesn't. You discover problems you must face sooner, while you can still do something about them.

Excellent.

Reduced time-to-market

You're in a worldwide competition.

The marketplace changes daily.

You may have to deliver capability far sooner than you'd like—to preempt the competition, or perhaps just to keep up with the competition.

With object technology and frequent, tangible, working results, soon after the project begins, you've got some working software.

Along the way, you see additional working results.

If you plan your "working results" milestones according to the importance of features in the marketplace, then you can reserve the option to choose to release core capabilities sooner, whenever you need to do so.

Justified cost

So what's the bottom-line impact? How do executives justify the cost?

There are many ways to justify the education, tool, and experience investment in object technology:

- competitive edge
- added value
- cost displacement, attract more talent
- cost avoidance
- obsolescence avoidance.

Competitive edge. Some organizations are early adopters of new technologies that may give them a strategic advantage over their competitors. Eventually, others join in.

Added value. Some organizations spend a lot of time considering cost and benefit. Hard data are hard to come by, and not so believable even when it is available. Expect the first project to cost about the same as what you do now. The project after the first one, especially in the same problem domain, is where the benefits will outweigh the costs.

Cost displacement. Other organizations adopt object technology even though they feel that the new technology costs are just going to displace current development costs. Why? They use object technology to attract more talent, within the organization and outside of the organization, to the development effort at hand.

Cost avoidance. Other organizations, faced with the incredible cost of developing GUIs or client-server applications using older technologies, finally make the leap to objects to avoid those upcoming costs.

Obsolescence avoidance. Other organizations wait, wait, and wait some more. Yet at some point, perhaps when embarking on a very long-term project, such organizations will adopt object technology, just to avoid falling off the trailing edge of technology.

One more thing. Who has made the move?

Leading firms in nearly every industry now use object technology, including aircraft, banking, electronics, engineering, government (business systems), government (real-time systems), insurance, investment, manufacturing, publishing, software, and telecommunications.

HOW TO GET STARTED WITH OBJECT TECHNOLOGY

Once the executive decision is made, then it's time to get started.

Devote resources to help your team get up to speed with object technology. That includes people, money for workshops, money for tools, and time to practice (becoming familiar with object technology and how to effectively apply it).

Here are some specific recommendations:

- select small teams of enthusiastic developers
- get hands-on workshops, delivering actual project results
- select a method, some tools, and a programming language
- keep your expectations modest
- just do it.

Select small teams of enthusiastic developers

Who should you start out with?

Select developers who love to learn and are very enthusiastic about applying object technology.

Why? The people will gain valuable experience and insights. You'll want them to carry their enthusiasm to others, both now and in the future.

Over time, you'll be able to put together teams with experience and enthusiasm. You'll be able to blend different levels of object technology experience: hands-on workshop experience, single project experience, experience on multiple projects within single problem domain, and experience on multiple projects across multiple problem domains.

Get hands-on workshops, delivering actual project results

Your teams need education and experience. Hands-on workshops deliver both.

Bring in some hands-on workshops, where your project is the "case study" around which the entire course revolves. (No lectures, no flip charts, no toy examples!)

Why? Object technology embodies a change in problem-solving style. Your team needs hands-on experience with that problem-solving style, in their own problem domain, to ensure effective technology transfer.

Note that this means that workshop leaders must have multidomain object-technology experience—in addition to the other skills and education that help one run an effective workshop.

Follow up the workshop with some mentoring, gaining practical advice and insights on a regular (typically, monthly) basis. Good mentors will save you time and headaches, move the team along, and help you build expertise into your team (right where you want it).

You might also follow up the workshop with a weekly object-model session. You can apply new strategies and patterns in an informal setting, continuing to build object technology expertise in your organization.

Be sure to include follow-up mentoring. Far too often, developers get caught up with incredible initial results and intense schedule pressures, and forget that education is a continual and much-needed improvement process.

Limited budget? Education is more important than tools. Simple tools with well-educated developers is a far better choice than the alternative. (A fool with a tool is still a fool.)

Select a method, some tools, and a programming language

You've got to make some initial choices. Go ahead and make them. Here are some facts you may find helpful.

Fact. If your team is good, they'll become literate in multiple object methods. They'll get past the differences in icon shapes. They'll focus on strategies and patterns—the heart and soul of any object method worth its salt.

Fact. If your team is good, they'll need a collection of tools to get their work done. Object technology tools tend to be smaller, low-cost tools that plug-and-play together (very different from the "one size fits all" tools from vendors in the 1980s).

Fact. If your team is good, they'll become literate in more than one object-oriented programming language.

Fact. Any developer who claims there is only one "right way" to do object technology needs some added practical experience with the technology itself.

Select a method, some tools, and a programming language. Make some initial choices. Move ahead.

Then, as time goes by, encourage literacy in multiple methods, multiple tools, and multiple languages.

Keep your expectations modest

In an industry where unpaid overtime is a time-honored tradition, it's time for some modest expectations.

Watch out for well-intentioned developer hype, fueled by industry hype!

Be modest in your schedule and cost expectations. For the first project, expect that the schedule and cost will be about the same as before. For the second and third project, expect that you may save 10 to 20 percent in schedule and cost, compared to the old way of building systems. For subsequent projects, expect that you may save 30 percent, compared to the old way of building systems.

Be reasonable about what you expect out of your teams. You'll gain some real advantages with object technology. If all you get out of it are the benefits of planning, measuring, and delivering frequent, tangible, working results—even at the same old cost—you will gain a lot.

When it comes to expectations, modesty is the best policy.

Just do it

Objects are mainstream development technology, no longer at the bleeding edge.

Reducing risk by managing with frequent, tangible, working results is motivation enough to adopt object technology.

Do it—now!

Appendix E
A Histogram Of Initial Object Modeling

This appendix presents a histogram of some initial object modeling by four object model builders (one was Peter Coad) and one domain expert—using the strategies and patterns in this book.

This histogram is for a commercial project, a planning system.

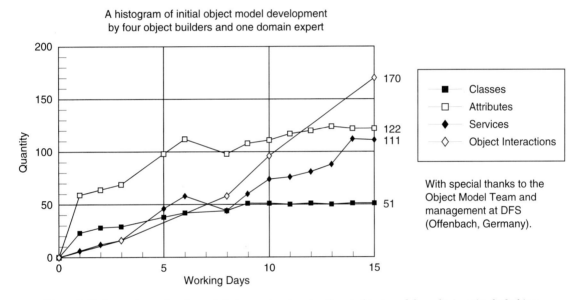

Figure 1–E: Strategies and patterns help teams develop significant object model results in a timely fashion.

Observations:

- The number of classes grew rapidly at first, gradually leveling off over time.

- The number of attributes also grew rapidly at first (that makes sense; "objects and their attributes" is a basic method of organization people use). Then the number of attributes gradually leveled off, too.

- The number of services grew much more slowly at first, yet after Day 8, the number of services grew rapidly. Indeed, the number of services was about the same as the number of services, by Day 14. This illustrates the extra emphasis on dynamics in the Coad method.

– The number of object interactions really ramped up, beginning at Day 8. Again, this illustrates the extra emphasis on dynamics.

You can use this histogram as a benchmark for your early object model development. Although the duration will vary, the basic pattern should follow:

– lots of classes and attributes at first, then gradually leveling off
– more and more services and object interactions over time (leveling off only when you've worked through all the scenarios you intend to work out).

Glossary

Words, words, words.

Words most certainly take on different meanings in different contexts.

This glossary is a convenient reference of words and their meanings within the context of building effective object models.

attribute

An attribute is something that an object knows. An attribute represents a value for which each object in a class has its own value. Regarding accessibility, an attribute is private; one must use "get" and "set" services to access its value.

attribute description

An attribute description is some text about an object's attribute. It is a filled-in template of information about an attribute, including: description, legal values, unit of measure, required (yes/no), get/set constraints, rules for getting a default value, applicable states, and traceability codes. For real-time systems, categorize each attribute as: state, state-dependent, or state-independent.

basic services

The basic services are services that each object in an object model provides. These basic services are not shown in a object model. However, they are included in a scenario view, as needed along the way. The basic services are: create an object, get and set attribute values, add and remove object connections, and delete.

class

A class is a description that applies to each of some number of objects that have the identical responsibilities.

class cohesion

Class cohesion describes the degree of relatedness of the responsibilities within a class. A class has strong cohesion if the attributes and services work well together and are well-described by the name of the class itself. Strong class cohesion is desirable; it indicates good object partitioning and greater resiliency to change over time.

class symbol

This is a symbol which represents a class that does not have any objects (also known as an abstract class). Such a class makes sense only as a generalization class within a generalization-specialization structure.

class-with-objects symbol

This is a symbol which represents both a class and some number of objects in that class.

data management component

The data management component contains objects that provide an interface between problem domain objects and a database or a file management system. In an object model, such objects most often correspond to specific problem domain objects that need support for persistence and searching.

domain expert

A domain expert is a person that has experience working within a specific area of concern. Ideally, the person is somewhat introspective, too (someone who has spent some time thinking about what he or she does, fitting that work within an overall scope or larger perspective.) You cannot possibly build an effective object model without domain experts on your team.

generalization-specialization (gen-spec)

Generalization-specialization is a relationship between classes. Informally, one can say, "a(n) <specialization name> is a kind of <generalization name>." A specialization class inherits the responsibilities of its generalization class(es).

human interaction component

The human interaction component contains objects that provide an interface between problem domain objects and people. In an object model, such objects most often correspond to specific windows and reports.

inheritance

Inheritance is a mechanism for explicitly expressing commonality. The best use of inheritance is when it follows generalization-specialization as the guiding principle (easier to understand; more likely to apply in the future, within the same domain). When a class inherits from another, it inherits responsibilities (who I know, what I know, and what I do).

message

A message is a request for a service to be performed, sent from a sender to a receiver. The sender sends a command and optionally some arguments; the receiver performs the service; the receiver returns control to the sender, along with optionally some results.

object

An object is a person, place, or thing (including a conceptual thing). An object in a software system is an abstraction or representation of a person, place, or thing.

object connection

An object connection represents that one object needs to know another object. There are two reasons for this knowing: (1) to know to whom to send a message (during a scenario); and (2) to support basic querying capabilities (given an object, tell me who the corresponding objects are). (In the OOA book, the term used for this concept was "instance connection.")

object connection constraint

An object connection constraint indicates the number of objects that an object knows. The constraint appears next to the object being so constrained. "I'm a cashier object; I know about some number of sale objects." Here, the constraint would be placed next to the object being constrained — the cashier object. Typical constraint values are: 1 (one), 0-1 (0 to one), 0-n (0 to n), n (0 or more), 1-n (1 to n), [XOR A] 1 (meaning, an exclusive "or" for all object connection constraints labeled "A"), [or B]; [C] ordered n, all.

object coupling

Object coupling describes the interdependence between two objects: the number of messages, the frequency of messages, and the number of arguments (making values visible to other objects). Low coupling is desirable (better encapsulation, fewer objects needlessly affected when making changes).

object model

An object model represents objects and their responsibilities.

object model component

An object model component is a grouping of classes. These model components are problem domain, human interaction, data management, and system interaction. Another model component is called "not this time" (documenting classes investigated yet not included in the current application). These components separate domain objects from technology-specific objects (those supporting human interaction, data management, or system interaction). The impact? Separation of concerns, simpler modeling, and an increased likelihood of reuse.

object model documentation set

The object model documentation set consists of an object model (usually presented with a number of views, highlighting different aspects of the model), scenario views (one for each feature of the system under consideration), and descriptions (for example: attribute descriptions, service descriptions, scenario descriptions, and an overall model description).

pattern (for object models)

A pattern is a template of objects with stereotypical responsibilities and interactions; the template may be applied again and again, by analogy. Pattern instances are building blocks, very helpful in building effective object models. Patterns are categorized into these pattern families:

- fundamental
- transactions
- aggregates
- path
- interaction.

pattern instance

A pattern instance is the outcome of applying a pattern. For example, cashier-sale is a pattern instance of participant-transaction.

pattern player

A pattern player is one of the participanting objects in a pattern. For example, "participant" and "transaction" are the pattern players in the participant-transaction pattern.

personification

Personification is a figure of speech, one that gives human characteristics to inanimate objects. Figures of speech are an age-old way of providing special emphasis. "I am an object. Here's what I know, who I know, and what I do." Personification helps developers think like an object (rather than remain somewhat aloof, at a distance, merely describing the data and functions that are needed in a model).

polymorphism

Polymorphism is giving the same name to services in different objects; those services may do the work differently; yet those services produce the same kind of results. (This is especially valuable when you want to send a message to each of some number of objects — without needing to know the specific kind of object you are sending a message to.)

postcondition

A postcondition is a something that must be true before a service may go to completion. If a postcondition applies, specify it in the applicable service description.

precondition

A precondition is something that must be true before a service may be executed. If a precondition applies, specify it in the applicable service description.

problem domain component

The problem domain component contains the objects that directly correspond to the problem being modeled. Objects in this component are technology-neutral. They have little (or no) knowledge about objects in the other components (human interaction, data management, and system interaction).

responsibility

A responsibility is something that an object knows or does ("what I know, who I know, what I do"). A responsibility may be expressed with an attribute, an object connection, or a service.

reuse

Reuse is using something again, in an object model, whether patterns, instances of patterns, some portion of an object model, or inheritance.

scenario

A scenario is a specific time-ordered sequence of object interactions, one that exists to fulfill a specific need.

scenario view

A scenario view presents a specific time-ordered sequence of object interactions.

scope

The scope of a system indicates what should be included in the system. It is expressed by the system purpose and a prioritized features list. Scope is also expressed by contrasting the objects in an object model with the objects in the "not this time" model component.

service

A service is something that an object does. (Language-specific synonyms: function, method, procedure.)

service description

A service description is some text about an object's service. It is a filled-in template of information about a service, including: inputs, outputs, description (including pseudo-code or actual code, detailing the algorithm to be applied), traceability codes, and visibility. For state-dependent services, additional information may be needed, including: precondition, postcondition, trigger, terminate, exception action, and performance constraints.

stereotypical responsibilities

Stereotypical responsibilities are the customary things that a pattern player (an object within a pattern) knows and does.

strategy

A strategy is a plan of action, intended to accomplish a specific objective. Object model strategies fall into four major categories, referred to as four major activities:

– identifying system purpose and features
– selecting objects
– establishing responsibilities
– working out dynamics with scenarios.

A few other strategies fit into one of two minor categories:
– working with activities and components
– discovering new strategies and patterns.

system interaction component

The system interaction component contains objects that provide an interface between problem domain objects and other systems or devices. A system interaction object encapsulates communication protocol, keeping its companion problem domain object free of such low-level, implementation-specific detail.

task

A task is a program that executes as if it were running at the same time as other programs. A task is complex. An object should encapsulate such complexity. When someone sends a message to an object, that object returns a response (at the very least, "I got the message.") Then the receiving object may start or stop one of its service as a separate task. This level of detail may be expressed in a scenario view and in a service specification.

terminate condition

A terminate condition identifies the circumstances upon which a service stops itself. A terminate condition, when applicable, is specified in a service specification.

transaction

A transaction is an "event remembered," an event that a system must remember through time. A transaction is a moment in time (for example, a sale) or an interval of time (for example, a rental).

trigger condition

A trigger condition identifies the circumstances upon which a service starts itself. A trigger condition, when applicable, is specified in a service specification.

whole-part object connection

A whole-part object connection is a kind of object connection. It carries the added meaning of container-content, group-member, or assembly-part.

Bibliography

This is a *working bibliography* of books and articles we used during the development of this book. This is not a comprehensive listing of current literature. On-line references do a much better job of that. There is so much good work in this field that deserves recognition. We cannot possibly hope to mention all the good work being done by our peers. Instead, we list those publications we found helpful, ones that you may want to pick up and read, for additional background and insight into the ideas that helped along the way.

SOFTWARE DEVELOPMENT

Anderson, Bruce. "Patterns: Building Blocks for Object-Oriented Architectures." *Software Engineering Notes*, January 1994.

Atkinson, Colin. *Object-Oriented Reuse, Concurrency and Distribution, an Ada-Based Approach*. ACM Press, 1991.

Barnes, J.G.P. *Programming in Ada Plus an Overview of Ada 9X*. Fourth edition. Addison-Wesley, 1994.

Beck, Kent, and Ward Cunningham. "A Laboratory for Teaching Object-Oriented Thinking." *OOPSLA Conference Proceedings*. ACM, 1989.

Ben-Ari, M. *Principles of Concurrent Programming*. Prentice Hall, 1982.

Booch, Grady. "Patterns." *Object Magazine*, September 1993.

———. *Object-Oriented Analysis and Design with Applications*. Second edition. Benjamin/Cummings, 1994.

Brinch Hansen, Per. *Operating System Principles*. Prentice Hall, 1973.

Buschmann, Frank, Claus Jäkel, Hans Rohnert, and Michael Stal. *Software Architecture* (working draft). Siemens Corporation, 1993.

Chandra, Rohit, Anoop Gupta, and John Hennessy. "COOL: An Object-Based Language for Parallel Programming." *IEEE Computer*, August 1994.

Jacobson, Ivar, Magnus Christerson, Patrik Jonsson, and Gunnar Overgaard. *Object-Oriented Software Engineering: A Use Case Driven Approach*. Addison-Wesley, 1992.

Papert, Seymour. *Mindstorms: Children, Computers, and Powerful Ideas*. Basic Books, 1980.

Rumbaugh, James, Michael Blaha, William Premerlani, Frederick Eddy, and William Lorensen. *Object-Oriented Modeling and Design*. Prentice Hall, 1991.

Selic, Bran, Garth Gullekson, and Paul T. Ward. *Real-Time Object-Oriented Modeling*. John Wiley & Sons, 1994.

Webster, Bruce. *Pitfalls of Object-Oriented Development*. M&T Books, 1995.

Wirfs-Brock, Rebecca, "Stereotyping: A Technique for Characterizing Objects and Their Interactions." *Object Magazine*, November-December 1993.

———, Brian Wilkerson, and Lauren Wiener. *Designing Object-Oriented Software*. Prentice Hall, 1991.

PATTERNS IN OTHER FIELDS

Alexander, Chris. *The Timeless Way of Building*: *A Pattern Language*. Oxford University Press, 1979. An oft-cited book, one that focuses on cataloging "solutions to a problem in a context"—something Alexander calls a "pattern" (although no dictionary defines the term that way).

Coward, L. Andrew. *Pattern Thinking*. Praeger Publishers, 1990.

DeBono, Edward. *Lateral Thinking: Creativity Step by Step*. Harper & Row, 1970.

Gardner, Howard. *Frames of Mind*. Basic Books, 1983.

Learning with Pattern Blocks. Cuisinaire Company of America, 1992. ("Pattern Blocks" are a hands-on learning system for exploring patterns and shapes.)

Muhlberger, Richard. *What Makes a Van Gogh a Van Gogh?* Metropolitan Museum of Art, 1993.

Murphy, Pat and William Neill. *By Nature's Design*. Chronicle Books, 1993. *If you buy one book on patterns in other fields, buy this one*. The patterns in nature—and the analogous use of a pattern across multiple domains—is truly inspiring.

Proctor, Richard M. *Principles of Pattern Design*. Dover Publications, 1990.

Texas Instruments, *Touch and Discover Educational Product*. The *New Discoveries* and *Advanced Discoveries* options include modules on classification of objects, part-whole relationships, and identification and matching of patterns for ages 2 to 5. Texas Instruments, 1993.

This-Evensen, Thomas, *Archetypes in Architecture*. Norwegian University Press and Oxford University Press, 1987. This book presents archetypes, visual templates, for twentieth-century architecture. The archetype categories are the floor, the wall, and the roof. The pattern summary, entirely in pictures, is awesome.

Uhr, Leonard (editor). *Pattern Recognition*. John Wiley, 1966.

OTHER PUBLICATIONS

Alexander, Chris. *A Foreshadowing of 21st Century Art*. Oxford Press, 1993.

"Automatic Pilots." *World Book Encyclopedia*. World Book, Inc., 1990.

Hayakawa, S.I. *Use the Right Word*. Funk & Wagnalls, 1968.

RELATED PUBLICATIONS BY THE AUTHORS

Coad, Peter. "Object-Oriented Patterns." *CACM*. ACM, September 1992.

———, and Mark Mayfield (with Bruce Anderson in 1993). "OOPSLA Patterns Workshop Report," *OOPSLA Proceedings Addendum*. ACM, 1992, 1993, and 1994.

———, and Jill Nicola. *Object-Oriented Programming*. Prentice Hall, 1993.

———, and Edward Yourdon. *Object-Oriented Analysis*, Second Edition. Prentice Hall, 1991.

———, and Edward Yourdon. *Object-Oriented Design*. Prentice Hall, 1991.

Index

Object International, Inc.
1720 Leigh Drive
Raleigh NC 27603-5159 USA

For **FASTER SERVICE,**
VISIT http://www.oi.com

COAD NOTATION

Object Model

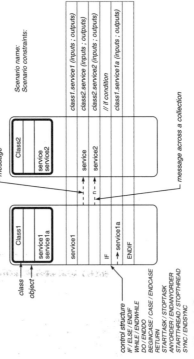

class name
attribute name
service name

specialization

whole-part object connection

object connection

class
object

generalization

object connection constraint

0-1	0-1
1	1
n	0 or more
1	1 or more
ordered n	ordered collection
[XOR A] n	XOR across connections labeled "A"

Scenario View

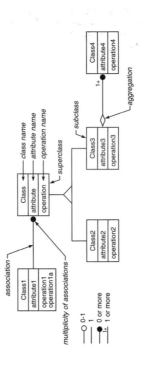

Scenario name:
Scenario constraints:

message

class
object

message across a collection

control structure
IF / ELSE / ENDIF
WHILE / ENDWHILE
DO / ENDDO
BEGINCASE / CASE / ENDCASE
RETURN
STARTTASK / STOPTASK
ANYORDER / ENDANYORDER
STARTTHREAD / STOPTHREAD
SYNC / ENDSYNC

Model Components

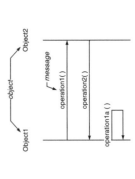

ProblemDomain
HumanInteraction
DataManagement
SystemInteraction

UNIFIED NOTATION

Class Diagram

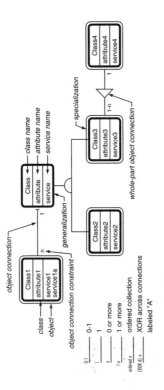

class name
class property
attribute name
operation name and parameters

association

superclass

subclass

inheritance

aggregation

multiplicity of associations

0-1	0-1
1	1
*	0 or more
1..*	1 or more

(Note: Based on Unified Version 0.8 Notation Summary)

OMT NOTATION

Object Model

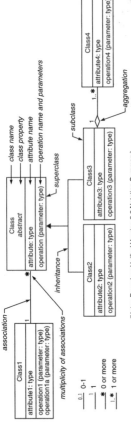

class name
attribute name
operation name

association

superclass

subclass

aggregation

multiplicity of associations

○	0-1
	1
●	0 or more
|+	1 or more

UNIFIED NOTATION, OMT NOTATION

Message Trace

object
Object1 Object2

message
operation1( )
operation2( )
operation1a ( )

(Note: OMT calls this an "Event Trace Diagram.")